960

D1576654

**FOR
REFERENCE ONLY**

WATERFORD CITY AND COUNTY
WITHDRAWN
LIBRARIES

Africa and Asia: Mapping Two Continents

WATERFORD CITY AND COUNTY WITHDRAWN LIBRARIES

Introduction

It was not that the people of Europe knew nothing about Asia and Africa. From ancient times travelers had returned from both mysterious continents with stories of people and places so magnificently exotic that even the wildest exaggeration seemed more likely than the bare facts. Honest reports by men trying to explain completely unfamiliar societies and customs became hopelessly intermingled with fantasy and speculation. That Asia and Africa were there, everyone knew. But what really lay within them? That was the question.

This book tells the story of how the question was answered. It was worked out by men frequently pushed to the edge of their endurance. Few of them arrived in those strange lands with any clear idea of the problems they would face. The climates and conditions were completely unfamiliar to them. Almost all of the territories were populated, and the local inhabitants presented yet another unknown quantity. Sometimes they helped the explorers; more often they simply observed them or actively tried to prevent them from going further. Sometimes they killed the curious outsiders.

The first part of this book tells the story of the exploration of the central part of Asia, a vast, often hostile expanse of land with people as fierce and uncomprising as their environment. Europeans began to penetrate the outer edges in the great burst of discovery during the 1500's. Approaching Asia by the north, the south, and the west, they moved slowly toward the interior. Many of them would never have thought of themselves as explorers—they were merchants, or missionaries, or adventurers. Not until the 1800's was there a consistent, organized effort to survey and produce accurate maps of the enormous heartland. Throughout the years each man had his own reasons for venturing into central Asia. Each—deliberately or inadvertently—added to our knowledge of that often barbaric, often splendid land.

A HISTORY OF DISCOVERY AND EXPLORATION

Africa and Asia:
Mapping Two Continents

WATERFORD

No. 124720 .

MUNICIPAL LIBRARY

Aldus Books / Jupiter Books

London

Contents

This edition published in 1973 by
Aldus Books and Jupiter Books, London

SBN 490 00293 5

Distributed by Jupiter Books
9-13 Cowcross Street, London EC1M 6DR

© 1971 Aldus Books Limited, London

Printed and bound in Yugoslavia by
Mladinska Knjiga, Ljubljana

Part 3 Seas of Sand

Below: a Persian miniature of a large banquet, painted in about 1440. It was such
pictures that gave Europeans the idea that
Asia was a land of gracious opulence.

PART ONE
The Heartland of Asia

BY NATHALIE ETTINGER

Left: an engraving of the arms of the
Company of Merchants of Russia, the
Muscovy Company that was incor-
porated by the young King Edward VI,
and later confirmed during the reign
of his elder sister, Elizabeth I.

Below: the plan of Moscow, as the city
was when Chancellor saw it in the
mid-1550's. At that time the buildings
were made of wood, as shown in this
plan, published in Cologne in 1572.

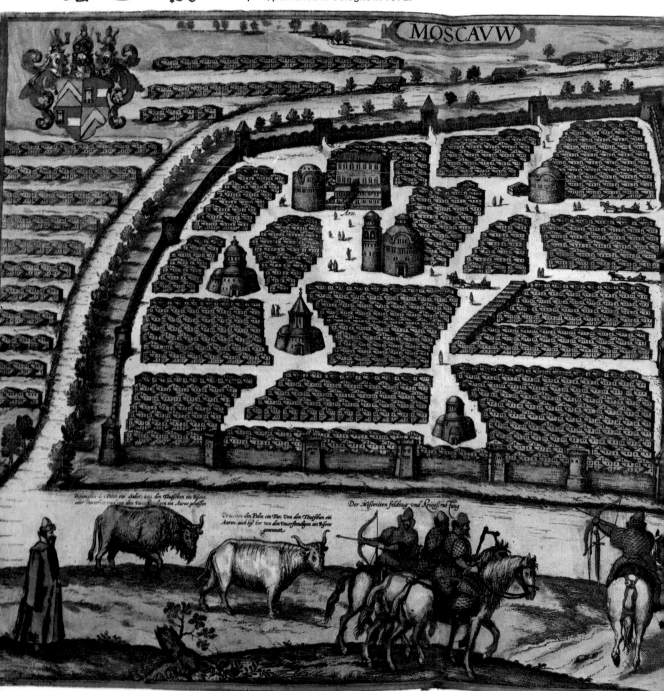

Northeast to Muscovy

1

MOSCOVIA, vrbs. regionis eiusdē nominis metropolitica, duplo maior; quā Praga Boiemiæ, lignea ædificia habet; multas plateas, sed dispersas, latissimi campi interiacent: Mosca amnis, ipsam irrigat.

On a bright May morning in 1553, an excited crowd began gathering at Greenwich, England, along the banks of the River Thames. All eyes were fixed on the fleet of ships just coming into view. In the vanguard was a throng of small boats rowed by men in sky-blue uniforms. Behind, at the end of stout towing ropes, were three tall-masted vessels, their rails and rigging alive with sailors. As the procession neared Greenwich Palace, the towing lines were cut, and the ships' sails were unfurled. Then all three vessels fired off a thunderous cannon salute. The crowd, now swelled by scores of courtiers from the palace, responded with wild enthusiasm, filling the air with shouts and cheers as the three ships gathered speed and moved off down the river to the sea.

It was a sendoff to make any mariner proud. But for Richard Chancellor, pilot-general of the fleet, it was less the cheers than the cries of "Farewell! Farewell! Godspeed!" that he remembered when the familiar shores of England had dropped out of sight. He was a widower, and had left behind two small sons. What would become of them, he wondered, if he should not come back? For this, he knew, would be no ordinary voyage. He and his commanding officer, Sir Hugh Willoughby, had been charged with the dangerous task of locating a Northeast Passage to the Orient. They were to sail through the cold, unknown waters beyond Norway, past the uppermost fringes of Asia, and then, hopefully, down the coast of Cathay (China) to the East Indies. No one knew what perils might lie along the way, let alone whether such a passage even existed.

Nevertheless, the hopes of many a man were pinned on the discovery of this Northeast Passage. The only other feasible route to the Orient—around the tip of Africa and through the Indian Ocean—had long been the exclusive monopoly of its discoverers, the Portuguese. Banned from using this vital seaway to the East, English merchants could neither compete for the spice trade nor find new markets for textiles, their own chief trading commodity. This was why the Northeast Passage held out such promise. At one and the same time, it would place the riches of the East within England's grasp, and open vital new outlets for England's manufactured goods.

The prime mover behind this search for the Northeast Passage was Sebastian Cabot, founder and governor of the London Company of Merchant Adventurers. It was he who had fitted out the three

Above: portrait of a gentleman presumed to be Sebastian Cabot, by Lorenzo Lotto. He had made voyages to the New World for both England and Spain as a young man, and later became the founder of the London Company of Merchant Adventurers.

vessels for the voyage, and he who had procured the royal letters of introduction carried by Willoughby and Chancellor. These documents were addressed—with more hope than certainty—to "the Kings, Princes, and other Potentates inhabiting the Northeast partes of the worlde, toward the mighty Empire of Cathay."

On their departure, Willoughby and Chancellor had been instructed to keep the ships within sight of one another at all times. This they did until they reached the Lofoten Islands, high up along the coast of Norway. But there, meeting first with thick, swirling mists and

then with violent winds, they became separated. Chancellor later wrote that he became "very pensive, heavy and sorrowful" as he sailed on alone in the coming weeks. How much more depressed he might have been had he known that he would never see Willoughby again! Within the next few months, Willoughby and all his men were to die of scurvy along the cold and barren coast of Lapland.

Chancellor continued northeast until he "came at last to the place where he found no night at all, but a continual light and brightness of the sun, shining clearly upon the huge and mighty sea."

Above: although Willoughby and Chancellor had instructions to remain together, they were separated by a wild storm along the coast of Norway. Such a furious storm is shown here, painted by Pieter Bruegel the Elder in about 1568, contemporary with the time of the voyage north to Russia.

Right: an icon with the portrait of Ivan the Terrible, the first Russian sovereign to take the title of czar.

Above: the Cap of Kazan, Ivan's crown, with its sable rim and peaked dome, worn by the czar on state occasions.

Left: the Throne Room in the Kremlin, the room in the royal residence where 'van received Richard Chancellor. The walls of the room were then crowded with tables and cupboards loaded with gold and silver plates and serving pieces. As this was the room where the czars received foreigners, it became the most famous of the Kremlin staterooms, and the one most talked of abroad.

Well within the Arctic Circle, he rounded the northern tip of Norway, where he found the coast curving southward, and soon came to a large bay (the White Sea). There he sighted a settlement and decided to land. When he stepped ashore, the inhabitants, awed "by the strange greatness" of his ship, fell before him to kiss his feet. Chancellor gently raised them up and asked to see their governor. He came, and gave Chancellor to understand that the town was Colmagro (near the present-day port of Archangel). The governor added modestly that it was but a small outpost of the great land of Muscovy, ruled by Czar Ivan IV.

At that time, few Englishmen had ever heard of Muscovy, or Russia, as it later came to be called. Chancellor had accidentally stumbled upon a whole new nation—and at a time when that nation was experiencing the rule of its very first czar, the man whom we call Ivan the Terrible.

Chancellor wanted to trade with the people of Colmagro, but they were afraid to do so without the permission of Czar Ivan. When Chancellor asked to see the czar, messengers were dispatched to the court at Moscow. After many days, they returned with an invitation from Ivan himself. Chancellor and his men at once set out for Moscow, traveling overland in horse-drawn sledges (heavy wooden sleighs), and escorted by strange men who wore sheepskin clothing

Right: an icon of the late 1400's or
early 1500's, showing an important
official of the Russian church, the
Metropolitan Alexey. This was used as
a holy image, and venerated in the
same way as a similar icon of a saint
or member of the Holy Family would be.

and spoke a wild, incomprehensible language. It was a frightening journey, one that took them 700 miles over endless fields of snow and ice, through dark, brooding forests, and across gleaming frozen rivers.

When at long last the travelers reached their destination, Chancellor was immediately struck by the size—and the primitiveness—of the Russian capital. Though much larger than London, he wrote later, "It is very rude and standeth without all order." The houses were no more than log cabins, a fact that helped to account for the numerous blazing buildings Chancellor saw in the city during his stay. Most of the citizens seemed to be living in dire poverty, their cheerless existence relieved only by their constant tobacco smoking and heavy reliance on vodka. Chancellor was appalled by the number of drunken men and women he saw in the streets. More than once he saw the body of a person who had fallen down drunk in the snow and been left there to freeze to death or to be eaten by wild dogs.

The drabness of the citizens' dwellings contrasted strongly with the lavish residence of the czar. Situated in a walled sector of the city called the Kremlin, Ivan's gaudy palace did not at first impress the English sea captain, who remarked sarcastically that its exterior was "not of the neatest." But once through its portals, he was dazzled by its splendor. In the gilded throne room stood 100 courtiers, each dressed in golden robes. But by far the grandest figure in the court was the czar himself. Ivan's robes were heavily encrusted with precious stones, and the gems that glittered from his golden scepter fairly blinded Chancellor with their brilliance.

Awed by all this magnificence, the English captain hesitated a moment, then strode resolutely forward and presented the letter

Below: the capture of Kazan, Ivan's first major victory over the Mongols. This picture of the mid-1500's—Kazan fell in 1552—shows the conquest as a triumph of the Cross over the Crescent.

from his own king, Edward VI. Ivan received it gravely, then motioned his guest to join him at dinner. The banquet table was in keeping with the richness of the court. All the plates and goblets were made of gold, and every course, from the roast swans to the great tankards of mead, was presented with lavish ceremony.

Chancellor was royally entertained at the czar's expense for several weeks. During this time, he had ample opportunity to observe the Russian way of life, and many things struck him as strange. One of these was the Russians' Eastern Orthodox religion, an elaborate and traditional form of Christianity unknown in Europe. A Protestant himself, Chancellor saw in this unfamiliar religion "such an excess of superstition as the like hath not been heard of." He considered the Russians' veneration of *icons* (religious pictures) idolatrous, and found their church services utterly baffling. Repeatedly kneeling and mumbling the words "Oh Lord, have mercy upon us," the congregation seemed to "gaggle and duck like so many geese." But what most distressed Chancellor was the behavior of the priests. As far as he could tell, they were illiterate, overbearing, and as fond of vodka as the rest of the populace. Nevertheless, he noted, the Church was held in great respect, and seemed to possess at least a third of the nation's wealth.

But if Chancellor found the customs of the Church curious, he found the might of the czar positively awesome. Less than 100 years had elapsed since the country had shaken off the harsh rule of the Tartars—the ruthless "Golden Horde" of Mongol tribes that had swept down upon Muscovy in the 1200's. For two centuries, while Western Europe experienced the flowering of the Renaissance, generations of Muscovites had suffered under the cruel yoke of Mongol domination. Towns and cities had been burned to the ground, and many thousands slaughtered. The art of living had been lost in the struggle for survival. At last, in 1480, the grand prince of Moscow, Ivan III, had succeeded in driving the Golden Horde out of Russia. But by that time, the kingdom had fallen far behind Western Europe in the development of technology, statecraft, art, and scholarship.

The Mongols' single contribution to Russian civilization had been the lesson of tyranny. Ivan IV (the Terrible), grandson of Ivan III, had learned that lesson well. The first Russian ruler to be crowned czar, Ivan wielded his power with a mailed fist. He created a small army of secret police and began a reign of terror, reducing the power of the country's nobility by having hundreds of aristocrats arrested and executed. He put whole towns and villages to the sword, and murdered any church officials who opposed him. He initiated a series of laws that bound the peasants to the land in a form of economic slavery called serfdom. Then, having got all Russia under his control, he turned his attention to his grandfather's old enemies, the Mongols, driving them out of Astrakhan, their stronghold on the Caspian Sea, and extending Russia's borders south to the lower Volga River Basin.

Right: the busy port of Hamburg in the late 1400's. Since the early 1200's, enterprising merchants from a group of north German cities known as the Hanseatic League had held a near-monopoly of trade in the Baltic, and in particular with Russia. Hamburg was one of the most important of these Hanseatic towns. Here Russian grain, honey, and furs were exchanged for European metal work and linens.

Left: Edward VI, the English king who began the diplomatic exchange with the czars. Shown with him, kneeling, is the Lord Mayor of London, Sir George Barnes, who was one of the first men to be consul of the Muscovy Company, as the Company of Merchant Adventurers came to be called.

The basis of Ivan's power lay in his absolute control over the immense Russian army. Made up of men who had nothing else in the world but what he chose to give them, it was a force to be reckoned with. Chancellor was deeply impressed by the iron discipline and physical stamina of the soldiers: "They are a kind of people most sparing in diet and most patient in extremity of cold," he wrote. "For when the ground is covered with snow and is grown terrible and hard with the frost, this Russ hangs up his mantle, or soldier's coat, against that part whence the wind and snow drives, and so, making a little fire, lies down with his back toward the weather; his drink is cold water from the river, mingled with oatmeal, and this is all his good cheer."

While Chancellor was busy admiring Russia's army and criticizing its religion, he was also engaged in appraising its trading possibilities. He had already found buyers for the woolen goods he had brought with him, and had taken a shrewd look at what the Russians had to offer in exchange. It was an impressive list: flax, hemp, wax, honey, salt, oil, and—most valuable of all—furs. Among these were fox, beaver, and seal, as well as luxurious mink, ermine, and sable.

But if Chancellor was delighted with the prospect of trade with Russia, Ivan was equally delighted with the prospect of ties with England. Anxious to pursue his wars against the Mongols, he was eager for powerful Western allies, and even more eager for the military supplies he knew England could provide. Thus, when Chancellor returned to England in 1554, he carried with him a warmly welcoming letter from the czar, promising England the most generous trading terms and privileges if her merchants would do him the honor of visiting his country.

Mary Tudor, who had become Queen of England during Chancellor's absence, was well pleased with the outcome of his voyage. She at once granted the Company of Merchant Adventurers a special charter and urged them to waste no time in sending traders to Russia. For the moment, the grand scheme of opening up a Northeast Passage was laid aside. In discovering Russia, Chancellor had located a vastly promising new market, one that was not only nearer than Cathay, but practically an English monopoly already.

Thus began a lively commercial romance between England and her new-found trading partner. The very next year, Richard Chancellor made a second voyage to Russia. Again he had no trouble

Left: Antony Jenkinson, shown in an Elizabethan miniature by Nicholas Hilliard in 1588. He was a young man, already very experienced in foreign travel, when he was chosen to take the place of Chancellor, who had drowned.

Right: a Russian church—the Church of the Intercession of the Virgin—in winter. In Jenkinson's time, and for years afterward, travel in Russia was only really easy during the winter, when the surfaces of roads and fields had frozen hard. During the summer almost all travel was stopped by mud.

selling his wares, and again he was royally entertained in Moscow. And this time, Chancellor obtained from the czar an official document granting the Muscovy Company—as the group of Merchant Adventurers now called themselves—the right to buy and sell wherever they liked in the czar's domains. But the brave captain did not live to carry the good news back to England himself. On the return voyage, his ship ran into a storm off the coast of Scotland, and Chancellor, along with many of his men, was drowned.

The man chosen to take Chancellor's place as merchant-ambassador to Russia was Antony Jenkinson, an experienced traveler who had already journeyed far and wide through Europe, Asia Minor, and northern Africa. Like Chancellor before him, Jenkinson was to serve both as an agent for the Muscovy Company and as Queen Mary's special representative to the court of the czar.

When he reached Colmagro in December, 1557, Jenkinson set out for Moscow, as Chancellor had done, in a convoy of horse-drawn sledges. By changing the horses every 40 miles, the travelers made rapid progress, gliding over the endless Russian plains in an eerie silence broken only by the tinkle of the harness bells. As they swept along, the runners of the sledges left a shimmering trail in the snow beneath the branches of bare, frost-covered birch trees that looked, as a later traveler put it, "like white coral encrusted with brilliant diamond dust."

Jenkinson arrived in Moscow just in time to attend the czar's lavish Christmas banquet, and a few days later he was invited to witness the Twelfth Night "Blessing of the Waters." This ceremony began with a long procession from the largest church in the city to the Moskva River. At the head marched the Church officials carrying icons and a large wooden cross. Behind them walked the czar, accompanied by all his *boyars* (high-ranking landowners). The candlelit procession slowly wound its way through the city streets and down to the river, where a great hole had been hacked in the ice. Before a hushed crowd, the *patriarch* (chief bishop of the Church)

MUNICIPAL LIBRARY

No. 124720
MUNICIPAL LIBRARY

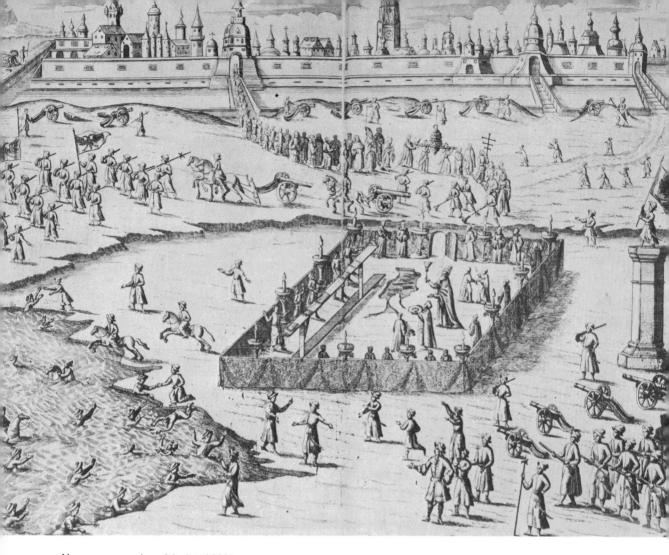

Above: an engraving of the late 1600's showing the Blessing of the Waters on the Twelfth Night of Christmas. Antony Jenkinson witnessed this annual ceremony when he visited Russia in 1558.

formally blessed the water, then sprinkled some of it on the czar and the boyars. "This done," reports Jenkinson, "divers children were thrown in, and sick people, and plucked out quickly again, and divers Tartars christened."

Jenkinson later learned that this type of enforced baptism was considered the surest—and the quickest—way to convert the heathen. It was common practice to drive newly conquered Mongols, fleeing for their lives, into the nearest river. Then, as they crawled back to shore, more dead than alive, a Russian priest standing on the bank would make the sign of the cross over them, officially turning them into Christians.

Instant conversion was not the only tradition Jenkinson took note of during his stay in Russia. He observed the country's marriage customs closely and found them "in most points abominable." He reports that, "One common rule is amongst them, that if the woman be not beaten with the whip at least once a week she will not be good, and the women say that if their husbands did not beat them they would not love them." Indeed, a Russian wife's position was exceedingly precarious at the best of times. If a man wished to marry

Left: by the time Jenkinson returned to England, Elizabeth I was on the throne. This portrait, by an unknown artist in 1560, shows her dressed for her coronation on January 15, 1559.

again, he simply disposed of the wife he already had by driving her into a nunnery or flogging her to death—a form of "correction" not punishable by law.

In April, 1558, Jenkinson received the czar's permission to travel south to Astrakhan. Because roving bandits made travel through the countryside hazardous, he made the journey by boat down the Volga River with an armed escort. When the party reached the lower Volga River Basin, Jenkinson had his first encounter with the Mongols. He was shocked by their primitive way of life. A nomadic people, they moved from place to place on horseback, and scorned the growing of crops. They said that it was the practice of eating bread, "made from the top of a weed [wheat]" that made the Christians so weak. They themselves lived on a diet of horsemeat, often eaten raw (the original form of modern-day "steak Tartare"), and on fermented mare's milk.

But the Mongols Jenkinson saw in Astrakhan were far from flourishing. Only four years had passed since Ivan's army had conquered the region, and the effects of the war were still being felt. Astrakhan was in the grip of famine and plague, and heaps of decaying bodies lay everywhere. Over 100,000 had died, and the miserable survivors were being sold as slaves. Jenkinson reports that he could have bought any number of Mongol children for the price of a single loaf of bread.

The Englishman's journey did not end at Astrakhan. Hoping to reach Cathay, he sailed across the Caspian Sea and traveled eastward by caravan to the Mongol *khanate* (princedom) of Bukhara. But there, 800 miles from the Caspian, the local *khan* (ruler) turned him back. Disappointed, he returned to Moscow, paid his respects to the czar, and set sail for England. He found the nation rejoicing over the recent accession of young Queen Elizabeth I. Like Queen Mary before her, Elizabeth heartily approved of the Muscovy Company's activities. And so it was with her blessing, in 1566, that Antony Jenkinson was again sent to Moscow. This time, his task was to negotiate for an exclusive English trading monopoly in Russia.

Jenkinson's mission was completely successful. Not only did the czar grant the wished-for monopoly, he also promised that merchants from any other country would have their goods confiscated. But Ivan wanted something in exchange. He was beginning to feel more and more menaced by his enemies, and, in 1567, Queen Elizabeth received a secret letter from him asking if she would grant him asylum in England if he were forced to flee. He also requested England's help in his wars against the Mongols. The queen was quite willing to give asylum to the czar, but she was not prepared to involve her country in a military alliance with him.

Elizabeth's answer reached Ivan at an unfortunate time. He had just learned of the queen's official proclamation forbidding Englishmen from wearing furs—Russia's chief export. Her motive in doing so was simply to protect England's own woolen industry, but Ivan took it as a personal insult. In retaliation he threatened to take away every trading privilege he had thus far granted to the Muscovy Company. It took a whole succession of English ambassadors to heal the breach and recoup the company's trading rights in Russia.

One of these ambassadors, an extraordinary man named Sir Jerome Bowes, soon became known far and wide for his boldness and bravado in the presence of the czar. On his very first meeting with Ivan, Bowes refused to doff his hat. Outraged, Ivan roared that the only other man who had ever refused to do so had been punished by having his hat nailed to his head. Bowes still would not comply, explaining that he was "the ambassador of the invincible Queen of England, who does not veil her bonnet nor bare her head to any Prince living." Ivan was impressed with this display of courage and loyalty. "Look you there!" he said to his boyars, "There is a brave fellow indeed that dares to do and say thus much for his mistress," and thereupon gave Bowes a hearty welcome. On another occasion, Bowes is said to have flatly refused to go up the stairs to the throne room until two boyars who had rushed ahead of him had been dragged all the way back down again, feet first.

The number of English ambassadors to the court at Moscow

Right: both England and Russia were eager to establish trade, with Russia desiring the fine English wool as much as the English wanted Russian furs. Here a table carpet of the 1500's is decorated in part with a scene of shepherds and their flocks, the raw materials of the important wool trade.

Below: this carved bench-end, also from the 1500's, shows an English cloth-weaver of the time, apparently at work pressing a piece of cloth.

declined during the later years of Ivan's rule. The czar was slowly going mad, and had begun a series of cruel persecutions and arbitrary executions. Following his death in 1584, there was a period of relative peace, but in 1605, after the death of Czar Boris Godunov, Russia was again thrown into turmoil by the start of a bloody civil war. This period, known as the "Time of Troubles," ended in 1613, with the accession of Czar Michael Romanov. The Romanovs were to rule Russia for the next 300 years, until the February Revolution of 1917 ended the monarchy.

Right: the reception of the foreign ambassadors by the Czar Alexis, as shown in Adam Olearius's account of his visits to Moscow, published in 1647. In the ceremonial chamber the boyars and court officials served mainly as decorative background.

Left: Sir Jerome Bowes, wearing his hat. His stubborn insistence on his queen's dignity—and his own, as her representative—won Ivan's respect.

It was during Czar Michael's reign that travelers from Western Europe began visiting Russia again. Among them were men from countries other than England, for by now, Russia was actively seeking trade with a variety of nations. One of these was the tiny German state of Holstein, which sent embassies to Moscow in 1634, 1636, and 1639. All three missions included a man named Adam Olearius, whose special duty it was to gather useful information about Russian customs.

Olearius was a keen observer, and wrote vividly about his experiences in Russia. He records that shortly after his arrival in 1634, while riding through one of the villages in the north of the empire, his party was suddenly set upon by swarms of bees. "The horses began to wince, stand upon their hinder feet, and beat the ground as if they were bewitched"—much to the alarm of their riders. Olearius later learned that "it was a strategem of the inhabitants, who had incensed the bees purposely to prevent our lodging in the village."

In his report, Olearius describes Russian men as "corpulent, fat and strong, and of the same color as other Europeans." About the women he says that they "are well-proportioned, having passable good faces, but they paint so palpable [i.e., use such heavy make-up], that if they had a handful of meal cast in their faces, they could not disfigure themselves as much as the paint does."

As in Chancellor's time, there were frequent fires in Moscow. A good many of them were caused by the carelessness of tobacco smokers, and during Olearius' first visit to Muscovy, a special proclamation was issued forbidding the smoking of tobacco. Perhaps it was this deprivation that made the Russians Olearius saw so irritable. They were, he concluded, "a very quarrelsome people, who assail each other like dogs, with fierce, harsh words."

Above: Adam Olearius. He was a well-educated German whose job on all three embassies to Russia was to gain information about the general life in Russia. He apparently was not able to read English and so was unfamiliar with the accounts of the English travelers. This makes his close agreement with their view of Russian life and habits all the more interesting to us today.

But the aspect of Russian life that most impressed Olearius was its extreme insularity. He records that the people were forbidden to travel abroad on pain of death, in order that "they might stay tranquil in slavery and not see the free institutions that exist in foreign lands." This was one reason why there was so little interest in learning or scholarship inside the empire. As Olearius puts it, "Just as they are ignorant of the praiseworthy sciences, they are little interested in memorable events or the history of their fathers, and they care little to find out the qualities of foreign peoples."

In fact, even the learning of a foreign language was officially banned in Russia at this time, and all foreign visitors were regarded with dark suspicion. Baron Augustine Meyerberg, the Austrian ambassador to Moscow from 1661 to 1663, voiced a familiar complaint when he said that the Russians made no distinction between peaceful diplomats and prisoners of war. Meyerberg himself was kept under virtual house arrest during the whole of his stay in Moscow.

But suspicion of foreigners and foreign ideas did not prevent the Russians from employing Western technicians to perform the tasks their own lack of learning rendered impossible. One such foreign expert was Samuel Collins, an English doctor who, in 1661, traveled to Moscow to become the czar's private physician. Collins spent nine years in Russia, and seems to have been well enough content there, despite the drawbacks of living in a society where "the people . . . look upon Learning as a Monster, and fear it no less than a Ship of Wildfire."

Certainly the good doctor found Russian justice no match for England's due process of law. As he wrote later, "Their judiciary proceedings are very confused. The accused cannot be condemned although a thousand witnesses come in against him, except he confesses the fact; and to this end they want not torments to extort confessions." The punishment meted out to those found plotting against the state was harsh in the extreme. "Traitors are severely tormented and afterward sent to Siberia, and [along] the way . . . softly put under the ice."

To us today, the very word "Siberia" has a forlorn ring to it, reminding us of the countless political prisoners who have died in its grim labor camps. But in Dr. Collins' day, there were as yet no official Siberian prison camps, and "Sibir," as it is called in Russian, generally had other, more hopeful connotations. To the majority of Russians, it was still "a vast, unknown province, reaching to the walls of Cathay," a frontier land as rich in potential as it was rife with danger.

As early as 1584, an English merchant named Antony Marsh had tried, unsuccessfully, to penetrate this harsh, mysterious land in the hope of reaching Cathay. But the iron gates to this wilderness were not to be breached by mere merchants—either English or Russian. The conquest of Siberia called for men as uncompromising as the land itself.

Above: one of the engravings made from sketches by Baron Augustine Meyerberg. During his time in Russia he made many drawings of the ambassadorial precinct in Moscow, where he complained that he was treated much like a prisoner of war.

Right: the trade between Russia and England continued fitfully—these English knives, dated 1607, were brought back to England from Russia where they were found in the 1800's. They carry the London Cutler's Company proof mark, and have carved ivory handles representing English monarchs.

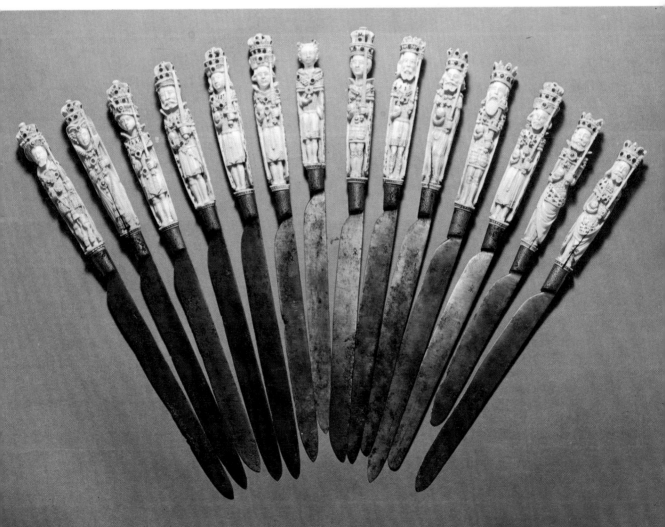

29

Below: Siberia, from a world map of 1550 by Pierre Desceliers. The topography is almost entirely imaginary, populated by strange monsters. In the center is the Mongol Khan.

The Siberian Frontier

2

However bleak and desolate northern Russia had appeared to English visitors in the mid-1500's, it was, in fact, a travelers' paradise compared to Siberia. Russia, after all, was an established kingdom with established frontiers. Within its confines, no traveler could journey far without finding a town or village where he might stop to warm up and ask directions. In fact, despite its newness to the English, Russia was really a "known" land, even a tamed land.

Not so Siberia; in the 1550's, this northern third of Asia loomed almost as mysterious as the dark side of the moon. Few travelers had ever been as far as the Ural Mountains, where Siberia begins, let alone into the 4 million square miles of *tundra* (flat, treeless plains), marshland, forest and *steppe* (grassland) beyond. How far east would a man have to travel through these trackless wastes to reach Cathay? What manner of strange people and places might he see along the way? These were questions even the Russians did not ask—and for a very good reason. Siberia—and, indeed, all of Central Asia—was still in the viselike grip of the Mongols, and few men were willing to risk an unnecessary encounter with them. Siberia might have remained "off limits" to the Russians for a long time to come, had it not been for one of those curious tricks of history that matches the right man to the right challenge at the right time.

The story begins in the 1560's, when a family of Russian merchants named Strogonov began trading with the Samoyeds, a group of Siberian tribes who occasionally traveled west to Russia to sell furs. Finding that the Samoyeds would accept mere trinkets for their ermines and sables, the Strogonovs established a brisk trade with them, and soon became very wealthy. To speed delivery of the pelts, the Strogonovs built trading posts nearer and nearer to Siberia, until, by 1578, they had reached the very foothills of the Urals. But the next year, their lucrative business came to an abrupt halt. The Mongols had swept down upon the Samoyeds in Siberia, and cut off their trade routes to Russia.

Maxim Strogonov, head of the Ural trading station, was about to close the post and go home, when an extraordinary collection of men arrived at his camp. He counted almost 800 of them, weary and bedraggled, and obviously on the run. He had no need to ask who they were. It was clear that they were Cossacks, fleeing from the armies of the czar.

The sight of Cossacks on the move was not unusual in Muscovy.

© Geographical Projects

Left: Eurasia. Its sprawling deserts,
frozen wastes, and lofty mountain
ranges make it one of the most bleak
and challenging regions in the world.

These "free laborers," or "freebooters," as some would have it,
were a law unto themselves, a rebel army of hard-riding brigands
who roamed at will throughout Russia. Their forefathers, runaway
serfs and outlaws from southwestern Russia and eastern Poland,
had banded together early in the 1400's to form their own fugitive
society. Always ready to give refuge to people in trouble, they had
soon been joined by many other brave and desperate men and, by
the mid-1500's, were numbered in the thousands.

Restless and venturesome, the Cossacks considered farming a
foolish waste of time, and possessed few permanent villages. Most
of them preferred the proud, free life of the wayfarer, moving
swiftly over the southern steppes on horseback, or scudding down
the rivers in the streamlined sailboats they called "seagulls." They
lived by piracy, swooping down on towns, estates, and rich
monasteries to loot and plunder. They were feared far and wide and,
as a Turkish chronicler later wrote, "It can be stated with confidence
that one cannot find bolder men on earth who care less about life . . .
and fear death less." But if, as another writer put it, a Cossack's life
was "rough, tough, short, and cheap," it was also vivid and joyful.
They loved to dance, drink, and make merry, and were known
everywhere for their haunting folk songs, which seemed to echo
the wild and lonely beauty of their beloved steppes.

From time to time, the Cossacks hired themselves out to the
czars as mercenary soldiers—but only on condition that they be
allowed to keep their independence. They fought the Mongols in
Astrakhan for Ivan the Terrible, and played a vital role in the region's
conquest. But the Cossacks' triumphs in Astrakhan did not make
up for the havoc they continued to wreak in Russia. Ivan was
prepared to let them rule themselves, but not to let them terrorize
the country. When the town of Nogoy was sacked and burned early
in 1578, the czar dispatched an army to find and destroy the Cossacks
responsible.

These were the hunted men who arrived at Maxim Strogonov's
camp in the summer of 1579. Their leader, a fierce-looking man
named Yermak, approached Strogonov and asked for employment
for himself and his men. To the Russian trader, it seemed a heaven-
sent opportunity. Who *but* the Cossacks could drive the Mongols
out of Samoyed territory? Strogonov offered Yermak and his
followers a supply of new muskets if they would take on the Mongols

33

beyond the mountains. The assignment was a daunting one, but Yermak did not hesitate to accept it. Behind, in Russia, were the dogged armies of the czar and almost certain capture. Ahead, in Siberia, were the Mongol barbarians and the possibility of a splendid conquest. It was a challenge no Cossack could resist.

Late in 1579, Yermak led his men across the Ural Mountains, built a fleet of boats, and then sailed down the Tura River into western Siberia. There, after a brief skirmish with a small band of Mongols, the Cossacks built a camp in which to wait out the winter. The cold was intense, often reaching temperatures of —40°F., and

Above: the Cossacks were traditionally scornful of authority from any quarter. Here, in an incident well known in Russian folklore, Cossacks compose a mocking letter to a sultan who had dared to offer them his protection.

Left: two Cossacks of the Caucasus, in a watercolor by Sir Robert Ker Porter. By the early 1800's, when this picture was painted, it was common for Cossack soldiers to make up special regiments in the czar's armies.

sometimes a man keeping the night watch would freeze to death in his tracks. But the Cossacks were a tough breed, and when they broke camp and set off again the following spring, there were very few gaps in the ranks.

Again they followed the Tura, moving swiftly down the river in their streamlined "seagulls." News of their prowess in battle had already reached the local Mongol ruler, Kutchum Khan, via the Mongol forces Yermak had routed the previous year. Kutchum had heard the Cossacks described as "invincible warriors in winged boats, with fiery unseen arrows [bullets] and death-bearing thunder." Determined to stop their advance, the khan prepared an ingenious ambush. He had heavy chains stretched across the lower Tura River, and stationed hundreds of bowmen along the banks. In due course, the boats were sighted coming down the river, and the assembled Mongols, facing upstream, prepared to rain a hail of arrows on the figures they could see crowding the gunwhales. Too late, they saw that the "men" in the boats were merely bundles of straw dressed in Cossack shirts! The real Cossacks had come around by land, and were already shooting and cutting their way through the Mongol ranks from behind.

Driving their fleeing enemies before them, Yermak and his men struck out for Sibir, Kutchum Khan's capital on the banks of the Irtysh River. There the khan had assembled a mighty army, many times the size of Yermak's. But the Cossacks possessed two advantages over their enemies: superior military strategy, and a fierce determination to win against all odds. These qualities won the day for them, and, on October 25, 1581, Yermak marched triumphantly into Sibir.

But the conquest of the Mongol capital did not mean the end of Mongol resistance. Garrisoned at Sibir, the Cossacks were surrounded by a countryside still in arms. More serious, Yermak had by now lost almost 500 of his men—the victims of disease and

Below: Samoyeds at the temporary market at Obdorsk. The Samoyed people were determinedly nomadic, and after some clashes with the Russians came to the agreement that they would hold a yearly market and sell their furs, but only on the condition that the Russians would build no permanent structure on Samoyed land. The market was held on the border, in February, so it was always dark. This picture shows the scene, with a Russian church in the background to indicate the sovereignty of Russia.

Right: a portrait of Yermak, the leader of the Cossack band that began the exploration of Siberia. He was born in 1540, of a Cossack family. He was reputedly the grandson of a destitute migrant named Afanasy Alenin, who became a bandit in Russia's forests. Alenin's grandson Vasili took up the tradition of banditry under the pseudonym of Yermak. He was 38 years old when he made the agreement with Strogonov to drive the Mongols out of the territory of the Samoyed people.

starvation, as well as of battle. Reinforcements were desperately needed. In 1582, Yermak sent a messenger to Moscow to lay the newly conquered realm at the czar's feet and beg for assistance in its defense.

Ivan's response to this astonishing news was instantaneous. At once he granted Yermak a full pardon for all his past sins, and bestowed upon him the highest honors in the land. In token of his gratitude, he sent the Cossack leader his own royal mantle. Lastly, he acknowledged Yermak as his special representative in Siberia, and informed him that 300 of his best soldiers were on their way.

Before these reinforcements could reach him, however, Yermak and some of his men were ambushed near Sibir and, in trying to make his escape, Yermak was drowned in the mighty Irtysh River. After the death of their leader, the last 150 Cossacks hung on at Sibir until 1584, when the czar's reinforcements finally arrived. With their help, the Cossacks built a new fortress at Tobolsk, 12 miles from Sibir, and began to extend their power eastward.

They soon reached the Ob River, which runs through the center of the West Siberian Plain. There they met the Samoyed tribes that Yermak had been sent to liberate some 10 years before. The

Above: the battle between the Mongols and Yermak's men on the banks of the Irtysh River. In the background is the Mongol stronghold of Isker, one of the many places captured by Yermak and his hard-riding Cossack forces.

Cossacks thought them a strange people because they rode on reindeer instead of horses, and followed a primitive religion that called for the bloody sacrifice of animals on crude stone altars. Nonetheless, the Samoyeds seemed friendly and well intentioned. They were anxious to please their visitors with gifts and demonstrations of magic, and anxious, too, to begin trading with the Russians again.

But the Samoyeds' usefulness as middlemen in the Siberian fur trade was past. Now that the Cossacks had forged a way into western Siberia, the Russians themselves could procure the ermines and sables that fetched such a handsome price back in Moscow. Russian traders were soon beating a path eastward over the Ural Mountains, and the traffic in furs grew so rapidly that, by 1600, more than a million pelts were pouring into Moscow from the Siberian outposts every year.

But the real exploration and conquest of this harsh new land remained in the hands of the Cossacks. Seeking excitement and adventure, they came by the hundreds, lured on by the sheer expanse of a territory that seemed to stretch away to the very edge of the world. There, in a realm of wolves and bears, blizzards and dust storms, lay a challenge formidable enough to test the bravest man. And many brave men died in taking up that challenge. On one occasion, a party of 129 Cossacks, caught by the sudden onset of winter, were forced to make camp on an icy marshland deep in the wilderness. Many soon starved to death. Driven mad by hunger, the others ate their dead companions, then took to killing one another for food. By spring, there were only 30 survivors. These stark facts speak tellingly of the grim choices to be made in a land where nature itself is savage and uncompromising.

By the early 1600's, the majority of the Mongols had drifted southward, but there were still scattered tribes ready to offer resistance as the Cossacks swept eastward to the Yenisey River, and thence over the Central Siberian Plateau to the Lena River and Lake

Below: an engraving showing a Russian embassy at Regensburg in 1576. At this time, embassies were actually trade missions. Behind the ambassador come the boyars carrying furs, the staple of Russia's foreign trade.

Right: a wooden fort at Bratsk, on the Angara River, which was built in 1631 as a collecting center for furs for the czars. Originally the men who took the furs for the czar were soldiers, some of them Yermak's surviving Cossacks, but later, other hunted men—runaways from central Russia and Cossacks from the Don River area—came to try their luck in the vast expanses of the Siberian forests.

Baykal. There, along the shores of the deepest lake in the world, they encountered tribes like the Tungus and Buriats—nomadic hunters and herdsmen who lived in caves and used primitive stone tools. More often than not, these tribes proved hostile, and the Cossacks frequently had to fight a series of pitched battles before they could move on.

In the wake of the Cossacks came the ever-eager fur traders, and behind them, government officials sent by the czar to collect tribute from conquered tribes. Lastly came a few brave settlers who saw the vast Siberian grazing lands as a place to build farms and villages. Market towns were established farther and farther east: Tomsk, on the Ob River in 1604; Krasnoyarsk on the Yenisey River in 1627; and Yakutsk, on the Lena River in 1632.

But always it was the Cossacks who led the way. In 1638, they began pioneering a route eastward from Yakutsk through the East Siberian Uplands. After many months of toiling through rough and rocky terrain, they found the land sloping away abruptly toward a vast body of water—the Sea of Okhotsk. There, nearly 4,000 miles from Moscow, they had reached the eastern limit of the Asian main-

land. In less than 60 years, the Cossacks had forged a path across the world's largest continent. Perhaps, when they reached the sea, these hardy Cossack pioneers experienced the same sense of frustration felt by America's frontiersmen when they reached the Pacific. Nevertheless, much of Siberia still remained to be explored, and the next 30 years witnessed a whole series of daring Cossack expeditions, both to the north and to the south.

In 1644, a small fleet commanded by a Cossack named Deshnef traveled north along the Kolyma River to the East Siberian Sea on the north coast of Asia. Following the coast, Deshnef reached and rounded the extreme northeast tip of the continent and, according to some sources, may even have explored the coast southward around the spoon-shaped peninsula now known as Kamchatka.

Meanwhile, other Cossacks were blazing a trail southeast through the uplands to an important river called the Amur, the northern-most limit of the great Manchu Empire of China. In 1643, the Cossack Poyarkov followed the river northeastward to its mouth on the Sea of Okhotsk. In 1649, he was followed by a band of Cossacks under a bold adventurer named Khabarov. This group not only reached the

Above left: a drawing of a shaman of the Tungus tribe, one of the most numerous groups in Siberia, from a book published around 1810. The shamans were medicine men, who knew something about medicinal herbs, but did most of their healing by means of dancing, dressed in elaborate clothing made of leather strips, with bells and cymbals attached.
Above: a tribal Siberian sorceress.

Above: Cossack troops in Switzerland in the year 1799, depicted in a gouache dated 1802 by Wilhelm von Kobell. The Cossacks retained their vigorous enjoyment of life wherever they went. This painting shows them dancing to music played by a band of their enemies, the French, on the opposite bank.

Amur River, but also traveled down its length, attacking villages along the way in the name of the czar. Word of Khabarov's maneuvers soon reached the Manchus, and a force of Chinese soldiers was sent to oust the invaders. But on this—and on several subsequent occasions—the Cossacks succeeded in routing the Chinese. For the moment, the Russians were in possession of the mighty river. To assert their claim, they built settlements along its banks and sent embassies southward to negotiate at the court of the Manchu rulers in Peking.

The Manchus, however, remained adamantly uncooperative, and in 1684 launched a full-scale attack on the Russian settlements in the Amur River Valley. Despite heroic resistance, the Cossacks were defeated and forced to evacuate the area. Five years later, by the Treaty of Nerchinsk, Russia officially gave up its claims to the eastern Amur River Valley. But there was one compensation. The treaty included a proviso granting the Russians certain trading rights in China. Russian merchants were quick to take up this offer, and

soon, caravans loaded with Chinese silks, bales of tea, and carefully packed porcelain were winding their way westward, through the deserts, steppes, and mountains, to Russia.

And what of Russia itself during this century of Siberian exploration and expansion? The "Time of Troubles" had come and gone, but still the nation remained bogged down in ignorance and tyranny. Serfdom was even more widespread and oppressive, and the czars continued to rule with an iron hand. Only the Cossacks retained real freedom and scope for action—both within the country and outside its borders. Not for them the prohibitions against travel outside of Russia. They cheerfully accepted offers from foreign governments to serve as mercenary soldiers, and took part in many a great battle in Western Europe. In 1683, for example, they helped the Hungarians drive an invading Turkish army away from the beseiged city of Vienna.

By far the most dashing and notorious Cossack in Russia at this time was a man named Stenka Razin. Exceptionally tall and strong, he practically became a legend in his own time for his daring exploits and his scorn of all authority. He led his men on brazen daylight raids up and down the Volga, and everywhere he went attracted flocks of loyal followers who called him *Batushka* (father).

Right: a group of Siberian merchants entertaining Chinese traders in the border town of Kiatcha. After some disagreements with the Russians about the terms of the trading arrangements, the Chinese would do business only with the Siberians, and only in Kiatcha.

His deeds both delighted and terrified the common people, for no one knew where he might strike next.

In 1668, Stenka arrived in Astrakhan and quickly won to his side a large number of officers and men from the czar's own army. When the czar sent another army against him, the deserters from the first infiltrated the second, and persuaded the soldiers to throw their officers into the river and join up with Stenka. The Cossack leader greeted his new troops with an impassioned speech of welcome: "At last my friends, you are free; what you have just done liberates

Right: "The Siege of Vienna in 1683," by Franz Geffels. The Cossacks became famous for their skill as mercenary soldiers, and when the papal nuncio in Cracow reported that Cossacks in the Polish service were coming to relieve Vienna from the Turkish siege, he added they were "reckoned to be the best infantry which one can send against the Turks."

you from the yoke of your tyrants. . . . It is to destroy them that Heaven has put you under my protection. Help me and we will finish what we have begun!"

Stenka Razin was not always so warlike. Sometimes he could be positively sentimental. On one of his southern raids, he had captured a Persian princess, whom he dearly loved. But one evening, while sailing down the Volga, he got very drunk and took it into his head that his affection for the girl would make the river jealous. After all, he told his companions, it was to the Volga that he owed his good

Left: the great Cossack Stenka Razin sitting in one of his longboats. A foreigner who met him described him as tall, well-built, a man who carried himself with dignity and haughtiness.

fortunes. Then, addressing the river, he said, "I seem to hear thy reproaches, that I have never given *thee* anything." Stenka paused for a moment. Then, with tears streaming down his face, he cried, "I offer thee with all my heart what is dearest to me in the world!" So saying, he seized the hapless princess and threw her into the river. There, weighted down with her jewels and golden robes, the poor girl sank to her death.

But such acts of reckless extravagance were not for the average Russian. Life for the common man was one of relentless, backbreaking toil, unrelieved by any hope of advancement. Russia had but two classes: the very rich and the very poor. It was not uncommon for estate owners to possess 100,000 serfs—men and women who slaved on the land year in and year out, and yet could not even call their miserable huts their own. Schools were unheard of, and even the rich were uneducated. Science and technology were still regarded with profound suspicion, and the whole Russian population remained as abysmally ignorant as it had been under Ivan the Terrible.

This was the state of affairs when Czar Peter I (later called Peter the Great) came to power in 1689. Peter, unlike his predecessors, was not content with things as they were. He wanted to modernize his benighted country and make it a great power along Western lines. As a boy, he had learned about the West from the foreign

Left: the drunken Stenka Razin throws his Persian princess from his ship into the waters of the Volga. This engraving of the incident is by the Dutch traveler Jan Struys, who was visiting the Cossack leader on his ship when the event occurred.

Right: Stenka Razin gathered a band of destitute Cossacks around him and they went out together on a rampage of reckless plundering that lasted for four years. Toward the end, Stenka began a "crusade" to rally the people against the boyars, whom he called traitors to the czar. His rebellion was finally crushed by the government and he and his brother, Frolka, shown here, were executed in 1671.

RAZIN the R

his Brother

Left: a portrait of Peter the Great as a ship's carpenter's apprentice. During much of his journey throughout Europe he traveled incognito. This picture was painted while he was in The Netherlands.

merchants and ambassadors living in Moscow. His interest in the West never waned, and in 1697, he assembled a special delegation to travel through Europe and learn about Western technology and statecraft. This in itself was novel enough, but the most extraordinary aspect of the mission was that it included Peter himself. As Voltaire put it, "It was a thing unparalleled in history, ancient or modern, for a sovereign to withdraw from his kingdom for the sole purpose of learning the art of government."

The art of government, however, was not the only thing Peter was interested in. In The Netherlands, posing as a junior member of the Russian delegation, he hired himself out to a shipbuilder, and earned his living under the humble name of Pieter Baas. On receiving his

Right: an engraving made in 1748 of the speech Peter the Great made to William III of England in Utrecht in 1697. The speech reads: " Most Renowned Emperor. It was not the desire of seeing the celebrated Cities of the German Empire, or the most potent Republic of the Universe that made me leave my throne in a distant Country & my victorious Armies; but the vehement passion alone of seeing the most brave and most generous Hero of the Age. I have my wish & am sufficiently re-compensed for my Travel, in being and admitted into your Presence; your kind Embraces have given me more satisfaction than the taking of Azoph & triumphing over the Tartars, but the conquest is yours; your Martial Genius directed my sword, and the generous emulation of your Exploits instill'd into my breast ye first thoughts I had of enlarging my dominions. I cannot ex-press in words the veneration I have for your sacred person; my unparalleled journey is one proof of it . . . if either in peace or war your industrious Subjects will trade to the most northern parts of the world, the ports of Russia shall be free to them; I will grant them greater immunities than ever they yet had and have them enrolled among the most precious accorde of my empire, to be a perpetual memorial of the Esteem I have for the worthiest of Kings."

first salary, he remarked, "This will serve to buy me a pair of shoes, of which I stand in great need." Peter also studied shipbuilding in England before going on to Vienna and then to Venice. But there, news of trouble at home forced him to cut short his visit. He returned to Moscow, asserted his mastery over the nobles who had tried to seize power in his absence, and then set to work on his task of modernizing Russia.

He began his program by sending a large number of young Russians abroad to study. He encouraged them to take their wives with them, an idea that scandalized the conservative Russian Church. He next attempted to update the old-fashioned appearance of his people by issuing a *ukase* (royal order) that all coats be trimmed to

Left: a woodcut cartoon showing Peter cutting off the beard of one of his subjects. It was part of the relentless campaign to Westernize the Russians.

Right: Northern Asia. The map shows the journeys of England's first merchant-ambassadors to Russia, as well as the routes followed by the fearless Cossack adventurers and devoted scientists who explored Siberia.

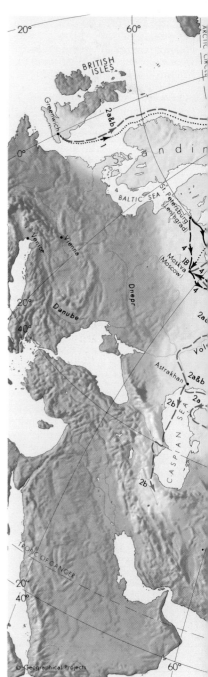

Western length. Those who refused were forced to kneel on the ground while soldiers cut the cloth to the right length.

By another ukase, Peter demanded that all Russian men shave off their traditional beards. But beards, somehow, were the hardest thing for the Russians to give up. Those who could afford it were willing to pay all manner of fines and "beard taxes" for the privilege of keeping them. The poor had to manage as best they could. John Perry, an Englishman hired to build a canal for Peter, reported that his best carpenter shared with all Russians "a kind of religious respect and veneration for their beards." Forced to shave because Peter was coming to inspect the canal, the carpenter carefully saved his shorn beard so that ultimately he might be buried with it. In heaven, he said, he would show it to St. Peter as proof that he had been a good son of the Russian Orthodox Church.

Peter also created many schools and universities, and stipulated that landowners' sons could inherit their fathers' estates only if they could read and write Latin or a modern European language.

Peter's most cherished ambition was to procure for Russia what he called "a window on the West"—a strip of land along the Baltic Sea. In the early 1700's, after a bitter war with Sweden, he gained what he wanted, the coastline of Livonia and southern Finland. There, at great cost—both in lives and in money—he built a splendid new capital, which he called St. Petersburg (now Leningrad).

Peter also took a keen interest in Russian holdings to the east,

Left: the centenary celebrations in
St. Petersburg, 100 years after Peter
had built the magnificent new city.
The Admiralty Bridge, a bridge of boats,
leads to Falconet's statue of Peter.

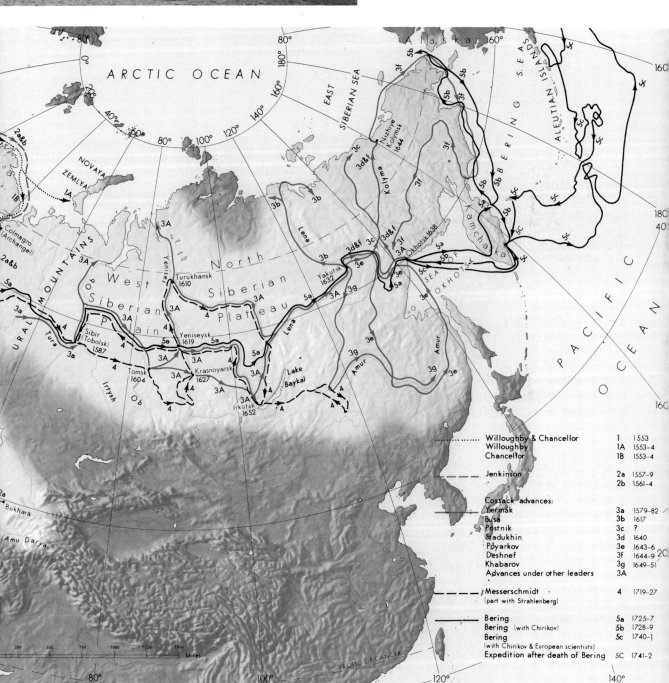

Willoughby & Chancellor	1	1553
Willoughby	1A	1553-4
Chancellor	1B	1553-4
Jenkinson	2a	1557-9
	2b	1561-4
Cossack advances:		
Yermak	3a	1579-82
Busa	3b	1617
Postnik	3c	?
Stadukhin	3d	1640
Poyarkov	3e	1643-6
Deshnef	3f	1644-9
Khabarov	3g	1649-51
Advances under other leaders	3A	
Messerschmidt	4	1719-27
(part with Strahlenberg)		
Bering	5a	1725-7
Bering (with Chirikov)	5b	1728-9
Bering	5c	1740-1
(with Chirikov & European scientists)		
Expedition after death of Bering	5C	1741-2

49

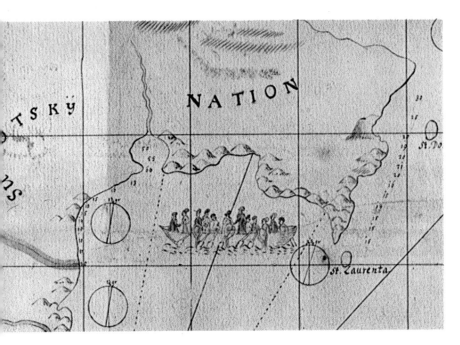

NATION

TSKY

St. Laurenta

Left: a detail from the map drawn by order of Bering in 1729, showing the small boat in which Bering sailed all along the coast of Kamchatka to find out if a strait existed between the continents of Asia and North America.

Right: a Russian peasant's house during the reign of Catherine the Great. Often the whole family slept on rugs on top of the household stove. Most houses had only one room, which was often shared by more than one family. It was usually terribly smoky and dirty.

Below: Catherine the Great and Joseph II of Austria, during a tour Catherine made of southern Russia in 1787. Unlike her subjects, Catherine lived in great luxury—even her expeditions to inspect newly annexed territories were made with all the conveniences of courtly life. This particular journey included such luxuries as peaches and champagne in the snow.

and it was he who prompted the first scientific exploration of Siberia. He wanted a comprehensive survey of his Asian dominion—its terrain and precise extent, its people and resources, its plants and animals. Peter did not hesitate to make use of foreigners to obtain the information he wanted. In the early 1720's, for example, he employed a Swedish adventurer named Strahlenberg and a Prussian naturalist named Messerschmidt to explore and map the Ob and Yenisey river valleys.

But Peter's greatest curiosity was about the mysterious Kamchatka Peninsula. Did this easternmost sector of Siberia join up with northwestern America, or was there a sea in between? In 1725, Peter, now ill and on the point of dying, summoned the well-known Danish navigator Vitus Bering to discuss the matter. "I have been thinking over the finding of a passage to China through the Arctic," he said. "On the map before me there is indicated such a passage bearing the name Anian. There must be some reason for that. Now that the country is in no danger, we should strive to win for her glory along the lines of the Arts and Sciences." The "Anian" passage Peter was referring to was the Bering Strait, which runs between the northeast corner of Siberia and the westernmost coast of North America. It

was Peter's wish that Bering sail northward up the coast of Kamchatka and discover whether such a passage really existed.

All the supplies for the voyage—stores and rigging, canvas and ironwork—had to be hauled over the Siberian steppes and uplands, and ships built along the southern coast of Kamchatka before Bering could begin his explorations. When at last he started out, he followed the east coast of the peninsula northward until he reached the strait that now bears his name. There, within sight of Alaska, severe gales forced him to turn back. But he had accomplished his mission. The nature of the territory between northeast Asia and northwest America was now known.

Scientific exploration in Siberia did not stop with the death of Peter the Great. In 1740, Bering headed another major expedition to the farthest reaches of Siberia. With him this time went many distinguished European scientists: the French astronomer De la Croyère, the German historian G. F. Muller, and the Swedish naturalists Johann Georg Gmelin and Georg Wilhelm Steller. The work of these men, and of Bering himself, contributed vastly to the growing body of knowledge about Siberia's geography, people, and resources.

Later in the 1700's, another series of important expeditions was launched by Catherine the Great. Imperious and tyrannical, this empress talked a lot about "enlightened rule," but did little to improve conditions in Russia. Indeed, the true extent of her "enlightenment" is shown by the fact that serfdom became almost universal in Russia during her reign. Nevertheless, she did recognize the value of science, and maintained the close association with the French Academy of Sciences that Peter had initiated early in the 1700's.

Catherine's mother, the Czarina Elizabeth, had made good use of this scientific body in 1760, when she requested the services of a French

Below: one of the midsummer camps of the abbé Chappe d'Auteroche, returning from Tobolsk to St. Petersburg after observing the transit of Venus.

Right: the famous Russian baths, much like the modern Finnish sauna. Nearly every traveler to Russia reported them, and even D'Auteroche said that they had a beneficial effect on the people, although he himself found, after one attempt at the bath, that the extreme heat of the steam was unbearable.

astronomer to observe the planet Venus as it passed close to earth the following spring. The astronomer, Chappe d'Auteroche, was to travel to Tobolsk in Siberia, where, on June 6, the planet's passage "could be viewed with more advantage than anywhere else."

Chappe d'Auteroche was a scholarly abbé, unused to travel, and he found the carriage journey through Russia extremely arduous. On one occasion, the snow was so deep that his carriage, breaking through the icy crust into a hole, "disappeared all at once, so that the horses' heads could but just be seen and we were buried!" The abbé and his companions, clutching their precious instruments, got out through a hole in the roof, and proceeded on foot to the next posting station, where they purchased sledges. In these, they were swept along rapidly through gloomy forests and across glittering frozen rivers eastward to Siberia.

All this time, the abbé was worried that he might not reach Tobolsk in time. His most anxious moments came when he was only 200 miles from his destination. The spring thaws were beginning, and the countryside was "overwhelmed with torrents pouring down on all sides." Ahead lay a large river, which his drivers refused to cross because the ice was already cracking. But the abbé had come too far to be turned back by a mere river. He promised his men double pay if they would take the risk, and frantically plied them with brandy until they agreed. They crossed the river safely, and D'Auteroche reached Tobolsk in plenty of time to set up his telescope and observe the planet's passage.

This kind of dedication to science took many other frail scholars deep into the Siberian wilds in the decades that followed. But however brave, the scientists of the 1700's could never match the sheer, reckless courage of the men who had stormed across the continent 200 years earlier. The first, vital step in Siberia's exploration had been taken by the Cossacks—rebels, outlaws, and soldiers of fortune who neither knew nor cared about "scientific method."

53

Below: a detail from a Persian rug made
in the 1500's that shows mysterious
foreigners sailing in a ship. Persia
was first opened up by the Portuguese,
who, sailing around the tip of Africa,
took the port of Hormuz in 1515.

Persia, Gateway to the East

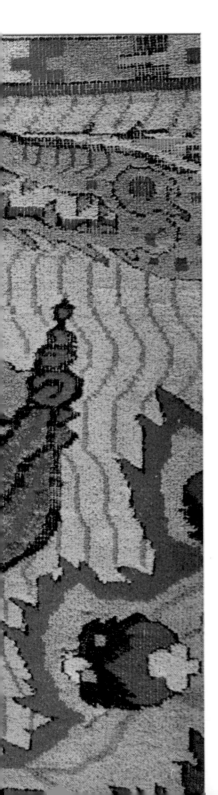

While the Cossacks were sweeping across Siberia, a hardy band of European merchants and adventurers were opening up another of Asia's hidden corners. This was the kingdom of Persia (now called Iran), tucked away between the Caspian Sea and the Persian Gulf in southwestern Asia.

A rugged land of mountains and narrow valleys, high plateaus and sweltering deserts, Persia was almost as forbidding as Siberia. Nonetheless, it had an irresistible appeal for Western travelers in the 1500's and 1600's. Located at the very crossroads of East and West, it offered exciting possibilities for trade. And, just as important, it possessed all the mystery and glamour of an utterly foreign world.

Before the 1500's, Europeans knew very little about Persia. For hundreds of years, the caravan routes connecting it to the Mediterranean had been jealously guarded by the Moslems, who possessed an exclusive monopoly over all trade with the East. Europeans did know that Persia was a vital link in the chain of sea and land routes by which the Moslems brought precious stones and spices from India and the Orient to Mediterranean markets. They also knew that Persia itself was the source of many luxuries: raw silk and dyes, wines and perfumes, delicate paintings, and rich brocades embroidered with roses, tulips, and lilies. Such luxuries suggested that Persia might be a fairy-tale land of Eastern romance. But was it? Fear of the Moslems—and of the unknown—had long kept Europeans from traveling east to find out.

And then, suddenly, early in the 1500's, the gates to Persia were flung open by the Portuguese. Using their new-found sea route around the tip of Africa, they sailed into the Persian Gulf and captured the strategic port of Hormuz in 1515. For the Portuguese, gaining control over this vital Persian port was just one step in their great eastward sweep to the Oriental lands of spice and treasure. But for other Europeans, it signaled the start of a whole new interest in Persia. If the Portuguese could outflank the Moslems by approaching it from the south, why couldn't other traders accomplish the same end by approaching it from the north?

The English were the first to try. In 1561, flushed with their success in Russia, the governors of the Muscovy Company sent their first merchant to Persia. This pioneer trader was Antony Jenkinson —the same Antony Jenkinson who, in 1558, had traveled from Moscow to Bukhara in search of Cathay. This time, his mission was

55

to investigate the rumor that "raw silk is as plentiful in Persia as flax is in Russia"—and, hopefully, to interest the Persians in trade.

With the blessing of the Russian czar, Jenkinson journeyed from Moscow to Astrakhan and boarded a ship bound for the southern shores of the Caspian Sea. On the way, a fierce seven-day storm nearly wrecked the vessel, and the captain was forced to make a landing halfway down the Caspian's west coast. Jenkinson—no doubt thankful to be safely back on dry land—unloaded his cargo of woolens, and hired a caravan to take him southward.

Below: Jenkinson's map, engraved in 1562, showing "Russia, Muscovy, and Tartarie." It shows his route down from Moscow to Astrakhan and across the Caspian Sea to Persia. The pictures are based on Marco Polo's accounts.

His first stop was the city of Shamakha, capital of a small Persian principality called Shirvan. The local ruler, Abdullah Khan, soon learned of his arrival, and asked to see him. When Jenkinson entered the palace, he found the khan seated in an elegant pavilion decorated with carpets of silver and gold. Surrounded by courtiers, the khan himself was the very picture of Eastern opulence. Jenkinson described him as being "richly apparelled with long garments of silk and cloth of gold, embroidered with pearls . . . his earrings had pendants of gold . . . with two rubies of great value set in the ends."

Below: an Indian miniature showing Abdullah Khan, who befriended Antony Jenkinson. When he saw Jenkinson sitting cross-legged before him, he ordered a stool so that Jenkinson could sit comfortably.

57

Above: a Persian miniature of 1590-1600 showing a man grooming one of the royal horses. Sometimes they were kept in solid gold stables, and equipped with jewel-studded gold saddles.

The khan took an immediate liking to the adventurous Englishman, and entertained him royally for several weeks. Jenkinson was treated to lavish banquets that sometimes consisted of as many as 290 different dishes, and learned to like coffee, a drink then unknown in Europe. Jenkinson was favorably impressed with everything about this glamorous way of life, except the harem system, which made it possible for princes such as the khan to have numerous wives. This not only shocked Jenkinson's sense of propriety, but also struck him as dangerous to the safety of the state. The more wives a man had, the more potential heirs he produced, and, as Jenkinson shrewdly observed, "one brother seeketh always to destroy another, having no natural love among them, by reason that they are begotten of divers women." In fact, this was a grave problem in the courts of Persia, and only one solution had been found: to keep male heirs cooped up in the women's quarters, thereby preventing them from learning anything about the arts of war.

From Shamakha, Jenkinson made his way 300 miles south to Qazvin, then the capital of Persia. All along the way, he encountered tribes of nomads. He described them as "pasturing people, which dwell in the summer season upon mountains, and in winter . . . re-

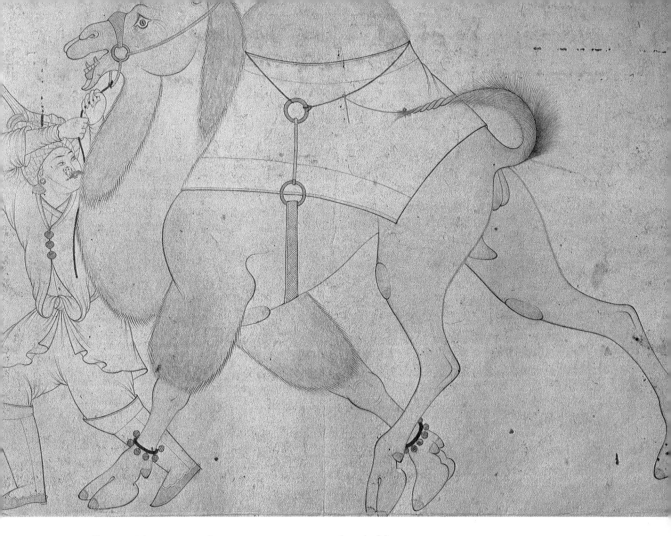

move into valleys, without resorting to towns or any other habitation." Possessing little but their flocks and their threadbare tents, these hardy tribesmen were a far cry from the luxury-loving courtiers Jenkinson had met at Shamakha.

The palace at Qazvin was, if anything, even more sumptuous than Abdullah Khan's. But the Persian king, Shah Tahmasp, was far less friendly than the khan. Jenkinson had barely presented his letter of introduction from Queen Elizabeth when the shah demanded to know his religion. When the merchant confessed that he was a Christian, the shah—who, like most Persians, was a Moslem—flew into a rage. "Oh thou unbeliever," he cried, "we have no need to have friendship with the unbelievers!" So saying, he ordered Jenkinson to leave his palace, instructing a retainer to follow him out and "purify" the ground he had walked on with fresh sand.

But Jenkinson was not one to give up easily. He stubbornly remained in Qazvin for several months, despite ugly rumors that the shah was thinking of sending his head as a present to the Sultan of Turkey. In the end, Jenkinson's friend Abdullah Khan intervened in his favor, and somehow even managed to convince the shah that it would do no harm to let the Englishman trade in his country.

Above: a Persian miniature, probably of the early 1500's, showing a camel with his driver. Horses were only for royalty—the ordinary people relied on the camel for all their traveling.

59

Below: seven men in an arid desert, from a Persian miniature of about 1495. The rigors of desert travel, such as heat, thirst, and attack by bandits, were familiar to the people living in Persia, but presented a formidable challenge to outsiders trying to make their way into the interior of the kingdom.

Jenkinson returned in triumph to Moscow late in 1562 with a rich cargo of silk and brocades, brilliant dyes and precious stones.

Over the next 20 years, the Muscovy Company sent six further missions to Persia over the route Jenkinson had pioneered. But none of them proved as successful as his had been, and the toll in lives was considerable. The northern route to Persia was fraught with perils for the unwary traveler: storms and pirates on the Caspian Sea, and the prevalence of plague in the region just south of it. By 1581, the English were beginning to consider a daring alternative route to the land of the shahs—via the Middle East.

The first English merchant to explore this possibility was John Newberry. Late in 1581, he crossed the deserts of present-day Syria and Iraq to the broad Euphrates River. Following the river southward, he reached the Persian Gulf, and traveled down its eastern shores to the great port of Hormuz. There, under the very noses of the suspicious Portuguese, he spent six weeks gathering information about the "trade and custom of the place." He then traveled widely through the interior of the country and, on his return to England, gave a glowing report of the merchandise to be found in the bustling bazaars of Persia's cities.

But few merchants were willing to undergo the hardships of desert travel to reach these cities, and it was not until 1598 that Persia again became the object of a major English expedition. This time, the travelers were not merchants, but "gentlemen-adventurers"—28 English noblemen under the leadership of two brothers named Sir Anthony and Sir Robert Sherley. Seeking romance and adventure, they visited Baghdad, then crossed the Zagros Mountains into Persia and headed straight for Qazvin in hopes of meeting the shah.

They were not disappointed. Their arrival in the city coincided with the triumphant return of Persia's new young ruler, Shah Abbas I, from a successful campaign against a warlike tribe in the north. The shah's festive entry into Qazvin made an impressive sight. One of the Englishmen, John Manwaring, reports that at the head of the returning army rode 1,200 horsemen, "carrying 1,200 heads of men on their lances, and some having the ears of men put on strings and hanged about their necks. . . . Then a good distance after them came the king, riding alone with a lance in his hand . . . being a man of low stature, but very strongly made, and swarthy of complexion. Next . . . came [the] lieutenant-general of the field, and all his bows

Right: rebellious tribesmen being burned, one of the sights witnessed by the Sherley expedition. They were amazed by the examples of casual savagery they often saw during their Persian tour in search of adventure.

Below right: a Persian picture of a captive Mongol. Not all the prisoners of war were mutilated or killed; many were kept as slaves. Here such a prisoner is shown in a symbolic form of restraint, that leaves his right hand free.

Above: Sir Robert Sherley, painted by Sir Anthony van Dyck while he and his wife were in Rome on their European tour of 1609-1616. Sherley posed in his turban and Persian cloak and tunic.

[archers] in rank like a half-moon to the number of 20,000 soldiers."

The Sherley brothers, as leaders of the English party, soon gained an audience with the shah. Telling him that they were English knights anxious to enter his service, they presented him with a tribute of gems and a golden goblet. Pleased and flattered, the shah gave them in return "40 horses all furnished, two with exceeding rich saddles plated with gold and set with rubies and turquoises."

After several months, most of the English party returned to Europe, but the Sherleys remained, and soon rose to a position of prominence in the Persian court. In 1599, Shah Abbas sent Anthony

Above: Teresa, the Persian princess that Robert Sherley married, painted by Van Dyck. They had stopped in Rome on their way to England, hoping to interest European powers in Persia.

Sherley as his ambassador to Europe to arrange a European alliance with Persia against their common enemy, the Turks. Anthony's mission was a complete failure, and he did not return to Persia. Robert Sherley, who had remained with the shah as a sort of hostage, was left in a very awkward position. He began writing mournful letters to his brother telling him that he had given up all hope of "delivery out of this country."

But Robert's time in Persia was not a complete loss, either for himself or for the shah. The young Englishman met and married a lovely Persian princess named Teresa, and began advising the shah on military matters. With Sherley's help, the shah reorganized his army, using European strategy against the Turks with great success.

In gratitude, the shah made Sherley his new ambassador. Between 1609 and 1627, Robert and his wife traveled around the courts of Europe, vainly trying to interest various monarchs in a military alliance with the shah. But despite his lack of success, Robert Sherley loyally returned to Persia. Over the years, he had come to regard the kingdom as his real home, and Shah Abbas as his closest friend. But in 1628, the shah repaid his years of devotion and service with a cruel rebuff. He publicly rejected the Englishman "wishing Robert Sherley to depart his kingdom as old and troublesome." This unfeeling declaration broke Sherley's heart, and a month later, he died.

There was a definite streak of cruelty in the shah, and his treatment of Robert Sherley was nothing compared to the way he dealt with his own children. When word reached him that his eldest son had become popular among his people, the jealous shah had him put to death, and even ordered that the young man's head be brought to him as proof. Mercifully, Abbas's second son died of natural causes, but the third and fourth were not so lucky. They, too, incurred their father's wrath, and were summarily executed.

But however barbaric he was as a father, Shah Abbas was remarkably progressive as a ruler. He had a genius for administration, and a keen eye for whatever would improve the efficiency of his government. One of his first acts as king was to build roads and bridges to link up the far-flung corners of his empire. The most famous of these causeways was the *Sang Farsh* (stone carpet), a road stretching almost all the way across northern Persia.

Abbas's most lasting monument, however, was the city of Isfahan. Located in the very heart of the kingdom on one of Persia's few

Right: Shah Abbas receives the envoy of Jahangir of India. Abbas was a great and skilled diplomat, and his court attracted many envoys from countries both to the east and west.

rivers, it became the shah's official capital early in the 1600's. At his command, Isfahan was almost completely rebuilt, and soon became one of the most beautiful cities in the East. The Persians were justly proud of their new capital. *Isfahan nusf-i Jihan,* they used to say: "Isfahan is half the world."

Leading into the center of the city were long avenues of trees bordered by gardens where little fountains sparkled in the sun. In the main square, or Maidan, were hundreds of market stalls overflowing with exotic merchandise: spices from the Orient, diamonds from India, delicate metalwork from Arabia, and the very cream of

Persia's own products. The fruits and flowers sold in the Maidan made it a kind of garden in its own right, and the air was perfumed with the fragrance of peaches, apricots, limes, and quinces, roses, violets, hyacinth, and jasmine.

Overlooking the Maidan were two splendid buildings. On one side stood the Lutfallah Mosque, its huge dome encrusted with blue and green stones intermingled with gold. Opposite the mosque stood the royal palace, a sumptuous concoction of marble and alabaster, ebony and ivory. The rooms of the palace were decorated with paintings and fine enamels, and furnished with the softest of Persian carpets.

Above: the Great Mosque at Isfahan, the city that Shah Abbas made his capital. The large central court of the mosque surrounds a pool, and the covered areas have blue tiled floors to give the impression of cool water.

Isfahan was just one of the cities seen and admired by a young Englishman named Sir Thomas Herbert, who traveled to Persia in 1627. Five years before, the English had driven the Portuguese out of Hormuz and established their own foothold in the Persian Gulf. And so it was by ship that Herbert reached the country, landing at the port of Bandar Abbas, just north of Hormuz. Like the Sherleys, Herbert was a "gentleman-adventurer," and he set off eagerly to explore the kingdom. His journey, which took him all the way to the Caspian Sea and back again, gave him ample opportunity to observe Persian life and manners at close hand.

Herbert was particularly impressed by the gentleness and courtesy of the Persian nobility. They seemed to live a charmed existence, and showed surprisingly little interest in the world beyond Persia. If they asked Herbert any questions at all about Europe, it was only to know whether "such and such a country had good wine, fair women, serviceable horses, and well-tempered swords." Herbert surmised that it was their own good wine—and their indulgence in opium—that made them so complacent. "But above all," he wrote, "poetry lulls them, that genius seeming properly to delight itself amongst them."

But not all visitors to Persia were as favorably impressed with its people as young Herbert. John Chardin, a French merchant who visited the country in the mid-1600's, wrote that "Luxury, sensuality, and licentiousness on the one hand, scholasticism and literature on the other, have made the Persians effeminate."

And another traveler, an English trader named John Fryer, who also visited Persia in the mid-1600's, found much to criticize. He complained bitterly about the climate which, he said, caused "rheumatisms, numbness, and periodical fevers," and scoffed at the Persians' naïve belief that washing in the public baths, or *hummums,* would cleanse them of their sins. Fryer was particularly critical of the reigning shah, Husain, who "lived like a tyrant in his den." In fact, Husain—like many of the kings who succeeded Abbas—was extremely vicious. He delighted in torturing his wives, and thought nothing of putting out a man's eyes if he displeased him.

But even the wickedness of the shahs could not dim the rosy light in which most European visitors viewed Persia in the 1600's. By the end of the century, there were merchants from many different countries either living in the country or making regular journeys

through it on their way to India. Many wrote rhapsodic accounts of Persian life, and all agreed that it was the most civilized in the East.

Even so, European interest in Persia began to diminish late in the 1600's. Portuguese power in the Orient was rapidly waning, and the traders of England, France and The Netherlands increasingly focused their attention on India and the Far East.

This gradual shift in European interest was speeded up early in the 1700's, when a series of major upheavals made access to Persia all but impossible. In 1722, the kingdom was suddenly invaded by Afghan tribes from the east. It took 14 stormy years for the Persian king, Nadir Shah, to drive them out. But no sooner had he done so than Persia itself erupted in a violent civil war between Nadir Shah and a rebellious group of tribes called the Qajars.

The Muscovy Company chose this unhappy moment to send a merchant named Jonas Hanway to Persia. His task was to explore the possibilities of reopening the old northern trade route to the kingdom. The expedition proved a disaster. Poor Hanway was

Above: an engraving from a drawing by John Chardin, a diamond merchant, of the city of Isfahan. He spent many years living in Persia in the 1600's.

Left: an engraved portrait of Thomas Herbert. Herbert went on to India and Ceylon after his visit to Persia, returning to Europe in 1629.

Above: John Fryer, a doctor who spent 10 years traveling through Persia and India. His *New Account of East India and Persia,* which was published in 1698, is one of the most interesting books describing the area at that time.

Right: Persian baths, as pictured in a Persian manuscript of 1566. It was these baths that Fryer was so skeptical about, reporting that the people firmly believed that washing there would be effective in cleansing them of sin.

robbed by highwaymen, imprisoned by the Qajars, and almost coerced into running a harem by the shah. It was only with great difficulty that he finally managed to obtain compensation for the goods he had lost and make his way back to England.

"How happy Persia might be," Hanway wrote later, "if a general depravity of manners did not involve her inhabitants in such an inextricable confusion." Indeed, peace did not return to the kingdom until the late 1700's, when the Qajars—having murdered Nadir Shah—succeeded in establishing themselves as the ruling dynasty. But by that time, the once-flourishing trade in Persian silk had dwindled away. European merchants, busy reaping a harvest of spice and treasure farther east, almost forgot about Persia. Even the English, who had done so much to pioneer new routes to the kingdom, paid it little heed in the second half of the 1700's. It was to take a whole new set of circumstances—the power-politics of the 1800's—to reawaken British interest in this exotic "gateway to the East."

Below: Jonas Hanway, painted by Arthur Devis. He unfortunately reached Astrabad just as it was captured by a rebel army, who took his merchandise and kept him locked in his lodgings. After his release he was nearly taken as a slave by highwaymen, and when he reached the shah in Meshed, he was told he could only be compensated for his goods if he went back to Astrabad.

The Mysterious Land of Tibet

4

Left: the Potala, the Dalai Lama's residence, in the Tibetan capital of Lhasa. This painting, done in the 1200's, shows the original Potala. In the mid-1600's, the Fifth Dalai Lama had it razed to the ground, and built a new and grander edifice in its place. The new building was the one seen and admired by the missionaries and explorers of the 1700's and 1800's. But, though different in outward appearance, the later Potala served the same functions as its predecessor. It was not only a palace, but also a monastery and a well-defended fortress.

The search for new markets had led English merchants deep into Russia and Persia; the Mongol challenge had drawn the Cossacks into the wilds of Siberia. But the motive that launched the exploration of Tibet was neither trade nor conquest: it was religion. The first Westerners to venture into this forbidding mountain realm were Jesuit missionaries, members of a Catholic order called the Society of Jesus. Quiet, scholarly men, they were often frail in health and old in years. Yet their dedication led them to achieve feats of bravery and endurance worthy of the toughest Cossack.

The Jesuits began arriving in the Orient in the 1500's, soon after the Portuguese had pioneered the sea route to Asia. By 1600, the hardworking fathers had founded a flourishing mission at Goa, on the west coast of India, and another at Peking, in northern China. From these two centers, they ventured farther and farther afield, activated not only by missionary zeal, but also by a growing interest in exploration for its own sake.

In the early 1600's, the Jesuits working in northern India began to hear intriguing stories about a strange land called "Tibet" beyond the mountains. In this land, they were told, dwelt priests who

Right: a monastery in Tibet, hugging the hilltop over a vast expanse of a valley landscape. The Tibetans are a very religious people, and their monasteries—as in Europe during the Middle Ages—were the main centers of education and intellectual development.

dressed and behaved much like the Jesuits themselves. They wore black robes, never married, and performed rites that sounded strangely like baptism, confession, and communion. Rumors of a mysterious Christian community somewhere in Asia had haunted Europe for centuries. Could the people of Tibet be the famous lost Christians?

The Jesuits longed to follow up the lead, but the soaring Himalayan mountains between India and Tibet presented a daunting obstacle. And, as they learned from the few merchants who ventured north, the terrain on the other side of the Himalaya was no less formidable. In fact, the inner recesses of Tibet are all but inaccessible. Most of the country's 500,000 square miles are slung over the world's highest mountains, highest passes, and highest plateaus. Except for a few nomads, this barren, windswept region is uninhabited. Most of the population is concentrated in the southern part of Tibet, where there are pockets of lush green grazing and agricultural land in the troughs between the Himalaya. But even these lovely valleys are perched at heights greater than the mountain summits of most other countries.

Yet despite what they had heard—and guessed—about the perils of Himalayan travel, the Jesuits' desire to reach the tantalizing land beyond the mountains only increased as the years went by. The possibility that the Tibetans might not be Christians after all did not deter them. On the contrary, as one industrious father put it, "a great harvest of heathens may be reaped."

No Jesuit was more eager to reach Tibet than Father Antonio de Andrade, a 44-year-old priest working in northern India in 1624. One day, in the city of Delhi, he met a group of Hindu pilgrims bound for the holy shrine of Badrinath, deep in the Himalaya near the Tibetan border. Here at last was the opportunity he had been waiting for! Without a moment's hesitation, he collected his two Christian Indian servants, donned the garb of a Hindu, and joined the pilgrim caravan.

Slowly, the long column of men wound its way northward—through forests thick with leeches, leopards, and tigers; through fields luxuriant with wild flowers; through fragrant groves of lemon, cinnamon, and cypress trees—to the foothills of the Himalaya. The weather grew steadily colder, and the pilgrims' path, which now followed the Ganges River, became increasingly narrow and more

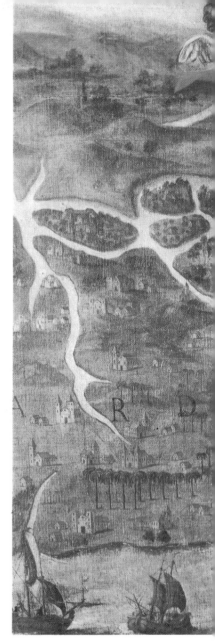

72

Above: a detail from a painting of the 1600's showing the Portuguese colony of Goa, on the coast of India. The vignette shows St. Francis Xavier arriving at the colony, which became the headquarters of missionary work.

Left: a contemporary portrait of Antonio de Andrade. He was convinced that hidden in the valleys of the Himalaya were pockets of forgotten Christians, and he was determined to make his way to the lost communities.

Right: a river gorge in the foothills of the eastern Himalaya. Father Antonio de Andrade traveled through this region on his journey to Tibet.

Above: present-day lamas outside a lamasery in Ladakh. Bordering on Tibet, Ladakh had, before the Chinese occupation, very close educational and religious links with the lamaseries of Tibet, sharing their culture.

dangerous. Sometimes the travelers had to creep along ledges that were only inches wide, clinging to the rough side of the river gorge hundreds of feet above the swirling waters.

Some 150 miles north of Delhi, they came to the tiny Indian state of Srinagar. Something about Andrade and his servants aroused the suspicion of Srinagar's ruler, but he let them pass on to Badrinath. There, Andrade and his companions left the caravan and made for Mana, the last village in Indian territory. When they reached the village, they found that orders had been received from Srinagar to have them arrested. But the Jesuit had come too far to be stopped now. Before him lay the Mana Pass, gateway to Tibet. When night fell, he and his servants escaped and headed for its summit.

Though it was summer, the pass was covered in snow so deep that the three men frequently sank up to their chests in it. At some points they could make their way forward only by lying prone on the snow and moving their arms and legs like swimmers. It was a terrifying ordeal, but they did not dare to stop, for to do so would have meant freezing to death. They lost all feeling in their hands and feet, and

Above: present-day lamas outside a lamasery in Ladakh. Bordering on Tibet, Ladakh had, before the Chinese occupation, very close educational and religious links with the lamaseries of Tibet, sharing their culture.

Right: Leh, the capital of Ladakh, where the 400 Christian converts were sent after their church in Tsaparang had been destroyed by the local lamas. The castle of the Leh kings is shown on the left. Azevado traveled there to beg for mercy for the Christian slaves.

Andrade in particular was so frostbitten that he knocked a finger off without feeling a thing. "Having no sense of pain I should not have believed it, had not a copious flow of blood shown it to be a fact!"

With the dawn came the glare of the sun on the snow, blinding the men so much that they could hardly see the ground in front of them. But somehow they managed to reach the summit of the pass and descend into the valley below. They found themselves in the town of Tsaparang, capital of the small Tibetan state of Guge. Andrade was conducted to the king, who received him kindly and took great pains to answer his religious questions. No, the Tibetans were not Christians; they were Buddhists. But, as the Jesuit learned, there *were* many fascinating similarities between the two religions. The Buddhist *lamas* (monks) not only performed baptisms and heard confession, but also observed fasts, officiated at weddings, and held Masslike ceremonies where they blessed sacramental bread and wine.

The king of Guge was a Buddhist too, of course, but he was so impressed by Father Andrade that he decided to become a Christian. Moreover, he asked the Jesuit to teach the faith to his people. Overjoyed, Andrade returned to India to arrange for a mission, and came back the next year with five other Jesuits. A church for the

Right: a lamasery of Likir in Ladakh. Endowed with a splendid view of the valley spread below it and the white-cloaked mountains in the distance, it looks as it did in the time of Azevado.

"lamas of the West" was built next to the king's palace, and officially opened on Easter Sunday, 1626.

During the next few years, the mission made 400 converts. In fact, all seemed to be going well in Tsaparang when Father Andrade left the city in 1630 to become the Jesuit superior at Goa. But shortly after his departure, disaster struck. The local lamas, furious at the Jesuits' growing power, rose up against the zealous Christian king and overthrew him. Guge was taken over by the ruler of the nearby Kashmiri state of Ladakh, and the 400 converts were enslaved and sent to Ladakh's capital of Leh. The church was razed to the ground and the five missionaries sent back to India.

When news of this catastrophe reached Andrade, he at once dispatched another priest to Tibet. The missionary, Father Francisco de Azevado, was to travel to Ladakh, visit the king at Leh, and persuade him to free his Christian slaves and permit the reopening

Below: vast caravans followed the old trading routes such as the one that Grueber and D'Orville traveled along. This Chinese roll painting of the 1600's shows part of one of these caravans.

Above: a wood model of the chief lama of Bhutan, who was of the Red Hat sect, which was the traditional party. At the time that Cabral and Cacella came to Shigatse, the Red Hats were locked in political combat with the Yellow Hats, the reform party. The Jesuits, aware of the air of tension, decided to seek counsel from their brethren.

of the Tsaparang mission. It was a daunting task, but the 53-year-old Azevado was a brave and determined man. He made his way to Tsaparang and from there followed a rough track through the mountains to Ladakh, 200 miles to the northeast. Along the way, he frequently had to cross yawning chasms by means of flimsy rope bridges. Just how terrifying this could be was described by another Jesuit, Ippolito Desideri, who journeyed to Ladakh some 85 years later: "From one mountain to the other two thick ropes of willow are stretched, nearly four feet apart, to which are attached hanging loops of smaller ropes of willow about one foot and a half distant from one another. One must stretch out one's arms and hold fast to the thicker ropes while putting one foot after the other into the hanging loops to reach the opposite side. With every step the bridge sways from right to left, and from left to right. Besides this, one is so high above the river and the bridge is so open on all sides that the rush of water beneath dazzles the eyes and makes one dizzy."

Azevado had no experienced companions to help him on his way. When he came to such a bridge, he simply commended himself to God, took hold of the ropes, and kept praying till he reached the other side. He reached Leh safely in October, 1631. All around the town were orchards, where apples, peaches, and apricots were grown amid a profusion of wild roses and forget-me-nots. In the capital itself lived some 800 families. They dwelt in terraced houses that seemed to melt into the slope of the little mountain on which the palace stood.

Father Azevado went directly to the palace to see the king. The Ladakh ruler was a man of "stern appearance," but he turned out to be quite sympathetic to the Jesuit's requests. He promised to release his Christian slaves and agreed to allow the missionaries back in Tsaparang. The Jesuit, anxious to carry the good news to Father Andrade, remained in Leh only a week before returning to India.

The Tsaparang mission was started up again the next year, but by now, the townsfolk were too frightened of the lamas to pay much heed to the Jesuits. In 1635, the mission had to be abandoned altogether. Meanwhile, 600 miles to the east, another mission had been established in the Tibetan city of Shigatse. In 1627, two brave Jesuits, Father Cabral and Father Cacella, had reached the area via the tiny Himalayan kingdom of Bhutan. But the mission they founded at Shigatse soon came under attack from two rival factions of lamas, the Red Hats and the Yellow Hats. The Jesuits were in doubt about how to handle the situation. To seek advice, Father Cabral made his way back over the mountains to a Jesuit mission in northeast India. Meanwhile, Father Cacella made a heroic, but unsuccessful, attempt to reach the Tsaparang mission. Forced back by heavy snows, he turned southward, rejoining Cabral at a town in northern India.

Having made their report to the Jesuit authorities, the two priests returned to Shigatse. Soon afterward, Father Cacella, worn out by his travels, fell ill and died. Father Cabral continued to work at the mission until 1631, when he was recalled to India. On this journey, he pioneered a new route over the mountains. The route—which lay over some of the highest passes in the Himalaya—took him through Nepal, where he became the first European to visit the Nepalese capital of Katmandu.

Not until 1661 did the Jesuits again penetrate into the hidden recesses of Tibet. In that year, two intrepid Jesuit travelers not only entered Tibet, but did so from an entirely new direction: China. By the late 1650's, Dutch merchants had broken the Portuguese monopoly on trade with Asia, and armed Dutch vessels had begun blockading the ports of call along the coast of China. This made it impossible for the Jesuits at Peking to maintain contact with their headquarters in Rome. They saw only one solution: to find an overland route to the West.

The Peking authorities chose two young Jesuits for this dangerous task, John Grueber and Albert d'Orville. Grueber, an Austrian, and D'Orville, a Belgian, were both trained geographers. Laden with surveying equipment, the two set out from Peking in April, 1661, and followed an ancient caravan route that took them west to the Great Wall of China. This wall had been erected by the Chinese in the 200's B.C., in an effort to keep out marauding barbarians from Central Asia. Stretching from China's east coast to the Gobi Desert, it was some 1,500 miles long and, as Grueber noted, was wide enough at some points for six horsemen to ride abreast on it.

The Great Wall has excited the admiration of travelers for hundreds of years. Some years after Grueber and D'Orville saw it, for example, another Jesuit named Father Verbiest had occasion to travel many miles along its length and wrote enthusiastically to a

Above: the Great Wall of China, which Grueber and D'Orville had to pass on their long journey from Peking to find an overland route to the West. Here, the wall is about 21 feet thick at the bottom and the parapet is 18 feet high. There are watchtowers at intervals of several hundred yards. The wall was first built by the expanding Tsin dynasty to keep out nomadic tribesmen from Central Asia.

Left: an engraving of the Potala of Lhasa, made in 1667 from sketches that Grueber made when he was in the city.

Right: an engraving of the Chinese emperor made by A. Kircher from a sketch by Grueber. Before Grueber left, Kircher, a Jesuit scholar, came to an arrangement that Grueber would keep a record of the journey which he would give to Kircher, who was then planning his monumental work, *China Illustrata*. Kircher's book, dated 1667, gave Grueber's story to the world.

Imperij
fino-Tartarici Supremus
MONARCHA.

friend that, "The seven wonders of the world condensed into one could not be compared with it. . . . It is carried in many places over the highest summits of the mountains from East to West, and follows all the acclivities, towers of a lasting construction rising into the air at intervals of two bow-shots apart."

Grueber and D'Orville headed southwest after leaving the Great Wall. They entered Tibet, and toiled on for three months over its endless mountains and high plateaus. Only the occasional sight of a nomad's black felt tent gave any indication that there were other human beings in this bleak and terrible domain.

In October, 1661, the two Jesuits reached Lhasa. This city had been the real heart and capital of Tibet for 20 years. In 1641, the Fifth Dalai Lama, head of the Yellow Hat sect, had invited a Mongol khan from the north to invade Tibet and, with his help, had subjugated the rival Red Hats. For the next 14 years, the khan and the "Great Lama" had ruled Tibet together, with the Mongol in charge of secular matters and the Dalai Lama in charge of religious affairs. But in 1655, the khan had died, and the lama had moved swiftly to assert his mastery over the political scene as well. A Mongol representative still lived in Lhasa, but he was completely subordinate to

79

Above: a prayer wheel. The use of these ingenious devices greatly interested Grueber. It is believed that when the small cylinder is spun the prayers on it are transmitted and it is not necessary to give any further thought or articulation. Below: a man standing near two small buildings called *chortens,* little shrines dedicated to famous lamas, at which people may stop and pray.

the Great Lama, and played only a minor role in Tibetan politics.

At the root of the priest-king's power was the Tibetans' belief that the Dalai Lama was the reincarnation (reappearance on earth) of the great Avalokitesvara, the original ancestor of all the Tibetans. The Dalai Lama was held to possess special powers, and before his death was supposed to indicate the time and place of his next incarnation by mystical signs. Following these clues, a council of high priests would find a young boy, question him closely about his "previous life," and, when satisfied that he was indeed the reincarnation of the Dalai Lama, prostrate themselves before him. Thereafter, no one would dare question his exalted position as the semi-divine ruler of Tibet.

On entering Lhasa, Grueber and D'Orville were immediately struck, as all later travelers have been, by the sight of a majestic palace called the Potala, which overlooks the city. Begun by the Fifth Dalai Lama in 1645, this awesome structure is built into the side of a mountain, and its soaring walls appear absolutely impregnable. At the time of the Jesuits' visit, it served as a combination palace and monastery, for in addition to the Great Lama and his court, it housed hundreds of studious Buddhist monks.

Grueber was greatly impressed by the elegance of the courtiers he saw going to and from the Potala. But he was appalled by the appearance of the common folk in Lhasa's crowded streets. He found them astonishingly dirty and wrote later that "neither men nor women wear shirts or lie in beds, but sleep on the ground." Worse still, they "eat their meat raw and never wash their hands or face."

Grueber, like Andrade before him, was struck by the similarities between Christianity and Buddhism. But there were no Christian parallels for some of the religious practices he witnessed. One of these was the use of prayer wheels. These ingenious devices were designed to ensure the endless—and effortless—repetition of a prayer. They were cylindrical in shape, and could be turned by the wind, by a watermill, or by hand. Inside each cylinder was a scroll of parchment bearing the Sanskrit words *Om mani padme hum.* Literally translated, the phrase means "Oh, the jewel in the lotus," but for Buddhists it has a mystical meaning, and they believe that its repetition is pleasing to God.

Another custom Grueber saw in Lhasa was an annual rite in which the high priests selected a youth and gave him free rein for a day to slay whomever he wished. The young man, wearing "a very gay habit, decked with little banners, and armed with a sword, quiver, and arrows, wandered at will through the streets killing people at his pleasure—none making any resistance." Grueber's horror at this barbaric practice was not lessened when the Tibetans assured him that everyone slain in this way was guaranteed "eternal happiness."

The two Jesuits could stay only a short while in Lhasa; they had to get on before the winter snows closed the Himalayan passes. To

reach Nepal, they had to travel a torturous route through the Bhotia River gorge. At some points the trail became nothing more than a series of jutting stone slabs supported by iron pegs—1,500 feet above the foaming river! It took the Jesuits 11 days to navigate the 775 steps that made up this part of the trail.

In November, they reached Katmandu, and were immediately conducted to the Nepalese king. He was on the outskirts of the city with his army, preparing to repel an attack by a rebel tribe. Grueber made him a present of one of his telescopes. Looking through it, the king saw the distant enemy forces magnified many times and, thinking that they were upon him, ordered his astonished troops to attack at once!

The Jesuits finally reached Agra in March, 1662, 11 months after leaving Peking. There, worn out by his travels, D'Orville died. Grueber, however, pressed on—through India, Afghanistan, Persia, and Turkey—and eventually reached Rome, where he made his report to the pope.

Grueber and D'Orville were the last Jesuits to see Tibet in the

Above: a group of Tibetan musicians, elegantly dressed in the fashion that impressed Grueber. But he was appalled by some of their customs: the drums, for instance, made of human skin, and the famous Tibetan horns that were often made out of human leg bones.

Below: Central Asia, showing the routes followed by the courageous missionary explorers. Only one of them, Father Bento de Goes, undertook his journey for purely exploratory reasons. The others were chiefly motivated by the desire to win souls for the Roman Catholic Church. Few of these adventurous priests were

still young men when they began their travels, and some — De Goes, Cacella, and D'Orville — died in the course of their work. Yet despite their relative frailty, each achieved remarkable feats of bravery and endurance, pioneering routes through forbidding terrain that even today remains a challenge for well-equipped explorers.

De Goes	1	1603–5
Messenger from De Goes to Ricci	1A	1605–7
Andrade	2	1624, 1625
Cabral & Cacella	3	1626–8
Cabral	3A	1631–2
Cacella	3B	1628
Azevado	4	1631–2
Grueber & D'Orville	5	1661–2
Desideri	6A	1713
Desideri & Freyre	6	1714–6
Freyre	6B	1716
Desideri	6C	1721–2
Desideri	6D	1725
Huc (with Gabet)	7a	1844–6
Huc	7b	1848–9

© Geographical Projects

1600's. But the authorities at Goa never quite gave up their dream of founding a permanent Jesuit mission in Tibet. In 1714, they took steps to realize that dream by sending two missionaries north to the Ladakhi capital of Leh. The two men they chose made an odd pair. The nominal leader of the team, Emanuel Freyre, was a crotchety old father in his late 50's. His companion, Ippolito Desideri, was a young, enthusiastic priest not yet 31. Through all the trials and tribulations that lay ahead, it was Desideri who was to provide the real driving force behind the expedition.

The pair set out from Delhi in the spring of 1715, intending to reach western Tibet by way of Kashmir. As they wound their way north through the Himalayan mountains, they often met shepherds tending flocks of sheep. These flocks provided the wool for the famous shawls made in Kashmir. Desideri described these lovely garments as being "so fine, delicate, and soft that, though very wide and long, they can be folded into so small a space as almost to be hidden in a closed hand."

The route through Kashmir to Leh involved terrible hardships. They were blinded by the glare of the sun on the snow, and often frightened out of their wits by the thunder of nearby avalanches. But they managed to reach their goal by June, 1715. Once there, Desideri

Left: a letter of patent given by Simon da Cunha, resident in Japan, to Grueber and Bernard Diestel (who was the man who had invited Grueber to join the China mission), charging them with finding a land route from Peking to Europe. This was the sort of license or passport that the Jesuits gave to their missionaries. In the lefthand corner, D'Orville's name was substituted for Diestel's, as Diestel had then died. In the righthand corner, Henri Roth's name is substituted for D'Orville's after his death in Agra in March, 1662.

84

was eager to begin the work of starting up a mission. But Father Freyre decided that he had had enough of Tibet already, and insisted that they return to India at once. Because Freyre was unwilling to go back the way they had come, the two set out to find an alternative route via eastern Tibet.

After several weeks of arduous travel, the pair managed to reach Gartok, a city some 200 miles southeast of Leh, and there they had a wonderful stroke of luck. A sizable caravan bound for Lhasa was just about to leave Gartok, and the Jesuits were invited to join it. Better still, the captain of this caravan was no rough barbarian, but a charming Mongol princess. She seems to have captured the heart of old Freyre from the first moment when, "the Lady, whose pretty face was radiant with our gifts, raised her eyes to ours." Again and

Above: a caravan of traders in Ladakh making their way through the mountains. The difficult terrain such caravans had to negotiate can be seen here. Even in summer the mountains are covered with snow, and huge glaciers continually grind down into the valleys.

Left: an Indian miniature of Mount Kailas, showing the holy family of Siva and Parvati with their children Karthikeya and Ganesa, sitting in a cave. The mountain is holy to both the Hindu and the Buddhist faiths.

again in the course of the journey, she offered help and encouragement to the two travelers. Freyre recorded that "the terrible cold and wind would chafe my face so severely as to make me exclaim (I confess it) 'A curse on this cold!' But at such trying moments Princess Casals would comfort us with hot *cha* [tea] and . . . tell us to have courage, for no dangers from mountains or avalanches had power to harm us if we kept to her side."

Late in 1715, the party came in sight of Mount Kailas. This snowy Himalayan peak is the Central Asian equivalent to the Greeks' Mount Olympus, and is believed to be the abode of the gods. Hindu and Buddhist pilgrims from all over India and Tibet go to worship at this shrine and make a ritual trip around the base of the mountain, sometimes on their knees.

In March, 1716, the caravan reached Lhasa. Father Freyre set off at once for India, But Desideri, asserting his independence, decided to stay on in the Tibetan capital. Soon after his arrival, he gained admission to the imposing Potala palace. In the throne room he found himself confronting—not the Dalai Lama, as he had expected —but a Mongol king named Latsang. Following the death of the Fifth Dalai Lama in the late 1690's, the Mongols had descended on Lhasa and ousted the Great Lama's successor. Latsang, who had led the invasion, had installed himself as king and, with the help of

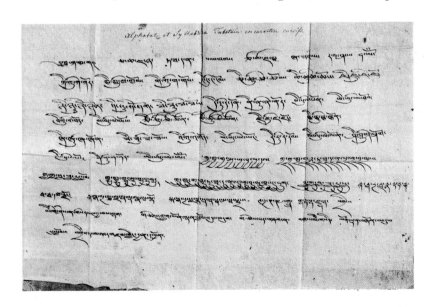

Right: the alphabet and syllables in Tibetan characters, a page from the material that Desideri brought back with him. He was the first European who learned to read and write Tibetan.

87

Left: a wooden Tibetan receptacle for blood, shaped like a devil's face. Although Desideri was impressed by some aspects of Tibetan culture, he considered that many of their customs were grossly barbarous.

the Emperor of China, had won complete control over Tibet.

Desideri liked Latsang. He found him "by nature gay, joyous, and affable . . . courteous to all [and] easy to approach." The Mongol king was equally impressed by the young priest, and promised to look after him "as a father cares for his son." The king gave him permission to found a church in the city, but encouraged him first to study Buddhism, "the better to refute it."

Desideri retired to a lamasery (Buddhist monastery) outside of Lhasa and began studying the language and religious customs of Tibet. He was shocked by many of the things he learned. The Tibetans did not bury their dead, for example. Because they believed in the passage of souls from one creature to another, they fed their dead to eagles, dogs, even fish. They regarded this practice as an

affirmation of man's oneness with the universe, a means of uniting the dead person's soul with that of other, living creatures.

Another practice Desideri found astonishing was the belief that a man's innocence or guilt could be proved by a physical test. Alleged criminals were forced to plunge their hands into a cauldron of boiling oil in which there were two stones, one black and one white. If a man was innocent, he would be able to pluck out the white one without burning his arm. Needless to say, most of the accused were found guilty.

But the practices Desideri found most deplorable were the Tibetans' marriage customs. On the wedding day, the groom's friends fetched the bride—who, until that moment, did not know that she was to be married—and carried her kicking and screaming

Right: lamas wearing aprons made of human bones. The Tibetans' traditional attitude toward the bodies of their dead was one aspect of Tibetan culture that Desideri found hard to accept.

Above: a cup made from a human skull, which was used by the lamas for ceremonial religious occasions. Many of the customs that so amazed Desideri continued long after his time in Tibet.

to her future husband. In the presence of a lama, the groom smeared pats of butter on his bride's hair, officially making her his wife. But she was not only *his* wife—the ceremony automatically made her the wife of all her husband's younger brothers as well!

Desideri, appalled by these customs, addressed himself to the task of refuting them in a long tract that he wrote in Tibetan. But before he could get very far with his great work, a terrible calamity befell the capital. The Yellow Hat lamas had long resented King Latsang's usurpation of the Dalai Lama's power. In 1717, they connived with the ruler of a rival Mongol horde, the Dzungar Mongols, to drive him out. The Dzungars undertook the task with relish, and swept down on Lhasa to kill Latsang and sack the city. But, in turn, the Dzungars, too, were driven out by a large Chinese army in 1720. The Chinese came in the guise of religious crusaders, alleging that their mission was to reinstate the next Dalai Lama in his rightful place as ruler. In fact, what they did was to establish themselves as Tibet's "patrons," and installed Chinese representatives in Lhasa to "advise" the new young Dalai Lama.

During all this upheaval, Desideri had remained safely closeted away in his lamasery. When he emerged with his written refutation of Buddhism in 1721, all was calm again in Lhasa. But his book created quite a stir. "My house suddenly became the scene of incessant comings and goings," he wrote. Learned lamas from all over came "to apply for permission to see and read the book."

But Desideri's day of triumph in Lhasa was short. In April, 1721, he received word that he was to leave Tibet. The pope at Rome had decided to give the missionaries of the Capuchin order (a branch of the Franciscans) the rights to carry on missionary work in Lhasa. Desideri, as a Jesuit, was forced to leave. Bitterly disappointed, the 37-year-old priest bade farewell to his friends in the capital and returned to India. He died, 12 years later, in Rome.

The founding of the Capuchin mission in Lhasa signaled the end of the Jesuits' Tibetan ventures. Though the Capuchins, too, were soon forced out of the capital by more political upheavals, the Jesuits did not make any further attempts to found a mission there. In their own eyes, their missionary efforts in the mountain kingdom had been a failure. But in the eyes of the world, the courageous Jesuit fathers had achieved something just as important: they had laid the groundwork for all future exploration of Tibet.

Below: a Tibetan *thanka,* a painting
of a sacred subject that is hung in
a temple, showing a celestial being.
Thankas are normally done on cotton,
and are therefore known as cotton-
drawings. The drawing itself is then
lavishly framed in silks or brocades.

Central Asia: Desert Challenge

5

Sandwiched in between Tibet and Siberia lies the giant desert waste of Central Asia. Roughly triangular in shape, it begins just east of Kashmir, with the Taklamakan Desert, and gradually widens out into a vast complex of wastelands that includes the Dzungaria, the Ordos, and the mighty Gobi deserts of central China and Mongolia. With the exception of its eastern fringes, the whole bleak region is enclosed and broken up by mountain ranges: the Pamirs in the west; the Tien Shan, Altai, and Khingan in the north; and the Kunlun, Astin Tagh, and Nan Shan in the south.

Back in the early 1600's, this vast, forbidding terrain was almost a complete mystery to Westerners. For 300 years, European access to the heartland had been cut off by the combined might of the Mongols and the Moslems. Even after the Portuguese had reached the Orient by sea in the early 1500's, it was a full century before any Western traveler ventured into Central Asia. The man who eventually did so was, like the first explorers of Tibet, a brave Jesuit priest.

The Jesuits at Peking had long been at odds with their brethren in India over a perplexing geographical riddle: Where was Cathay? In the late 1200's, the great traveler Marco Polo had visited this Eastern realm and glowingly described it. But by the time the Portuguese arrived in the Orient, it seemed to have vanished into thin air. Matteo Ricci, head of the Jesuit mission at Peking, stoutly maintained that "Cathay" was simply an old name for China. This was true, and, in fact, some of China's land neighbors were still calling the Chinese empire "Cathay." But the Jesuits in India were convinced that Marco Polo's fabled Asian realm was a different country from

Left: a detail from a Turkoman tent band, used to decorate the interior walls of the round tentlike structures that the Turkoman people lived in and carried with them on their travels. The design here is a caravan scene of men, horses, and camels.

Below: Matteo Ricci, who was the head of the Jesuit mission in Peking. He maintained that the mysterious "Cathay" was an old name for China.

China. To settle the issue once and for all, they decided to send an explorer deep into the Asian heartland to find Cathay.

The man they picked for this hazardous mission was a 41-year-old priest named Bento de Goes. He had started his career in India as a Portuguese soldier, and even after becoming a Jesuit—at the age of 27—had eagerly seized every opportunity for travel and adventure. De Goes was serving as the Jesuits' emissary to the glittering court of India's Mogul ruler at Agra when, in 1603, he received his orders to set out in search of Cathay.

De Goes' first stop was the bustling city of Lahore, in present-day West Pakistan. Knowing that he would be traveling through fanatically Moslem lands, he disguised himself as a Moslem merchant, and joined a large caravan bound for Kabul in eastern Afghanistan. The region between Lahore and Kabul was infested with bandits, and despite the size of the caravan—500 men with wagons, camels, and pack horses—an escort of 400 soldiers was necessary to get them through without too much loss of lives and property. De Goes himself was cut off from the caravan one day by four bloodthirsty robbers. He managed to escape their clutches only by throwing his jeweled cap to the ground and galloping off while they fought for possession of it.

After six grueling months, the party reached Kabul, and there the Jesuit joined another caravan, this one bound for Yarkand in western Turkestan (now the Chinese province of Sinkiang). Along the way, they had to cross the high, windswept passes of the Pamirs, and five of De Goes' seven horses died from the intense cold and the difficulty of breathing in the rarified air.

Left: an Indian miniature depicting the Mogul ruler Akbar with Jesuit missionaries. Akbar was much impressed by De Goes, who at one time became Akbar's ambassador to the Portuguese viceroy at Goa, under instructions to improve the strained relations between the Portuguese and the Indian court.

Late in 1603, the caravan reached Yarkand, and De Goes settled down to wait for the departure of another large caravan which, he learned, was going to travel east "to Cathay." Shortly after his arrival in the city, he was almost murdered by an angry mob of Moslems who had seen through his disguise. At the last minute, the city's more tolerant ruler intervened, and placed the Jesuit under his protection. With the help of another local potentate, De Goes became the first European to see the fabulous Khotan jade mines, 200 miles to the south.

Ready at last, the caravan set out in 1604 and began winding its way eastward along the foothills of the Tien Shan. Occasionally, it made stops at such obscure places as Aksu, Turfan, and Hami. At Aksu, De Goes was introduced to the king—a boy of 12—and gave him some sugar lumps. The boy was so delighted with this novel gift that he ordered a special dance in the traveler's honor. To please the king, De Goes danced too—much to the boy's amusement.

Above: Bento de Goes' caravan being set upon by bandits. The perils of travel were so well known that a small army had to travel with every large caravan to protect them from raiders.

But such moments of gaiety were few and far between on the long road to China. In eastern Turkestan, there was the ever-present danger of a Mongol attack. De Goes recorded that passage through the region could be made only "in the greatest fear, sometimes even under cover of night, and in the strictest silence." The going got even rougher when they reached the outskirts of the Gobi Desert. There, all along the trail, lay the bleached bones of men and animals—grim reminders of the fate that awaited stragglers.

Late in 1605, the caravan reached its destination, a dusty trading station called Suchow, just north of the Nan Shan. De Goes learned from his traveling companions that this outpost marked the western-most limit of Cathay. So he had reached his objective! But had he also reached China? He put the question to a party of Peking merchants who arrived in Suchow a few days later. To his great joy, they assured him that he was indeed standing on Chinese soil.

Right: an engraving of the early 1700's, showing De Goes being poisoned by his fellow travelers. He lies dying in bed while the Moslems attack his servant and go through his papers. His diary was stolen, probably by men who wanted to remove all evidence of their indebtedness to De Goes. The only account of his journey comes from his servant, who managed to reach Ricci.

Left: the Gobi Desert. Covering vast areas in Mongolia and central China, the desert was a formidable buffer between China and the world to the west. Here the dangers of bandits receded in the face of the difficulties of finding a way across the arid waste.

Better still, one of the merchants happened to be a friend of Father Ricci, and offered to carry a letter to him from De Goes.

It took over a year for Ricci's answer to reach De Goes, and during that time the explorer was persecuted—and probably even poisoned—by his Moslem traveling companions. The priest was a dying man when, in April, 1607, he finally received Ricci's reply, urging him to proceed eastward through Cathay-China to Peking. But it was too late for De Goes. A few days later, the brave Jesuit died. "Seeking Cathay," one of his fellow priests wrote later, "he found heaven."

It was to be a long, long time before De Goes' harrowing journey was repeated by another European. In fact, the western half of Central Asia remained a blank on the map for another 200 years. In the meantime, however, a number of intrepid explorers made their way through the eastern deserts of the heartland.

The first of these daring travelers were, of course, the Jesuits Grueber and D'Orville, who journeyed from Peking to Agra in 1661. They were followed by a Dutch adventurer named Samuel Van de Putte, who traveled from Europe to Peking—via Persia, India, and Tibet—*and back again,* in the 1720's. But Van de Putte was a strange man. He seemed not to want to tell anyone about his journey, and even burned his diaries before he died in 1745. All he left to the world as a record of his journey was a rough map of his

route, and ironically, that, too, was later destroyed in a World War II bombing raid.

The next European to venture into Central Asia was the distinguished German geographer Alexander von Humboldt. In 1829, he traveled to the western edge of the mighty Altai Mountains on a scientific expedition for the Russian government. But like Van de Putte, the German was curiously modest about his exploits in the heartland. Having made his official report, he refrained from writing a personal account of his experiences in Central Asia.

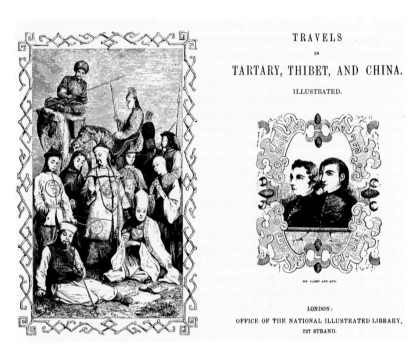

TRAVELS

IN

TARTARY, THIBET, AND CHINA.

ILLUSTRATED.

MM. GABET AND HUC.

LONDON:
OFFICE OF THE NATIONAL ILLUSTRATED LIBRARY,
227 STRAND.

Left: the frontispiece and title page of Huc's account of his journey, *Travels in Tartary, Thibet, and China*. On the title page are pictured Huc and his traveling companion Gabet, and the frontispiece shows men in Tartar and Chinese dress, improbably grouped. His story was so entertainingly told that for years few scholars believed it.

Modesty was definitely not a characteristic of the next European traveler in the heartland. This was a French missionary named Father Evarist Huc, who, with a companion named Joseph Gabet, made an epic two-year tour of Mongolia, China, and Tibet in the mid-1800's. On his return, Huc published a long and colorful account of his travels—so colorful, in fact, that for years no one believed a word of it.

Huc and Gabet were working at a mission in northern China when they began their great adventure. They had had some success in converting the Buddhist Mongols of the Chinese interior, and decided to try their luck in Tibet. They knew it had been nearly 100 years since any missionaries had been allowed inside the country. But they hoped that by approaching Tibet from China, rather than from India, they would succeed where others had failed.

Having first disguised themselves as lamas—complete with shaven heads—the two set out from Hei-shui, north of Peking, in 1844. They had decided to make a brief circuit through Tartary (Inner Mongolia), so they headed due north. Their route took them through a rugged, heavily forrested terrain which, they soon learned, was

Right: the interior of a Mongol tent, with the hole at the top to let out the smoke. Abbé Huc wrote about them, "The odor pervading the interior of the Mongol tents is, to those not accustomed to it, disgusting and almost insupportable. This smell, so potent sometimes that it seems to make one's heart rise to one's throat, is occasioned by the mutton grease and butter with which everything on or about a Tartar is impregnated."

notoriously infested with thieves. According to Huc, these bandits operated with a kind of sinister politeness. "Venerable elder brother," they would say as they held up a traveler, "I am on foot; pray lend me your horse." So saying, they would rob him of horse, money, and any other valuables he had with him, thanking him profusely all the while.

Huc and Gabet managed to get through this region safely, and proceeded west to the high plains of Tartary. Huc found the grasslands strangely beautiful. "The aspect of the prairies," he wrote,

"excites neither joy nor sorrow, but rather a mixture of the two, a sentiment of gentle, religious melancholy." These rolling plains were the home of the Mongol nomads, whose round felt tents looked from a distance "like balloons newly inflated and just about to take flight."

The missionaries found the nomads kindly and hospitable, and often stopped to rest with them. The scene at each camp was the same: "Children with a sort of hood at their backs run about collecting *argols* [dried dung used for fuel] which they pile in heaps

Below: a Mongol camp in the 1800's. The nomadic Mongols were completely at home in the steppes, being superb horsemen. They kept large herds of cattle and horses, and lived in tents— the famous Mongol *yurts*—that they could easily dismantle for traveling.

around their respective tents. The matrons look after the calves, make tea in the open air, or prepare milk in various ways. The men, mounted on fiery horses and armed with a long pole, gallop about, guiding to the best pastures the great herds of cattle which undulate in the distance all around like waves of the sea."

During their sojourn among the Mongols, Huc recorded many of their customs and beliefs. One of these—a tradition that horrified the missionary—was their practice of supplying dead kings with slaves. Just before the tomb was sealed, the Mongols "take children of both sexes remarkable for their beauty, and make them swallow mercury until they are suffocated. In this way they preserve the freshness and ruddiness of their countenances so as to make them appear still alive." The Mongols placed these unfortunate children in the tomb together with the king, in the belief that they would serve him in the afterlife.

Huc and Gabet traveled some 300 miles through the prairies before turning south into the bleak wastes of the Ordos Desert.

Right: Mongol herdsmen of today, little changed from the Mongols abbé Huc described, riding horses and using long poles to guide their herds.

There, Nature inspired no sentiments of "religious melancholy." The Ordos was more like a giant enemy armed with a variety of fiendish weapons. It was the middle of winter, and the missionaries found the nights almost unbearably cold. During the day, fierce winds often drove blinding clouds of sand into the eyes of the men and their camels. But worst of all were the frequent hailstorms. Like everything else about this desert, the hailstones were Gargantuan—rocks of ice as big as a fist.

The only refuge from the elements was the occasional *serai*, or

Above: an engraving from the English edition of Huc's book showing the Tree of Ten Thousand Images. Huc wrote,"More profound intellects than ours may, perhaps, be able to supply a satisfactory explanation of the mysteries of this singular tree; but as to us, we altogether give it up."

desert inn. These welcome havens were no more than rough huts, but they offered warmth, shelter, and companionship to weary travelers after a long day's march in the desert. At such waystations, Huc and Gabet would join caravan merchants around long tables called *khangs,* smoking, swapping stories, and philosophizing far into the night.

Twice during their journey southward, the missionaries had to cross the great Hwang Ho River. The second time, it was in flood, and proved a formidable obstacle. The camels could not swim, and had to be pushed and hauled through the swirling waters. But once across the river, the travelers made fairly rapid progress southward. Early in 1845, after "ascending many hills and twice passing the Great Wall," Huc and Gabet reached Kumbum, a Buddhist sanctuary in the northwest corner of the Tibetan plateau. There the missionaries made the acquaintance of a learned lama, and gained his permission to enter the famous Kumbum lamasery.

Kumbum was the sacred birthplace of Tsong Khapa, a great Buddhist teacher of the 1300's. Tsong Khapa had become a lama at the age of three, and legend has it that when his shorn locks were thrown on the ground, a miraculous tree sprang up. On each one of its leaves was the sacred Buddhist prayer *Om mani padme hum.*

Huc and Gabet, who spent several months at the Kumbum lamasery, were convinced of the genuineness of this "Tree of Ten Thousand Images." Huc wrote that "We were filled with an absolute consternation of astonishment at finding that there were upon each of these leaves well-formed Tibetan characters, all of a green character." The two men examined the tree minutely, and found that "when you remove a piece of the old bark, the young bark under it exhibits the indistinct outlines of characters in a germinating state."

For two devout Catholic priests to acknowledge a "heathen" miracle was practically a miracle in itself. Yet they had the evidence before their very eyes. Was it genuine? We shall never know, for by the time the next European traveler reached Kumbum, 50 years later, the miraculous tree had died.

The Kumbum lamasery was both a shrine and a medical center. Huc watched the lama-physicians at work, and describes how they would diagnose a patient's illness by listening to a sample of his urine, "to ascertain how much noise it makes; for in their view a

...se for sale in Peking. When we met the first
...river, we asked him how far it was from
... Enclosure. "You see here," said he with a

grin, "one end of our caravan; the other extremity
is still within the town." "Thanks," cried we; "in
that case we shall soon be there." "Well, you've
not more than fifteen lis to go." "Fifteen lis! why
you've just told us that the other end of your
caravan is still in the town." "So it is, but our

Above: a page from Huc's book showing one of the immense caravans he and
Gabet had seen. This particular one
was on its way to Lhasa from Peking.

Right: a drawing of the Potala at
Lhasa in crayon, showing it as it
looked in 1904. Huc, like those who
came to the city before him, was
much impressed by its magnificence.

The Pota-la Palace: Lhasa
9.VIII.04.

patient's water is mute or silent according to the state of his health."
The missionary also watched the lamas making the herbal medicines
for which Kumbum was famous. "The Tartar-Mongols never return
home without an ample supply of them, having an unlimited
confidence in whatever emanates from Kumbum, even though the
very same roots and grasses grow in abundance in their own lands."

At the end of October, 1845, a large caravan from Peking passed
through Kumbum on its way to Lhasa. Here was a golden opportunity, and the two priests were quick to take advantage of it.
When they joined the caravan, their presence was hardly noticed

amid the throng of 2,000 men and 4,000 animals that made up the entourage.

The long column of men and beasts slowly made its way south over the high rim of mountains guarding the Tibetan plateau. Winter was setting in, and the wind cut through them like a knife as they stumbled along through deep drifts of snow. To keep from losing their way in blizzards, the men walked behind their horses, holding on to their tails and trusting to their instinct. "Death now hovered over the unfortunate caravan," writes Huc. "Each day we had to abandon beasts of burden that could drag themselves no further. The turn of the men came somewhat later. . . ." But still the caravan pressed on, and at long last, on January 29, 1846, the travelers reached Lhasa.

Like Grueber and Desideri before him, Huc was deeply impressed by the Potala palace. "Two fine avenues of magnificent trees lead from Lhasa to the Buddha-la [Potala], and there you always find crowds of foreign pilgrims. . . . The Potala inspires a strange silence." But the atmosphere in the city itself was very different. In the streets, "all is excitement and noise and pushing . . . every single soul in the place being ardently occupied in the business of buying and selling."

The missionaries' arrival in the "forbidden city" created a sensation. Word went round that they were foreign spies, and they were summoned to the palace for a confrontation with the reigning regent. For a long time, the regent stared silently at the two men before him. Finally, just the hint of a smile on the man's face prompted Huc to whisper to Gabet, "This gentleman seems a good fellow." The regent immediately wanted to know what he had said, so Huc repeated his remark in Tibetan. At this, the regent burst out laughing, for in truth, he said, he was really bad-tempered. But the ice had been broken, and thereafter, the ruler often invited Huc and Gabet to the palace to discuss religion and tell him about the outside world.

One day, the regent asked Huc to show him the microscope that the missionary had brought with him from Peking. The Tibetan wanted to know how it worked. Accordingly, writes Huc, "We asked if one of the company would be so good as to produce us a louse. A lama had merely to put his hand under his silk dress to his armpit, and an extremely vigorous louse was at our disposal. . . . We requested the regent to apply his right eye, shutting his left, to the glass top of the machine. 'Tsong Khapa!' exclaimed the regent, 'The louse is as big as a rat!'"

The priests' friendship with the regent led them to hope that sooner or later they would succeed in converting him to Catholicism. And if he became a Christian, who could tell how many other Tibetans might follow suit? But it was not to be. Three months after their arrival, the resident Chinese ambassador—who had been suspicious of them from the start—ordered them to leave Tibet.

The regent was genuinely sorry to see them go, and provided them with a military escort to ensure their safe return to Peking.

Left: the regent of Lhasa, shown with pen in hand. Huc said of his writing that he was not able to judge of its literary merit, but that he had never seen such beautiful calligraphy.

The Tibetans helped them find a shorter and easier route back, and by June, 1846, the missionaries were once again on the warm plains of eastern China. They had not succeeded in converting Tibet, but they had traveled deeper into the heartland than any European since the mysterious Samuel Van de Putte, 120 years before.

Huc and Gabet were the last Europeans to venture into Asia in the hope of winning souls. From 1850 onward, the Asian interior increasingly became the haunt of explorers with a more worldly end in view. This was particularly true of the explorers in northern India and the Himalaya. There, in the region first penetrated by the Jesuits, a wave of British merchants, surveyors, and military officers had already begun writing a spectacular new chapter in the history of Asian exploration.

Below: two Ladakh lamas blowing their beautiful ceremonial long brass horns. Often the only sounds Tibetan travelers hear are the wind and the eerie traditional music of these horns.

Penetrating the Himalaya

6

In May, 1774, a young Scotsman named George Bogle set out from northeast India on a crucial diplomatic mission. His task was nothing less than to gain access to Tibet, to learn all that he could about it, and to persuade its rulers to open their gates to the British.

Why were the British interested in Tibet? The answer lies in their phenomenal rise to power on the subcontinent below it. As far back as the early 1600's, English merchants of the East India Company had won powerful trading concessions in India. Year by year, the company had grown in wealth and power, aggressively extending its sphere of influence by scooping up hundreds of tiny Indian states. So successful were its political intrigues—and outright

conquests—that by the late 1700's, the East India Company was virtually master of India.

With almost the whole of the subcontinent in its pocket, the company naturally began to look beyond India's frontiers, to the remote Himalayan kingdoms. Tibet in particular intrigued the British. What trading opportunities did it offer? How close were its ties with China? Would it consider a trade alliance with Britain?

These were just some of the questions that George Bogle was to answer on his Himalayan mission. It was a tough assignment, for as yet no Englishman had penetrated beyond Nepal and Bhutan. Little was known about the Tibetan terrain—and still less about Tibetan

Above left: the East India Company had gradually gained wealth and power in India until, in the late 1700's it virtually controlled the subcontinent. In about 1790 the chess set from which these pieces are taken was carved of ivory in Bengal, and depicts the East India Company men pitted against the soldiers of an Indian army.

Above: Warren Hastings, the governor general who sent George Bogle off to establish contact with Tibet, and hopefully to persuade the Tibetans to permit the British to trade with them.

politics. But Bogle was a daring and cool-headed young man, and Warren Hastings, the company's governor general, was confident that he would make the right decisions whatever happened.

Bogle almost failed to get into Tibet. On the very borders of the kingdom, he was turned back by an emissary from the Panchen Lama—Tibet's second most powerful Buddhist leader—who strongly urged him to return to India. But Bogle was not ready to give up. He began a lively correspondence with the lama, petitioning him for a special audience. At last, his persistence paid off. In October, 1774, he received an invitation to visit the Panchen Lama at his lamasery near Shigatse.

No European had seen this city in southern Tibet since 1635, when the Jesuits had been forced to abandon their mission there. Bogle's arrival caused a sensation. Crowds of people came running out to watch as he walked slowly through the streets to the lamasery. This made Bogle very nervous. How would he be received by the Panchen Lama? But he found the great man astonishingly open and kindly. Within a few moments, the two were talking like old friends. They discussed the purpose of Bogle's mission, and soon came to an agreement about British trade with Tibet. The agreement, however, could not be put into practice without the consent of the Lhasa authorities. And it would take some careful negotiating, the lama assured Bogle, to get their approval.

In fact, Bogle was to wait almost a year before Lhasa made up its mind about trade with the British. But it was a year of fascinating experiences in a world unlike anything Bogle had ever known. Soon after his arrival, the Panchen Lama moved to a much grander lamasery at Tashilhumpo. Hundreds of high-ranking priests came from all over to pay homage to the lama at his new quarters, and a great banquet was held. Bogle and the other guests dined on such strange delicacies as dried sheep's carcasses and tea buttered with yak fat. While they ate, they were entertained by scores of brightly garbed dancers who performed "to the music of flutes, kettledrums, and bells, keeping time with hoppings and twirlings."

Above: a watercolor by Lieutenant Samuel Davis who accompanied Turner on the journey to Tibet. The drawing shows a scene in Bhutan, with the mountain tops covered with clouds.

Left: the Director's Court Room of the East India House in Leadenhall Street, London. From this room the decision went out that the Company should try to make contact with the rulers of Tibet, as the area showed promise as a new market for goods from England.

Right: George Bogle, who managed to reach Tibet and became a friend of the Panchen Lama. When he set out he was only 28 years old.

Bogle's own quarters consisted of a dim monastery hall supported by nine square pillars painted red and white. There he was visited by a seemingly endless procession of curious Tibetans who came to stare at him as though he were an animal in a zoo. On his side, Bogle was amazed at the filthiness of the Tibetans' hands and faces. "It is directly contrary to custom for the inhabitants, whether male or female, high or low, ever to wash," he wrote. He did his best to interest Tibetans in washing, but met with little success. One day, Bogle's Tibetan servant happened to come in while he was shaving. "I prevailed on him," writes Bogle, "for once to scrub himself with the help of soap and water. I gave him a new complexion, and he seemed to view himself in my shaving glass with some satisfaction. But he was exposed to so much ridicule . . . that I could never get him to repeat the experiment!"

Left: a young Incarnate Lama of the Yellow Hat sect. He is a 17th incarnate, a lama of Kye monastery in Spiti on the border of Tibet and Ladakh. Tibetans believe that when a great lama dies, his soul is reborn in another body, and a search is undertaken for auspicious signs that will direct the remaining lamas to their reborn leader. When Turner was there the new Panchen Lama was only 18 months old.

Bogle whiled away his days at Tashilhumpo playing chess with the monks and writing a history of Europe for his friend the Panchen Lama. Over the months he became increasingly fond of the Lama. "He is extremely merry and entertaining in conversations," Bogle wrote, "and so universally beloved . . . that not a man could find in his heart to speak ill of him."

The young Scotsman was equally enchanted by one of the Lama's pretty young cousins. He married her, and later took her back to India with him. His family, horrified at this exotic alliance, tried to suppress the fact after his death. But we do know that Bogle and his Tibetan wife had two daughters, both of whom were later brought up in Scotland.

All during his stay at Tashilhumpo, Bogle hoped that Lhasa would ultimately agree to the trade arrangement he had worked out with the Panchen Lama. But it never came through. The Dalai Lama's regent refused to sanction it, no doubt at the Chinese ambassadors' insistence. After all, it was in China's best interests to keep any other foreign influences out of the kingdom.

At last, Bogle was forced to give up and return to India. The Panchen Lama bade him a sad farewell, throwing a ceremonial white scarf around his neck and gently laying his hand upon his head in a last blessing. Six years later, both men were dead, struck down suddenly by illness within six months of each other.

The East India Company made no further attempts to negotiate with Tibet until 1783, when Warren Hastings sent another young envoy to Tashilhumpo. This envoy, Samuel Turner, was no more successful than Bogle in gaining trade concessions for the British. But he did meet the new Panchen Lama. Like the Dalai Lama, the new potentate of Tashilhumpo was chosen by divine signs, and Turner found himself confronting an 18-month-old child. But however skeptical he might have been before he met the boy, he came away profoundly impressed by his apparent wisdom. Seated on a high pile of cushions, the child listened attentively to all that Turner said and, "while unable to speak . . . made the most expressive signs and conducted himself with astonishing dignity and decorum."

Whatever faint hopes the British still had for establishing trade links with Tibet were finally extinguished in 1788. In that year, the East India Company's new governor general, Charles Cornwallis, made a grave tactical error. He received a desperate letter from the

Above: Charles Cornwallis, governor general of the East India Company. One result of his refusal to help the Tibetans when they were invaded by Nepalese forces was that Tibet closed its doors to all British explorers.

Panchen Lama's regent begging for the company's help against a Nepalese army that was heading for Tashilhumpo. Warren Hastings would have leapt at this chance to "save Tibet" and thereby win a British foothold in the kingdom. But Cornwallis was a cautious man. He decided not to risk company soldiers so far from India.

As a result, Tibet had to turn to China for assistance. A massive Chinese army arrived in 1792, swept away the Nepalese invaders, and placed Tibet under its "protection." Thereafter, Tibet could never really call itself independent again.

Another consequence of Cornwallis' decision was that the Tibetans began to regard the British as treacherous. As far as they were concerned, the East India Company had proved itself a false friend. Tibet officially closed its gates to the British, and became more of a forbidden land than ever. During the whole of the 1800's, only one Englishman was to gain access to Lhasa—and he was so eccentric that his exploits were not taken seriously.

This odd and unsung hero was Thomas Manning. From boyhood he had been devoured by curiosity about the exotic lands of Tartary. In 1807, his dream of visiting them came true when he won an appointment to the East India Company's offices in China. But this only increased his wanderlust, and in 1811, he turned up at Calcutta and asked if he might serve as the company's representative to Lhasa. The British officials refused his petition, and laughed at him behind his back. How could this bizarre person, sporting a long flowing beard and exotic "Tartary" robes, be expected to achieve anything significant?

But achieve it he did. In December, 1811, three months after leaving Calcutta, Thomas Manning became the first Englishman to enter Lhasa. How did he accomplish this remarkable feat? His diary offers few details about the journey itself. Mostly it is full of complaints about his rascally Chinese servant, and the occasional quip about Tibetan peculiarities. On seeing a long funeral procession carrying a corpse to the top of a hill for the vultures to feed on, Manning remarked, "The people of Tibet eat no birds . . . on the contrary, they let the birds eat them!"

While still some distance from Lhasa, Manning made the acquaintance of a Chinese general. Right away, he won the general's favor with a gift of two bottles of cherry brandy. Never has a bribe worked faster. After one sip, the general "promised to write immedi-

Left: Thomas Manning, the casual and unsponsored explorer who became the first Englishman to reach Lhasa in 1811. He was a brilliant but eccentric man who had long been fascinated by China and the mysterious land of Tibet

Below: a watercolor by Hyder Jung Hearsey of three Tibetan musicians at Ghertope, in the western sector of Tibet. Hearsey and his companion William Moorcroft traveled there in 1812 disguised as Indian holy men.

ately to the Lhasa Mandarin [Chinese ambassador] for permission for me to proceed."

Once in Lhasa, Manning went to visit the seven-year-old Dalai Lama. He was deeply moved by the interview and wrote in his diary, "This day I saluted the Grand Lama! Beautiful youth. Face poetically affecting. Very happy to have seen him and his blessed smile. Hope often to see him again." Whether he did or not is not clear. From then on, Manning's diary is devoted to his growing fear of the sinister Chinese officials in the city. They kept him under constant surveillance and made it pointedly clear that he was not

Left: Colonel Colin Mackenzie, one of the British surveyor generals, with his pundits, the Indians who were trained to carry out secret surveys in areas where Englishmen could not go.

welcome. At last, in April, 1812, Manning took the hint and left the city. By June he was back in India recounting his adventures to the open-mouthed officials of the East India Company.

The very year Manning returned from Lhasa, two young company officers named Moorcroft and Hearsey became the first Englishmen to explore the interior of western Tibet. Dressed as Indian *fakirs* (holy men), they made their way deep into the Himalaya and brought back the first accurate geographical data about India's northwest mountain frontier.

Moorcroft and Hearsey's findings contributed to an ambitious undertaking called the Great Trigonometrical Survey of India. Launched in 1802, its objective was no less than the mapping of the entire subcontinent, including the 2,000-mile arc of mountains beyond it. An accurate map of India and the Himalayan kingdoms north of it was essential if the British were to maintain and extend their Indian empire.

But getting the information—particularly in the jagged mountains of northern India, Kashmir, and Nepal—was often difficult and dangerous. There the surveyors had to contend with hostile tribesmen, as well as with all the perils and hardships of mountain travel. But the work went on, and by 1863, most of the region south and west of Tibet had been accurately mapped. Not the least of the surveyors' achievements was to calculate the height of the world's loftiest peak, Mount Everest, on the Nepal-Tibet border.

But Tibet itself remained an enigma. As the years went by, the Tibetan authorities increased their vigilence, and it became impossible for British surveyors—no matter how well disguised—to gain access to the country. This was doubly frustrating because knowledge of Tibet had assumed a momentous strategic importance. Beyond it lay the powerful empires of Russia and China. Edgy about the security of their Indian holdings, the British were anxious to learn all they could about the mountain fortress that guarded the northern approaches to the subcontinent. But how were they to do so if the Tibetans would not let them enter their kingdom?

It was a surveyor named T. C. Montgomerie who found the solution. He hit upon the idea of training Indians to carry out a secret survey of Tibet. Traveling in the guise of merchants or pilgrims, such native explorers could enter the forbidden land and obtain the vital information needed to fill the blanks on the map.

The Indians chosen for this important task were given an intensive course of training in the use of various surveying instruments, as well as in the techniques of navigational astronomy. But scientific method was not the only thing these "pundit-explorers" learned. Because, in effect, they were British spies, they were taught a variety of ingenious techniques to conceal their real identity and purpose. They were given code names, clothes with secret pockets, and Tibetan prayer wheels with hidden compartments for storing notes. They were encouraged to memorize important information in the form of cryptic verses, and taught special methods of measuring distance, using prayer beads as counting markers and regulating their stride so that each step could be counted as a unit of measure.

All these clandestine techniques were used to great effect by a remarkable pundit named Nain Singh. Traveling as a Tibetan trader, he journeyed through Nepal, and reached Tashilhumpo late in 1865. From there, he traveled north to Lhasa. Soon after his arrival in the city, some resident merchants saw through his disguise, but for reasons best known to themselves, decided not to inform the authorities. Nain Singh kept off the streets as much as possible, and carried out his survey in the strictest secrecy. Working at night from the roof of his humble accommodation, he made a series of astronomical observations that enabled him to plot the exact location of Lhasa for the first time in history.

From Lhasa, Nain Singh journeyed to Tibet's sacred Lake Manasarowar, just beyond the northwest corner of Nepal, and then returned to India. In all, he had covered some 1,200 miles—each of them laboriously measured in footsteps—and obtained crucial information about Tibet's southern trade routes. On his next mission, in 1867, he explored western Tibet, and visited the fabled Thok-Jalung gold mines. There, at an encampment guarded by fierce Tibetan mastiffs, he saw a group of black-clad workers digging out lumps of gold as much as two pounds in weight. He noted that they only mined the surface of the soil, because they believed that to dig for gold deep underground would rob the soil of its fertility.

The next great pundit-explorer was Kishen Singh. In 1878 he made his way to Lhasa, and joined a caravan of Tibetan and Mongolian merchants bound for Chinese Turkestan. His object was to make a thorough survey of the route north, but it was an immensely difficult task. All the while he was making his observations, he had

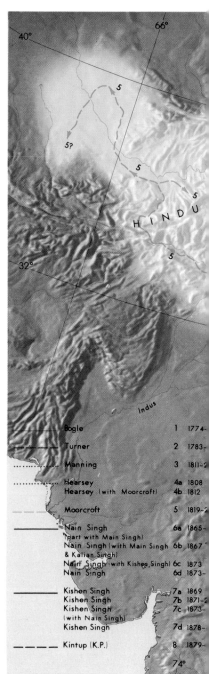

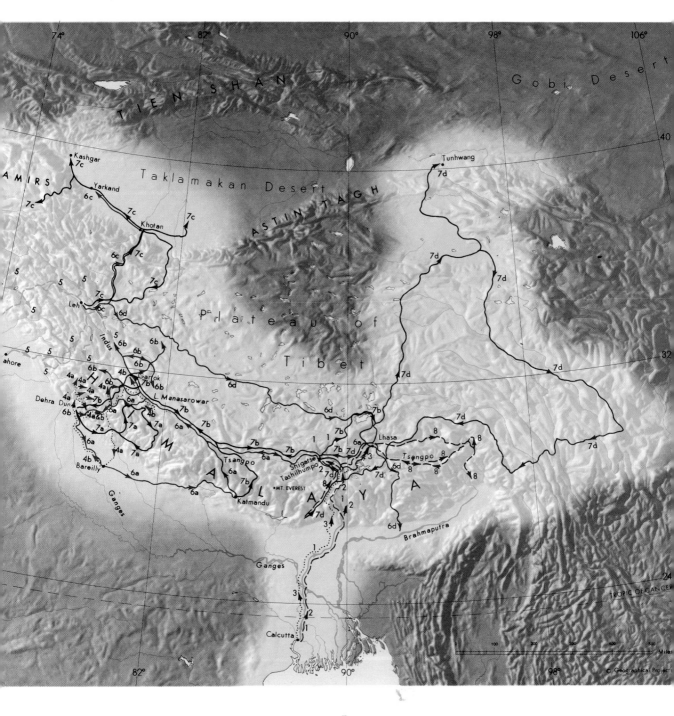

TIEN SHAN

Gobi Desert

Taklamakan Desert

ASTIN TAGH

AMIRS

• Kashgar
7c

7c

Yarkand
6c

7c

Khotan

7c

• Tunhwang
7d

7d

7d

7d

P l a t e a u   o f

7c

6c

7c

5

5

5

7c

Leh
6c

6d

7d

T i b e t

5

5

ahore

5

Indus
6b
6b
6b

6b

6b
4b
4a
4a
4a
4a
H
6b
4a
4b
6b
Gartok
6b

7d

7d

Dehra Dun

4a
7b
6a
6a

L. Manasarowar

6a
6a
4b
7b
7a
7a
6a
7b

6d

7b

4a&b
6b
7a
7a

M
7a
6a

7a
6a

7b

7b

7b

4b
Bareilly

6a
6a

A
Tsangpo

7b
6a

7b
6a
6a

Shigatse
Tashilhumpo

1 1
6a
7b
7b 7d

Lhasa

8

7d

8

3
Tsangpo
6d
8

8

8

8

6a

• MT. EVEREST

8
7d

2
2
1

L
A
2

7d

Katmandu

Ganges

6a

6a

Y
7d
3

A

6d
Brahmaputra

1

Ganges

TROPIC OF CANCER

3

2

Calcutta
1

100   200   300   400   500
Miles

© Geographical Projects

82°   90°   98°

117

to keep up the pretense that he was just a simple merchant who happened to enjoy star-gazing. Fortunately, the party was traveling on foot, so he was able to measure distances fairly accurately. But on one occasion, the caravan leader insisted that they ride horses to speed up their journey through a bandit-infested area. Undaunted, the pundit "set at once to work counting the beast's paces," reckoning the distance in this way for almost 230 miles.

With the caravan, Kishen Singh traveled all the way to Tunhwang, at the western end of the Gobi Desert. He then made his way back to Tibet, visiting most of the principal towns in the eastern sector. He finally returned to India in 1882, after a remarkable journey of several thousand miles through hitherto unknown territories.

Another four-year Tibetan odyssey was made by a dogged pundit named Kintup—or K.P., as he was known in the survey code. In 1879, he set out to explore the Tsangpo River in southern Tibet. Early on in his journey, he attached himself to a Mongolian lama as a servant, hoping thereby to reduce the risk of detection. This, however, soon proved to be a dire mistake. Kintup's Mongolian master promptly sold him to a Tibetan lama, who kept him under almost constant surveillance. It was only after two years of bondage that the pundit managed to make his escape. But despite the indig-

Above: a portrait of Nain Singh, one of the earliest and most famous of all the pundits. His training lasted for two years, during which time he became expert in the use of the compass and sextant, and learned to measure his steps so that every pace was exactly uniform for calculating distances.

nities he had suffered in the cause of the survey, Kintup was determined to complete his mission. He set off for the Tsangpo, and spent over a year exploring it before returning to India in 1883.

The work of Nain Singh, Kishen Singh, and Kintup—together with that of many other, lesser known, pundits—contributed immeasurably to the knowledge of the mysterious lands northeast of India. Meanwhile, to the northwest, British surveyors and explorers were hard at work mapping the strategic territory between India and the exotic land of Persia.

Right: K.P., the pundit Kintup, who doggedly stuck to his task in spite of a series of mishaps and difficulties. His mission was to explore the Tsangpo River and see if it did indeed become the Brahmaputra River of India. He was enslaved, but managed to escape and eventually completed his mission.

Left: a small pocket sextant, made in England in about 1790, of the type that the pundits would have used. They were taught to remember their notes by transcribing them into verse and constantly reciting them as they walked, as pilgrims did the Buddhist prayers.

Above: a detail from a painting of the court of Fath Ali, shah of Persia, in the early 1800's, showing all the foreign ambassadors who had suddenly surged into Persia. Sir John Malcolm is the figure in European dress nearest to the king on his righthand side.

Far right: the imposing portrait of Fath Ali with his magnificent full beard and jewel-encrusted robes. He reigned as shah from 1797 to 1834.

Persia and the "Great Game"

7

During the late 1700's, while the British were building up their vast Indian empire, they all but forgot about Persia. Ravaged and impoverished by civil war, the kingdom had long since lost its appeal for British merchants. And in any case, why should they bother with this dusty corner of Asia when the riches of India lay at their feet? In fact, the British might well have gone on ignoring Persia, had it not suddenly become vital to the security of India itself.

In earlier times, Persia had been famous as a "gateway to the East." In 1800, that phrase abruptly took on a new and sinister meaning for the British. Word had reached them that the Russian czar was eying the kingdom as a possible gateway to India. Already, a Cossack army had conquered the Persian province of Georgia, between the Black and the Caspian seas. If the Russians gained control over the rest of the kingdom, nothing would stand between them and India but the rugged terrain of Afghanistan. And there the Russians would have the full support of the Afghans, who for years past had been making their own attacks on India. Thoroughly alarmed by these possibilities, the British decided it was high time they established their own sphere of influence in Persia.

The man picked to spearhead this move was a young officer in the East India Company's army, Captain John Malcolm. Armed with gifts for the shah, he traveled by ship from Calcutta to the Persian Gulf, and then he set off for the new Persian capital of Teheran. When

he reached the city, late in 1800, he found himself the object of wonder and suspicion. It was hardly surprising, because many, many years had passed since any European had sought an audience with the shah. The Persian courtiers wanted to know why he was not dressed like the Englishmen who had visited the kingdom in the 1600's. They had seen a painting of an English traveler of that time, and expected Malcolm to copy the old style of dress for his presentation to the shah.

Malcolm willingly complied with this odd request, for he was a born diplomat. Discreet and persuasive, he soon won the confidence of the shah, Fath Ali, and convinced him that it would be in his best interests to ally himself with the British. Then, playing on the shah's fear of further Russian attacks, he promised to send British soldiers to train the Persian army in modern fighting methods. In return, the shah agreed to bring pressure on the Afghan ruler to make peace with the British in India.

Over the next 10 years, 2 more visits by Malcolm and one by another envoy, Sir Harford Jones Brydges, clinched this new friendship between Britain and Persia. A permanent British embassy was set up in Teheran, and the soldiers Malcolm had promised duly arrived. But, to the dismay of the British, even the expert advice of these officers could not prevent the shah's army from losing more ground to the Russians.

Above: a Persian miniature showing a battle between the Persian and Russian armies. Fath Ali is shown leading the Persian forces to victory, although on most of the occasions when the Persians fought the Russians, it was the czar's armies who won the day.

Hopelessly undisciplined, the Persian troops did not know how to seize the advantage even when they had it. On one occasion, with victory practically in sight, the Persian commander suddenly lost his head, gave a series of wildly contradictory orders, and ended by calling a retreat. Another time, when the Persians had actually won a battle, they wasted so much time cutting off the heads of a few captives that they let the main body of the enemy force escape.

Part of the trouble lay with the shah himself. Fath Ali was an incorrigibly selfish man, and he simply could not be persuaded to spend money on equipment for his army. Worse still, he seemed to be unaware of just how serious the situation was. His reaction to the news of one particularly crushing defeat was to appear before his courtiers dressed all in red. Fantastic as it may seem, he imagined

that word of his wearing his "robes of wrath" would reach the Russians and frighten them off!

Fortunately, the Russians ceased their attacks on Persia in 1828. For the moment, they were content with the strategic gains they had made along the southeastern shores of the Caspian Sea. But the end of the conflict by no means marked the end of British fears. Persia was now under Russia's thumb in some respects, and there was a powerful Russian embassy in Teheran. Countering Russian influence in Persia became a full-time job for British diplomats.

As a result of this renewed interest in Persia, European merchants and travelers were lured back to the country. Among these travelers was the artist Robert Ker Porter, who journeyed to Persia to paint and sketch in 1818. One of his first stops was the fabled city of

Above: a watercolor of Persia by Robert Ker Porter, here the View of Guz Kala and the Pass of the Koflan-Kou Mountains. Ker Porter writes that the road to the pass was steep, winding, intricate, and very dangerous because of the slipperiness of the ice surface.

Above: Fath Ali receiving Sir Harford Jones Brydges in 1809. The painting is possibly by James Morier, shown standing behind the ambassador. He took part in three missions to Persia.

Right: James Morier's diaries. One, opened, describes a visit to a Russian camp in October, 1813, and the incident illustrated by a watercolor sketch. Many of the travelers of the 1800's and 1900's kept detailed diaries.

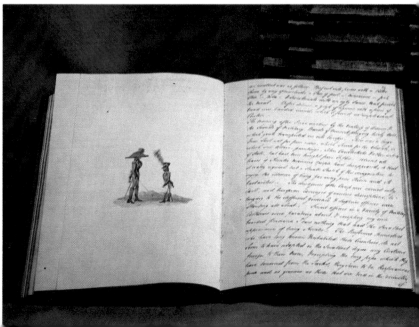

Isfahan. Alas, the city had lost much of its splendor since the days of Shah Abbas. Years of civil war and neglect had turned Isfahan into a waste of ruins and abandoned houses. Though it was still inhabited, Porter recorded sadly that "its palaces [are] solitary and forlorn. . . . The nocturnal laugh and song which used to echo from every part of the gardens [are] now succeeded by the yells of jackalls and the howls of famishing dogs."

And what of the new Persian capital, Teheran? Set at the very foot of the snow-clad Elburz Mountains, the city looked from a distance every bit as romantic as European tourists expected it to be. But once inside its gates, they found to their astonishment that the capital was little more than a squalid, overgrown market town, a hodgepodge of low, flat-roofed houses and crowded bazaars.

James Morier, a British diplomat who spent many years in Teheran, vividly captured the typical European's first impressions of this strange city. "In vain he looks for a street. . . . He makes his way through the narrowest lanes, incumbered with filth, dead animals, and mangy dogs. He hears a language totally new . . . spoken by people whose looks and dress are equally extraordinary—rough faces masked with beards and moustachios, in long flapping clothes . . . . At dawn the *muezzins* [Moslem criers] are heard in a great variety of .tones, calling the people to prayer from the top of the mosques; these are mixed with the sounds of cow horns . . . to inform the women, who bathe before the men . . . that the *hummums* [public baths] are ready. The cow horns set all the dogs to barking in a frightful manner. The asses of the town generally begin to bray about the same time. . . ."

James Morier, like most British visitors to Persia in the early 1800's, found little to praise in the country. But Morier spiced his criticisms with wit. One of his most amusing—and uncomplimentary —books about life in Persia was a satire called *Hajji Baba*. It describes the adventures of a young man, the Hajji Baba of the title, as he passes through a wild variety of careers—as a slave, a dervish, an executioner, a holy man, a scribe, a tobacco dealer, and finally an assistant to an ambassador. Morier was a shrewd observer, and the

Right: an engraving made from one of Morier's sketches of Persian musicians. These he saw at one of the entertainments during a journey he took with the ambassador Sir Gore Ouseley.

Left: a harem lady tumbling, in an oil painting of the early 1800's, from the shah's palace. The strange position of the lady shows clearly her voluminous trousers. The more noble a woman was, the more layers of trousers she wore. When Lady Shiel first appeared wearing a dress she caused a great flurry as the Persians thought she was wearing trousers with only one leg.

fictional characters in the story were, in fact, only thinly disguised versions of real people. The ambassador in the tale, for example, was based on the Persian envoy whom Morier himself had accompanied to London in 1809.

This ambassador, a man named Mirza Abul Hassan Khan, was so outraged when he read the book that he sat down and wrote Morier an angry letter. "What for you write Hajji Baba, sir?" he demanded. "That very bad book, sir. All lies, sir. Who tell you these lies, sir? What for you not speak to me? Very bad business, sir. Persian people very bad people, perhaps, but very good to you, sir. What for you abuse them so bad?"

But there was a good deal of truth in Morier's account. Persia at this time was rife with corruption and governmental abuses. Extortion was the rule all the way up the ladder of authority, and the shah maintained his tyrannical grip over the country with arbitrary acts of extreme cruelty. Lady Shiel, the wife of a British ambassador in Persia in the mid-1800's, recounts how the shah used to levy a fine in the form of eyes from those cities that incurred his displeasure. The eyes had to be brought to him on a platter, and he would count them, in the presence of all his courtiers, with the tip of his jeweled sword. On one occasion, no less than 70,000 pairs of eyes were exacted from the province of Kerman as a punishment for sheltering a rival prince.

Rival princes abounded, for by the 1800's, it was common for the shah to have literally hundreds of sons. James Morier recorded that on a single night in 1808, the shah, who already had 65 sons, was presented with another four sons and two daughters. And when Lady Shiel visited the country, 30 years later, she was astonished to discover that the shah's "family" included some 2,500 people! Most of the shah's children lived at the royal palace as his dependants. But some of the princes were permitted to take charge of distant provinces. If and when they acquired too much power and began to intrigue against their father, they were promptly killed or blinded.

The shah stocked his harem with beautiful women from all over Persia. Government officials used to roam the kingdom seeking pretty virgins to please the king, and Persian nobles were expected to offer their wives to him as potential mistresses. All the women in the royal harem were kept in strict seclusion, under the care of a man

Above: a papier-mâché Persian pen box, decorated with the picture of the court of a eunuch who had become a governor. The shah put the royal princes in the care of the eunuchs in the harem to keep them uninvolved in the world of politics and therefore less of a threat to his own position.

Below: a watercolor drawing by Robert Ker Porter of one of the harem women. He wrote that their personal beauty seldom lasted longer than eight or ten years, and then faded quickly.

called a eunuch, who could be trusted because he had been castrated.

The keeping of women in seclusion—or *purdah*, as it was called—was standard practice throughout Persia. A woman was allowed to be seen only by her family. If she ventured out of the house, she had to wear a *bourkha*, a tent-like garment that covered her from head to toe. While in Persia, Lady Shiel was forced to adopt this garb lest she be thought indecent. She resented the custom at first, but later came to the conclusion that it gave Persian women a freedom and anonymity their British sisters might well envy. Hidden under the folds of their bourkhas, they could travel incognito wherever they wanted.

In spite of the interest she took in Persian customs, however, Lady Shiel found life in Persia very dull. There was only one other educated European woman in Teheran, and she was the wife of the Russian minister. Since their husbands were political enemies, it was impossible for the two women to become friends. Lady Shiel occasionally accompanied her husband on diplomatic missions to other parts of the country, but these journeys could hardly be described as pleasure trips. As she herself put it, Persia was divided into "two portions—one being desert with salt, and the other desert without salt." Nor was the Persian climate endearing. The winters were extremely cold, and often accompanied by severe blizzards. In summer, the whole country baked in a sweltering heat so intense that "ivory split, mathematical rulers curled up, and the mercury overran the boxes which contained it."

But if life in Persia was dull for diplomats' wives, it was frustrating and difficult for the diplomats themselves—particularly during the second half of the 1800's. Shah Nasiru'd Din, who ruled from 1848 to 1896, stubbornly refused to commit himself to either the British

Left: Abdel Samud, the Afghan official responsible for having two Englishmen put to death in Bukhara in 1842. He had them thrown from the top of a minaret for having ventured too far into Afghanistan. Such incidents made later travelers, like the French explorer J. P. Ferrier, fear for their own safety while in Afghanistan.

or the Russians. Instead, he played one power off against the other, and kept them both guessing as to where his real loyalties lay. He granted concessions to each, sought "advice" from each, and accepted handsome gifts—in the form of loans, railroads, and telegraph lines—from each. Neither the British nor the Russians could ever be sure of Nasiru'd Din, and so both were forced to maintain their vigilance at the Persian court, constantly striving to prevent one another from gaining the upper hand.

This war of nerves in Teheran was just one aspect of the increasing rivalry between Britain and Russia for supremacy in southwest Asia. With grim humor, the British writer Rudyard Kipling dubbed this contest the "Great Game." It was an apt phrase, for the rivalry between the two powers never reached the point of actual combat. Instead, it consisted of a series of moves and countermoves in the

Above: nomads with their flocks in Afghanistan, pursuing a way of life that has remained the same for hundreds of years. The mountainous area was sparsely populated then as now, and the towns were small and primitive.

Above: J. P. Ferrier, who had been sent originally by the French to help organize the Persian army. When he left Persia he went to Afghanistan, where he was promptly placed under house arrest by a local ruler, Yar Mohamed, who was convinced he was English. The Afghans were then still very bitter about the British attack on their land.

strategic territories separating their two spheres of influence.

Early in the 1800's, the British had begun exploring Afghanistan. They justified their activities there as an extension of their geographical survey of northern India. But their real reason for exploring the country was political. The security of India depended on their knowing the sort of people and terrain that lay beyond it.

The first British explorers in Afghanistan were two surveyors named Christie and Pottinger. Disguised as horse-dealers, they crossed the country from east to west in 1810, and returned to India with the first rough sketch of the route to Herat, Afghanistan's largest city. Over the next 25 years, a number of other British survey teams made their way through the country, penetrating deep into the Hindu Kush mountains that link Afghanistan to Kashmir.

These expeditions paved the way for a successful British military campaign against Afghanistan in 1839. The campaign was launched in response to rumors that the Afghan ruler, Dost Mohamed, was considering an alliance with Russia. The very idea was enough to send shivers up British spines, and the East India Company promptly sent an armed force to change Dost Mohamed's mind. So swift was the British advance that they took the Afghans by surprise, captured the capital city of Kabul, and forced Dost Mohamed to agree to a treaty with Britain.

The Afghans were extremely bitter about this act of aggression, as a French explorer named J. P. Ferrier discovered some years later. In 1845, he set out from Persia with the idea of reaching India by way of Afghanistan. His first stop was Herat, and there he was immediately put under house arrest by the local ruler, Yar Mohamed, who believed him to be an Englishman. For many days, Ferrier lived in fear of his life. He witnessed the hideous execution of a prisoner who had tried to escape. The man was blown from a gun: "A horrid spectacle. . . . The broken limbs . . . scattered in all directions [and] were in an instant devoured by the dogs that were loitering about the spot."

Fortunately, Ferrier himself was spared. Somehow he managed to convince Yar Mohamed that he was not British after all, and was granted leave to depart. He set off once more, making his way through a sweltering desert where the temperature in the sun was close to 175°F., and where he actually saw people poaching eggs on the ground.

As Ferrier traveled east, he was constantly harassed by bandits and hostile tribesmen, and on one occasion, was even attacked by his own guide. In fact, the only reason he was not actually killed was that the Afghans were Moslems, and according to the Moslem code of hospitality, even an uninvited guest is sacred. A tribal chieftain who coveted Ferrier's pistols sighed, "You are my guest . . . may your shadow never be less! But it would have been a fine piece of good luck to meet you [far] from this place. Those pistols, that gun . . . would soon have been hung up in my house!"

Right: the Russian Prince Soltykoff on a visit to Persia, painting a young Persian prince. The Russians and the British vied with each other for years to gain influence over the Persian shah, Nasiru'd Din, who managed to extract the maximum benefit without committing himself to either side.

But not all Afghans felt as strongly about the rules of hospitality as this chieftain. When Ferrier reached the little principality of Mahmoodabad, he was thrown into jail and robbed of his pistols. For three weeks he was starved and tortured until he finally agreed to give the local ruler a receipt for the "sale" of the guns.

Ferrier pressed on to the city of Kandahar, in southern Afghanistan. There he was once again placed under house arrest. Unfortunately, his arrival in the city coincided with the outbreak of a cholera epidemic. The populace, believing that Allah had sent the

Above: Sir Percy Sykes, the Englishman who spent many years in Persia making six major expeditions to fill in large blank spaces on the map. During all his time there he remained enthusiastic about the quality of life in Persia.

epidemic because their ruler was harboring an unbeliever, rose up in arms and stormed the palace. Ferrier, who had had years of experience in the French army, persuaded the ruler to let him take charge of the palace troops, and under his expert guidance, they repelled the attack.

But even this act of heroism did not prevent Ferrier from ultimately being sent back to Herat as a "trouble-maker." Disgusted, Ferrier left Afghanistan, concluding that the only way to deal with the Afghans was "by force or by the hope of gain."

Force was the method used by the Russians in dealing with the Moslem people who dwelt in the vast region of steppes and deserts east of the Caspian Sea and south of Siberia. These people, like the Afghans, were nomadic tribesmen. They were no match for the

fierce Cossack armies that began sweeping down on them in the mid-1800's.

Russian expansion in this region was both systematic and relentless. It began in the 1840's, when teams of explorers were sent out to make a careful survey of the area between the northern shores of the Caspian Sea, the Aral Sea, and Lake Balkhash. From there, they worked their way south to the Syr-Darya River, and thence on down to the cluster of cities just north of Afghanistan. Inexorably, the work of the scientist was followed up by the work of the soldier, as the armies of the czar moved south to secure the newly explored territories. The city of Tashkent fell to the Russians in 1864, and the city of Bukhara in 1865. Samarkand, Khiva, and Kokand followed in quick succession. By 1880, only the region now called Turkmen-

Above: the Persian ambassador, Mirza Abul Hassan Khan, making a splendid entrance into St. Petersburg in the early 1800's, during the period when Britain and Russia were struggling for influence over the shah. He had also represented the shah in London.

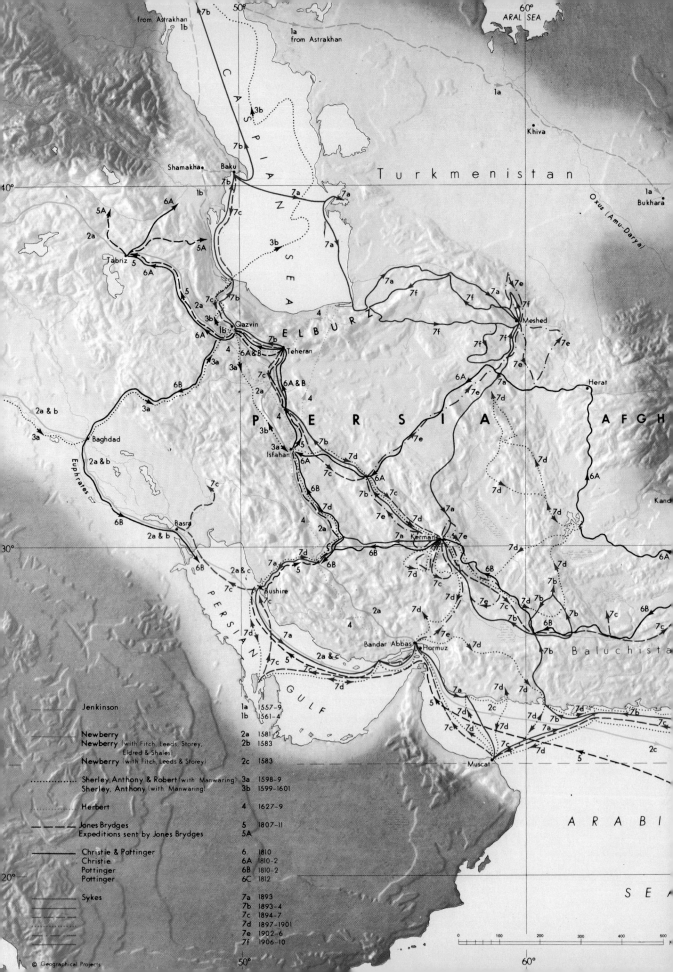

ARAL SEA

from Astrakhan
1b

1a
from Astrakhan

1a

Khiva

CASPIAN SEA

Shamakha
Baku

Turkmenistan

Oxus (Amu-Darya)

Bukhara
1a

Tabriz

Meshed

Qazvin

ELBURZ

Teheran

Herat

Baghdad

PERSIA

AFGH

Isfahan

Kand

Euphrates

Basra

Kerman

Bushire

Bandar Abbas
Hormuz

Baluchista

PERSIAN GULF

Muscat

ARABI

SEA

© Geographical Projects

Left: Persia and Afghanistan, showing the journeys of some of the most important British merchants, travelers, and explorers who visited the region between 1558 and 1910. Britain's purely mercantile interest in the area swiftly changed to political concern early in the 1800's, when Russia's aggressive policy of expansion began to threaten the security of Persia, and therefore the security of Britain's Indian empire as well.

istan—between the Aral Sea and northern Persia—remained unconquered. And by 1884, that region, too, was in Russia's pocket.

These developments caused grave concern in British India. Suddenly, alarmingly, Russia was at the very gates of Kashmir, Afghanistan, *and* Persia. The British stepped up their own explorations west of India, and waged a new war against Afghanistan. By 1880, they were as much the masters of that country as the Russians were of the lands beyond it. This gave the British some measure of security, but they could not rest until they had mapped every corner of accessible ground between India and northwest Persia.

This new phase of British exploration began in 1870, with the expedition of a man named Sir Frederick Goldsmid. He and his party crisscrossed Persia and Afghanistan, as well as Baluchistan (a smaller kingdom along the shores of the Arabian Sea), which today forms a part of West Pakistan. During the next 40 years, scores of other British explorers made their way through the three kingdoms, and, slowly but surely, the blank spaces on the map were filled in.

Among all the explorers of this difficult terrain, none ranks higher than Sir Percy Sykes. Between 1893 and 1910, he made no fewer than six major expeditions through Persia and Baluchistan. Each contributed significantly to British knowledge of the region, and each confirmed and increased Sykes's own love of Persia. His writings about the kingdom are full of glowing accounts of its romantic beauty. About one particularly lovely Persian garden, luxuriant with flowers and fruit trees, fountains and pavilions, he wrote that, "the singing of the nightingales, added to the murmur of the water and the scent of the roses, made us travelers . . . feel that we had reached an earthly Paradise."

But Sykes's romantic view of Persia was not shared by the majority of British travelers in the late 1800's. What they saw was a backward country "even more incapable than Turkey of adopting European habits," as one diplomat put it. Persia was in fact badly in need of modernization and reform. But neither the British nor the Russians were prepared to devote their time to improving conditions in the kingdom. They were too busy vying with each other for influence over the shah. On his side, Shah Nasiru'd Din graciously accepted the vast loans they offered him, and even went so far as to pay a series of state visits to London and St. Petersburg. But to the

The arrival of Shah Nasiru'd Din at Windsor Castle in 1873. Queen Victoria, standing on the steps, is greeting the shah. The Prince of Wales is with her, in the ceremonial uniform of a general of the British army.

exasperation of both sides, he still refused to commit himself one way or the other.

And then, in 1896, Nasiru'd Din was assassinated. A wave of agitation for governmental reform swept through the country and, in 1906, Nasiru'd Din's successor, Muzaffar al-Din, was forced to grant his people a constitution. The Persian reformists wanted to oust the British and the Russians once and for all. But the kingdom was still too weak to stand up to them, and in 1907, it fell still further into their clutches. In a high-handed agreement called the Anglo-

M. Chevalier 1874

Russian Convention, the two powers settled their rivalry by dividing
up the country. There was a Russian zone in the north, containing
most of Persia's main cities; a neutral zone in the center; and a
British zone in the south, including many of Persia's new oil fields.

Persia remained in this unhappy state of dependency until 1919,
when Britain and Russia finally agreed to "give Persia back to the
Persians." Nonetheless, the kingdom's strategic location and vast
reserves of oil continued to make it the target of imperialism by
Russia and the major Western powers until long after World War II.

In Oſtaſien

Confrontation in the Heartland

8

Nowhere did Russia and Britain play the "Great Game" of the 180c's as fiercely as they did in Central Asia and Tibet. There, knowledge was power—the power to protect and consolidate their rival empires. And, as the two nations jockeyed for position in this strategic corner of Asia, the work of their explorers took on a deadly political significance.

The Russian advance on the heartland began in 1851, when an adventurous scientist named Semenov crossed the Tien Shan mountains into Chinese Turkestan. His expedition fired the imagination of other Russian explorers, and over the next 50 years, they made a full-scale assault on the deserts and mountains south of Siberia. Some of these hardy pioneers mapped the rough Mongolian plateau and the southern reaches of the Altai mountain range. Others explored the Tien Shan and the bleak Taklamakan Desert.

The British were understandably alarmed by these maneuvers. Ostensibly, the Russians were exploring Central Asia in the pure interests of science. But the British knew only too well that earlier Russian exploration—in the region east of the Caspian—had heralded a series of conquests. Now Russian scientists were reconnoitering the region north of Tibet, and it was only too clear that the czar had his eye on the very mountain kingdom Britain needed to defend her Indian empire. This was a shattering prospect for the British. If Russia gained dominion over Tibet, there would be no stopping her—sooner or later, she would make a bid for India itself.

To a large degree, British fears were justified. For the previous 300 years, the Russian Empire had been growing at the phenomenal rate of 55 square miles a day. And if anything, Russian imperial ambitions had only grown stronger over the years. As India's British viceroy, Lord Curzon, put it, "Each morsel but whets her appetite for more, and inflames the passion for pan-Asiatic domination." Indeed, by the late 1800's, Russia had begun to regard the whole continent as her natural sphere of influence. And Tibet—strategically placed between China and India—was high on the czar's list of Asian priorities. Curzon guessed rightly when he surmised that the czar was encouraging Russian explorers to aim for Lhasa.

But access to the Tibetan capital proved just as problematical for the Russians as it was for Montgomerie's pundits. The forbidding rim of mountains along Tibet's northern plateau, combined with

Above: Nicholas I, czar of Russia. It was under his rule that major Russian expansion began, based in large part on the work of explorers charting the territory in Central Asia. Under his successor, Nicholas II, this led to the confrontation of the "Great Game."

Far left: a cartoon from a German political magazine showing an enormous Russian shoving a thin aristocratic Englishman along the bench of Central Asia, asking, "Do you mind moving?"

Left: Przhevalski was the giant of Russian exploration in Central Asia. Among other firsts, he was the first modern traveler to delineate the Astin Tagh mountains that form a barrier to northern Tibet, and the first man to make a systematic survey of the sources of the Hwang Ho River.

the Tibetans' morbid fear of foreigners, made the kingdom practically inaccessible. By 1900, only one Russian scientist had even succeeded in getting close to the sacred citadel. That man was Nikolai Przhevalski. Between 1871 and 1885, this tireless geographer made four attempts to reach Tibet, and, in the process, added more to the knowledge of Central Asia than any man before him.

With a small Cossack guard, Przhevalski began his first journey in northeastern Mongolia. From there he traveled to Peking, and then set out across the Ordos Desert, roughly following the route taken by Huc and Gabet 30 years before. Travel through this desert was never easy, especially for men making maps. "In the daytime," wrote Przhevalski, "the heat enveloped us on all sides, above from the sun, below from the burning ground. . . . To avoid the heat as much as possible, we rose before daybreak; tea-drinking and loading the camels, however, took up so much time that we never got away before four or even five o'clock in the morning. We might have lightened the fatigue considerably by night-marching, but in that case we would have had to forego the survey which formed so important a part of our labors."

At last, in October, 1872, the party reached the sparkling waters of Lake Koko Nor, just south of the Nan Shan mountains. But winter was setting in, and the pitiful state of his camels forced Przhevalski to turn back halfway across the vast Tibetan plateau. Ironically, he met precisely the same difficulties four years later, when he tried to penetrate Tibet from the direction of the Astin Tagh mountains,

Below: Przhevalski's Cossack guard, an engraving from his book about his explorations. The Cossacks were loaned to him by the czar for the expedition, as part of the discreet backing the czar gave to Przhevalski's travels.

which lie west of the Nan Shan and south of the Taklamakan Desert.

In 1879, Przhevalski made his third—and most successful—journey to Tibet. This time he breached the mountain barrier, and began marching steadily southward through the plateau. But the Chinese ambassadors in Lhasa, learning of his approach, spread a rumor that the Russian was on his way to kidnap the Dalai Lama. Outraged, the Tibetans organized a small militia and began harassing the travelers. Finally, at a village just 170 miles from Lhasa, the explorer was met by a deputation of Tibetan officials, who absolutely forbade him to go a step farther. Practically within sight of his goal, the disappointed Russian was once more forced to turn back.

In 1884, the indefatigable geographer mustered a new party of 21 men for what was to be his last expedition. Though he was yet again turned back in northern Tibet, he returned to Russia with a wealth of information about the northern reaches of the mountain kingdom.

All the time Przhevalski was trying to reach Lhasa from the north, the British were trying to reach it from the south. But so far, only the pundits had succeeded. And meanwhile, the Russians were

Above: an engraving from Przhevalski's book showing the heartbreaking end of his expedition in 1879, when a force of Tibetan guards attacked his camp and forced him to turn back when only 170 miles from his goal of Lhasa.

Above: Sir Francis Younghusband, the young British explorer who crossed Central Asia. He came of a conventional colonial background—his father and four of his uncles were in the Indian Army—and he went to India to serve as an officer in the cavalry in 1882.

Above right: Younghusband (on the left) with his two companions on the journey across the barren Gobi Desert.

making steady progress in Central Asia. Not to be outdone, the British, too, began exploring the heartland. Between 1873 and 1900, a number of expeditions traveled north from India and west from China into the Taklamakan and Gobi deserts. But none of them made as long—or as daring—a journey into the heartland as a youthful British officer named Francis Younghusband.

Younghusband was a born adventurer. In 1886, at the age of 23, he accompanied a British expedition from Peking to Manchuria, and the very next year, set off on an epic journey across Central Asia. His plan was to pioneer a new route from Peking to Kashgar, at the western end of the Tien Shan. It was an enormous undertaking for someone who had never even been in a desert before. But Younghusband was a daredevil, and actually relished the prospect of danger and hardship.

Two weeks out of Peking, Younghusband and his two companions, a cook and an interpreter, reached the edge of the Gobi Desert. Here, at a small waystation, the young explorer obtained five camels and a guide to take his party westward. But before they could set out, they had to consult the Chinese calendar to fix the correct moment for their departure. "The guide was very particular about this," wrote Younghusband later, "He said it would never do to start in a casual way on a journey like this."

Finally, on April 26, 1887, the auspicious moment arrived, and the four men plunged into the desert oven. To escape the worst of the

FORCED FAVOURS.

The Grand Lama of Thibet. "NOW THEN, WHAT'S YOUR BUSINESS?"
British Lion. "I'VE COME TO BRING YOU THE BLESSINGS OF FREE TRADE."
The Grand L. "I'M A PROTECTIONIST. DON'T WANT 'EM."
British Lion. "WELL, YOU'VE *GOT TO HAVE* 'EM!"

["The advisers of the Dalai Lama, having ignored their obligations to us under the Convention of 1890, have now ignored the British Mission;"... "an advance is to be made into the Chumbi Valley on the frontier of Thibet."—*Daily Paper.*]

Above: a cartoon from the English satirical magazine *Punch,* ridiculing the British determination to open Tibet to the glories of British trade.

heat, the party traveled mostly at night, but even then the air was as dry as a bone. The men's belongings became charged with static electricity, so that "in opening a sheepskin coat or a blanket, a loud crackling noise would be given out, accompanied by a sheet of fire."

Toward the end of June, the tiny caravan reached the eastern end of the Nomin Gobi Desert, a tongue of wasteland between the Altai and the Tien Shan mountains. Crossing this desert was to prove the worst part of their journey. In his journal, Younghusband recorded that, "Nothing we have passed hitherto can compare with it—a succession of gravel ranges without any sign of life, animal or vegetable, and not a drop of water. . . ." But at long last, they reached the shade of the Karlik Tagh mountains, and dragged themselves into the town of Hami. Younghusband and his exhausted companions rested there for a few days, then set off once more. It took them another two months to reach Kashgar, 1,000 miles southwest of Hami. But even at Kashgar, Younghusband's journey was not over. Proceeding south, he crossed the mighty Karakoram mountains— becoming the first European to ascend the lofty Mustagh Pass in Kashmir—and at long last, in the fall of 1887, rejoined his regiment in India.

Over the next 10 years, Younghusband was to make a number of other exploratory journeys, mostly in the complex of ranges northwest of India. But his real ambition—like that of so many other British officers in India—was to explore Tibet. His chance to do so finally came in 1903, when he was chosen to head a crucial diplomatic mission to Lhasa.

By 1903, British anxiety about Russian activities in Tibet had reached fever pitch. Word had begun filtering through diplomatic channels that the czar now had a secret agent in the very palace of the Dalai Lama. The name of this sinister character was Arguan Dorjiev. Born a Buriat-Mongol in southeastern Siberia, he was a Russian only by nationality, but he had been working for the czar since the late 1880's. In his youth, Dorjiev had been trained as a Buddhist monk, so he had no trouble gaining access to Lhasa. Once there, he had insinuated himself among the lamas, risen rapidly in the ranks, and won the coveted job of tutor to the young Dalai Lama.

According to a Japanese observer then in the capital, the crafty Dorjiev had "omitted no pains to win the heart of his little pupil," and early on had begun advising him to make friends with Russia. Dorjiev told the boy that the czar was a Buddhist too, and would be only too happy to defend Tibet against the evil machinations of the British. Dorjiev was so convincing that by 1902, the Dalai Lama

Right: George Nathaniel Curzon, then viceroy of India and the instigator of Younghusband's expedition into Tibet. Lord Curzon was determined to provide a frontier-in-depth for India, a safe buffer area beyond the actual border.

Below: one of the Tibetan wounded at Guru. The battle—which was the result of a minor incident—quickly turned into a massacre, as the Tibetans were mowed down by British-led forces.

was thinking of visiting St. Petersburg, and plans were afoot to link Tibet to Russia with a branch of the Trans-Siberian Railroad.

In 1903, Lord Curzon, viceroy of India, decided to counter Russian influence in Tibet with direct British pressure. He would send a mission to Lhasa and force the Dalai Lama to renounce his Russian affiliations. In Curzon's view, it was the only way to guarantee the safety of British India. Younghusband, picked to head the mission, gladly seized this opportunity to play the Great Game. "Here indeed, I felt, was the chance of my life. I was once more alive," he wrote.

The expedition that set out for Lhasa in 1903 was almost an invasionary force. Younghusband had a military "escort" of 3,000 Indian soldiers under the command of a British general named Macdonald. In addition, there were 10,000 Indian tribesmen to carry baggage, and no fewer than 20,000 animals. Included in this traveling

Below: a pencil drawing by N. Rybot of Lieutenant Hadow at Gyantse, on the mission roof. Hadow had also been at Guru, of which he wrote, "I hope I shall never have to shoot down men *walking* away again," as the Tibetans retreated.

zoo were mules, yaks, camels, buffalo, bullocks, horses, pack ponies, and even two "zebrules"—experimental animals half mule and half zebra. Sadly, many of the animals perished in the long climb from the hot forests of northern India to the icy passes of the Himalaya.

When Younghusband reached southern Tibet, he was greeted by a party of Tibetan officials who told him that any Anglo-Tibetan negotiations were out of the question. Never, never, they said, would foreigners be allowed inside their sacred city. But the British kept advancing, and by January, 1904, were on the Guru plain, 150 miles southwest of Lhasa. There they were met by an armed force of 2,000 Tibetan warriors.

There was a curious moment of indecision as the two armies faced each other; neither side seemed willing to open fire. Then the British began trying to shoulder their way through the Tibetan ranks like policemen handling an unruly crowd. This was too much for the Tibetan general; he pulled out his revolver and shot one of the Indian soldiers. At once the British attacked and, with a thundering volley of rifle shots, mowed down the Tibetan soldiers.

This crushing defeat was repeated 50 miles farther north on July 4, 1904, when Macdonald led a full-scale attack on the Tibetan *dzong* (fort) outside the town of Gyantse. Although vastly outnumbered, the British soon gained the upper hand. Younghusband

Above: a drawing in crayon by N. Rybot of the Tsechen lamasery near Gyantse, which the British took. Rybot noted on the drawing, "Captured 28 June 04 Looted 29 June 04 Burnt 5 July 04."

reports that, "Tier after tier of the fortification was crowned, and at last our men were seen placing the Union Jack on the highest pinnacle of the Dzong. The Tibetans had fled precipitously, and Gyantse was ours."

Triumphant, the British marched into Lhasa on August 2, 1904. They were the first Europeans to see the forbidden city since Huc and Gabet, over 50 years before. It was a glorious moment for Younghusband: "The goal of so many travelers' ambitions was actually in sight. . . . The sacred city, hidden so far and deep behind the Himalayan ramparts, and so jealously guarded from strangers, was full before our eyes."

Both the Dalai Lama and the treacherous Dorjiev had fled the country by the time Younghusband arrived. The Tibetan regent, left to deal with the conquerors, was bitter about Russia's failure to protect the kingdom. Where were the czar's forces when the Dalai Lama really needed them? Now the regent had no choice but to grant the sweeping demands Younghusband made on behalf of Britain.

But ironically, as Younghusband learned when he returned to India, he had gained *too much* for Britain. The almost insurmountable problem of maintaining communication links with India made it

Left: a photograph of the 13th Dalai Lama (1876-1933) when he was 24. He fled with his tutor, the Russian agent Dorjiev, as Younghusband's British forces neared the Tibetan capital.

Below: Central Asia. In this forbidding terrain of burning sands and
rocky wastes, jagged peaks and windswept plateaus, Nikolai Przhevalski,
Francis Younghusband, and Sven Hedin
carried out extensive explorations,
pioneering routes through territories
never before seen by any European.

ALTAI

98°

in Gobi
2c

Gobi   Desert   106°
                                                   1a&c
                                                        1d   114°
                                                                          1a   3f   122°   2b   40°

ami   3e   2b
                                              2c   3b   1a
         3E   2c   3e
1c   3f   3E   3e&f   1a&c   1a   3f   3e&f   1a
              3f   3e   Peking 2b
         3E   1a   Ordos   3b 1a   3f
3f   3b   Desert   3e
    3f   NAN   SHAN   1a&d   3f
1c   3f   3e
                        3b   1c   3f   32°
                   Koko   Hwang Ho   3f
1d   3b   Nor   3f   3f
    1c   1c   1a&d 3f   3f
         1a&d   1c 1c   3f   3e   3f
1c   1c   3f   Shanghai
         1a   1d   1c   3e
    1d   Hangchow
                                                                          Yangtze R.   122°

gpo   24°
                                                                              TROPIC OF CANCER

Brahmaputra

                                                                        _____ Przhevalski   1a   1871–3
                                                                                                       1b   1876–7
                                                                                                       1c   1879–80
                                                                                                       1d   1884–5
                                                                                                       1e   1888

Mandalay 2a   _____ Younghusband   2a   1886
Irrawaddy   2b   1886
              2a   2c   1887
                        Mekong   2d   1889   16°
    Salween   2e   1890–1
                                                                                                       2f   1892–5

2a   Younghusband (with Macdonald) 2g   1903–4

              2a   Mekong   _____ Hedin   3a   1890–1
                                                                       _____ Hedin   3b   1893–7
                                                                       – – – – – – Hedin   3c   1899–1902
2a   –·–·–·–·– Hedin   3d   1906–8
Rangoon   Moulmein   ·········· Other members of the 3e   1927–33
                                                                                  Sino-Swedish expedition 3E
98°   106°   _____ Hedin   3f   1933–5

                                                                       © Geographical Projects   114°

Top: a watercolor drawing by Sven Hedin of one of his mountain camps. The drawing, dated 1908, was made during his second journey to Tibet. Above: Sven Hedin sitting on a camel outside a yurt in Mongolia, on his way to Peking. Hedin managed to learn the rudiments of the Mongolian language by persuading a Mongol yak-hunter to act as his tutor, miming the words that he wanted to learn.

impossible to keep a British garrison in Tibet. Moreover, British dominion over the mountain kingdom would upset the delicate balance of power in Asia. There was only one answer: Younghusband's agreement with Tibet must be modified. In 1906, Britain made a treaty with Peking giving *China* full sovereignty over the kingdom. This arrangement somehow suited the czar as well, and in 1907, Russia and Britain signed a treaty in which they formally recognized this diplomatic solution to the "problem" of Tibet.

The Great Game in Central Asia was now officially over. But exploration in the heartland continued, and, if anything, became more ambitious and more spectacular in the early decades of the 1900's. The two leading figures in this period of exploration were Sven Hedin and Sir Aurel Stein. The two men were as different from one another as night and day, but each was to make discoveries in Central Asia that astonished the world.

Sven Hedin was a bit like Francis Younghusband. Rugged, fearless, and supremely self-confident, he had an unquenchable thirst for adventure. In 1890, as a 25-year-old member of the Swedish embassy in Persia, he made a trip eastward to Kashgar, and crossed the Tien Shan mountains. This taste of Asian travel merely whetted his appetite for more, and in 1893 he was off again, seeking "the road to wild adventure" in the Taklamakan Desert. But young Hedin was still a relatively inexperienced traveler, and he almost perished during his first few weeks in the desert.

Some 200 miles out of Kashgar, his caravan began to run short of water. Hedin was prepared to turn back, but his guides, believing that the Khotan River was not far off, persuaded him to press on. He strictly rationed their remaining water, but even so, the last of their meagre supply was soon gone. A week went by, and still they saw no sign of the river. They were lost! One by one, the expedition's animals began to die. The men themselves were so desperate for liquid that they killed a sheep and tried to drink its blood. But the fluid was so thick that none of them could swallow it. During the next few gruesome days, death struck down man after man. At last, only Hedin and his faithful servant Kasim had strength enough to continue the struggle.

The two survivors dragged themselves forward over the dunes, toiling on "for life—bare life," writes Hedin. At last, like a miracle, a dark green line showed itself on the horizon. It was the poplar wood along the banks of the Khotan River. But Kasim could go no farther. He fell down in the sand, his eyes vacant, waiting for death. Alone, Hedin staggered forward to the promise of water. But when he reached the Khotan, he found the river bed dry! Somehow, this awful discovery only made the young Swede more determined than ever not to die—especially not in the very bed of a river. Grimly, he plodded on, as if "led by an unseen, but irresistible hand." Then, suddenly, he heard a splash, and saw a wild duck fly up into the air. A few paces farther on, he found a clear pool in the deepest part of the river bed. "I drank, and drank, and drank," he wrote later. Then, having filled his boots with water, he returned to revive Kasim. Soon afterward, the two were rescued by some passing shepherds.

Hedin returned to Kashgar, organized a new party, and immediately set off again. By now, he was more familiar with the perils of the Taklamakan, but the desert still had some grim challenges in store. One of these was the *kara-buran* (black desert-storm). When a kara-buran hit the caravan, there was nothing to do but wrap up

Above: two Tibetan youths exchanging a traditional form of greeting. These illustrations and those overleaf are taken from a portfolio of many hundreds of drawings and watercolors made by Sven Hedin during his travels.

Below: a Tibetan woman wearing traditional multicolored woolen garments.

and lay low while the wind screamed around the tents and the sky grew dark with flying sand. Hedin reports that one of these storms "lasted all day, all night, and part of the next day, and when at last it had shot past . . . we felt queerly dazed, as after a long illness."

One day, halfway across the Taklamakan, Hedin spotted what appeared to be bleached bones sticking up from the sand. He bent down to examine them, and found that they were the remains of timber posts. He and his men started digging and, to their great amazement, discovered the relics of a 2,000-year-old city. Hedin carefully marked the site before proceeding eastward. In the course of his long march to the Gobi, he found two other ancient cities buried in the sand—discoveries that brought him world fame on his return to Europe in 1897.

But Hedin was essentially an explorer, not an archaeologist, and he was content to leave the scientific examination of his cities to other men. He now wanted to explore Tibet, and on his third expedition, in 1899, made a heroic attempt to reach Lhasa from Kashgar. But a mere 100 miles from the forbidden city, he was turned back, as Przhevalski had been, by a party of Tibetan officials. "It is quite beyond any need," they declared quaintly, "for Europeans to enter the Land of the Holy Books." Hedin was forced to turn west, making

Above: a lama at the door of a Tibetan mausoleum. Like Przhevalski, Hedin was forced to turn away before he reached the forbidden city of Lhasa, and had to go to India by way of Leh.

Left: a Tibetan soldier, armed with an old-fashioned type of musket. It was this sort of weapon that the Tibetans tried to use to repulse the British.

Right: a beggar pleading for alms.

his way over the mountains to India via the Kashmiri city of Leh.

It was from Leh that Hedin started on his fourth and greatest expedition in 1906. His object this time was to explore the valley of the Tsangpo River (sometimes also called the Upper Brahmaputra) which flows through southern Tibet. But first he had to cross the Himalaya, and winter overtook his party as they struggled over the high passes. Several of his pack horses died in the heights, and only hastily improvised felt jackets saved the lives of his faithful dogs.

But at last Hedin reached the beautiful valley of the Tsangpo and began following the river eastward, past flowering orchards and fields of barley, to the town of Shigatse—last visited by Samuel Turner of the British East India Company in 1783. Hedin was granted permission to enter the nearby lamasery of Tashilhumpo. The head lama conducted him through long musty corridors to the sacred

Above: a photograph taken by Sir Aurel Stein during his excavations in Khotan. The local workmen he employed are shown in the emerging ruins. Stein was first attracted to the desert by reading Hedin's report of ancient cities still lying beneath dry desert sands.

library, a vast hall filled with Buddhist holy books, and showed him the cavernous kitchen where tea was brewed for the building's 3,800 lamas. But the most amazing thing Hedin saw was 50 miles beyond the lamasery. This was a *dupkang,* or hermit cave. The entrance was sealed up, leaving only a small hole through which the man inside received his daily ration of food. Hedin was told that voluntary imprisonment of this kind earned a man *nirvana* (the "blessed oblivion") after death. One poor soul who had been locked up for 69 years asked to be let out just before he died, to see the sun once more. But when the old hermit emerged, he was found to be stone-blind, and died almost immediately.

After leaving Shigatse, Hedin turned west again, and made two major discoveries. The first was the source of the Tsangpo River: a blue-green glacier high in the mountains of western Tibet. The second was the source of the Indus River: a little stream gushing from a shelf of rock just north of the sacred Lake Manasarowar in southwestern Tibet. These two discoveries—made within the space of a few months—placed Hedin among the ranks of Tibet's most distinguished explorers.

While the Swedish adventurer was cutting a swathe through the

Above: Aurel Stein (1862-1943). He was a quiet and unassuming man who took great pains to record all his discoveries carefully, taking many thousands of photographs and writing numerous books about his amazing finds.

deserts and mountains of the heartland, another remarkable explorer was also at work in Central Asia. This was Sir Aurel Stein. A shy, unassuming scholar, Stein was Hedin's complete opposite in every respect except one: he, too, was fascinated by the mysteries of the Asian interior. Born in Budapest, Stein had emigrated to England as a young man, and taken up Asian studies. He was particularly interested in the early history of the continent, and was enthralled in 1897 by Hedin's report of ancient cities beneath the sands of the desert corridor. In 1900, Stein himself made a brief reconnaissance of the Taklamakan, and returned convinced that it held a wealth of archaeological treasures.

In 1906, Stein returned to the Taklamakan in charge of a large expedition. At a site just beyond Khotan, he found a collection of ancient wooden tablets still bearing their original clay seals. The seals depicted the gods Eros and Hercules—proof that once, long ago, the people of Central Asia had had tangible links with Greece and Rome. At Loulan, the first city discovered by Hedin, Stein unearthed bales of yellow silk, bronze mirrors, rings, bells, and scraps of manuscript. These relics indicated that Loulan had been a frontier town on the ancient Silk Road between China and Rome.

Where now there was desert, there had once been a bustling city, complete with a hospital, a post office, a large Buddhist temple, and numerous warehouses. Southwest of Loulan, at an ancient ruin called Miran, Stein found several giant statues of the Buddha, and a crumbling bit of manuscript that, when later deciphered, turned out to be a recipe for a medicine concocted of butter, barley, and boiled sheep's dung!

All these finds were excavated by Stein and his men under grueling desert conditions—the same intensely dry heat, in fact, that had preserved these buried cities for almost 2,000 years. Stein's work proved conclusively that hundreds of years ago, Central Asia had been a fertile plain, watered by numerous rivers and inhabited by a thriving population. One of the ruins Stein explored was 100 miles from any drinkable water, an indication of how dramatically the climate and geography of the region had changed since ancient times.

Slowly, Stein worked his way from one site to another. Then, one day, as he was approaching the western end of the Gobi Desert, he spied a solid mass of brickwork, 23 feet high. Was it an ancient watchtower? After clearing away the sand at the base of the tower, the archaeologist found the remains of a regular wall made of reed bundles set in a mixture of clay and gravel. An old inscription on a piece of wood inside one of the bundles proved that the wall was an early portion of the Great Wall of China.

But Stein's greatest discovery still lay ahead. Following the reed wall, he came to a towering cliff-face just outside the Chinese outpost of Tunhwang. The cliff was honeycombed with small caves, linked together by crumbling flights of steps. All these so-called "Caves of the Thousand Buddhas" had once been shrines, and many were lavishly decorated with wall paintings. In Tunhwang, Stein learned that a hoard of manuscripts had recently been found in one of the caves. With some difficulty, he persuaded the keeper of the shrines to show him a few of these *chings*, or sacred texts. The man brought out a few specimens. All were of great antiquity, and in remarkably good condition. There were manuscripts, scroll paintings on fine Chinese silk, and packets of long, brilliantly colored temple banners.

What Stein held in his hands were the remnants of a long-forgotten library, a priceless record of China's past greatness. Excitedly, the scholar asked if he might remove some of the manuscripts for closer inspection. The priest was dubious, but Stein overcame his objections with a generous donation of silver "for the upkeep of the shrines." A bargain was struck, and Stein came away with 29 cases containing 9,000 manuscripts and countless works of art. Much of this treasure trove is now housed in London's British Museum.

Stein's return from Central Asia in 1908 coincided with Hedin's return from Tibet. The paths of the two men were to cross many times during the next 25 years, as both men continued their ex-

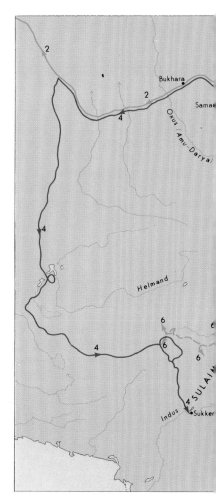

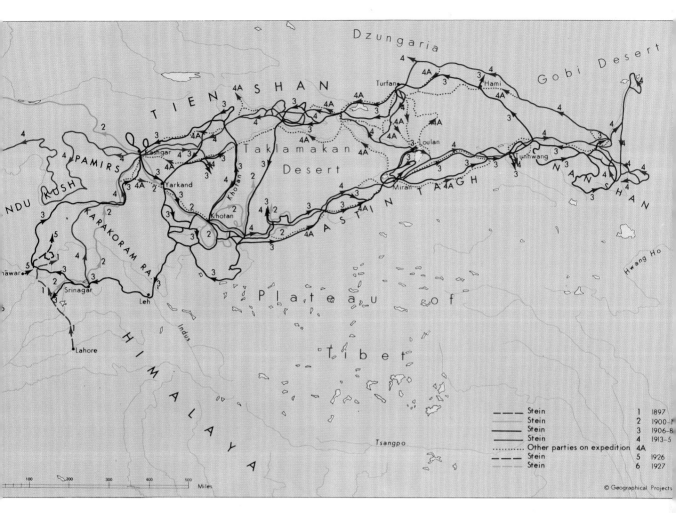

Above: the expeditions of Sir Aurel Stein, 1897-1915. In the course of his four major journeys, this remarkable scientist ranged far and wide through the Asian heartland, criss-crossing the whole region between the western borders of Afghanistan and the Nan Shan mountains of China.

Left: a Chinese wooden votive tablet that Stein found at Khotan. Like many of his archaeological finds, it is now kept in the British Museum in London.

plorations in the heartland. But Stein and Hedin were to be among the very last Europeans in Central Asia. After the Chinese Communists came to power in 1949, access to the heartland was again denied to Europeans.

In a curious way, history had repeated itself. It was like a flashback to the Middle Ages—only instead of the hard-riding Mongols, there were efficient Chinese border patrols to seal off the interior. And as China strengthened its grip on Central Asia, only Russia, secure in its Siberian holdings, could rival it for territorial supremacy in Asia. Even remote Tibet was sucked into China's maw in the 1950's, when a Chinese army swept down on the kingdom and wrested away its last shreds of independence. Only the countries along Asia's southern perimeter remained free and open to Western travelers.

But there are signs now that the long Red curtain may be lifted. And when it is, explorers will once more find themselves drawn to the hidden corners of the Asian wilderness. For, despite all the stunning achievements of the Cossacks and merchants, missionaries and scientists, few regions of the world still remain as mysterious and challenging as the heartland of Asia.

Acknowledgments

Abbey Museum, Barnet/Michael Holford Library 88; Aldus Archives 27(L), 52, 67, 72, 79(B), 102, 103(L), 104, 109(L), 125, 130, 142(T)(B), 143, 145(L)(R), 149; Archivium Romanum Societatis Jesu, Roma/Photo Mauro Pucciarelli, Rome 78, 84, 87; Department of Eastern Art, Ashmolean Museum, Oxford 77, 80(T), 90; Simplicissimus/BPC Library 140; Reproduced by permission of the Trustees of the British Museum 8(T), 30, 34(B), 45, 57, 58, 60, 76(B), 123, 124(B), 127(B), 158; British Museum/Photo R.B. Fleming © Aldus Books 8(B), 22, 29(T), 44(B), 50(T), 51(T), 56, 61(T), 64, 66, 68(L)(R), 95, 97; Count Brobinskoy/Michael Holford Library 46; Chester Beatty Library, Dublin/Photo Rex Roberts 94; Chiesa del Jesu, Roma/Photo Mauro Pucciarelli 93(B); The Cleveland Museum of Art, Purchase, John L. Severance Fund 6; The Cleveland Museum of Art, Purchase, J.H. Wade Fund 7; The Cleveland Museum of Art/Photo André Held 59; Photo Jeremy Whitaker © Aldus Books, courtesy Reverend J.O.E. Coffee, Spaxton Church, Bridgwater, Somerset 24; Det Nationalhistoriske Museum, Frederiskborg, Denmark 27(R); Photo by David Douglas Duncan 12(T), 12-13; From *Tresors de l'Art Russe*, Editions Cercle d'Art, Paris 14(T), 14-15, 21; Photo Werner Forman 65, 91; Geographical Projects Limited, London 33, 49(B), 82-83, 117, 137, 150-51, 159; Photo Bertram Unné © Aldus Books, reproduced by kind permission of the Earl of Harewood 10(L); Sven Hedin Foundation, Stockholm 98, 152(T), 153(T)(B), 154, 155(T)(B); Her Britannic Majesty's Treasury and the National Trust, Petworth House (Egremont Collection)/Photo John Webb © Aldus Books 62(L), 62-3; Reproduced by Gracious Permission of Her Majesty Queen Elizabeth II 40, 139; Fred Mayer/The John Hillelson Agency 160; Historisches Museum der Stadt Wien/Photo Erwin Meyer 42-3, 50-1(B); India Office Library and Records, London 122; India Office Library and Records, London/Photo R.B. Fleming © Aldus Books 73(B), 75, 80(B), 103(R), 107, 108, 111, 113, 114, 147(R), 148; Photo Romi Khosla 74, 76(T), 85, 105, 110; Photo © Aldus Books reproduced by courtesy of The Governors of King Edward's School, Witley, Surrey 18; Kunsthistorisches Museum, Wien/Photo Erwin Meyer 10-11; Photo A.C. Cooper © Aldus Books from the Private Collection of Professor W. Bruce Lincoln, Northern Illinois University, DeKalb 141; London Borough of Lewisham Library Service/Photo Mike Busselle © Aldus Books 47; By permission of J.H.S. Lucas-Scudamore 124(T); Musée d'Historie de Berne, Propriété de la fondation Gottfried Keller 48-9(T); Musée Guimet/Michael Holford Library 70; Musée Historique des Tissus de Lyon/Photo Denise Bourbonnais © Aldus Books 54; Museo Nacional de Arte Antigua, Lisbon/Photo Michael Holford © Aldus Books 73(T); National Army Museum, London 146; National Maritime Museum, Greenwich/Michael Holford Library 118(B); National Museum, Copenhagen 33(T); National Portrait Gallery, London 144, 147(L), 157; Captain John Noel 71, 81, 89; Novosti 48(L); In the possession of Boies Penrose 69; The Pierpont Morgan Library, New York 61(L); Roland Michaud from Rapho Guillumette 129, 131; Royal Asiatic Society/Photo John Webb © Aldus Books 112, 120-21(T); By the late Lt. Colonel F.M. Bailey C.I.E., courtesy of The Royal Central Asian Society 119; Reproduced by permission of the Royal Geographical Society 118(T), 134, 152(B), 156; Photo R.B. Fleming © Aldus Books reproduced by permission of the Royal Geographical Society 109(R); Emil Schulthess 79(T); From the collection of Rodney Searight 128, 133, 135; Staatsarchiv, Hamburg 19; John Massey Stewart 34(T), 36(L), 38, 44(T), 96, 101(B); Photo © Aldus Books reproduced by kind permission of Rt. Hon. The Earl of Suffolk & Berkshire 26; Textile Museum Collection of Washington, D.C./Photo Allan C. Marceron 92-3(T); Reproduced by permission of the Trustees of the Victoria & Albert Museum, London 20; Victoria & Albert Museum, London/Michael Holford Library 106; Victoria & Albert Museum, London/Photo John Webb © Aldus Books 25, 29(B), 36(R), 86, 121(B), 126, 127(T); Photo John Wright © Aldus Books, courtesy The Trustees of the Warwick Castle Resettlement 23; Photo John Webb © Aldus Books 37; Photo John Webb © Aldus Books, courtesy Taya Zinkin 35, 39(L)(R), 41, 53, 99, 100-01(T).

Left: Tibetan refugees from the Chinese now living in Switzerland, Many of the refugees are being trained for industrial work so that if it does become possible for them to return to Tibet, they will be more self-reliant.

PART TWO

The Challenge of Africa

Below: Livingstone sails up the Shire River in the *Ma-Robert*. The artist who painted this picture, Thomas Baines, used the fiercely trumpeting elephant as an illustration of the strange sights and dangers that awaited all the explorers of Africa.

The Challenge of Africa

BY ELSPETH HUXLEY

Right: a proud Masai warrior. The Masai are still a basically nomadic people who roam the grassy plains of East Africa.

Foreword

African exploration, unlike the mapping of the heartland of Asia, had a certain logical progression. The intrepid men who first ventured into the high mountains and vast deserts of Asia traveled there in pursuit of their own goals, which seldom included exploration. In Africa, however, the acquisition of knowledge was a conscious aim. Almost all the exploration was done during the 1700's and 1800's, with each man consciously building on the body of knowledge painfully acquired by his predecessors. The explorers of Africa had an enormous advantage: by this time books were a conspicuous part of European civilization, and all the explorers wrote books. As each installment of the story of the opening of Africa was completed, the weary explorer returned home and rushed into print. Almost invariably he had an avid audience. The fascinating stories, the engravings from drawings often executed in the most hazardous situations, all were snatched up by the stay-at-homes, thrilled by the vicarious contact with the savage interior. Some of the young men who read the tales of far-off adventure resolved to join in the quest to fit the great puzzle together, to define the courses of rivers, to map the wilds. A few of them eventually came to Africa, disappearing for years, and returning with their own reports that would add to the burgeoning literature about Africa. In turn, other young men would be inspired by them.

Africa: it was a magical name, promising an infinity of possibilities. It beckoned men like Livingstone, determined to bring the heathen within the fold of Christianity; Harris, who was equally determined to expand the barbarity of unrestricted slaughter of the wild animals; and Burton, who was more at home in the wilds than in the civilization that produced him. This is the story of their struggles.

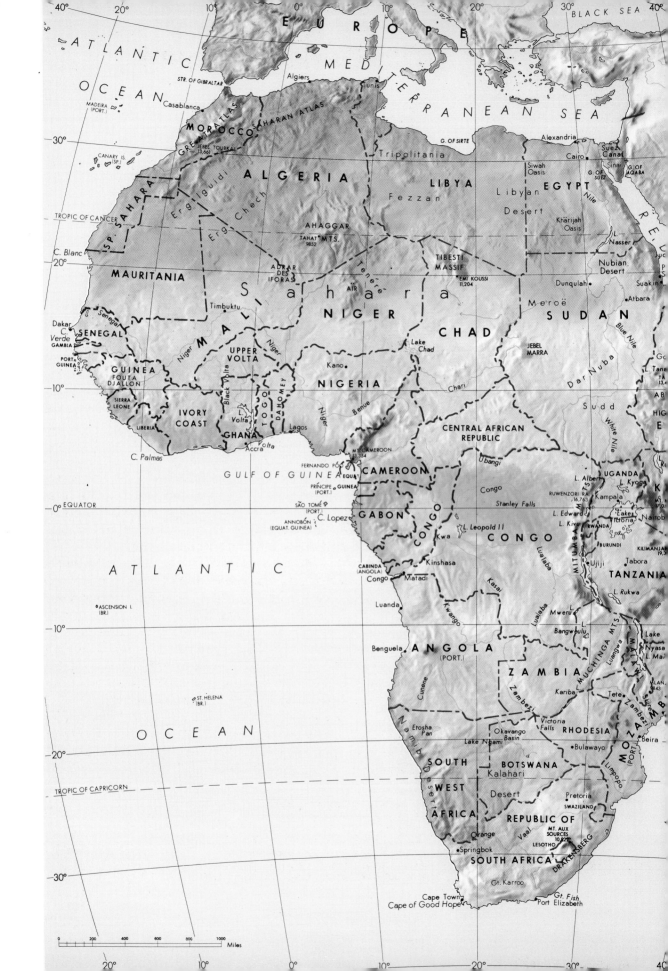

The Dark Continent

1

In 1434 Henry the Navigator, prince of Portugal, sent his ships sailing southward past Cape Bojador on the coast of Africa. For the first time the barrier of fear and superstition surrounding the Dark Continent and the seas guarding its shores had been broken. Now, in time, the exploration of Africa would become possible.

By 1800, however, more than 350 years later, the great African land mass had still not surrendered all its secrets to the mapmakers and geographers of the Western world. The Portuguese and those who followed had mapped the African coastline, all 22,921 miles of it. And here and there on the Atlantic and Indian Ocean shores the trading nations of Europe had scattered a handful of forts, trading posts, slaving stations and even a colony or two. The Portuguese, from their settlements in Mozambique on the southeast coast, had explored 300 miles or so up the Zambezi River looking for gold. And the Dutch settlers from Cape Colony on Africa's southern tip had pushed east to the Fish River, northeast to the border of present-day Botswana and northwest to the mouth of the Orange River on the South Atlantic. But after three-and-a-half centuries of exploration the map of tropical Africa from Kuruman in South Africa to Timbuktu in what is today Mali, was virtually a blank.

In the early centuries of African exploration most of what Europeans knew—or thought they knew—about the interior was based on legend, rumor, and speculation. Many believed that unknown Africa was savage and sinister, populated by dwarfs and cannibals. Scholars and savants wrote knowingly of strange creatures such as unicorns, werewolves, and "men whose heads did grow beneath their shoulders." But others held a contrary view. They believed that Africa was the home of the *Noble Savage,* the innocent, simple man living in golden joy. But no matter what position they took on Africans, there were few who doubted that gold and other riches were concealed in the mighty continent. The Bible told them that ivory, apes, and peacocks had been shipped from there to the Queen of Sheba. What was the truth? No one knew.

Left: Africa, showing the continent's most important geographical features. Many explorers of Africa named their discoveries for people or places in their homelands. Some have since been given African names, but many European names still appear on the map of Africa.

Below: Masai tribesmen at a water tank. It is Masai belief that when the supreme gods divided the land of Africa between their children, they decreed that the Masai should be the keepers of cattle and goats in the open plains of East Africa.

Left: A Masai elder. Traditionally Masai society was divided into age groups. Children tended cattle; boys from 14 to 20 played games and hunted; young men were the warriors; old men remained at home instructing their juniors who paid them great respect.

There was more than a grain of truth in most of these tales. The Africans may not have been innocent, but some of them were undoubtedly noble in appearance, particularly the proud Masai and the stately Tusi peoples. And there were dwarfs and cannibals. To be sure, unicorns turned out to be rhinoceroses, but at least their horns were located in the right spot. There was, and still is, a good business in powdered rhinoceros—or unicorn—horn. It is believed to restore health and vitality to aging men.

Of riches—gold and diamonds—there is no doubt. Today, Africa produces 70 per cent of the world's gold, 82 per cent of its diamonds and much of its natural, or live, ivory. But up till the late 1800's the greatest wealth of Africa lay in none of these. The greatest fortunes in African trade were made by dealing in human beings. Between about 1450 and 1880, when the trade ended officially, as many as 10 million black Africans were captured and sold into bondage.

Before the late 1700's, the Europeans simply waited for the treasures and the endless stream of slaves to work their way to the coasts, for the interior of Africa did not welcome intruders. Of those who dared to push inland from the European-controlled outposts, few returned. Those who did come back had no great opinion of the place. It was a white man's grave. And because of the slave raiding, tribal warfare, its seasons of burning drought and starvation, and rampant diseases, life in Africa was nearly as hard for its black inhabitants.

When the Europeans who had clung so long to Africa's shores began to succumb to the irresistible urge to find out what lay hidden within the unknown continent there were enormous difficulties to overcome. One was the sheer size of the area. Unexplored Africa was larger than all of Europe. Except for slave routes which penetrated only a few hundred miles inland and game trails that led nowhere useful, there were no roads, and of course no detailed maps.

Guides were available but they were notoriously unreliable. Many explorers were completely on their own with only the stars to guide them. Furthermore, the terrain was rugged. They had to cross deserts almost totally without water, and swamps and tropical rain forest with too much. Rivers are often the explorers' best routes, but the African rivers flowing eastward into the Indian Ocean could not be navigated for more than a few hundred miles—a relatively short distance into the 2,400 mile width of the continent at the equator.

Left: the Olduvai Gorge in northern Tanzania is the source of important information on an early form of man, who lived about 1½ million years ago. The gorge lies in the Serengeti Plain.

Apart from the size and type of country to be explored, there were other hazards. Many African peoples were ferocious warriors. Some had been drilled by warrior kings into powerful military forces constantly at readiness to repel intruders. The Africans were often merciless, and some ate the flesh of their fallen enemies, either to show contempt or because they believed they would gain their strength. War between the white intruders and the black defenders of the land was terrible and bloody. But not all Africans fought the white intruders. Many of the coastal tribes cooperated and some enlisted the whites in wars against their enemies.

The greatest obstacle of all to exploration was disease, the most widespread being malaria. The explorers also suffered from yellow fever, dysentery, typhus, tropical ulcers, and bubonic plague. When Europeans began to move inland, medical science had not yet discovered the causes of the deadly malaria and blackwater fevers. Some decades were yet to pass before scientists and physicians learned to prevent these and the others. The diseases of tropical Africa were as hard on animals as on men. Pack animals seldom survived for long the fatal infections carried by ticks and tsetse flies. This meant that the explorers' baggage usually had to be carried on the heads of human porters who were also vulnerable to accident and disease.

Besides food and scientific supplies, the porters' loads included quantities of beads, cloth, and copper wire for bartering with the tribes in the country they passed through. When food ran out, explorers and their porters alike had to live off the country. In places where crops had failed or in areas where there was no game, they starved.

Once they left the coast explorers simply vanished, at least as far as the outside world was concerned. They might reappear in two, three, six, or sometimes seven years. Some did not return at all. That so many did, despite all the hazards and danger, was a measure of their determination and courage—their sheer grit.

Below: Bushmen in the Kalahari Desert. There are probably about 50,000 of these people living in the deserts of southern and southwestern Africa. The basic social unit is still the small hunting band, made up of only two or three families.

The explorers came from many nations, professions, and social classes. There were noblemen and commoners, rich men and poor. Some were gentle scholars and others were blood-lusting big game hunters—one missionary explorer called these "itinerant butchers." Devout Christian missionaries went out as did adventure-seeking army officers. Each explorer was an individualist, yet one characteristic united them all—an unquenchable curiosity, a determination, whatever the danger, to find out who and what was there.

As it turned out, the "who was there" was as unexpected as the "what." The explorers found and duly mapped rivers, lakes, mountains, savannas, and forests. They also found people of a bewildering range of sizes and colors living in almost as infinite a variety of ways. The ancestors of the Africans had been there a long time, longer perhaps than the Europeans in Europe, the Indians in the Americas, or the Chinese in China.

Mankind it now seems may have had its beginnings in Africa. If so, our ancestors migrated out of Africa to the rest of the world, and —tens or hundreds of thousands of years ago—some wandered back again. The theory of man's African origins is based on the discovery in Kenya of the fossil remains of what may prove to be our most remote ancestor, dating to 14 million or more years ago. According to the theory, there gradually evolved in the same region some one-and-three-quarter million years ago manlike creatures who walked upright and may have used crude stone tools. If, as many anthropologists claim, the ability to fashion tools and use them is the criterion that separates man from the apes, this scavenger turned hunter

was a true man. Possibly he was a direct ancestor of the animals we now call the human species.

Just how these fossil "near-men" of Africa are related—if they are —to the Africans of historic times remains a mystery. But man's long residence in Africa has been proved conclusively by the discovery in Kenya and Ethiopia of the fossil bones of *Homo sapiens,* the species to which all men belong. These bones date back perhaps as far as 100,000 years.

As man in Africa embarked on the long, slow business of coming to terms with his environment, the original African stock must have divided into several groups. To these groups were added by intermarriage other stocks who migrated into Africa from Asia. From these mixtures that divided and intermarried again and again rose the peoples—the races—who were occupying the lands of Africa when the Europeans forced themselves on the ancient continent.

Race, however, is hard to define. And any definition—always a matter for dispute—is constantly blurred by intermarriage. The Europeans who arrived in tropical Africa after 1500 or so were not concerned with these problems. They quickly learned that Africa was a black man's country. *Afrique noir,* black Africa, the French called it. Four, possibly five, main groups or stocks of Negroid Africans have been defined. Among the most ancient of these are the Bushmen, although some anthropologists do not consider them to be Negroid. Standing less than five feet tall, these yellowish-brown people are hunters. They wander in small family groups and obtain their food by hunting and digging for insects, reptiles, and roots. By the time the Europeans encountered them in the 1600's, the Bushmen had been pushed south by more aggressive Africans to the deserts where they still live, tenaciously clinging to their ancient ways. The "gentle people," as they were called by one anthropologist who lived with them, are a dying race. Only 50,000 or so still survive.

The Bushmen speak a "click" language, making sounds that strike strangely on European ears by sucking in air as they speak. This trait they share with another yellowish-skinned people called Hottentots. Because the cattle-herding Hottentots came often to the shores to fish and salvage what edible meat they could from the carcasses of stranded seals and whales, the Dutch settlers on the Cape of Good Hope called them *strandloopers,* or beachcombers. When the Dutch met the Hottentots in the region of the Cape, the Hottentots were also being pushed south and west.

The peoples responsible for the migration of the click language speakers were the larger, darker "true" Negroes. The oldest skeletons that can be identified as Negro have been found in the Sudan and the equatorial forests on the southern fringe of the Sahara, and date back to around 4500 B.C. Fishhooks and harpoon heads found in the ancient graves suggest the Negroes may originally have been fishermen. They were, however, the first Africans to take to the settled life of cultivators.

The Sudan and central Africa are also the home regions of yet

Above: an old Berber. Anthropologists disagree about the use of the term Hamitic, but in general it is taken to indicate a group related to the Caucasoid stocks that entered Africa from Asia in ancient times. The Berbers and most Ethiopians are Hamites.

another Negroid people, the tall, slender Nilotes. In contrast to the Nilotes, who are often as much as 7 feet tall, the Pygmies of the Congo forests are the smallest of all Negro peoples. Smaller even than Bushmen, few Pygmies grow taller than 4 feet 10 inches, and they are normally between 4 feet 5 inches and 4 feet 8 inches tall.

Not all the Africans were of Negro stock. The brown-skinned Hamites are related to the Caucasoid (white) stocks. They came to Africa in widely-spaced migrations, probably from southwest Asia, to settle in the northern and eastern regions of Africa. The ancient Egyptians were Hamites as are the Ethiopians and Galla of Somalia.

Around the dawn of the Christian era, the Bantu-speaking Negro peoples in what is now eastern Nigeria began to multiply and move into central Africa. After more than 1,000 years, they had spread south, occupying almost all of Africa's great southern bulge. Bantu speakers are the predominant peoples of eastern and southern Africa. They are not a true race but a group of many millions of people divided into hundreds—perhaps thousands—of tribes linked by sharing dialects of a common ancestral language, Aba'ntu.

Already, long before the birth of Christ, the unknown regions of Africa called to adventurous spirits. The first explorer of tropical Africa we know by name was Herkhuf, governor of Egypt's southern province under Mernere who ruled about 2275 B.C. Herkhuf made at least four expeditions to a country he called Yam, probably in the southern Sudan. On his last recorded visit, he set off with a pack train of 300 donkeys loaded with trade goods, water, and food. He returned with his donkeys laden with ivory, ebony, frankincense, and skins. He also brought back a Pygmy.

Herkhuf sent reports of his profitable expedition down the Nile by

Far right: a Namaqua woman collecting firewood. Racially Hottentots have become mixed in the last two centuries, and the Namaquas of South West Africa are one of the purest strains left.

Right: Mbulu woman, tattooed with her tribal markings. She is a Negro, one of the major groupings of the human race. Negroes form the largest part of the population of Africa, and the group includes several distinct races.

boat to the Egyptian capital at Memphis. News of the "dwarf" greatly excited Mernere who sent back instructions that the "living, prosperous, and healthy" Pygmy should be brought down river to the court without delay under maximum security conditions. Herkhuf was ordered to "appoint excellent people who shall be beside the dwarf on each side of the vessel . . . take care lest he fall into the water. When he sleeps at night appoint excellent people who shall sleep beside him in the tent . . . inspect ten times a night. My majesty desires to see this dwarf more than the gifts of Sima and Punt."

Nearly 300 years after Herkhuf's last expedition, another Egyptian, called Hennu, led a group of his fellow-countrymen on a voyage to the land of Punt. Punt lay somewhere on the Red Sea coast of Somaliland and to get there the travelers had to trek across the desert to the northern end of the Red Sea. Here they built boats and set sail for Punt. On their safe return, Hennu had the story of his journey carved on a stone and this stone still exists.

During the next 1,500 years, other Egyptian explorers followed Herkhuf and Hennu south. Gradually the influence of the great Egyptian civilization began to spread southward too. It was from Egypt that the use of iron first penetrated into what is now the Sudan, probably by about 600 B.C. By 300 B.C. iron ore had been discovered in the region of Meroe, near present-day Khartoum, capital of the kingdom of Kush. The Kushites learned to smelt iron and work it,

Above: the Nile River. The fertile silt deposited on the plains of the Nile Valley by the flooding of the river has enabled the Egyptians to grow fine crops.

and the contours of the enormous slag-heaps produced by their operations can still be traced under the sand.

From Meroe the use of iron spread gradually throughout the middle belt of Africa and then southeast toward the Cape of Good Hope. Its spread coincided with the migration of the Bantu peoples, who worked their way southward by degrees from sub-Saharan regions. The Bantu tribes were approaching the southern tip of Africa, pushing the Hottentots and Bushmen before them, when the Dutch took possession of the Cape of Good Hope in 1652. In the next hundred years the Dutch going north and the Bantu coming south were to meet on the Great Fish River in South Africa. There in 1799 the first skirmishes took place in the Bantu wars, which lasted for nearly 100 years, and finally subdued the warlike Bantu peoples.

By this time, the peoples of tropical Africa had split into a large number of tribes. A tribe is not so much a racial unit as a social one, usually occupying a territory with recognized boundaries. It forms a closely knit, exclusive community bound by rules that are broken only on pain of death or banishment. The tribesmen share a tradition

Below: the great cemetery of Meroe, standing a mile outside the city, where the nobles were buried. Within the city itself are the remains of the enclosure for royal palaces, dating from about 590 B.C. Later Meroe had close ties with Egypt, and Egyptian-style temples were built about A.D. 100.

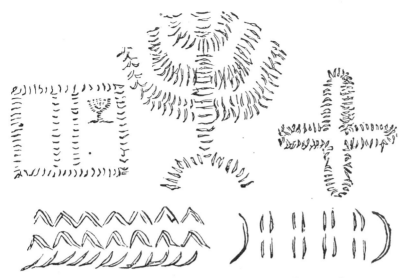

Left: tattooes of the Matambwe tribe, drawn by David Livingstone. The son took the tattoo of his father, so that it was possible to tell at a glance not only to which tribe a man belonged, but to which family within that tribe.

of descent from a common ancestor, a folklore, and a set of customs and behavior patterns that have the force of law. Tribe-members acknowledge a common system of government and unite for defense or aggression.

There is often some hostility between different tribes, and although tribes linked by language and origin sometimes join forces in confederacies, the hostility between them can be deep and hard to overcome. Even in modern times when a number of unrelated tribes find themselves politically bound together in a single nation, hostilities and quarrels may break out into intertribal wars.

The belongings and dwelling places of most tropical African tribes in olden times were simple. The people dressed in skins, bark cloth, or occasionally in handwoven cotton. They dwelt, as a rule, in windowless huts of mud and wattles, which they shared with goats and fowl. Africans had few of the things Europeans thought essential—they sat on three-legged stools and ate with their fingers. They dressed their hair with grease and earth and bedecked themselves with beads and coils of copper wire as anklets or bracelets. Womenfolk did the work—they cared for the crops and carried loads on their heads or backs. Men and boys herded the cattle and hunted and fought with assagais (iron-tipped wooden spears) and poisoned arrows, and dug pits to trap their prey. Their primitive way of life had changed little in hundreds of years—they had not discovered gunpowder, nor did they know the arts of reading, mathematics, astronomy, or the uses of the wheel or the plow.

The cultural gap between Africans and Europeans was wide, but it was also misleading. The absence in Africa of a complex technology on European lines, partly due to a relative lack of raw materials, did not imply failure in other fields. The Africans were skilled in the practice of the arts, the uses of leisure, personal relationships, and the rule of law. Crime was controlled by fines or instant execution. There was no need for policemen and jails. The tribe provided a complete cradle-to-grave system of social security. Orphans, widows, and the old were taken care of, and no one went hungry except when all did,

Above: a stool from Uganda, light, strong, and easy to carry around. John Speke was told of the Watiti people, who "have small stools fixed on behind, always ready for sitting."

in times of famine. Africans had learned, if not to master, at least not to be mastered by an environment that was sometimes harsh, and always full of danger.

The Europeans came from Christian countries. In their eyes the tribesmen of tropical Africa were pagans whose enlightenment by means of the Gospels was expected to follow the "opening up" of the continent. The tribesmen had their own religions—not one but many, having their base in a belief in ancestral spirits who had continually to be appeased. They worshiped a number of gods instead of only one. In European opinion all these were false. Sometimes the African creeds involved dark practices such as human sacrifice which Christians strove to eradicate, and thus drastically to change African lives.

So the explorers and those who followed them were—not always

intentionally—agents of change. Many wanted to alter African society, or to open the way for others to do so, and to alter it so as to conform to European beliefs and ways. Missionaries wanted to convert the heathen. Soldiers wanted to establish their kind of law and order. Humanitarians wanted to abolish slavery. Geographers wanted to make maps. Adventurers looked for fame and fortune. Nearly all shared a belief in the superiority of the "civilized" societies from which they came, over the "primitive" societies they found in the "heart of darkness," the mysterious African continent. The explorers opened the way for a flood of Western ideas, practices, skills, and beliefs that, for good or ill, have, in a remarkably short space of time, irrevocably changed African society.

Above: an engraving of the 1700's, of Hottentots worshiping the moon. They would shout prayers to the moon, as they danced and clapped their hands. The celebration would go on all night.

First Reports
2

The ancient Greeks were the first people of mainland Europe to bring back reports from Africa. Around 430 B.C., the historian Herodotus went up the Nile as far as Elephantine, near present-day Aswan. In his reports he tells of the kingdom of Kush 1,000 miles up the Nile which he heard about but never reached. About four centuries later, an unknown Greek seaman wrote the *Periplus of the Erythrean Sea,* a mariner's guide to the Red Sea ports and the East African coast as far south as a harbor he called Rhapta. Possibly the unidentified Rhapta was near a town in present-day Tanzania that the Arabs were to call Kilwa, and we know as Kilwa Kivinje.

Even then, 2,000 years ago, Rhapta and the other East African coastal towns were in regular touch with Arabia. "The Arab kings," wrote the author of the *Periplus*, "sent thither many large ships, with Arab captains and agents. These are familiar with the inhabitants, and both dwell and intermarry with them; they know all their villages and speak their languages." The Arabs and other Near Eastern peoples—particularly the Persians and Turks—were to play a leading role in the history of East Africa right down to the present day. The marriages between the Arabs and Negroes, who were mainly Bantus, were the origin of the brown-skinned Swahili people who still occupy the East African coast. Their language—Swahili—became the most widely spoken in eastern Africa and served as a trade language among people whose own languages were mutually unintelligible. Together with English, Swahili is today the official language of Tanzania.

After the *Periplus of the Erythrean Sea* the next record of East Africa tells of the voyage of an Arab traveler, Abdul Hassan ibn Ali al-Mas'udi. In about A.D. 916 al-Mas'udi sailed from Oman in Arabia down the Indian Ocean or, as he called it, the Sea of Zinj, probably as far as the port of Kilwa. The term *Zinj,* the Arabic word for East Africa, originally referred to black people in general, and in particular the Negroes who live on the East African coast.

"The Sea of Zinj," wrote al-Mas'udi, "reaches down to the coun-

Left: Elephantine (elephant town) was the Greek name for the now ruined Egyptian city of Yeb. The most southerly city of the Old Kingdom (2700–2200 B.C.), it was probably so named for the thriving trade in ivory that was centered there.

try of Sofala [near Beira in Mozambique], and of the Wak-Wak which produce gold in abundance and other marvels; its climate is warm and its soil fertile." He went on to note that the people's staple food was the banana, but they also ate a plant "which they take from the ground like a truffle," as well as meat, honey, and coconuts.

More than 400 years later another Arab traveler, Ibn-Batuta, sailed down the coast and wrote of his experience in *Travels in Africa and Asia 1325–1354*. By the time of Ibn-Batuta's visit in 1331, Kilwa had been under Arab control for more than 300 years and had become one of the richest and most important of all the Arab ports on the Zinj coast. It even had its own currency and mint. In Ibn-Batuta's opinion Kilwa was "one of the most beautiful and well-constructed towns in the world. The whole of it is elegantly built." Like most traveler-writers, he commented on the weather ". . . there is very much rain." And then as a devout Moslem he noted, "the people are engaged in holy war, for their country lies beside that of the pagan Zinj. The chief qualities are devotion and piety." The Arabs and most of the coastal Swahili were Moslems, and the war was a *jihad,* a holy war of Islam against the infidel.

Kilwa, located so that ships to and from the gold fields near Sofala had to stop there, became the commercial capital of the southwestern Indian Ocean. It carried on regular trade with India and Arabia and was visited by ships from China and from Indonesia.

By the 1400's there were 37 Arab-dominated Moslem towns strung along the East African coast between Kilwa in the south and Mogadiscio in the north. The latter, still a predominantly Moslem town on the Indian Ocean coast of Somalia, was even larger than Kilwa. It, too, was visited by Ibn-Batuta, who reported that its king "walked under a canopy supported by four staves, each surmounted by a golden bird."

In 1501, about 170 years after Ibn-Batuta's visit, Duarte Barbosa, the first Portuguese traveler to see Kilwa, was equally impressed. "In this town," he reported, "was great plenty of gold, as no ships passed toward Sofala without coming here first. . . . Of the Moors [as Europeans of the time called Arabs] there are some fair and some black, they are finely clad in many rich garments of gold and silver cotton, and the women as well; also with much gold and silver on their legs and arms, and many jeweled earrings."

The Portuguese who brought news of Africa's east coast to Europe were navigators searching for a sea route to the Indies. In 1487, Bartolomeu Dias sailed from Lisbon with three small ships on such a voyage of exploration. He rounded the Cape of Good Hope in 1488 before returning to Lisbon to report that he had found a route around Africa. Nine years later another expedition set out from Lisbon under a Portuguese nobleman, Vasco da Gama. The vessels carried trade goods to barter for gold, gems, and spices with the inhabitants of the Indies. Each sail, however, was painted with a red crucifix to proclaim that Portugal's mission was also to bring the blessings of Christianity to the heathens. Their total crew comprised

Right: Sofala, one of the trading posts established by the Portuguese, from an early map of the 1600's. The strong central fort was surrounded by groups of houses, and several churches.

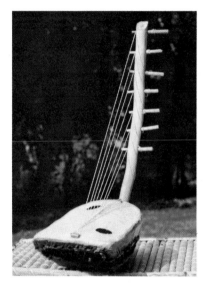

Above: a bow-harp played by the women of the court of a king of Buganda. In Luganda, a language of the country, the bow-harp is called *ennanga*.

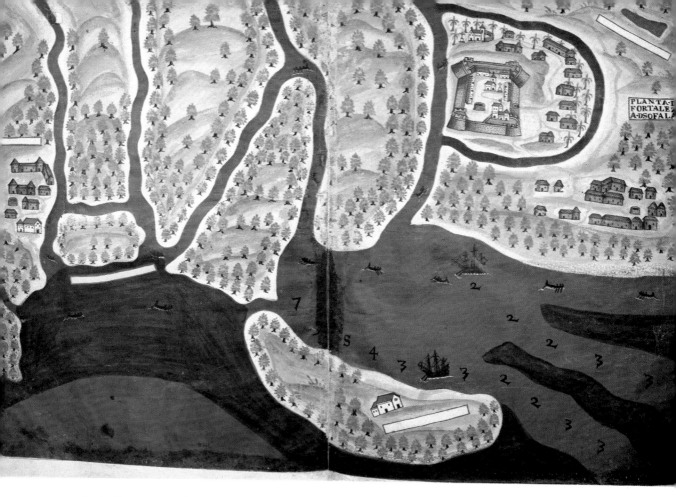

170 men, including 12 condemned convicts to be used as scouts in situations of danger. Da Gama's ships put to sea on July 8, 1497, rounded the Cape on November 22, and on Christmas Day gave the name Natal to the stretch of African coastline they were passing.

On the eastern coast of Africa, a surprise awaited them. Instead of encountering wild men and wilderness, they found prosperous Arab cities well laid out and civilized, ruled by well-dressed sultans living in elegant abundance. At Sofala, the Portuguese encountered four merchant vessels carrying "gold, silver, and cloth, and cloves, pepper and ginger, and rings of silver with many pearls, and seed-pearls and rubies, and the like." The voyagers were also astonished to learn that "farther on, where we were going, there was so much, and the stones and seed-pearls and spices were in such quantity, that it was not necessary to trade for them but simply to gather them by the basketfulls." Neither Da Gama nor his successors ever located that place. Wherever they went they had to trade. But the European clothes and foodstuffs, intended to excite the wonder of savage peoples, created no interest at all among the wealthy Arab and Swahili sheiks of these civilized cities on the coast of Zinj.

The people of these East African towns were generally hostile to Da Gama but the Sultan of Malindi, on the coast of Kenya north of Mombasa, did prove friendly and provided Da Gama with an

Indian Ocean pilot. He took the Portuguese to the port of Calicut in India in less than four weeks. After a three-month stay in Calicut the way for the spice trade was open. The Portuguese loaded up with spices and sailed for home, sighting the East African coast of Mogadiscio early in January, 1499. At Malindi, they erected a commemorative stone pillar.

Early in September, 1499, Da Gama reached Lisbon. Of the 170 men who had started out, 2 years earlier, only 55 returned. Some of them were broken men both in body and mind. But commercially the voyage had been a great success. A new trade route to India had been opened up, and reports of the prosperous East African seaports had been brought to Europe for the first time.

The Portuguese quickly followed up with a more ambitious expedition. They hoped to make treaties with the rulers of Moçambique and Kilwa but found them suspicious and unwilling to trade. The Portuguese then decided to use force. They sent out an even larger fleet, again under the command of Vasco da Gama, who compelled the Sheik of Kilwa to submit and pay tribute. In 1505, yet another fleet under Francisco de Almeida captured Kilwa, and built a fort there. He also went on to storm, capture, and destroy Mombasa, leaving the city a wreck, its streets piled with over 1,500 corpses.

Within a few years, the whole seacoast of Zinj between Sofala and Mogadiscio was in Portuguese hands. But their rule was continually challenged by the Arabs, by Turkish raiders, and by warlike tribes from the interior. In 1587, warriors of the Zimba tribe sacked Kilwa, slaughtered 3,000 of its inhabitants, and advanced up the coast "killing and eating every living thing, men, women, children, dogs, cats, rats, snakes, lizards, sparing nothing." Fear of such tribesmen, the barren and forbidding nature of the interior, and the lack of

Left: for centuries Arab dhows have sailed down to Africa on the northeast monsoon winds between November and March, returning with the southwest monsoon from May to September. Today the dhows still sweep across the Indian Ocean, and in Mombasa, where this dhow is being unloaded, there are big carpet sales when the boats arrive.

navigable rivers all combined to discourage inland exploration.

In 1505, the Portuguese established a trading outpost at Sofala, but soon found that the gold they had hoped to get by barter was not forthcoming, nor was sufficient food. So they sent Antonio Fernandes, one of the convicted criminals the Portuguese brought along for such particularly hazardous tasks, to the interior in search of both. Between 1505 and 1514 he made at least two journeys inland, and must have been the first European to explore the area called Mashonaland in what is now eastern Rhodesia.

Above: Zimbabwe is an anglicized form of *Dzimbahwe*, which means a stone house, or venerated place. There the chiefs were buried, and the people gathered for intercession with their ancestral spirits. In the 1800's the Mashona were invaded by the Zulus. Since then they have refused to speak of their sacred place, and so little traditional information is available.

Fernandes reported that the Zambezi River offered the easiest route inland. It was, in fact, the only East African river navigable for any significant distance. Canoes could be paddled 300 miles upstream. The Portuguese explored the navigable reaches of the Zambezi and established outposts at the settlements of Sena, in 1531, and Tete, in 1560. At Sena they were the first Europeans to make contact with the Bantu kingdom of the Mwanamutapa, the hereditary title given to the superior chieftain of a group of tribes then occupying much of what was later to become Rhodesia.

Right: the Kafue River, one of the longest of the many tributaries of the Zambezi. It rises in the copper belt on the borders of Zambia and Katanga, and joins the Zambezi north of Lake Kariba. Below: an Italian fresco of the 1400's showing Solomon receiving the Queen of Sheba. Scholars have failed to agree on where she came from, but according to tradition it was from Ethiopia. Ethiopians believe that their royal family is descended from the Queen of Sheba and King Solomon.

The first Portuguese to be received by the Mwanamutapa's court was Antonio Gaiado, a trader, who went to live there in 1550. The Portuguese viceroy gave him the title of keeper of the gates and the right to one-twentieth of all the cloth sent inland for barter. Ten years later the Mwanamutapa received the first Jesuit missionary, Gonzalo da Silveira. Da Silveira baptized the Bantu king, but was later murdered at the instigation of the Moslem Arabs, who saw a threat to their religion and trade in the encroachment of Christians.

The main town of the Mwanamutapa's kingdom then lay about 300 miles north of the fortified stone citadel now called Great Zimbabwe. According to their own account, the Mwanamutapa's people had once dwelt at Great Zimbabwe, but had left about a century earlier because their salt supplies had failed. In the 1700's, Great Zimbabwe fell into decay. When the ruins were rediscovered in 1868 the origin of these substantial stone ruins long intrigued and baffled historians. They were thought by Europeans to be the work of Arabs or perhaps Phoenicians. Some linked the stones of Great Zimbabwe with the legendary land of Ophir, the Biblical land from which came the rich gifts sent by the Queen of Sheba to King Solomon. Modern research has shown that Great Zimbabwe was built by Bantu-speaking Mashona peoples at various times between the 1000's and 1400's. It was the headquarters of a wealthy kingdom whose gold, silver, and copper were transported to Sofala and sold to Arab and Swahili traders. Great Zimbabwe is the largest, but by no means the only, structure of its kind. Over 300 similar stone ruins, sites of former dwellings and perhaps temples, have been found in Rhodesia and Mozambique.

A Dominican priest, João dos Santos, published in 1609 the earliest travel book about these Bantu kingdoms. He visited a king called the Quiteve, a son of the Mwanamutapa, ruling at the time.

Dos Santos described the court rituals: "If the Cafres [his subjects] have a suit, and seeke to speake with the king, they creepe to the place where he is, having prostrated themselves at the entrance, and looke not on him all the while they speake, but lying on one side clap their hands all the time and having finished, they creepe out of the doors as they came in." The "Portugals" had to go through a similar ritual. Dos Santos also commented wryly on required etiquette at the court, "both Cafres and Portugals are entertained by him with wine of Mays, or their Wheate, called Pombe, which they

Right: the British consulate in Zanzibar. Sir John Kirk, who negotiated the treaty with the Sultan of Zanzibar for the suppression of the slave trade in his dominions, lived here in 1883.

must drinke, although against stomacke, not to contemn the King's bountie."

These first explorers were already asking questions that were not to be answered for 250 years. For instance, where did the Zambezi rise? The source, Dos Santos wrote, "is so farre within lande that none of them [the Bantu] know it, but say it comes from a lake in the midst of the Continent, which yields also other great Rivers."

No Portuguese, so far as we know, reached the source from the east coast. But traders are thought to have gone up the river some 800 miles from its mouth, and they established trading "faires" inland in what is now Rhodesia.

In 1644, the Mwanamutapa was forced to declare himself a servant of the King of Portugal, to agree to the building of a Christian church, and to receive a resident priest in his kingdom. In the 1700's, the Portuguese brought out families of settlers to establish colonies. But during the 1700's, probably there were never more than 400 Portuguese living in the colony of Mozambique, either along the 1,500-mile coast or inland. And as it turned out the Portuguese were never able to obtain the gold and silver they had hoped for.

Farther north, the Portuguese hold weakened. Fort Jesus in Mombasa fell in 1697 to the Arabian Sultan of Muscat, and the Arabs re-established their influence over the coastal cities. They were traders, not explorers, and the interior remained more or less undisturbed. Often the Arab cities, which were much like small independent nations, fought one another. Finally, in 1840, a dominant personality in the shape of Sayyid Said ibn Sultan, the ruler of Oman, won control of the Swahili coast north of Mozambique and controlled the area from his capital on the island of Zanzibar, off the coast south of Mombasa.

During the 1800's, Zanzibar became the great slave market of the east coast. Arab and Swahili caravans marched far inland to the East African lakes in search of "black ivory." The enslaved tribesmen were brought down to the coastal markets, yoked and fettered, and then exported to Arabia and the Turkish domains. The slave trade was part of African life, but was exploited and enlarged by non-Africans—in East Africa by the Arabs—to meet a world demand. One of the main differences between the role of Europeans in West Africa and in East Africa was that in the West they came as slavers, but in the East, from the 1800's onward, as liberators of the slaves.

Below: the Zanzibar market place, where bargaining is the rule. In some seasons, the hot, pungent smell of the market is overlaid with the scent of cloves, for which the island is noted.

Tracking the Nile

3

Left: James Bruce of Kinnaird. Bruce was 38 years old when he set out to find the source of the Nile River.

Below: verses from the Bible translated by Bruce into Amharic and Ge'ez. Early Ethiopian literature was in Ge'ez, the language of the Kushite shepherds. About 1100, the king set up his court in the province of Amhara, and slowly Amharic became the national language of Ethiopia.

መሕልየ፡ መሕልየ፡ ዘወስቱ፡ ዘለስሎዎን፡ ይስዐሙኒ፡ በስዐመተ፡ አፉሁ፡ አደም፡ አጣባቲከ፡ እምወይን፡ ወኍ፤ ዐፈርትቢ፡ እምጦሉ፡ ስፈው፡ ዐፈረት፡ ዘተወመጠ፡ ስምከ፡ ወበእንተዝ፡ ይናገል፡ አፈፈሪብ፡ ፍርዐ፡ ስብስፈ፡ ፃጉ፡ ወስት፡ ፃርሑ፡ ንትፈዋሕ፡ ወንትሐሠይ፡ ብብ፡ ናፈቅር፡ አጣባተh፡ እምወይን፡ ወርቱዐ፡ አፈቅርተከ፡ ፃለም፡ አና፡ ወውናይት፡ እዶስ ዋለይ፡ ኢየሩሳሌም፡ ብ፡ ምዳላላ፡ ተፈር፡ ወፃይመተት፡ ሰሎዎን፡ ኢትርእያኒ፡ እስም፡ አና፡ ፃለም፡ እስም፡ ኢርእፈኒ፡ ፀሕ፡፡

ይህ፡ ብዎአጋና፡ የሚበለጽ፡ ዎአጋና፡ የስሎዎን፡ ናው፡ ብሩ፡ አአም፡ ይስመኛል፡ ብዐይኝ፡ ይለት፡ ጦቸሻ፡ ይስ፡ ይለሉ፡ የኍቀሾዎ፡ ሾኀ፡ ብቸተ፡ ኍለ፡ የፃለል፡ በሰል፡ የተለተለ፡ አዎህ፡አጓ፡ ሾቸ፡ ያስዎይፀዎል፡ ብለኍ፡ ፃ፱ቸቱ፡ ወፈሩ፡ ኍፀለዋኘ፡ ተበተሉ፡ በቸሉ፡ ሾቸ፡ አፃሒ፡ ለኝ፡ ፃ፪ሠ፡ በገኘቸ፡ አገነፀ፡ በፃ፵፡ ይስ፡ ይስጎ፡ ወቸሻኘ፡ ብዎፀ፡ ይለት፡ እንዎለኘ፡ አጋ፵ኘ፡ ዎወረ፡ ቅን፡ ፃገኘ፡ ፀው፡፡ ብየሩሳሌም፡ ተፃኀት፡ ይለት፡ ጦዳረስስ፡ ፡፡ኍ፵ፈ፡ ዘለኝ፡ ሰኝ፡ እንፈ፡ ስለ ዎን፡ ይ፪ኟኘ፡፡

In the 1700's.a new breed of explorers came to Africa. They came not to enrich themselves by trading in gold or slaves, nor to bring the good news of the Gospel to the pagan tribesmen. Instead they were driven by the desire to unravel the mysteries of the Dark Continent's geography. They explored for the sake of curiosity and adventure. And they were—many of them—seekers of fame. Most of them were not scientists or professional explorers, but gifted amateurs. Such a man was James Bruce, a Scottish aristocrat, laird of Kinnaird.

Born in 1730, Bruce came from an old Scottish family. He was 6 feet 4 inches in height, handsome and well-built, with dark red hair and considerable charm of manner. Charming as he was, Bruce had a quick temper. In his own words he was "of a sanguine, passionate disposition, very sensible of injury."

Bruce married when he was 24. Nine months later his young wife tragically died of tuberculosis. In order to take his mind off his loss Bruce decided to travel abroad. On a visit to Spain he became very interested in the Moors—the Arabic-speaking people who had conquered Spain during the 700's, ruled over most of it until the late 1200's and were finally expelled in 1492—and began his studies of Arabic. Shortly after, Bruce was appointed British consul general to the Moorish city of Algiers. To prepare himself for this new job he perfected his Arabic, and because part of his official mission was to learn all he could about Africa, he began to study the little-known Ethiopian tongues of Amharic and Ge'ez. After two years in Algiers he spent the next seven years traveling in North Africa and the Near East, looking, learning, and equipping himself for an enterprise which, in the words of his first biographer, "had taken deeper possession of Mr. Bruce's mind than any other project." His goal was to reach Ethiopia and find the springs which were said to be the source of the Nile.

Instead of traveling, like most well-to-do Europeans of the day, in luxury and aloofness, Bruce lived and dressed as an Arab. In North Africa he learned to ride in the Arab style and proved to be a brilliant horseman. During an attack of malaria while he was staying at Aleppo in Syria he came under the care of a doctor, Patrick Russel, who had made a study of tropical diseases. Bruce picked up so much medical knowledge from Russel that he could pass himself off as a physician. When he started off for Ethiopia the Sherif of Mecca gave him the closest thing in those days to a passport, saying Bruce was "a Christian physician accustomed to wander over the world in search of herbs and trees beneficial to the health of man."

In 1768, Bruce, now 38, was in Cairo ready to embark on his quest. With Luigi Balugani, a young Italian he had hired as secretary and artist to make sketches and maps, Bruce set off up the Nile by boat. The party got as far as Aswan only to find that tribal wars to the south made it too dangerous to go on. Bruce, however, was determined. Turning eastward, he left the Nile and crossed the desert and the Red Sea to the port of Juddah on the coast of Arabia. From there he sailed south to Massaua, a port on Ethiopia's coast. Massaua was then under the control of the Turks who detained Bruce for two months.

On November 10, 1768, Bruce set out from Massaua for Gondar, the Ethiopian capital. He was accompanied by Balugani, some guards he had hired and armed, three servants, and a guide. The most important item in his baggage was a quadrant—an instrument for measuring the altitude of the sun or stars and used in determining position—so that when he found the source of the Nile he could work out its latitude. The quadrant was so heavy that two teams of four men were needed to carry it over the mountains that rise so quickly from the coast to the high plateau of Ethiopia. Traveling over the plateau the party passed through immense flocks of antelopes that scarcely moved aside to let them by. The Ethiopians were herdsmen and Bruce wrote that cattle were "here in great plenty, cows and bulls, of exquisite beauty, for the most part completely white."

The usual diet of the Ethiopians consisted of honey and bread made from *dhurra,* a kind of millet. When they ate meat, it was taken raw from living animals. Bruce first experienced this when his party overtook three soldiers herding a cow along with them. When they reached a river bank the soldiers tied the cow and proceeded to cut two large portions of flesh from her flanks. After this they folded the skin back over the wound and fastened it with small skewers, untied the cow and drove her on.

After three months the expedition reached Gondar, where smallpox had broken out. Because of his reputation as a physician, Bruce was summoned to the palace of the Iteghe, the queen mother, and commanded to treat her grandchildren. Following Russel's procedures he had all the doors and windows opened, the rooms fumigated with incense and myrrh, and the walls washed with vinegar. The children recovered, and the Iteghe's gratitude and protection opened the way to Bruce's success. A close friendship grew up between him and the ladies of the court. Bruce spoke their language fluently, charmed them with his manners, and took care to dress to please them. "My hair was cut round, curled, and perfumed in the Amharic fashion, and I was thenceforward, in all outward appearance, a perfect Abyssinian."

But Bruce's way to the source of the Nile was blocked by political strife. Ethiopia was in a state of civil war caused by a rising against

Below: a Coptic priest instructing his students at Lalibela. Traditionally teaching has been an important part of the church's function in Ethiopia.

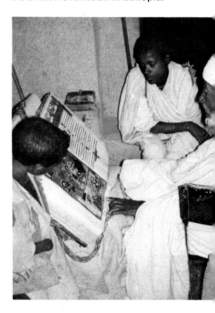

Right: Ethiopian soldiers, taken from an Abyssinian drawing by a traveler, Henry Salt, in 1814. He reported that figures were always drawn full face, except for Jews, who were always shown in profile, but he was unable to find the logic in the distinction. Otherwise he said that the dress of the warriors and the equipment of their horses were very faithfully pictured.

the 15-year-old king of the country, Takla Haymanot. The real ruler of Ethiopia, however, was not Takla but his adviser, Ras Michael, who was away campaigning against the rebels when Bruce arrived. Upon his return Ras Michael paraded through the capital at the head of 30,000 men. Every soldier who had killed an enemy decorated his lance or musket with a strip of red rag. One soldier "had been so fortunate in combat that his whole lance and javelin, horse and person, were covered over with shreds of scarlet cloth." Held high in the procession was the "stuffed skin" of a rebel chief who had been flayed alive. One of Ras Michael's first acts on his return was to have the eyes of 44 captive chiefs torn out and "the unfortunate sufferers turned out into the fields, to be devoured at night by the hyenas." Bruce rescued three of the chiefs and nursed them back to health.

Ras Michael, apart from his brutality, was an intelligent man. He was about 70 years old with "an air perfectly free from constraint," and he saw in Bruce a possible ally in the civil war and court intrigue. He appointed the Scot master of the king's horse, groom of the bedchamber, and titular governor of the province of Geesh where the fabled spring that Bruce hoped to find was located.

It was while Bruce was in the employ of the Ethiopian court that he got his first view of the Blue Nile. The river's source is the Little Abbai River, a stream that rises about 70 miles south of Lake Tana in Ethiopia, and some 2,750 miles from the Nile Delta. The stream enters Lake Tana, emerges from the lake's southeast corner, and then—as the Blue Nile—flows in a great curve, first to the southeast and then northwest to enter the Sudan. Bruce first saw the Blue Nile where it thunders over the Tisisat Falls 20 miles below Lake Tana, but he was campaigning with the king's army. As they were returning to court he had to turn back with them.

Bruce was determined to attempt to reach the source of the river. Eventually, in October, 1770, he received royal permission to undertake his search, and he left Gondar with a small party of men and his precious astronomical instruments. Just as they approached the stream, his party climbed a steep, rugged mountain populated by great numbers of baboons. Although these long-toothed powerful animals can be dangerous, Bruce was not deterred. From the mountain's 9,500 foot summit he looked down on "the Nile itself . . . now only a brook that had scarcely water to turn a mill."

Below the mountain, at the tiny town of Geesh, lay a shallow ford and beyond that a deserted Ethiopian church where the small party paused in the shade of a grove of cedars. Before them lay the swamp from which the river drained. The guide now turned difficult and bargained for Bruce's scarlet silk sash in return for revealing the spring which was the ultimate source of the Blue Nile. Throwing off his shoes, Bruce raced toward the little island in the marsh the guide had pointed to, and there he found his prize. The spring, which was sacred to the local people, appeared to Bruce "as in the form of an altar. . . . I stood in rapture over the principal fountain which rises in the middle." Bruce indulged himself in a moment of triumph "standing in that spot which had baffled the genius, industry, and enquiry of both ancients and moderns for the course of near three thousand years. Kings had attempted this discovery at the head of armies. . . . " But Bruce had at last triumphed and reached his goal.

For all his exuberance, Bruce was mistaken on two counts. This spring was not the true source of the Nile, nor was he the first European to reach it. Of the two branches that unite to form Africa's greatest river, the White Nile is the longer, and the place where it

Right: Tisisat Falls. The river approaches gently and then suddenly vanishes in a tremendous, foaming downpour of water. From above it appears to be a narrow gorge with water racing through in a terrifying turmoil. It remains spectacular to this day. For Bruce it must have been an unexpectedly overpowering sight.

issues from Lake Victoria is now generally accepted as "the source of the Nile." The Blue Nile is, in this sense, a tributary, although a mighty one, supplying six-sevenths of the water that flows through Upper Egypt as well as the fertile silt upon which Egypt's civilization was founded.

The first European to set eyes on the spring at Geesh had been a Spanish Jesuit, Pedro Páez, in 1618. About 10 years later another Jesuit, Jeronimo Lobo, had passed through the district and visited the Tisisat Falls. But Bruce was the first to verify the source and to fix the spring s position, and the first to follow the river from Sennar, where the Sennar Dam now blocks its path, down to its confluence with the White Nile where Khartoum now stands.

Bruce's mood of euphoria quickly gave way to one of gloom. Having achieved his object, he wanted to go home, but this was not allowed by the Ethiopian court. As master of the king's horse he found himself caught up in campaigns against the rebels, and for his part in one of them was rewarded with a massive gold chain. But the intrigues, bloodshed, torture, and executions sickened him. "Blood continued to be spilt as water, day after day," he wrote. "Priests and laymen, young and old, noble and vile, daily found their end by the knife or the cord. Bodies were left to rot where they lay, and by night the capital was filled with scavenging hyenas." Bruce fell sick with malaria. His Italian draughtsman, Balugani, died of dysentery. "Nothing occupied my thoughts but how to escape from this bloody country by way of Sennar."

Eventually, because of Bruce's ill-health, the king reluctantly allowed him to depart. More than a year after his return from the spring at Geesh Bruce rode out of Gondar accompanied only by

Below: Fasildas Castle, in the imperial compound at Gondar. From the 1600's Gondar was the Ethiopian capital, and the emperors built castles and palaces within a walled enclosure. Bruce lived in the castle of Koosquam, outside Gondar. He estimated that the city then had a population of 10,000 families.

three Greeks, one of them almost blind, an elderly Turk, and a few grooms. He headed for Sennar in the Sudan both to follow the Nile and to avoid the Turks at Massaua. He was to take just over a year on the journey, which began on December 26, 1771, and ended at Cairo, a total of 2,000 miles, on January 10, 1773.

At this period the authority of the Ottoman Turks who controlled Egypt extended no farther up the Nile than Aswan, at the first cataract. South of this lay an immense and sparsely-populated region where independent kingdoms waxed and waned according to the strength and fortunes of their rulers. These desert kings were of Arab blood mixed with the native Negro or Hamitic. They were Moslems who spoke and wrote Arabic, and kept to some Arab customs and traditions. Their subjects were either nomadic herders of long-horned cattle or peasants barely able to survive because of the taxes imposed upon them by their landlords.

Despite the remoteness of these kingdoms, cut off by cruel deserts and even more cruel bandits from the rest of the world, they had not lost all touch with civilization. To such markets as Shandi and Barbar on the Nile came silks from the Indies, swords from Syria, rugs from Iran, glass from Venice, brass and beads from India, and spices from many other parts of the world. From them went spirited desert-bred horses, ivory, leopard skins, ostrich feathers, gold-dust, and a great number of slaves. There was a regular slave trade with Egypt, and with Arabia via the port of Suakin on the Red Sea.

After a four-month journey—part of it taken up with a two-month bout of malaria—Bruce reached Sennar. The courts of the sheiks kept up a barbaric sort of splendor. One traveler recorded in 1409

Below: a hyena, drawn by Bruce. Like all scavengers, hyenas perform a useful function, but they are ugly animals and generally despised. It is easy to imagine the horror they must have evoked when the carcasses they fought over were human, often the dead left abandoned on some bloody battlefield.

Below: a female antelope, or greater kudu, running through the desert near Sennar. The kudu lives on grass and the young leaves of shrubs, and in the dry season goes from the desert to the cooler fertile country close to the rivers.

that the ladies of Sennar wore robes of silk or fine calico with sleeves falling to the ground, "their hair is twisted and set with rings of silver, copper, brass, and ivory, or glass of different colours. These rings are fastened to their locks in form of crowns; their arms, legs, ears, and even nostrils are covered with these rings."

Bruce was less flattering to the King of Sennar's favorite wife. She was, he wrote, "about six feet high, and corpulent beyond all proportion. A ring of gold passed through under her lip, and weighed it down, till, like a flap, it covered her chin, and left her teeth bare." Her ears reached to her shoulders, tugged down by more rings, and "she had on her ankles two manacles of gold, larger than any I had ever seen upon the feet of felons." It was not surprising that all the royal ladies needed treatment for some ailment.

In Sennar the king's authority was enforced by a small but highly trained corps of cavalry, the Black Horse, who fought, like medieval knights, in chain mail. Bruce was deeply impressed by the Black Horse of Sennar, known and dreaded throughout a kingdom stretching from the Ethiopian foothills to Kordofan, west of the White Nile. Bruce admired the 400 famous horses, "all above sixteen hands high, of the breed of the old Saracen horses, all

Above: the plains west of the Blue Nile, near Sennar. For a short time after the rains this semidesert country blossoms, grass and flowers spring up as if by a miracle, bushes grow green, and the animals return. In the dry season, when Bruce crossed it, the sun blazes all day on burning rocks, hot soft sand, and naked thorns that tear the flesh, in a shimmering heat.

finely made." The soldiers slept beside their horses, and each man hung up on its stall his suit of chain mail, his copper helmet, a broadsword in a red leather scabbard, and a pair of thick leather gloves.

Despite the splendor of the horses, the beauty of the country, and the hospitality of the people, Bruce soon grew tired of Sennar which, in the rainy season, became unbearably hot and unhealthy. Once again the king refused to let him go. Bruce ran out of goods and money, and was forced to sell all but six links of his massive gold chain to buy food to keep himself and his men alive. But after four months, he managed to escape with the three Greeks, the old Turk, an unreliable guide, and five camels. Ahead lay 800 miles of unknown country, mostly desert, separating Sennar from the borders of Egypt at Aswan.

After passing the junction of the two Niles and then Shandi and Barbar, Bruce and his party reached the point where the Nile turns west to make an 800-mile loop before it turns north again. Rather than follow the great curve, they struck out on the direct but dangerous route north across the desert toward Aswan, a distance of about 350 miles. On November 11, 1772, they filled their waterskins and Bruce had his last bathe in the Nile, "and thus took leave of my old acquaintance, very doubtful if we should ever meet again."

His doubts were nearly justified. The men's shoes wore out and they trudged on through burning sand and over jagged rock, barefooted, and in pain. There was no food for the camels. Then, to add fear to physical discomfort, the struggling group came on the remains of a large caravan that had left Sennar a few days before them and had been wiped out by robbers. "In this whole desert," wrote Bruce, "there is neither worm, nor fly, nor anything that has the breath of life."

Whirlwinds and the dreaded *simoom,* the burning dust-laden wind of the desert, almost suffocated them. Bruce's feet were so badly blistered and swollen that he could scarcely walk. As a last desperate resort Bruce and his companions killed the camels and drained their stomachs to replenish their water supplies. They set off on foot, leaving Bruce's instruments and the records of his four years of travel.

When all hope seemed lost, Bruce saw two hawks in the sky—signs that water was not far away. The party staggered on, and in the evening heard the distant sound of a cataract. "Christians, Moors, and Turks all burst into floods of tears, kissing and embracing one another, and thanking God for his mercy in this deliverance." Next morning, November 29, 1772, they limped into Aswan.

Despite his desperate condition, Bruce's first thought was for his papers. He begged camels from the governor, retraced his steps, and found his baggage untouched. From Aswan he went by boat to Cairo, sick and with feet so swollen that he could not stand.

Now Bruce was ready to reap his reward. He set out for home. Before going to England, however, he went to France to receive treatment for a leg infected by the parasitic Guinea worm he had picked up in Sennar. Several months elapsed before he arrived back

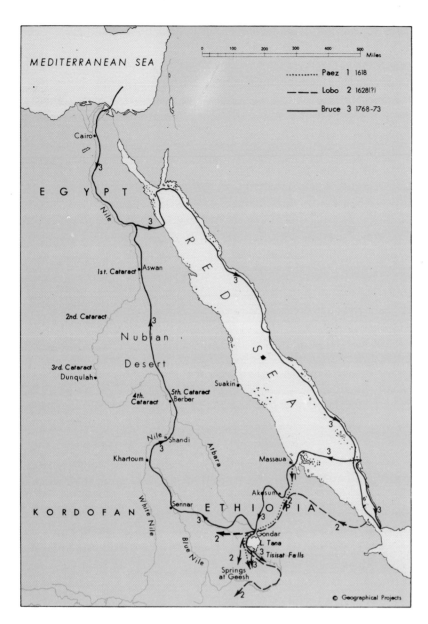

Left: the Nile Valley and Ethiopia.
This map shows the routes Páez, Lobo,
and Bruce took to the Spring at
Geesh, the source of the Blue Nile.

in London, expecting recognition and praise for his great achievement. At first, people listened to his story. George III received him and accepted a present of some of Balugani's drawings. Then the mood changed.

In 1774, London society was dominated by polished, skeptical wits. This bluff, noisy Scot, full of what seemed to be tall stories, was an irresistible target. London society just did not believe Bruce's tales of meat cut from living cows and served raw and bleeding, and of fat princesses with golden rings in their noses. Moreover Bruce fell foul of Samuel Johnson, one of the great figures of London who greatly influenced popular opinion. Johnson's first published work had been a translation of Jeronimo Lobo's account of his Ethiopian travels, and he had written a novel, *Rasselas, Prince of Abyssinia,* set in an imaginary Ethiopia very different from the reality described by Bruce. Johnson, who disliked Scots anyway, made it known that he did not believe that Bruce had ever been to Ethiopia at all. This was a sentence of death to the explorer's reputation. None of the honors Bruce had hoped for came his way.

Hurt, angry, and humiliated, Bruce retreated to his estate in Scotland, remarried, raised a family, and enjoyed the social and sporting life of a Scottish laird. Only after his wife died in 1785 did he begin to work on the notes and journals he had brought home at so high a cost and then locked away in disgust at his treatment. And it was not until 1790 that his *Travels to Discover the Source of the Nile* appeared. The public did not question the author's truthfulness, but delighted in his racy style, and admired his courage and tenacity. He did not, however, live long to enjoy his popular success. On April 27, 1794, Bruce, the gentleman-adventurer, died at the age of 64 as a result of an accident the day before.

T R A V E L S

TO DISCOVER THE

SOURCE OF THE NILE,

In the Years 1768, 1769, 1770, 1771, 1772, and 1773.

IN FIVE VOLUMES.

BY JAMES BRUCE OF KINNAIRD, ESQ. F.R.S.

VOL. I.

*Opus aggredior opimum casibus, atrox præliis, discors seditionibus,
Ipsâ etiam pace sævum.* TACIT. Lib. iv. Ann.

EDINBURGH:
PRINTED BY J. RUTHVEN,
FOR G. G. J. AND J. ROBINSON, PATERNOSTER-ROW,
LONDON.

M.DCC.XC.

Left: the title page of Bruce's *Travels.* He had no illusions about the dangers he would encounter when he set out in 1768, and on his return felt justifiable pride at his accomplishment. He dedicated his book to King George III, and wrote, "I humbly hope I have shown the world of what value the efforts of every individual of your Majesty's subjects may be; that numbers are not always necessary to the performance of brilliant actions."

The Dutch and British in South Africa 4

The first explorers of South Africa were Dutch hunters and traders. On April 7, 1652, a party of about 90 Dutchmen led by Jan van Riebeeck ran up the flag of the Dutch East India Company beside Table Bay at the Cape of Good Hope. They had come to establish a settlement as a victualling station to supply food, fresh water, and firewood for the company's ships plying between The Netherlands and the East Indies. The gardens they planted thrived, but the task of obtaining meat was more difficult. The Dutch were forced to move inland and along the coast to hunt game and to barter for cattle. The Hottentots, who valued cattle as wealth and not as meat, were reluctant traders. The Dutch had little to offer that seemed as valuable as a fat cow or strong bull. So, in time, the Dutch brought their own cattle to the Cape and farmers (Boers) to raise them.

In 1681, a party of Namaquas, a branch of the Hottentots, who lived northwest of the Cape south of the Orange River, arrived at the Dutch settlement. They brought with them lumps of copper ore dug out of a mountain near a big river. The Namaquas claimed that beyond the river lived a different sort of man—tall and black. Both were of interest to the Dutch who saw potential wealth in the copper. They wondered whether "these different men" were subjects of the Mwanamutapa whose fame had spread even to the Cape. The river could be the *Vigiti Magna* which they believed to form the southern border of the Mwanamutapa's kingdom. In the next few years three parties went northwest to investigate, but had to turn back without success because they ran out of supplies before reaching Namaqualand. In August, 1685, the governor himself, Simon van der Stel, set out with a retinue of 57 white men and a number of Hottentot and Bushman servants with riding horses, donkeys, 7 wagons, and oxen. They had a boat with them to cross the river into the kingdom of the Mwanamutapa. That was, if they found it.

Their guides led them into steep mountains with boulder-filled ravines where their wagons overturned, and swamps in which the wheels sunk to the hubs. In Namaqualand, Van der Stel made a pact with the chiefs to "live forever in a salutary state of peace with one

Left: Van Riebeeck and his men first meeting the Hottentots, against a background of Devil's Peak, part of Table Mountain. It served as an unmistakable landmark for mariners rounding the Cape of Good Hope.

another." A week later the expedition found the Copper Mountain, near the site of modern Springbok, and began to prospect and dig. The rock yielded good copper and a crude smelting furnace was constructed. The expedition returned intact with samples of metal.

It turned out, however, that the mountain was too remote for the copper to be mined profitably. And the Vigiti Magna—no doubt the Orange River, about 50 miles farther north—remained undiscovered.

Relations between Hottentots and Dutch did not continue on such a friendly footing. As more Europeans arrived at the settlement and more land was given out, the Boers went farther afield and began to raid instead of trade for Hottentot cattle. The nomadic Hottentots were not organized for fighting, and in any case their assagais were no match for the Boers' muskets. So they retreated north and west. Many were impressed into slavery or a form of domestic bondage amounting to the same thing.

As the colony at the Cape grew, the Dutch pushed eastward toward the Indian Ocean. In 1736, a party of Dutch elephant hunters led by Hermanus Hubner crossed the Great Fish and Kei rivers to the east into the Transkei (beyond the Kei). Here lived the Xhosa and Tembu Bantu nations who displayed a different temper altogether from the Hottentots. Hubner's party was attacked by these Kaffirs, as the Dutch called the Bantus. The skirmish was a foretaste of things to come. In 1752 an official expedition sent to explore beyond the Great Fish River managed to get as far as the Kei but was forced to turn back by Bantu warriors soon after crossing the river. The party, despite Bantu attacks, made an eight months' exploration and returned with the first accurate maps, surveys, and reports of the eastern Cape.

Interest had never died in the Vigiti Magna which the practical minded Dutch translated into their own language as the Groote (big) River, and which is now called the Orange. The first European known to have crossed the Groote River north of the settlement was elephant hunter Jacobus Coetsee, in 1760, while looking for ivory. The following year Coetsee returned with an official expedition led by Henrik Hop. Setting out with 15 wagons, the men passed the Copper Mountain, crossed the Groote River, and were successful in shooting a *camelopard* (giraffe). They then drove their teams northward in search of "a nation who went clad in linen and who were of a tawny complexion." When they came to a parched, semidesert country with dried-up river-beds and baking heat, they were forced

Above: in the 1700's parties of Dutch elephant hunters were among the first Europeans to explore the interior of what is now South Africa. The African elephant, shown here, is larger and has bigger ears and longer tusks than the Asian elephant.

Left: a Xhosa man, wearing a colored blanket. This has become the modern replacement for the original robe made of cowhide, which was greased and rubbed until soft. The Xhosas still live in the eastern Cape Province, where Hubner first saw them in 1736.

to turn back; the "different" people, reported on many years before by the Namaquas, remained unseen.

In the late 1700's, travelers in the Bruce mold appeared in Cape Colony. These were men who, like the Scot, traveled not to hunt, trade, or look for minerals, but simply to see what was there and to bring back specimens of plants, beasts, birds, insects, and rocks. A Swedish naturalist, Anders Sparrman, traveled widely in South Africa in 1775 and 1776, and made one of the first scientific studies of the Bushmen. The "boosies men," he wrote, were "pursued and exterminated like wild beasts," by the Boers, or else "kept alive and made slaves of." These small, yellowish-brown-skinned hunters

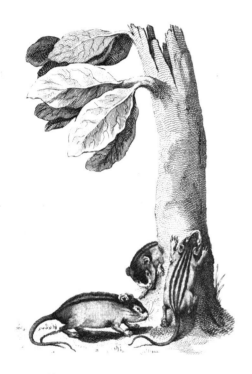

Above: drawing of dwarf mice, from Sparrman's book. He was fascinated by the variety in size of African animals, and calculated that a hippopotamus was 25,000 times larger than this 1½-inch-long mouse.

were, Sparrman noted, "ignorant of agriculture. . . . Their table is sometimes composed of the larvae of insects, a sort of white ant, grasshoppers, snakes, and some sorts of spiders." Sparrman was not surprised that they were often "famished to such a degree, as to waste almost to a shadow." In this state they were easily captured by white farmers who rounded them up to become domestic slaves, fattening them in a few weeks on a diet of "meat, buttermilk, frumenty [a spiced cereal], and hasty pudding."

Contemporary with Sparrman was William Paterson, a 21-year-old Scot, sent to the Cape in 1777 by a Scottish noblewoman, the Countess of Strathmore, to collect plants for her estate. Paterson's journal published in 1789 was a first on-the-spot account in English of South African travel. On the last four journeys he rode in company with Colonel R. J. Gordon, a Dutchman despite his

Scots-sounding name. On August 17, 1779, they reached the long-undiscovered mouth of the Groote River on the South Atlantic. Paterson's book tells of renaming the river in honor of the ruling house of The Netherlands. "In the evening we launched Colonel Gordon's boat, and hoisted Dutch colours. Colonel Gordon proposed to drink first the States' [of The Netherlands] health and then that of the Prince of Orange, and the Company; after which he gave the name of the Orange River in honour of that Prince."

On the return journey Paterson saw a sight soon to disappear, herds of migrating Springbok antelopes in numbers of at least 20,000 to 30,000 in each flock.

Paterson's older companion Robert Jacob Gordon became commander of the Dutch garrison at the Cape, and an expert on "the manners and customs of the most Savage Nations of Africa." He

Above: a painting of Table Bay in 1720. By that time Cape Town had a permanent garrison, and was a port of call for the Dutch East India fleet. Though the bay is in some ways a natural harbor, the mountain formations surrounding it create baffling winds. When Burchell reached the Cape in 1810, his ship was blown out to sea by a storm, and it took the captain 12 days before he could make a landing.

Above: painting by William Burchell made near the Orange River on September 16, 1811. Burchell said that while he was painting, some of the Hottentots, glad to be able to shelter from the scorching sun, lay naked in little groups in the shade, while others had a swim, some going fearlessly right into the middle of the stream.

mapped the course of the Orange River from its confluence with the Vaal River to the sea and sent back to The Netherlands the first skin and skeleton of a giraffe. In 1795, when the Cape was temporarily occupied by the British forces to keep it out of Napoleon's hands, Gordon was so deeply humiliated to feel he needed British troops to protect him that he committed suicide.

In the regions north of the Orange and east of the Kei river lived many Bantu tribes who were cattle raisers but who, unlike the Hottentots, cultivated the land and dwelt in tribal villages or even large towns organized in a centralized form of government under the rule of chiefs. They worked in iron and other metals, used beads as currency, and, in some cases, maintained well-disciplined standing armies. The first Europeans to visit the large Bantu villages were amazed at what they found. One of the first to report on the Bantu was the Englishman John Barrow.

Above: Sir John Barrow. In 1801, then secretary to the governor of the Cape, he was sent north to buy cattle from the Batswana people. Barrow visited Lattakoo, the Batswana capital. He was much impressed both by the town itself and by the life of its inhabitants.

Barrow had come to Cape Town as secretary to the governor and in 1801 was a member of an official mission sent north of the Orange River to buy cattle from the "Booshuana," the modern Batswana people of Botswana. When they arrived at the chief's *kraal* (village), called Lattakoo (near the present-day South African town of Kuruman), the mission was astonished at its size, neatness, and good order. The chief received the travelers "in a most friendly manner," accepting their gifts and giving them curdled milk, a local delicacy.

Barrow reckoned that Lattakoo had between 10,000 and 15,000 inhabitants and was just as large as Cape Town. The houses were round with clay floors and neatly thatched roofs. Earthenware granaries stood on stilts throughout the town. "In elegance and solidity" wrote Barrow, the houses were "as good as the *casae* or first houses that were built in imperial Rome, and in every respect superior in construction and comfort to most of the Irish cabins."

The village was clean, well drained, and built with comfort in mind. Each house, surrounded by a palissade, was shaded by a spreading acacia "every twig of which is preserved with religious care." The inhabitants' dress, also, was superior. They wore pliant, soft leather cloaks sometimes lined with "fur skins of tyger-cats," and carried ostrich-feather sunshades. They used snuff and tobacco, ornamented their bodies, and made iron tools so skillfully that they spurned those of the Europeans, "observing that their own were at least twice as good because they were made to cut with two edges."

The English visitor was impressed by the "regularity and decorum" of a wedding ceremony and by "the uninterrupted harmony that seemed to prevail in this happy society." He considered that the Batswana had "in every respect passed the boundary which divides the savage from the civilized state of society." The Europeans bought cattle with their beads and left "this friendly and hospitable people" with much regret. They were invited by the chief to come back the following year.

Barrow never did go back. But in 1811 another Englishman, 29-year-old ex-schoolmaster William Burchell, reached Lattakoo and proceeded northward to the edge of the Kalahari Desert "solely for the purpose of acquiring knowledge." Trudging behind his oxwagon, he gathered plants, shot birds, and collected insects which he classified by his camp fire at night. Burchell's search for specimens also led him south to the confluence of the Vaal River with the Orange. In 1812, he again visited the Batswana capital which had been moved to a new location closer to the Kuruman River because of failing water supplies. It had been renamed New Lattakoo.

During his travels Burchell encountered many parties of Bushmen whose pitifully meager belongings and apparent melancholy moved him to tears. Burchell tried to cheer the Bushmen up by playing to them on his flute. In return, their leader played an air on his own musical instrument, a kind of bow. Despite the hardship of the Bushmen's lives, they were skilled and enthusiastic dancers, and had created in their cave paintings some of the finest primitive art in the world.

Burchell succeeded in his aim of acquiring knowledge, and brought back the skins of 80 different species of mammal, 265 species of bird, some quite new to science, over 500 drawings, and a vast number of botanical specimens. He was the first to describe a species of zebra which is named after him.

Above: Lattakoo from Burchell's book, *Travels in South Africa.* This view shows only about a third of the town. The large house on the left is that of the youngest wife of the chief's uncle.

Right: Burchell's Zebra. The stripes of this species are dark brown, often with a shadow stripe between. Other zebras have narrower black stripes against a white background.

Left: mission house and church at New Lattakoo, from Campbell's book. From this center the missionaries covered a large area, teaching and preaching, and trying to persuade the tribes to stop fighting and live peaceably together.

Below: giraffes and zebras running. Giraffes are strange-looking animals, and early naturalists considered the reports of them to be pure fiction.

Early Missionaries

5

Many of the early explorers of tropical Africa were primarily prospectors, ivory hunters, traders, botanists, even shipwrecked sailors. What they discovered was often of great importance but, unlike Bruce, their first objective was not exploration for its own sake. Among the explorers who came to Africa for some purpose other than exploration none were more important than the Christian missionaries. One of the first missionaries sent to South Africa was a Presbyterian minister, John Campbell. He was sent out by the London Missionary Society in 1812 to the Batswana capital at New Lattakoo.

Nine elders received him, their faces painted red and their hair dusted with blue powder. One of them "had as noble an appearance as any person I recollect to have seen anywhere." Campbell found the elders' opinions, however, less encouraging. When he asked them why they thought man had been created, they simply replied: "To go on plundering expeditions against other people."

Seeking new souls to win to the Gospel, Campbell often traveled with a cavalcade of wagons, oxen, dogs, sheep, and Hottentot guides. On one trip eastward from New Lattakoo Campbell and another minister, James Read, reached the Hartz River and followed it south to its confluence with the Vaal. There were "sea cows" (hippopotamuses) in the river, giraffe in the bush, and in the valleys an immense profusion of many kinds of antelope grazing, as yet, in peace and safety from man, except for occasional small groups of wandering Bushmen. Campbell was elated by the reflection that "no European eye had ever surveyed these plains, and mountains, and rivers, and that I was ten thousand miles from home."

In 1820, the enthusiastic Campbell explored north of the Vaal to seek out Bantu tribes hitherto known to Europeans only by rumor. On the way his party discovered one of the sources of the Limpopo River, the large river which runs along the border of South Africa with Botswana and Rhodesia and then down through Mozambique into the Indian Ocean.

Campbell was aiming for the country of the Hurutshe, a branch of the Tswana people, living roughly between modern Pretoria and the Botswana border. The Hurutshe's capital was at Kaditshwene near the modern city of Mafeking. After weeks of jolting in wagons over hills and plains Campbell's party came to a range where many footpaths converged to make a sort of highway. Then came the fields of millet and then "part of the long-desired city was seen standing on top of one of the highest hills in that part of Africa." People poured out of the town to see the wagons, which amazed and terrified them. In the town "the sight of white men threw them into fits of convulsive laughter; they screamed, and . . . fled."

But the regent, who was governing the country for a young king, made them welcome. White men he had heard of, if not seen. Campbell was deeply impressed by the size, neatness, and organization of this African town. He estimated the population at 16,000. "They are indeed an ingenious people. Every part of their houses and yards is kept very clean. They smelt both iron and copper. . . . The chief employments of the men are dressing skins and making cloaks in public places."

The missionaries presented the regent with their presents: a mirror, some red handkerchiefs, a red nightcap, scissors, and various trinkets. The regent put on the nightcap but was not interested in the other presents. Later Campbell realized that he would have much preferred beads, "the only circulating money or medium in the interior of South Africa." The regent and his councilors knew little of the world more distant than five or six days' journey, and displayed no curiosity. They were, however, enthralled by a candle, and "astonished that the flame continued for so long. They had long discussions concerning it, which I much wished to have understood."

Campbell preached the Gospel to them but found, to his regret, that "the number who attended to witness our mode of taking dinner was at least three times greater than attended the worship in the morning." He recorded that the townspeople boiled their tobacco leaves before smoking them, made ivory whistles, copper earrings, iron awls and knives, and stone pipes. When they were dressed in their best, they wore "a kind of white turban made from the skin of wild hogs." Despite the fact that Campbell preached the Gospel of peace, he left the Hurutshe making preparations for a raid on a neighboring tribe.

When Campbell returned to the mission at Lattakoo, he was met by Robert Moffat, a fellow Scot, a newly arrived recruit to the service of the London Missionary Society. Born in 1795, Moffat had been a gardener before he took up missionary work. He was to remain 50 years among the Batswana peoples. During those years he built the Batswana mission, which he moved to Kuruman, into a thriving community, translated the entire Bible into the Batswana language, and raised a family of 10.

Within a decade after Campbell's visit to Kaditshwene, a scourge of death and destruction fell on the prosperous countryside he had so admired. Kaditshwene and other large towns of the Hurutshe and other Bantu tribes in the region of the Limpopo and Vaal were laid waste and the region depopulated. This holocaust was caused by tribal wars, as successive waves of Bantus pushed along the east coast toward southern Africa. In Natal on the east coast of southern Africa, Chaka, warrior king of the Zulus, had organized the Zulu

Below: contemporary drawing of John Campbell by W. T. Strutt, a fellow minister. When Campbell went to South Africa, the secretary of the London Missionary Society told him that as well as working for their greatest object, the conversion of the heathen, missionaries materially contributed to general science, and particularly to geographical knowledge.

Yours truly

John Campbell.

Right: Zulu necklace and armlet of beads, brought from South Africa in 1864. In Africa beads have always been prized as currency and for adornment, with even the warriors wearing them.

Below: a map from John Campbell's book, with his routes, showing the types of country, sources of water, and tribal areas. He records with amusement that "on one occasion he advised the Bush people, who were extremely dirty, to wash themselves sometimes. They were much diverted with the idea of washing, but seemed unable to comprehend what end could be answered by it."

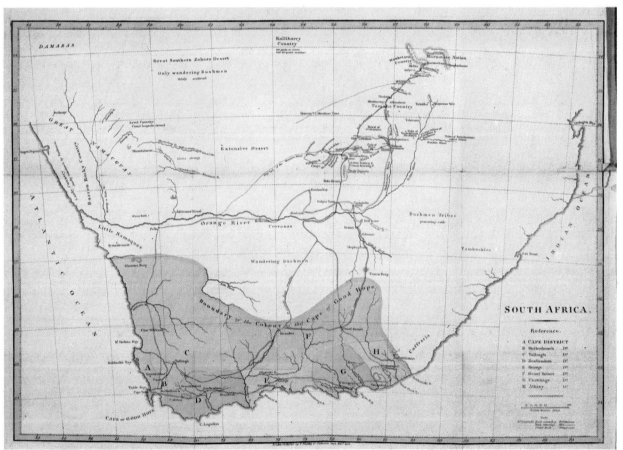

Above: portrait of Robert Moffat by John Baxter, published in 1843. The scene shows the country on the banks of the Kuruman River, a small tributary of the Orange. Moffat's daughter married David Livingstone.

warriors into highly disciplined regiments called *impis*. Chaka drilled his impis in new tactics, based on mass attacks with the short stabbing spear, the assagai. The Zulu impis quickly conquered the tribes between Natal's Drakensberg Mountains and the sea. One of Chaka's chiefs, Mzilikazi, fell into royal disfavor. Rather than face death, which was the only penalty Chaka ever exacted, Mzilikazi and his impis of two or three hundred warriors crossed the Drakensberg into the eastern Transvaal. Now Mzilikazi, who was as proud and warlike as Chaka, proceeded to conquer the tribes of the interior and lay waste their towns.

Zulu tactics worked just as well for Mzilikazi as they had for Chaka. The victorious Mzilikazi took the women of the defeated tribes as wives for himself and his men, and pressed the surviving warriors into his regiments. By 1830, Mzilikazi's warriors, who now numbered more than 1,000 and called themselves the Matabele, were raiding westward into Batswana country and northward into Rhodesia. Few tribes could stand before the well-drilled impis of the Matabele armed with their assagais and throwing clubs.

Mzilikazi realized that the white men who traveled about in

"moving houses" (as he called their wagons), with firearms and horses, were a greater threat to him than all Chaka's Zulu regiments had been. In 1829, he sent two *indunas* (chiefs who commanded impis) to Moffat's mission station at Kuruman to make contact and spy out the land. Moffat made the chiefs welcome, and decided to escort them on their return journey in order to prevent the revenge-seeking Batswana from attacking them on the way. They headed northeast in wagons toward Mzilikazi's kraal north of the Limpopo. When they crossed the Vaal into Hurutshe territory, Moffat found the once-prosperous villages and millet fields in ruins. "Where thousands once made the country alive . . . the extirpating invasions of the Matabele had left to beasts of prey the undisputed rights of these lovely woodland glens."

Lions had, in fact, become so numerous and bold that they had driven the surviving people literally into the trees. Moffat tells how he climbed one of these trees "by the notched trunk, and found no less than 17 aerial abodes. On reaching the topmost hut, about 30 feet from the ground, I entered, and sat down. Its only furniture was the hay which covered the floor, a spear, a spoon, and

Above: the interior of Sinosee's house, drawn by John Campbell. Sinosee was a captain of a district of the city of Kaditshwene, and his house was considered appropriately elegant for his official position.

217

W.C Harris.

a bowl full of locusts." Of Kaditshwene and the other large Hurutshe towns Campbell had previously seen "nothing now remained but dilapidated walls, heaps of stone, and . . . human skulls."

At last Moffat's wagons reached the Limpopo. Three more days' hard travel brought them to the great chief's kraal, which was located near the river south of modern Pretoria. To greet the whites and his safely returned indunas—and possibly to impress Moffat— Mzilikazi turned out his regiments for a war dance. Each warrior held a painted oxhide shield as tall as himself and wore a tossing headdress of ostrich feathers. Moffat was impressed. "They must conquer or die, and if one returns without his spear or shield, at the frown of his sovereign he is instantly dispatched."

Moffat spent 10 days at Mzilikazi's kraal being feasted and treated like a fellow king. "You have made my heart as white as milk," the warrior king told the missionary. "I cease not to wonder at the love of a stranger. You fed me when I was hungry; you carried me in your bosom, your arm shielded me from my enemies." Moffat replied that he had done the chief no such service. Mzilikazi pointed to his two indunas. On his orders, they had put themselves in the white man's power. Moffat had fed, clothed, and protected them from the Batswana. "You did it unto me," said the chief.

Despite Mzilikazi's pride, ferocity, and delight in bloodshed and in the fleshly pleasures—he had over 100 wives—the man of war and the man of God struck up an odd and enduring friendship. Moffat was to return several times to the Matabele kraal and to try, without success, to convert Mzilikazi to the cause of peace and humility.

The missionary made such a favorable impression that Mzilikazi

W. C. Harris.

Left: Harris' wagon train leaving Mosega. He prepared for his journey by purchasing 2 horses and a comfortable traveling wagon, 17 feet long, with a span of 12 little oxen.

used him as a sort of filter through which all Europeans who wished to visit him had to pass. Seven years after Moffat's first visit a British army officer, Sir William Cornwallis Harris, arrived at Kuruman, where the mission had been moved from New Lattakoo. His aim was to get Mzilikazi's permission to hunt elephants in Matabele country and return by the Vaal River.

On September 29, 1836, Harris with Moffat's introduction headed for Matabeleland with a companion, Richard Williamson, several wagons, and some Hottentots. Scattered remnants of various tribes despoiled by Mzilikazi surrounded their camps begging for meat and tobacco. En route to the Vaal the hunters saw wild animals in such abundance that "the landscape literally presented the appearance of a moving mass of game." Harris "left the ground strewed with the slain. Still unsatisfied, I could not resist the temptation of mixing with the fugitives, loading and firing, until my jaded horse exhibited symptoms of distress." Harris, who wrote the first book on big game hunting in Africa, was one of the "itinerant butchers."

In the region near South Africa's Magaliesberg Mountains, Harris came upon a sight which, he wrote, "beggars all description. The whole face of the landscape was actually covered by wild elephants— every height and green knoll was dotted over with groups of them,

Below: hunting the wild elephant, from Harris' book, *Wild Sports of Africa.* From his boyhood, Harris reports, he was "taxed by the facetious with 'shooting madness'," but he thought it a most delightful mania.

HUNTING THE WILD ELEPHANT

whilst the bottom of the glen exhibited a dense sable [dark] living mass . . . a picture at once soul-stirring and sublime." Harris and his companions lost no time in discharging broadsides into a herd whose members "all proved to be ladies, and most of them mothers, followed by their little old-fashioned calves." They found a calf which "ran round its mother's corpse piping sorrowfully, and vainly attempting to raise her with its tiny trunk." When their wagons could hold no more ivory the hunters were "reluctantly compelled to leave the ground strewed with that valuable commodity."

Harris' most thrilling moment came when he counted 32 giraffes peacefully browsing on acacia leaves. Harris, who was obviously not a marksman, picked a large bull and fired 17 shots into it before he killed the "towering giraffe." Harris threw his hat into the air and killed three more giraffes next day, and at least two out of every group they encountered thereafter.

The two Englishmen hunted north to a tributary of the Limpopo River, and then back to the Magaliesberg, where they were met by one of Mzilikazi's indunas who conducted them to the king.

Harris found Mzilikazi "of dignified and reserved manner; the searching quickness of his eye, the point of his questions, and the extreme caution of his replies, stamping him at once as a man capable of ruling the wild and sanguinary spirits by which he was surrounded." At first the chief refused to give Harris permission to take the Vaal route. But after the conversational ice was broken and

Left: copy in his own handwriting of the oath taken by David Livingstone when admitted to the medical profession. The point of his medical studies had always been to prepare him for becoming a medical missionary.

Mzilikazi was one day "reclining on Williamson's bed, his little dark eyes moving with restless activity in every direction," he spotted a chest full of beads. In a flash he had thrust both arms into the contents. "Never shall I forget the triumphant expression of his face at that moment," said Harris. In exchange for all the beads plus a tent, Harris won the permission he sought. Mzilikazi insisted also on being given a pair of shoes, and sent after the expedition when it had left for more wax candles.

Although Harris' main interest was in killing and collecting trophies, much of the territory he covered had not been seen before by Europeans. Thus he too helped fill in the map. On his way to the Vaal Harris discovered the source of the Mariqua River, one of the headwaters of the Limpopo. Many hippopotamuses fell to his musket. A careful keeper of records that now give us a picture of South African wildlife as it once was, Harris noted that "the host of rhinoceroses that daily exhibited themselves almost exceeded belief . . . an ugly head might be seen protruding from every bush." On their way south to Kuruman Harris made sure that the innumerable elephants "browsing in indolent security" were indolent no longer, but in flight screaming with fear and pain. Harris' greatest triumph was to shoot an antelope of a previously unrecorded species—the splendid sable antelope. This trophy, with sweeping horns three feet long, ended up in the British Museum.

Robert Moffat had been in charge of the mission at Kuruman for

Above: lions resting. Lions often hunt at night, and spend the day lying in the shade of rocks and trees. When they rouse themselves at dusk, their roar warns all animals around that they are starting their nightly hunt. Early travelers reported that other animals feared lions instinctively, and were aware of them at a distance, even when the lions had not roared.

Above: the Livingstone family in 1857. The children are (left to right) Oswell, born 1851, Thomas, born 1849, Agnes, born 1847, and Robert, born 1846. David Livingstone was aware of the hardships his family had to endure, and on April 30, 1851, wrote, "I look at my little ones and ask shall I return with this or that one alive."

20 years when he was joined by a young Scottish assistant—dark, bony, spare as whipcord, with piercing, intense brown eyes. This lean young man was David Livingstone, the greatest of Africa's explorers. "Livingstone stood middlesized," wrote a contemporary, "firm upon his feet, light in the undertrunk, round and full in the chest. His face wore at all times the strongly marked lines of potent will." That will was to drive him to feats of almost unbelievable endurance.

David Livingstone was born near Glasgow on March 19, 1813. The Livingstone family was poor, and at the age of 10 David went to work in a cotton mill. The boy made good use of his 14-hour day, 6-day week. At work he read "everything I could lay my hands on except novels . . . placing the book on a portion of the spinning jenny, so that I could catch sentence after sentence as I went by." In this way he taught himself Greek, Latin, and mathematics, and soon qualified to study medicine and divinity at a Glasgow college.

A deep and simple religious faith formed the basis of David Livingstone's character. After gaining his medical degree he became connected with the London Missionary Society and was ordained.

In 1840, the 27-year-old missionary doctor arrived in Cape Town. A 700-mile journey by oxwagon from the coast took him to Kuru-

man. From Kuruman he set out northward with two African converts and two ox-drivers. "In order to obtain an accurate knowledge of the language, I cut myself off from all European society for about six months, and gained by this ordeal an insight into the habits, ways of thinking, laws, and language of the Botswana [Batswana] people which proved of incalculable advantage in my intercourse with them ever since." In 1843, Livingstone opened a new mission station at Kolobeng, 220 miles north of Kuruman. Some months later he was severely mauled by a wounded lion. So bad was the wound that he was never able to raise his left arm above his shoulder.

Livingstone returned to Kuruman to recover. During his convalescence, he met and fell in love with Robert Moffat's eldest daughter Mary. They were married in 1845. "She was," wrote Livingstone, "a little, thick, blackhaired girl, sturdy, and all I ask."

Livingstone's purpose in going to Africa had been to spread the word of God among the African people. Six years after the opening of his mission station in Kolobeng he felt that the time had come to go even farther afield. North of Kolobeng lay 300 miles of arid waste, the Kalahari Desert. No European had as yet crossed the Kalahari, and a Batswana chief told Livingstone: "It is utterly im-

Above: the Kalahari Desert in the dry season, showing a dried-up salt pan. When Livingstone first crossed the desert, he saw one of these pans, which "burst upon our view, the setting sun was casting a beautiful blue haze over the white incrustations." He thought that he had found the water he so desperately needed.

possible even for us black men." At the northern edge of the desert
lay Lake Ngami, known by repute to Europeans but never seen by
one, although several parties had attempted to reach it. Beyond the
lake dwelt the Makololo, a Batswana tribe, ruled over by a respected
chief, Sebituane. Livingstone planned to contact Sebituane and seek
his permission to open a mission among the Makololo.

On June 1, 1849, Livingstone with two companions, Cotton
Oswell and Mungo Murray, and a guide set out from Kolobeng for
Lake Ngami. They faced a journey of about 600 miles. Soon they
found themselves struggling through a sea of soft white sand.

Above: the Zambezi River at Tete. The river is 1,600 miles long, the fourth longest in Africa. It was described to Livingstone by the Barotse tribe, who told him "when you look up the river the sun rises on one chief and sets on the other," to express its unimaginable size.

Wagons sank to the wheel hubs, and at the day's end there was nothing for the oxen but "grass so dry as to crumble into powder in the hands; so the poor brutes stood wearily chewing, and lowing painfully at the smell of our water in the wagons." Their guide lost his way, and all would have perished had not Oswell galloped after what he thought was a lion, to find it was a Bushman woman running away. She led them to a pool, and they were saved. They came to a hitherto unknown river, the Zouga (now Botletle), and followed it for 100 miles. Then, in a single wagon, they left the Zouga to make a 12-day dash across the desert to the lake.

The Makololo lived another 200 miles to the north. The three men felt they could never make it and returned to Kolobeng. The following year Livingstone took his pregnant wife and three small children with him to recross the desert and seek out the chief. They followed the Zouga "with great labour, having to cut down trees to allow the wagons to pass," and losing oxen which fell into pits dug by local tribesmen to trap game. Then they struck an even deadlier obstacle: the tsetse fly, carrier of the parasites which cause sleeping sickness. Abandoning the river bank, they took to the desert and found the lake. The party, including Mary Livingstone and her children, became so ill with malaria that they could not go on. Back in Kolobeng Mary's fourth baby was born and, not surprisingly, soon died. She herself was gravely ill.

"I mean to follow a useful motto," Livingstone wrote soon after, "and *try again*." So he did. The following year found Livingstone with Mary and the children headed once more across the wilderness of the Kalahari. This time they took a different route and their hardships were even more severe. Their staunch friend Cotton Oswell went with them and paid most of the expenses. He was a crack shot and kept them in meat whenever there was anything to shoot, but Livingstone's journals tell that in places there was nothing but "low scrub in deep sand: not a bird or insect enlivened that landscape; it was without exception the most uninviting prospect I ever beheld."

Once again their guide lost his way and this time he made off completely. A few days later they ran out of water, and the Livingstones had to face the prospect of their three children "perishing before our eyes." Only just in time did one of the drivers sent out to seek for water return "with a supply of that fluid of which we had never before felt the true value." Five days later they reached the

	Beutler	1	1752
	Paterson (with Gordon)	2a	1777
	Gordon (after leaving Paterson)	2A	1777
	Paterson (with Van Reenan)	2b	1778
	Paterson (with Van Reenan)	2c	1778–
	Paterson (with Gordon & Van Reenan)	2d	1779
	Gordon (after leaving Paterson)	2D	1779
	De Lacerda	3a	1787
		3b	1798

Mogadiscio

EQUATOR 0°

INDIAN

OCEAN

10°

MADAGASCAR 20°

TROPIC OF CAPRICORN

30°

Chobe (or Linyanti) River, a tributary of the Zambezi. Livingstone left his family and pushed on by canoe with Oswell 20 miles to meet the Makololo chief at last. He was "upon an island with all his principal men around him, and engaged in singing when we arrived."

Sebituane, "a gentleman in thought and manner," and the missionary took to each other at once. The Makololo was also a warrior of great renown, the only chief to have defeated one of Mzilikazi's impis. He welcomed Livingstone, and looked with favor on his project to set up a Christian mission in hope that it would help to put an end to tribal warfare and stop the spread of the slave trade, which was creeping inland. During Livingstone's stay with the Makololo, Sebituane fell sick and died. "I never felt so much grieved by the loss of a black man before," wrote the missionary, unconsciously revealing the great gap between the two races.

After the burial Livingstone and Oswell traveled 130 miles to the northeast and toward the end of June, 1851, they were rewarded by the discovery of a great river flowing eastward. It could only be the Zambezi. "This was an important point," wrote Livingstone later, "for this river was not previously known to exist there at all."

On the Zambezi, Livingstone discovered something even more important to him than a great river—his true vocation. In Oswell's words: "He suddenly announced his intention of going down to the west coast. We were about 1,800 miles off it. To my reiterated objection that it would be impossible—'I'm going down. I mean to go down,' was the only answer." In his own journal the explorer put it more soberly. "I at once resolved to save my family from exposure to this unhealthy region by sending them home to England, and to return alone, with a view to exploring the country in search of a healthy district that might prove a centre of civilization, and to open up by the interior a path to either the east or west coast."

Oswell and Livingstone rejoined Mary and the children on the Chobe and harnessed the oxen for the long journey home to Kolobeng. First they had to cross the desert to the Zouga, where Livingstone insisted on a halt. Oswell protested, but Livingstone refused to give his reasons. "What's the matter?" Oswell insisted. "Oh, nothing . . . Mrs. L. had a little son last night." It was her fifth child. He lived and thrived and was named Oswell. After six months of oxwagon-travel they reached Cape Town. In April, 1852, Mary and her brood sailed for Britain, leaving her husband to pursue his African destiny.

Livingstone and the Zambezi

6

Left: David Livingstone in 1864, by General Need. Livingstone's self-reliant determination impressed all who met him. As a friend, Cotton Oswell, said, "One trait in his character was to do exactly what he set his mind on . . . without feeling himself bound to give any reason."

Below: Livingstone's sextant, used in mapping much of southern Africa.

David Livingstone was to make three more major journeys. The first of these began at Cape Town in June, 1852, and took four years. Once again he crossed the Kalahari to Linyanti, the town of the Makololo in what is now northern Botswana. He found that Sekeletu, the 18-year-old Makololo chief who had succeeded Sebituane, was every bit as friendly as his father. The young chief provided 27 men, whose loyalty and fortitude proved outstanding, and canoes for the journey up the Zambezi. The Makololo became, and remained, Livingstone's favorite African people.

His aim was simple but audacious. He would follow the Zambezi to its sources, continue to the west coast, turn around, rejoin the river and follow it down to its mouth near the Portuguese city of Quelimane in Mozambique on the Mozambique Channel.

The journey across the continent would be over 3,000 miles, and the total distance covered nearly 5,000. For weapons Livingstone had three muskets and a shotgun, on which the expedition must depend for food. For trading, the Makololo carried 20 pounds of beads. For comfort, Livingstone had a small tent and one spare suit of clothes tied in a bag. His most precious possessions were scientific instruments for finding his position and accurately locating discoveries, a journal for recording his many detailed observations, and a magic lantern. The last item he used to illustrate, with Biblical scenes, the Christian message that he delivered at every stop to anyone who would come to listen. When he set off from Linyanti the magic lantern was left with one of Sekeletu's wives for safe keeping.

Livingstone and the Makololo left Linyanti in January, 1854. Trouble started at once. A severe attack of malaria prostrated the missionary. Then there were drenching rains, unpopulated country, and no game. Livingstone's small tent was reduced to shreds and he slept on the sodden ground. Either he trudged on foot, or, when the path allowed it, rode on the back of an ox. But as he later wrote "vertigo produced by frequent fevers made it as much as I could do to stick on my ox." When they at last reached inhabited regions, local chiefs extorted what little they had, including even Livingstone's tattered shirts, and the copper bangles on the Makololos' arms.

After tracing the Zambezi to its limits and crossing the divide —where the streams began to drain toward the Atlantic—the explorers were in Portuguese territory (modern Angola) and in touch with the slave trade. Livingstone was horrified when chiefs demanded men as well as possessions from him—wrongly assuming the Makololo with him to be slaves. At last, sick and exhausted, the party reached the coast at Luanda. It was now May. In four months they had covered over 1,500 miles through previously unexplored and unmapped country.

The Portuguese fed, sheltered, and re-equipped the expedition generously and without thought of payment. The Archbishop of Luanda, at his own expense, gave the Makololo clothing, blankets, and presents to take to their chief, including a horse with saddle and bridle, and the ornate full-dress uniform of a Portuguese colonel. Sailors from a British cruiser that was visiting Luanda made Livingstone a new tent.

Livingstone lingered on the coast to rest and explore, and take notes on the slave trade. In September the little expedition started back toward the headwaters of the Zambezi, taking a route inland along the Cuanza River. "I sit on my ox and think," Livingstone wrote. He thought sadly of the contrast between nature's beauty and innocence and the cruelties and ignorance of men. "The more intimately I become acquainted with barbarism, the more disgusting does heathenism become. It is inconceivably vile."

The return was no easier than the first leg. At one point rheumatic fever forced Livingstone to lie delirious for eight days on sodden ground in pouring rain. After nearly a year of slogging through the wilderness, the missionary and his Makololo finally struggled back to Linyanti and gave Sekeletu the colonel's uniform. The horse had died and so had Livingstone's ox, Sinbad.

Less than a month later Livingstone set off again with a larger retinue of Makololo volunteers, this time to follow the Zambezi downstream. On November 17, 1855, they came to the great falls called "smoke that thunders" by the Africans but named by Livingstone the Victoria Falls for the Queen of England. "It had never before been seen by European eyes; but scenes so lovely must have been gazed upon by angels in their flight."

Continuing eastward, the men circled the Quebrabasa Rapids without seeing them. Six months later they were still fighting their way downstream. By this time they had once again run out of food and had to scour the bush for roots and honey. Eight miles from the Portuguese Zambezi outpost at Tete they could go no farther.

Above: riding an ox. Livingstone did much of his traveling on oxback. Whether from lack of skill or because the ox is by nature a recalcitrant mount, he usually had a rough ride.

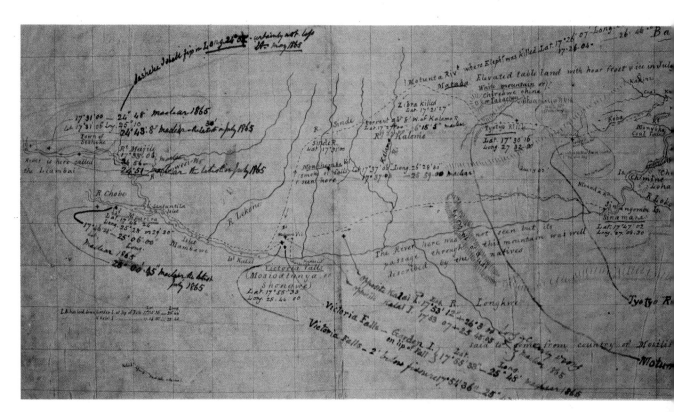

Livingstone and the Makololo would have perished almost in sight of their goal had word not been sent down to the Portuguese commandant, who sent men out with a litter and "the most refreshing breakfast I ever partook of." The expedition reached Quelimane on May 20, 1856, almost exactly four years after Livingstone's departure from Cape Town. He had become the first known European to walk across the continent.

When news of his exploits reached England, a ship of the Royal Navy was sent to bring him home. Livingstone left his Makololo companions at Tete, promising to be back in three months' time to restore them to their homes in Linyanti. In fact, it was to be four years before they reached home.

In England, fame, unsought and undesired, took David Livingstone by surprise. "They laud me till I shut my eyes," he wrote. The cities of London and Edinburgh conferred honors upon him. Queen Victoria received him at court. Most flattering of all, he was elected a Fellow of the Royal Geographical Society. Despite all this—"It does not look as if I reached the goal," he wrote. "I view the end of the geographical feat as the beginning of missionary enterprise." In an address at Cambridge University he concluded: "I beg to direct your attention to Africa . . . which is now open. Do not let it be shut again! I go back to Africa to try to make an open path for commerce and for Christianity."

Livingstone returned to Africa as British consul at Quelimane, commissioned "to make the Zambezi a path for commerce into the interior and thus end the slave trade." He had become convinced

Right: Victoria Falls. The Africans called the falls "smoke that thunders" but Livingstone renamed them after the Queen of England. He calculated that "the depth down which the river leaps without a break is 310 feet, or, if I remember correctly, double the depth of Niagara." He still found the scene the most remarkable in the world, and his measurements have since been proved nearly accurate.

Above: the Murchison Cataracts. This stretch of tumbling water—33 miles long—on the Shire River was called by the local people *Mamvera,* and renamed by Livingstone. Above the cataracts, the river flows smoothly from Lake Nyasa in Malawi, now renamed Lake Malawi.

that the trader must precede the evangelist. The British government voted £5,000 (about $50,000 in today's currency) to fit out an expedition which was to proceed up the Zambezi in a steam launch, the *Ma-Robert*—the Africans' name for Mary Livingstone. The expedition, backed by the government and the Royal Geographical Society, included a geologist, a botanist, an artist, and a "moral agent," Livingstone's brother Charles. It was with high hopes that the party reached the mouth of the Zambezi in May, 1858, and proceeded upstream in the launch to establish a base about 80 miles inland at Shupanga, just below the junction of the Zambezi with the Shire River.

In August, 1858, they steamed up the river to Tete and came to the foot of the Quebrabasa Rapids beyond. These were the rapids Livingstone had circled on his way to Quelimane two years before. He had been completely misinformed about their formidable size and extent, and thought a channel for the launch could be blasted through the rocks. Exploring the rapids on foot, he and one of his party, John Kirk, jumping like goats from boulder to boulder with hands and feet blistered by the sun-scorched rocks, had "as tough a bit of travel as they ever had in Africa." It was clear that the *Ma-Robert* would never get through.

This was a bitter blow, but instead of dwelling on it Livingstone turned his attention to the Shire River whose source had not been accurately located and mapped. In January, 1859, the Livingstone expedition started up the Shire River in the *Ma-Robert.* First they were harassed by hostile warriors. Then about 200 miles upstream the *Ma-Robert* was again turned back by rapids and returned to Tete.

Livingstone and three companions set out on foot to the Shire Highlands in the northeast. On April 18, 1859 amid magnificent scenery, with 8,000-feet-high mountain peaks and rich vegetation, he discovered Lake Shirwa in modern Malawi. Ahead, said his guides, lay a great water, "the lake of stars," Lake Nyasa. Yet again

233

Above: some of Livingstone's notes. He would write his observations on any paper available—sometimes on sheets of old newspaper or magazine pages, or on little booklets of cutoff margins from books, as on the right. Later he transcribed his notes carefully into a locked diary.

Livingstone and his party returned to Tete, but later in the same year they returned northeast.

A party of 4 Europeans, 36 Makololo, and 2 guides were hauled up the Shire River to the rapids in the *Ma-Robert*. On August 28, 1859, they struck out overland for the discovery of Lake Nyasa, now also known as Lake Malawi. "On a shoulder of Mount Milange [Mlanje] we slept under the trees; by early dawn our camp was in motion. After a cup of coffee and a bit of biscuit, we were on the way. The air was deliciously cool. . . ."

In the valleys were fresh green pastures, thriving crops, and prosperous villages not yet laid waste by the slavers. The women wore large ivory or wooden rings in their upper lips. "It was frightfully ugly," Livingstone noted, "to see the upper lip projecting two inches beyond the tip of the nose . . . the exposed teeth show how carefully they have been chipped to look like those of a cat or crocodile." The men "brew large quantities of beer, and like it well."

"We discovered Lake Nyasa a little before noon on September 16, 1859." They discovered something else as well—one of the principal slave routes from the interior to the coast. At a lakeside village they slept comfortably among the roots of an enormous banyan tree, while an Arab slave-party was encamped nearby. Some of the slavers came and offered to sell the explorers several children. "We might have released these slaves, but did not know what to do with

them afterwards . . . the chiefs [of the region] sell their own people."
The slavers paid 4 yards of cloth for a man, 3 for a woman, and 2
for a child. Livingstone reckoned that only 1 in 10 of the slaves
would live to reach the slave-market in Zanzibar. He felt that a
single well-armed vessel on the lake could put an end to the whole
business.

To end slavery now became Livingstone's overriding aim. He sent
an engineer to England to supervise the building of a new vessel that
could be taken to pieces, carried past the cataracts on the Shire, and
reassembled on Lake Nyasa, "so entirely to change the wretched
system of the trade."

Meanwhile he had to redeem his promise to the Makololo who
were still at Tete. With John Kirk, his brother Charles, and those
Makololo who wanted to go, Livingstone set out to walk up the
Zambezi to Linyanti. They were constantly sick with fever and
always hungry, living on what they could find. At one point the
Makololo shot an elephant. They buried one of its feet in hot ashes,
kept a fire alight on top of it all night and the group "had the foot
thus cooked for breakfast next morning, and found it delicious; it
is a whitish mass, slightly gelatinous, and sweet, like marrow."

After 10 weeks of hardship they again reached the Victoria Falls
on August 9, 1860. Livingstone's party went on to Sekeletu's kraal.
There they found the young chief sick with leprosy. The travelers
applied what remedies they could, recovered boxes of medicines,
papers, and the magic lantern that had been kept safe for seven
years. They returned to Tete on November 23, 1860.

After the publication of Livingstone's *Expedition to the Zambezi,*
a Portuguese scholar advanced arguments to refute Livingstone's
claims to be the first to explore the river. It is possible that the Portuguese had done more exploration than they are credited with. They
had been on the Zambezi since the early 1500's and had certainly
explored some way in from the river's mouth. In 1798 the governor
of the rivers of Sena, Francisco Lacerda, had visited a chief known as
Kazembe and died in his kingdom. Jesuit and Dominican missionaries had gone inland from Tete but no direct records survived of
their journeys, and in 1831–1832 two Portuguese majors, Jose Correia
Monteiro and Antonio Pedroso Gamitto, had traveled through
Kazembe's kingdom. However, the Portuguese of Mozambique
were implicated in the slave trade and it is possible that Livingstone's

Above: Arab dhow on Lake Nyasa
(Lake Malawi). In Livingstone's time,
dhows looking much like this carried
cargoes of slaves across the lake.

Above: a gang of captives met at Mbame's on their way to Tete, from Livingstone's *Expedition to the Zambezi*. Livingstone wrote that the black drivers, armed with muskets, seemed to feel that "they were doing a very noble thing, and might proudly march with an air of triumph."

Below: Livingstone's magic lantern, a primitive slide projector which he used when delivering his Gospel message. Whether his audiences fully understood what he was saying is questionable, but they certainly thought that the lantern was powerful magic.

hatred of the trade and all it involved led him to underestimate or disregard the Portuguese achievements.

Soon after Livingstone's return to Tete the new steam vessel, the *Pioneer,* arrived in sections in two naval cruisers. The cruisers also brought a party of missionaries, headed by the bishop of central Africa, Charles Mackenzie, bound for the Shire Highlands in response to Livingstone's appeal.

Livingstone was convinced that the only way to end the fast-spreading slave trade in east Africa was to "open" and develop the Shire Highlands for trade. But access to this fertile region lay up the Shire and Zambezi rivers which were under Portuguese control. The Portuguese, in his opinion, were too deeply involved in the trade themselves to have any heart for fighting it. Could the Ruvuma River, on the border of modern Tanzania and Mozambique, north of the Portuguese sphere of influence, be used as an alternative route to Lake Nyasa? To find the answer the *Pioneer* was navigated 30 miles up the Ruvuma, but at that point the water became too shallow to go farther. The boat was sent down the coast to the Zambezi and up the Shire while the party set out on foot to select a site for the mission that was to be the first step in ending the trade in human chattels.

The slave traders were devastating the country. On their way inland Livingstone's party saw a common sight. "A long line of manacled men, women, and children, came wending their way round the hill and into the valley." The black drivers were "blowing exultant notes out of their long tin horns." On seeing the party from the *Pioneer* they fled, and "knives were soon at work cutting the women and children loose. It was more difficult to cut the men adrift as each had his neck in the fork of a stout stick, kept in by an iron rod riveted at both ends." Luckily, the bishop had a saw and "one by one the men were sawed out into freedom."

Livingstone had a small naval launch, or gig, carried round the

Above: a cup and saucer from Mary Livingstone's best china. However well prepared she was for her rugged life—and as a missionary's daughter she knew what to expect of her life with Livingstone—her personal, dainty, domestic possessions must have been a source of great pleasure.

Below: Mary Livingstone's grave, under a baobab tree at Shupanga. Livingstone's reaction to her death was bewildered incredulity, and he said to her parents, "I have felt her to be so much part of myself that I felt less anxiety for her than ... worthless blackguards. She seemed so strong too."

cataracts to Lake Nyasa, whose bays and inlets he explored with his brother, Charles, and John Kirk. They saw the slave trade "going on at a terrible rate," with Arab dhows carrying captives across the lake. Livingstone had ordered yet another vessel to be built at his own expense, intending to put it on the lake to frighten away the slavers. At the end of 1861 he returned to the coast to supervise its arrival and assembly.

The naval vessel that brought out the new little steamer, the *Lady Nyasa,* also brought Mary Livingstone to rejoin her husband. It was a brief and tragic reunion. Malaria in its most malignant form struck down the whole party at Shupanga, and on April 27 Mary died. "I feel as if I had lost all heart now," Livingstone wrote. "I shall do my duty still, but with a darkened horizon. . . ."

The horizon remained dark until the end. Even the *Lady Nyasa* failed to get more than 156 miles up the Ruvuma. She was taken back and up the Shire to be carried in sections past the cataracts, where the slavers were busier than ever. "Dead bodies floated past us daily, and in the mornings the paddles had to be cleared of corpses caught by the floats during the night." The villages were sacked and abandoned. More members of the expedition died, including Bishop Mackenzie. Both John Kirk and Charles Livingstone became too ill to go any farther. They could hire no labor to cut a road round the cataracts and could buy no food. Armed slavers threatened them.

On July 2, 1863, a dispatch reached them from the British government recalling the expedition. Although it had failed in its main objectives, it had put Lake Nyasa and the Shire Highlands on the map, and exposed the horrors of the slave trade. "I beg to direct your attention to Africa," Livingstone had said. That attention had been well and truly directed.

South of Aswan
7

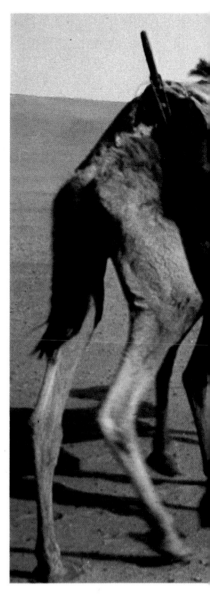

While one set of explorers probed northward from the Cape toward the equator, another set inched southward from Egypt up the Nile. Discovery of the source of that most ancient and mysterious of rivers would be the explorers' crown. James Bruce thought that he had won it, but he had discovered only part of the story—Africa still held the White Nile as its secret.

Egypt had been conquered by the Turks in 1517 and made into a province of the Ottoman Empire, but effective Turkish rule stopped at Aswan. In the 1800's in the region farther south all was confusion, lawlessness, and intermittent warfare, just as it had been in Bruce's day. To travelers the whole region was, in Livingstone's words, "closed." Nevertheless a few bold spirits ventured south of Aswan. The strangest of these men was Swiss, John Lewis Burckhardt. Born at Lausanne in 1784, he had studied at universities in Germany and then at Cambridge, England. At Cambridge, Burckhardt wore Turkish dress, studied astronomy, chemistry, mineralogy, and medicine, and trained himself for exploration by taking long walks, sleeping in the open, and living on vegetables and water.

An organization in London called the Association for Promoting the Discovery of the Interior Parts of Africa engaged this learned, conscientious, and eccentric young man to go in search of the sources of the Niger River in the west. He decided to start the quest from Cairo, by joining one of the caravans that set out at intervals to cross the Libyan Desert into Fezzan and continue to Timbuktu. To do this he had to pose as a Moslem and speak perfect Arabic. So before starting on his journey Burckhardt studied Arabic and lived for two and a half years in Syria "in the garb of a pauper." To master the language he translated Defoe's *Robinson Crusoe* into Arabic, classified and described 150 Arab tribes, and wrote on Bedouin customs.

In 1812, the 28-year-old Burckhardt, now calling himself Ibrahim ibn Abdullah, felt ready to join a caravan bound for Fezzan. But first, he thought he would visit Nubia, the northern area of the Sudan, south of Aswan. Early in 1813 he left Cairo with one servant, a donkey, and a total wealth of 60 Spanish dollars. In Nubia he was at the mercy of plundering tribesmen and only his obvious poverty protected him. He existed on a daily meal of millet porridge and a few dates, slept in the open among rocks, and rode all day under a broiling sun. At Dunqulah, Burckhardt could go no farther. Ahead lay only savage tribesmen and certain death. On his return he

Above: John Lewis Burckhardt. He said truly of himself, "I care very little about personal fatigue."

became the first European to see the magnificent rock temples of Abu Simbel in the area now flooded by the waters of Lake Nasser behind the Aswan Dam. (While the dam was under construction, the temples were cut into huge blocks and moved to higher ground.)

Back at Aswan there was still no news of caravans to West Africa, so Burckhardt decided to return upstream to Shandi and from there cross the mountains to the Red Sea, almost as Bruce had done. From the coast he would go on to Arabia and make the pilgrimage to Mecca, the holy city of Islam, a journey forbidden to non-Moslems on pain of death. His only possessions were a plate, two cups, a knife and spoon, a coffee roaster and mortar, and a few necessities such as a needle, thread, a comb, a blanket, and a packet of medicines. To this Burckhardt added a handful of trade goods: sugar, soap, nutmegs, razor blades, red caps, and wooden beads. Everything went into five leather bags. In his purse he had 50

Above: camels moving across the Sahara, one of the world's most unwelcoming areas. For centuries camels have crossed by traditional routes, stopping at oases and wells sometimes hundreds of miles apart. Even experienced Arabs thought four or five crossings in a lifetime the most that any single man could do.

Left: Abu Simbel, two ancient temples on the Nile, built during the reign of Ramses II in about 1280 B.C. The principal temple, discovered by Burckhardt, was hewn out of sandstone cliffs, and the hillside was recessed to form a background for four vast figures.

Below: Cairo today. Old Cairo was one of the most romantic cities of the Middle East, with narrow winding alleys, canals, and flat-roofed houses bleached to a pale cream color by the sun. Today much of it has been demolished to make way for skyscrapers and wide thoroughfares, but some of the old quarters remain.

Spanish dollars. Thus equipped, Ibrahim ibn Abdullah the Turk, otherwise John Lewis Burckhardt, set out on donkeyback for Shandi on the Upper Nile on March 1, 1814, in the company of 80 slave traders.

The journey was miserable. The Arabs hated him as a Turk and despised him as a poor man, and "not an hour passed without my receiving some insult, even from the meanest servants of these people." Ibrahim ibn Abdullah had no servant. While others rested he had to cut wood, light a fire, and cook his humble fare in the burning desert sun. To make his notes unobserved he had to ride ahead on his donkey and hide behind a rock with pen and ink until the caravan caught up. The constant glare injured his eyes.

Burckhardt never gave himself away and arrived safely at Shandi, a crossroads of trade routes leading north to Egypt, east to Arabia, south to Ethiopia, and west to Lake Chad. Its market offered camels and slaves, meat, milk, tobacco, and coffee. The shopkeepers in the bazaar hawked ostrich feathers, spices, charms, and saddles. The famous Dunqulah horses could be bought there, as could gold from Ethiopia, beads from Egypt, fine cloth from India, Arabian perfumes, Venetian glassware, German razors, and Italian paper—temptations from all over the world. But of all the goods in the market of Shandi none compared in value with the slaves. At least 5,000, Burckhardt estimated, were exported through Shandi every year. Girls under 15 fetched up to 25 Spanish dollars, boys were sold for 15. There was a brisk trade in children 4 or 5 years old.

For 16 Spanish dollars Burckhardt bought a slave boy as a companion, a strong camel for 11 dollars, and set out with a caravan bound for Suakin on the Red Sea. He reached it with 2 dollars left to get him to Arabia. He got there, wandered for a year, made the pilgrimage to Mecca and managed to get to Cairo in 1816. Sickness and poverty broke his health, and he was "chained to my carpet" by

chronic malaria and dysentery. There was still no Fezzan caravan. Burckhardt waited for 16 months, worrying lest his London employers should think he was shirking his duties. He had spent eight years preparing for a journey still as far away as ever. In October, 1817, at the age of 33, Burckhardt died. He had made no geographical discoveries. But he was the first European, since Bruce more than 40 years before, to bring back accurate reports from regions on the Upper Nile.

Egypt was ruled at this time by a man we would now call a military dictator. Mehemet Ali was an Albanian, a self-made man of ruthless ability who restructured the ramshackle Turkish administration of Egypt, and went on to conquer most of the Sudan. In 1824, he established a garrison at Khartoum, at the junction of the White and Blue Niles. In 1839, he sent an expedition under a Turkish officer, Selim Bimbashi, up river in sailing boats to seek the source of the White Nile. The boats found a way through the *sudd*—a mass of floating vegetable matter which blocks the river in some places—and got as far as present-day Bor. Two more expeditions followed, in

1841 and 1842, also under Selim. A German, Ferdinand Werne, went with the first of these and made scientific observations. The boats reached the latitude of Gondokoro, near modern Juba in the Republic of Sudan, but were halted by impassable rapids.

All Mehemet Ali's drive and ambition failed to settle the question of the White Nile's origin. In the end it was solved not by the logical course of following the river up to its source, but by striking across from the east coast to the center of the continent. Two German missionaries, Johann Ludwig Krapf and Johann Rebmann, made the first blazes on the trail. In 1844, Krapf established a mission at Rabai, near Mombasa on the coast of modern Kenya. Within a year he had translated the whole of the New Testament into Swahili and was ready to carry the news of the Gospel inland.

Krapf set out to minister to the people in a region known as Ukambani about 200 miles inland. He was shocked by the nakedness of the Kamba people. They in turn took alarm at his appearance. Later when he learned the Kamba tongue, Krapf found they had thought his shoes were made of iron, his hair was like an ape's, and his spectacles ridiculous. During his first visit to Kamba, Krapf's reading from the Gospel did not help matters, since the Kamba understood no Swahili and Krapf was ignorant of Kamba. But this was the first peaceable contact between Europeans and tribes of the interior of what is now Kenya, and it passed off amicably enough.

Krapf was joined at Rabai in 1846 by a fellow missionary Johann Rebmann. Evangelism in the soft, relaxing, and malarial airs of the coast of Zinj was uphill work. "All too often," wrote Rebmann, "heathenism showed itself in its most gloomy and immoral colors." There were festivals which "begin and end with gluttony and drunkenness." Few people came to Sunday services, and most of them drifted away before the end. "The indifference and dullness of the people toward the Gospel often depresses me."

The missionary preached for two years and then decided it was time to go off exploring on his own. He made for a large mountain he had heard of in the northwest. Drawing away from the humid and unhealthy coast, Rebmann and his bearers marched through uplands where "mountains and all hills; fruitful trees; beasts and all cattle; creeping things and flying things with varied melody of their song, praised their Creator with me." On May 11, 1848 he reported, "I fancied I saw the summit of one of them [the mountains] covered with a dazzlingly white cloud. My guide called the white which I saw merely 'Beredi,' cold; it was perfectly clear to me, however, that it could be nothing else but snow." Rebmann read the 111th Psalm, whose sixth verse perfectly expressed his feelings. "He hath showed his people the power of his works, that he may give them the heritage of the heathen." He was the first European to see Africa's highest mountain, the 19,340-foot Kilimanjaro with its flattened top and tablecloth of perpetual snow.

After a difficult march through Kilimanjaro's rugged stream-laced foothills, Rebmann met one of the chiefs of the Chagga tribe through

Above: Mehemet Ali in his palace at Alexandria in 1839, listening to a proposal for improving the passage across the Isthmus of Suez. He is shown in his informal costume.

Above: Mount Kilimanjaro, perpetually snowcapped, rising from the scorching plains. According to Krapf, the name might mean mountain of caravans (*kilima*—mountain, *jaro*—caravan), as it was a notable landmark for caravans.

whose territory he was passing. The Swahili-speaking Chagga chief could not understand how this white man and his small party of bearers had appeared from nowhere. Where was his retinue of soldiers and slaves? What weapons had he? "Only an umbrella," Rebmann replied, pointing it to the sky to indicate the whereabouts of his protector. The chief still could not understand how he had managed without a spear or shield.

Farther on, on the westward slopes of the mountain, lived a superior chief of the Chagga who had "thought of sending to the coast for some European to remain with him as one of his sorcerers, a class of whom he is extremely fond." Hearing that Rebmann was in his territory he sent warriors to fetch the missionary, who was thus able to reach the far side of the mountain. Rebmann found it cold, bleak, and wet. The chief's sorcerers killed a goat, mixed the contents of its stomach with various powders and plastered the mixture over Rebmann's face and chest with a cow's tail. In spite of this treatment, Rebmann managed to keep his temper and showed a

Bible to the chief, who pressed him to come back to teach his sons.

Rebmann returned a year later with a supply of trade goods, intending to continue into the unexplored regions beyond. The same chief extorted from him all his beads and calico. Then while still in the chief's village Rebmann was stricken with the explorer's afflictions, malaria and dysentery, and had to abandon his plan. When the explorer's plundered party at last started homeward with some of the bearers, stripped even of their clothing, they almost starved in the rain-soaked forest before limping back to Rabai 20 days later.

When Rebmann reported to his fellow Europeans at the Royal Geographical Society in London, they proved almost as spiteful as the Chagga chiefs. Instead of acclaiming his reports of Kilimanjaro as a great geographical discovery, they called him a liar. Desborough Cooley, an eminent member of the society who conducted researches in African geography from a London armchair, dismissed "his eternal snows as figments of imagination; no one has as yet witnessed their eternity . . . of reasonable evidence of perpetual snow there is not a tittle offered."

Krapf now took another turn. In November, 1849, he started out with 11 men to revisit the Kamba. The plains between their hilly country and the coast were dominated by roving bands of Masai warriors, and only large, well-armed caravans were thought to have a chance of survival. Moreover there was very little water on this route, which the slave and ivory traders avoided. Krapf put his

Below: Rebmann preaching at the mission house at Kisulutini, sketched by Richard Burton. Of these services Krapf said, "I endeavored to organize a regular congregation, which was joined every morning by some neighboring families and my servants."

faith in God, and hoped that the smallness of his party offered no threat and no prize. Seventeen days' strenuous marching brought them to the edge of Ukambani, at an altitude of over 5,000 feet.

The chief, Kivoi, received Krapf well and the chief's wives were delighted with the umbrella, which he had continually to open and shut. Kivoi invited the missionary to go with him to collect ivory from the banks of the Tana River. The chief said he had often seen a mountain which he called Kegnia (Kenya) and which "contained Kirira, a white substance producing very great cold." He invited Krapf to view it from a nearby hilltop, but the peak was covered by clouds. However, Krapf wrote that "on the 3rd of December, 1849, I could see the Kegnia most distinctly, and observed two large horns or pillars rising over an enormous mountain to the northwest of the Kilimanjaro, and covered with a white substance." Krapf had become the first European to sight the 17,058-foot Mount Kenya.

Although Krapf returned to Ukambani intending to found his mission and explore the "Kegnia" he never saw it again. He set off with Kivoi, but they were attacked by marauding warriors, possibly the Masai. The chief and the Kambas were killed. Krapf fled into the bush without food, water, compass, or a serviceable gun. He was reduced to eating ants and finally to chewing gun-powder. With great presence of mind, hiding by day and setting course at night by the stars, he eventually found his way back to Rabai.

The following year Krapf and a fellow missionary minister, J. J. Erhardt, explored the coast between Mombasa and Moçambique. In an area that is now Tanzania, they questioned ivory traders closely about a great inland sea, the Sea of Unyamwesi, of which Krapf had heard rumors in 1844. Beyond it, the traders said, was a range of mountains. Erhardt believed these might be the legendary Mountains of the Moon. Ptolemy, in his map made about 150 years after the birth of Christ, had placed these mountains near two lakes, from each of which a stream issued to unite and form the Nile. Back in Zanzibar, now part of Tanzania, Erhardt and Rebmann talked it over, and "at one and the same moment the problem flashed on both of us as solved by the simple proposition that, where geographical hypotheses had hitherto supposed an enormous mountainland, we must now look for an enormous valley and inland sea." Assuming that the valley and sea were blocked by snow-capped mountains to the south and opened to the north, two great problems fell into place: why the river should flow north rather than south, and the late summer flooding of the Nile thousands of miles to the north.

Krapf and Rebmann drew a map indicating the position of their two snow-capped mountains and the inland sea, and sent it to London. Some geographers, such as Cooley, derided both map and theory. Others supported it. Largely as a result of the controversy, the Royal Geographical Society raised money for an expedition whose leader was instructed to "penetrate inland from some place on the east coast and make the best of your way to the reputed great lake of the interior." Richard Burton was selected for the task.

Above: Mount Kenya from 15,000 feet. Although the beliefs of the people who live near this mountain are complex, and vary in detail, they have some features in common: that the supreme being placed a foundling father on the mountain, and that he and a woman produced the progenitors of the surrounding tribes, the Masai, Kikuyu, and Kamba. Some of these tribes moved away, but the Kikuyu still live near Mount Kenya.

Below: a map by Erhardt and Rebmann.
Dated 1855, it shows "the probable
position and extent of the sea of
Uniamesi as being the continuation
of the Lake Niasa." Uniamesi is
probably Lake Tanganyika.

"That Mighty Stream the Nile"
8

At the time of his appointment to lead the Nile expedition in 1856, Richard Burton was 35-years-old and already famous. He was a many-sided man—flamboyant, bold, brilliant. Before he was 18, he had mastered half a dozen languages. In all he learned 29, as well as various dialects to bring the total up to 40. Impulsive, hot-tempered, fearless, proud, and independent, Burton was a natural rebel. He began his career by getting expelled from Oxford University.

At 21, Burton landed in Bombay as an army lieutenant, and spent the next seven years in India, where he mastered Hindi, Gujarāti, Marathi, and Sanskrit. Serving in the army intelligence, he started to wear Indian dress and stained his face with walnut juice in order to pass as an Indian. In the bazaars of Bombay, Karachi, and Sind, Burton learned secrets of Indian customs and religious rites that had been hidden from most Europeans. Eventually he left India under a cloud. There were rumors about unbecoming and questionable conduct.

In 1853, in the disguise of a Moslem holy man, Burton visited Mecca, still forbidden to non-Moslems. Then he reached the Ethiopian city of Hārar, the "forbidden holy city" of the Moslem Somalis. On his return to the Red Sea coast, he survived a night attack by 350 Somalis but was wounded by a javelin that pierced his cheeks and jaw. With him, and even more severely wounded, was a lieutenant of the Indian army, John Hanning Speke. He had enlisted in the Indian army to enjoy the sport of big game hunting, and had joined Burton in search of adventure.

Speke had come to the right man. During his years in the East, Burton's ambition had become to seek and win the explorers' "crown," to discover what he called the "Coy Fountains" (the source) of the Nile. Now with finances supplied by the Royal Geographical Society, he and Speke sailed from the Red Sea to Zanzibar where they would pick up supplies and put their expedition together. They left Zanzibar on June 16, 1857, and crossed over to the mainland with about 130 porters, 30 donkeys, and trade goods to last for 2 years. Burton took as his headman an African ex-slave named Sidi Bombay, who became almost as famous as his successive masters—in turn Burton, Speke, and Verney Cameron.

The expedition struck out westward from the coast along the slavers' route to what the Arabs called the Sea of Ujiji. The usual

Above: Burton's Arab shoes, loose and comfortable, with worn-down heels.

Right: Richard Burton in Arab dress. Burton's gift for languages and his thorough knowledge of Islam made it possible for him to pass as a Moslem among Moslems. He identified himself with every aspect of their life and faith so that he simply *became* a Moslem. After his journey to Mecca he was accepted as a *hajji* – one who has made the pilgrimage to the holy city.

Left: John Hanning Speke. Unlike Burton, Speke was an orthodox army officer, efficient, reliable, and undoubtedly brave and tenacious. His habit of recording the details of even the smallest incidents of daily life provides a most informative record of the Africa he knew.

troubles beset the group—flooded rivers, bogs and forests, dying animals, absconding porters, and chronic fever. By August, both Englishmen were almost deaf from ear infections. Too weak to walk, they could barely even sit on their donkeys. Smallpox broke out, they had to abandon many loads, their chronometers failed, and they ran short of food. Not until November 7, did they reach Kazé (near modern Tabora), some 500 miles inland. It was an oasis of civilization, with well-built houses owned by rich and courteous Arabs, plenty of fresh fruit and vegetables, milk and butter, coffee and tobacco. Burton wrote, "The Arabs live comfortably and even splendidly, surrounded by troops of concubines and slaves; rich men have riding-asses from Zanzibar, and even the poorest keep flocks and herds." Here the traveler could have his musket repaired, bullets cast, or a pair of stirrups made.

They resumed their journey with a caravan depleted by sickness, and Burton more dead than alive. Soon afterward he was struck by a paralysis which crippled him for more than a year. Then Speke went almost totally blind. "The route lay through a howling wilderness, once populous and fertile, but now laid waste by the fierce

Watuta [local tribesmen]." They forded rivers, struggled through swamps, and stumbled over broken hills on exhausted donkeys.

On February 13, 1858, they climbed a hill so steep that it killed Speke's donkey. "What is that streak of light that lies below?" Burton asked. By now he, too, was more than half blind. "That is *the* water," Bombay exclaimed, "the Sea of Ujiji." Burton and Speke were the first Europeans to reach its shores, and their vision was so blurred that they could scarcely see it. But on approaching more closely, Burton was delighted with the vast Sea of Ujiji—the lake we call Tanganyika—that "lay in the lap of the mountains, basking in the tropical sunshine. . . . Truly it was a revel for soul and sight!"

The Arab town of Ujiji, a slaving station, was a squalid disappointment, its inhabitants rapacious and rude. Both Britons continued to be racked by sickness. Nevertheless they were determined to reach the north end of the lake. There, according to the Arabs, was a river, the Ruzizi, flowing out to the north. If this were true, then it must surely be, Burton believed, part of the Nile system and perhaps the great prize, its main source.

Burton succeeded in hiring 2 large canoes with 55 paddlers. Still unable to walk, he had to be carried to the canoe. The crews continually emitted a "long, monotonous, melancholy howl" to scare off spirits and crocodiles. On April 26, 1858, the travelers reached the most northerly trading post on the shore. Here all their hopes were dashed. Three sons of the local chief "unanimously asserted, and every man in the host of bystanders confirmed their words, that the Ruzizi enters into, and does not flow out of, the Tanganyika."

Due to ulcers of the tongue Burton was unable to speak and persuade his crew, who were terrified of cannibals, to go any farther. It was a bitter blow to be forced to turn back. When, after many troubles, they re-entered Kazé on June 20, 1858, Burton was still semiparalyzed and Speke still nearly deaf from the painful abscesses in his ears. Yet neither man would give up the quest. Burton had heard the Arabs talk of another lake, even larger, only 15 or 16 days' march north of Kazé. Might this be the birthplace of the "Coy Fountains"? Too sick to go himself he sent his young companion.

Speke left Kazé in July, 1858. After a surprisingly easy 16 days' journey, he reached an enormous sheet of water which a local tribesman said "probably extended to the end of the world." In a flash of inspiration Speke decided that he had found "the fountainhead of that mighty stream . . . the Nile." Speke named the lake for Queen Victoria. He then proceeded to shoot some red geese. The first gunshot to be heard on the shores of Africa's largest lake was fired by the first European ever to see it.

Burton greeted Speke's claims coldly. Speke had seen a lake, but no sign of any river. Burton later wrote that, "the fortunate discoverer's conviction was strong, his reasons weak," and he proceeded to demolish them. By tacit agreement, the two men avoided

Above: an engraving of Ujiji from a photograph by Stanley, taken from the flat roof of an Arab house facing the market place. Since then the waters of Lake Tanganyika have fallen, and Ujiji is now some distance from the lake.

any further mention of the great lake, the Nile, and what Burton called Speke's *trouvaille* (windfall).

There seemed no end to sickness and pain. On the way back to the coast, Speke was attacked by violent fever-induced fits that very nearly killed him. Burton never left his side. But as they approached the coast, they began slowly to recover. On February 2, 1859, they cheered at the sight of the Indian Ocean. On March 4, they were in Zanzibar.

On their way back to England Burton paused to recuperate in Aden on the Red Sea, while Speke went on ahead. "Goodbye, old

Above: a modern photograph of the plains of Tanzania, showing how little they have changed since Speke was there in 1861. Roads now cross them, but from a few yards away are invisible in the endless bush.

Above: Speke's drawing of Unyan-yembe, made in September, 1858.

fellow," was Speke's farewell, according to Burton, "you may be quite sure I shall not go up to the Royal Geographical Society until you come to the fore and we appear together. Make your mind easy about that." Either Burton had not heard him correctly, or Speke's word was not his bond, for on May 10, 1859, the day after his arrival in England, Speke called on the president of the society and put forward his claim.

Burton reached London only 12 days later. By then it was too late. Speke had already lectured to the society and was by now a popular hero. Burton found "the ground completely cut from under my feet," and their joint discovery of Lake Tanganyika was almost ignored. Burton went off in disgust to his sister's home at Boulogne in France to write his version of their journey in *The Lake Regions of Central Africa*.

The following year, in the spring of 1860, Speke set out to prove that Lake Victoria was the White Nile's source. His partner was a brother-officer, James Augustus Grant, a tall, good-looking, amiable young man, who got on with Speke very well. They reached Zanzibar in August. Their plan was to proceed to Kazé as before, circle Lake Victoria on the western side and find the spot where, Speke was convinced, the Nile issued from the lake. They would then follow the river down through the Sudan and Egypt to the sea. In London Speke had met an ivory trader, John Petherick, who was familiar with the Upper Nile region. He had promised to assemble some boats at Gondokoro, a Sudanese trading post near modern Jūbā, to await Speke's arrival. If possible Petherick promised to send a party on foot up the river beyond Gondokoro to help him down.

The explorers left the coast near Bagamoyo in Tanzania on October 2, 1860 with 217 men and a long train of donkeys, mules and goats. By the time they reached Kazé, about 500 miles, over 130 porters had deserted taking half their goods. War had broken out between Arabs and Africans, the country was in turmoil, and porters were almost impossible to recruit. Both men fell sick. They made several false starts but got off at last in detachments, taking 75 days to cover the first 90 miles.

Grant was laid up for nearly four months in a village while Speke vainly scoured the countryside for porters. Eventually they were able to leave in separate parties, but Grant was attacked and his goods plundered by an armed band. Speke went ahead, so weak from

Below: Burton's gift for adopting the manners and customs of any country he visited was rewarded by this present from an African king, a delicate necklace of human bones.

Below: Grant in the clothes he wore in Africa. Although Speke and Grant took a camera on their expedition, the principal record of the sights they saw on their journey was made in water-color paintings by Grant.

a chest complaint that he was unable to stand. "I would rather have died than have failed," he said. On November 25, 1861, they reached Karagwe, located between the western shore of Lake Victoria and the Virunga Mountains. It was one of several former kingdoms in what is now the Republic of Uganda.

Karagwe had a most delightful king, Ruwanika. He was a tall, good-looking man with fine features, an "open, mild expression," and an "ever-smiling countenance." He displayed the greatest interest in the wonders and customs of Europe, and "time flew like magic, the king's mind was so quick and enquiring."

Ruwanika liked his women fat. His wives and daughters were forced to drink such quantities of milk that some of the royal ladies were so obese they could move only their hands and knees. One of Ruwanika's sisters-in-law "could not rise; and so large were her arms that, between the joints, the flesh hung down like loose-stuffed puddings." The explorers spent a month with Ruwanika, and Speke enjoyed every moment. But Grant's leg broke out in ugly abscesses and he was incapacitated for five months.

All the while they were in Karagwe, the explorers had not set eyes on the lake which was their goal. To do so they would have to move on to the neighboring territory of Mutesa, the Kabaka, or king, of Buganda. Mutesa sent a party of warriors with drums, reed pipes, and dogs to escort the white men to his capital, located on the site of Kampala, the present capital of Uganda. Speke went on ahead and his first sight of the Kabaka's palace astonished him. "The whole brow and sides of the hill were covered with gigantic grass huts, thatched as neatly as so many heads dressed by a London barber, and fenced all round with tall yellow reeds." The palace was partitioned into courtyards where most of the king's three or four hundred women were kept. "Men, women, bulls, dogs, and goats, were led about by strings; and little pages, with rope-turbans, rushed about conveying messages . . . every one holding his skin-cloak tightly round him lest his naked legs by accident be shown."

Above: Lake Victoria from Mwanza. It is not certain from which exact spot Speke first caught sight of the lake, but it cannot have been far from Mwanza, which is the nearest point when approaching from Zanzibar.

Below: a sketch of the guards at the palace gateway, Buganda, by Grant. These are the guards who kept watch outside the fence of tall yellow reeds around Mutesa's palace.

Should such a breach of etiquette occur in Mutesa's presence, the offender was instantly executed. The Kabaka's rule was absolute and despotic. Everyone groveled face-downward in his presence, and anyone who gave offence was dragged out and killed. Grant saw a man speared to death because he had spoken too loudly in Mutesa's presence.

Speke's first meeting with the Kabaka did not go well. Speke was not going to grovel or be kept waiting, and Mutesa did not know what to make of the European. Mutesa was a tall, well-built young man of 25. He was dressed in a clean new bark cloth with bead ornaments. Behind him stood a number of wives who kept him supplied with copious draughts of *pombe* (beer). The royal emblems of Buganda—a dog, a spear, and a woman—were at his side.

Speke presented him with several rifles, and Mutesa asked the

explorer to demonstrate the rifles by shooting four cows which were wandering about the enclosure. The king then loaded one of the carbines and handed it to a page. As Speke tells it, "Mutesa ordered the boy to go out and shoot a man in the outer court; which was no sooner accomplished than the little urchin returned, to announce his success, with a look of glee such as one would see in the face of a boy who has robbed a bird's nest."

Speke was detained for nearly five months, needling away at Mutesa with requests for guides and porters to take him down the river to Gondokoro, where he hoped Petnerick was waiting. All Speke's attempts were turned aside. His men lacked food and had to live by stealing. Eventually Grant was carried on a stretcher around the lake from Karagwe to rejoin his companion. Although Mutesa was reluctant to let them go, on July 7, 1862, they left his court, accompanied by a large escort who looted every village they came to.

Perhaps the most curious aspect of Speke's five-month sojourn in the Buganda kingdom is that, in all that time, he had not looked at the lake or searched for an outlet to prove his contention that the Nile rose from it. So before going down the river, Speke had to see its source with his own eyes. On July 28, 1862, he stood beside the rocky falls about 40 miles east of Mutesa's capital and gazed entranced at the leaping fish, the basking crocodiles and hippopotamuses, fishermen in boats, and cattle drinking—a happy, pastoral scene. He named the falls for Lord Ripon, president of the Royal Geographical Society when Speke and Grant set out.

Mutesa had ordered canoes to take Speke and his party to Bunyoro, which lay between his own kingdom and Gondokoro. Speke hoped that now "there was nothing left but to float quietly down the Nile." But "this hope shared the fate of so many others in Africa." Bunyoro warriors halted the boats, and Kamrasi, their king, kept the white men waiting in the bush for an anxious month before receiving them.

According to Speke, Kamrasi was churlish, mean, suspicious, and grasping. He told the travelers he had heard that white men drank rivers and ate mountains seasoned with the tender parts of human beings. Nevertheless he was anxious to have anything he could extract from the whites. He commanded Speke to hand over his last remaining chronometer, and then visited the explorers' camp to commandeer mosquito nets, camp-beds, knives and forks,

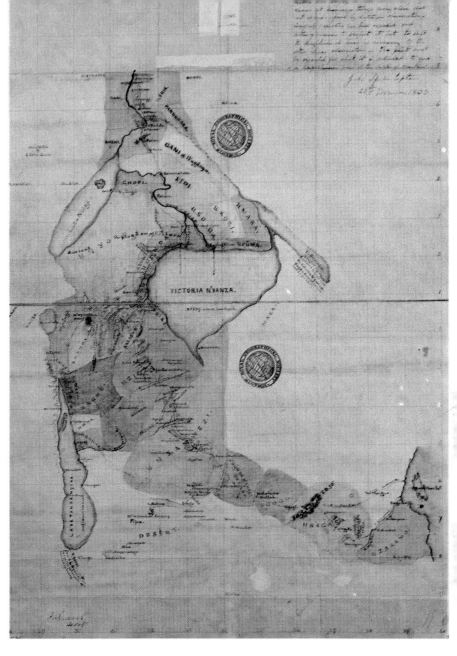

Below: a drawing by Speke of the Ripon Falls, on this drawing given their African name. When he first saw the falls, he was surprised to find that they were only about 12 feet high.

Right: Grant's map. Speke's note to the map added, "This miniature map is the result of a foot march with compass in hand ... compass variation has been regarded and nothing remains to perfect it but to shift the longitudinal line if necessary to the other lunar observations."

their cooking pots, and books—almost everything they possessed.

Kamrasi's capital was shadeless, wet, and infested with rats and lizards. It was so dirty that Speke considered stilts and respirators would be needed to explore it in comfort. "This horrid king" kept them waiting for two months, stripping them almost bare of possessions. In November he let them head down the Nile in canoes. The river was in flood and full of floating islands of reeds and grasses. At the Karuma Falls, the party had again to leave the river and march overland through grass eight feet high that tore their clothes to ribbons. When Speke and Grant regained the river, with only 20 surviving men, at Gondokoro on February 15, 1863, they had not seen it for two months.

As they marched into Gondokoro, they saw on the riverbank a

Above: Speke and Grant addressing the Royal Geographical Society, London. From Khartoum Speke telegraphed that all was well and the Nile River was traced to its source. His return was a triumph, with a public reception organized for his landing in England.

tall, burly Englishman hurrying toward them. "With a hearty cheer," Grant recorded, "we waved our hats and rushed into the arms, not of Petherick, but of [Samuel] Baker, the elephant hunter of Ceylon, who had bravely come in search of us."

Baker was also seeking his share of glory and had hoped to win the crown of discovery by locating the Coy Fountains. When Speke told him the puzzle had been solved, Baker asked whether there was not "one little leaf of the laurel" left for him. Speke told him that he had heard of a lake in Bunyoro called the Luta Ngizé and drew Baker a rough map. Speke had some idea that a tributary of the Nile might flow from it. But when he had learned of the Luta Ngizé both he and Grant had been too exhausted to go in search of it. Their only hope of survival had been to get to Gondokoro as soon as possible.

Accepting Baker's offer of his three boats, the survivors left Gondokoro on February 25, 1863, to sail and paddle slowly through the sudd to reach Khartoum on March 30, 1863. In Cairo, Speke and his group paid off Bombay and the remaining 18 men and 4 women who had accompanied them down the Nile.

"The Nile is settled," so Speke telegraphed to Sir Roderick Murchison, who had succeeded Lord Ripon as president of the Royal Geographical Society. In London he found that it was not. Explorers in the 1800's enjoyed the same sort of public adulation as pop singers do today, and the handsome Speke was at first a great hero. On June 22, 1863, he told his story at a public meeting organized by the society. But now he came up against his old companion Burton who had some difficult questions. Where was Speke's proof of his claim? He had seen a river flowing out of Lake Victoria to the north, but how could he be sure it was the Nile? He had not gone round Lake Victoria or sailed across it, and could not even prove it to be the same stretch of water he had seen north of Kazé in 1858. A number of geographers supported Burton's counter-claim.

Matters were brought to a head in September, 1864, when the British Association for the Advancement of Science arranged for the two rivals to confront each other at a public meeting in the resort city of Bath. Burton took his place on the platform, confident that he would destroy Speke's claims and reopen the whole question. There was a long delay, then a friend came up and whispered a message. Speke had died of gunshot wounds the previous afternoon, when out partridge-shooting with a cousin.

"My God, he's killed himself!" Burton exclaimed. But the verdict at the inquest was accidental death. It was thought Speke's shotgun went off when he was lifting it over a wall.

In spite of the official verdict many people wondered. Was Speke afraid to debate with the more experienced, fluent, brilliant Burton? If so, there was a further irony—for he was right and Burton wrong.

Left: Richard Burton's tomb, near London. Isobel Arundell was a young girl when she first saw Burton and said, "That man will marry me." It was 10 years before she became his wife. When he died in Trieste in 1890, she brought his body back to England, and buried him in this marble tent, fringed and gilded, surmounted by a nine pointed golden star. When she was laid beside him a few years later, by her direction only the simple words "and Isobel his wife" were added.

Lake Albert

9

Samuel Baker shared a birth-year with Burton and a passion for shooting with Speke. The son of a wealthy shipowner and banker who owned plantations in Mauritius and the West Indies, Baker led the life of a rich, Victorian gentleman adventurer. He had spent eight years farming and hunting in Ceylon. His lovely second wife, who was with him at Gondokoro to greet Speke and Grant, was a golden-haired Hungarian girl 15 years younger than the 38-year-old Baker. Florence Baker shared her husband's love of adventure. "Mrs. Baker was not a screamer," Samuel wrote. "She never even whispered." This was just as well, because during their marriage there was much she might have screamed about. The Bakers had been married the year before Speke and Grant disappeared into central Africa. In March, 1861, they went to Egypt to shoot big game, but Samuel had a secret plan. Later he wrote: "I commenced an expedition to discover the sources of the Nile, with the hope of meeting the East African expedition of Captains Speke and Grant . . . I had inwardly determined to accomplish this difficult task or to die in the attempt."

The Bakers spent a year in preparation for their journey, learning Arabic, tracing tributaries of the Blue Nile that rose in Ethiopia and, of course, hunting. In the Sudan the couple went elephant hunting with pony-mounted Arabs who slew the animals with swords. And then Florence Baker first displayed her genius for homemaking in the wilderness. In a round hut they built for two shillings she achieved "the perfection of neatness," with green mosquito nets, a table covered with muslin and chintz, walls hung with woven baskets, hunting knives, and fishing tackle.

On December 18, 1862, the Bakers set sail from Khartoum up the Nile in 3 boats laden with provisions for 4 weeks, pack animals, and 96 porters, bound for Gondokoro 1,000 miles south. After sailing for more than 500 miles through flat, barren country they approached the sudd. Here they were forced to haul the boats along with the aid of ropes. Malaria was rife and at night the air vibrated with mosquitoes, "the nightingales of the White Nile." The inhabitants of these swamps were "so emaciated that they have no visible posteriors"—their food was a kind of porridge pounded from the bones of dead animals.

At Gondokoro, "merely a station of the traders, occupied for about two months of the year" they found about 600 traders who

Above: papyrus chokes the upper reaches of the Nile River. An aquatic plant, papyrus was used by the ancient Egyptians to make both paper and boats. The seaworthiness of papyrus boats was recently proved by Thor Heyerdahl's voyage across the Atlantic Ocean on a boat made from the papyrus of Lakes Tana and Chad.

Right: the papyrus reed is a spectacular plant growing as high as 10 feet, and crowned by a lovely flower head in the shape of a feather duster.

Above: the Bakers' boat being hauled through the sudd, a huge mass of decaying vegetation, mostly matted grass and papyrus from the surrounding swamps. It formed an obstacle that defeated many efforts to trace the Nile to its source. When the mass of vegetation reaches the main channel of the river it forms a dam up to 25 miles long and 20 feet deep.

spent most of their time drinking, quarreling, and ill-treating their slaves. The Bakers had been there for 12 days when "My men rushed madly to my boat, with a report that two white men had come from the *sea!* Could they be Speke and Grant? Off I ran, and soon met them in reality; hurrah for old England! . . . The mystery of ages solved."

The Luta Ngizé had been left for the Bakers. After seeing Speke and Grant off, they mounted their Abyssinian ponies and, with 17 disgruntled men, 21 donkeys, some camels, and a pet monkey, set out at sunset on March 26, 1863. Because the Bakers' party was too weak and small to travel alone, they had to join forces with an ivory trader, Ibrahim, who was in no hurry. Rain began to fall, rivers became unfordable, and they were all marooned in the mountains for six months. Florence made a hut of mud and sticks eight feet in diameter into a "snug little dwelling" that became less snug as the rain came down. Now it was the Bakers' turn to discover just how unwelcoming Africa could be. They were prostrated with malaria, the baggage animals died, smallpox broke out among the porters. To add to their troubles, the Bakers

Above: Sir Samuel and Lady Baker. Samuel Baker's character is summed up well by his own words: "I could not conceive that anything in this world had power to resist a determined will, so long as health and life remained."

could buy scarcely any food. "I shall be truly thankful to quit this abominable land," Baker wrote. "But I shall plod onward with dogged obstinacy; God only knows the end."

At last the rivers fell. In January, 1864, riding on oxen they were able to start again for Bunyoro with Ibrahim and his men. But, as it turned out, their troubles had hardly begun. The rain fell in torrents, they were knocked out by fever, and nearly all their porters deserted. When they reached Kamrasi's court at M'ruli, Florence was traveling in a litter and Samuel had to be carried into the king's presence and laid at his feet. Baker's persistent requests for guides to take them to the Luta Ngizé were met by Kamrasi's even more persistently repeated demands for everything still in Baker's possession—his watch, his sword, his compass, his "beautiful little Fletcher 24 rifle."

Finally the King of Bunyoro seemed ready to give in. In return for a royal promise of guides next day, Baker gave Kamrasi his sword. Next day there were no guides, but a new demand. The king insisted that Baker repair Speke's chronometer which had stopped when Kamrasi had prodded at its works to find the tick.

Eventually they were allowed to leave. But as a parting gesture Kamrasi had them taken to a shed outside the village where he again appeared "to peel the last skin off the onion." He demanded the "pretty yellow muslin Turkish handkerchief fringed with silver drops that Mrs. Baker wore upon her head." This was surrendered. Then more handkerchiefs were required. In answer to Baker's protest that they had none left, Kamrasi insisted on having all their baggage unpacked to see for himself. Finally the demand came for Baker's ultimate possession: his wife.

This was the last straw. Baker pointed his pistol at the king. "If this were to be the end of the expedition I resolved that it should also be the end of Kamrasi." Mrs. Baker joined in "with a little speech in Arabic (not a word of which he understood) and a countenance almost as amiable as that of the Medusa." Kamrasi was astonished. He had merely been suggesting an exchange of wives, an old Bunyoro custom—he had plenty of pretty ones for Baker to choose from. Baker demanded an immediate start for the lake. This time Kamrasi gave way, the onion was peeled. A number of women onlookers were ordered to shoulder their remaining baggage. Baker then "assisted my wife upon her ox, and with a very cold adieu to Kamrasi, I turned my back most gladly on M'ruli!"

They were not out of trouble yet. Wading waist-deep through a swamp, Baker looked round to see his wife sinking through the weeds, "her face distorted and perfectly purple." In the nick of time he grabbed her and with the help of some of their men "dragged her like a corpse through the yielding· vegetation" and laid her unconscious under a tree. Florence's teeth and fists were clenched and there was "a painful rattle in her throat as she was carried forward in a litter." Baker opened her jaws with a wedge and moistened her tongue, but the next day she was still unconscious.

On they went toward the lake. Baker trudged by the side of his wife's litter and by night, coated with mud and shivering with ague, watched by her side. On the third morning, Florence regained consciousness, but only to fall into a delirium. "She spoke, but the brain had gone." After seven nearly foodless days of marching through continual rain, they reached a village. Baker covered Florence with a rug, lay down beside her and fell unconscious from exhaustion. His men looked for a dry spot to dig her grave.

Above: an elaborate ceremonial form of the African wooden stool, used by Baker on his explorations of the Upper Nile. It was probably presented to him by one of the many chiefs he met.

Next morning, the sun was shining, and Baker awoke to a miracle. Florence was sleeping naturally. She opened her eyes and they were calm and clear. After two days' rest they moved on, and on March 14, 1864, reached a hilltop where "The glory of our prize burst suddenly upon me! There, like a sea of quick-silver, lay far beneath the grand expanse of water—a boundless sea horizon glittering in the noon-day sun. . . . It is impossible to describe the triumph of that moment; here was the reward of all our labour—for the years of tenacity with which we had toiled through Africa. England had won the source of the Nile!" Baker renamed Luta Ngizé Albert Nyanza or Lake Albert after the late Prince Consort, the beloved husband of Queen Victoria. Thus "the Victoria and the Albert are the two sources of the Nile."

Lake Albert is no longer regarded as an actual source of the Nile, since that river runs into it and out again at the same northerly end. But this does not detract from Baker's achievement. He was the first European to see the lake, fix its position, and so fill in the last important gap in knowledge of the White Nile's origins. Florence Baker tottered down the hill and watched her husband wade in and "with a heart full of gratitude, drink deeply from the Sources of the Nile." Next morning they were all prostrated with fever and unable to rise.

The explorer's work was not quite done. He had to find the spot where Speke's river entered the lake, and verify its course upstream as far as the Karuma Falls where Speke had left the river to start overland. With difficulty he hired canoes and paddlers to take them

Above: after the Bakers had bid "a very cold adieu" to Kamrasi, out rushed their escort—about 600 men dressed in leopard skins, with antelope horns strapped to their heads, dancing and yelling. The drawing is by Sir Samuel Baker.

to the northern tip of the lake. Narrowly escaping death in a storm, they found the entrance, but were so weak with fever that they had to be lifted in and out of the canoe. They continued upstream to reach, on the second day, a spot where the river narrowed. Great rocks appeared ahead of them, and on rounding a bend they saw ahead a waterfall which Baker named the Murchison Falls, in honor of Sir Roderick Murchison.

Now with only one problem remaining—how to get home again—their plight became really desperate. A civil war between Kamrasi and one of his brothers had devastated Bunyoro. The people had fled into the bush, and the Bakers could get neither food nor guides for the long trip back to Gondokoro. They kept alive on a store of moldy grain they found buried in a deserted village, on a kind of bush spinach, and "tea" made from wild thyme. This diet, plus malaria, so weakened them that for two months the Bakers lay side by side on the floor of a hut unable to move, dreaming of beef and ale.

Kamrasi knew of their condition and was trying to starve them out. Suddenly he changed his mind and had them carried to his camp. The king greeted them roaring with laughter at a joke he now revealed—he was not Kamrasi after all but a younger brother

Right: Murchison Falls, edged on both sides by wooded cliffs. The river roars through a narrow rock-bound pass, and plunges into the dark abyss below in a single leap of about 120 feet.

Left: the sandy spit where the Victoria Nile actually enters Lake Albert. When Baker discovered Lake Albert he was sure that he had found a source of the Nile. Today the lake is no longer regarded as one of the river's true sources, as the Nile flows in and out again at the same end.

Below: when Baker reached Kamrasi's capital, he changed into a suit, similar to that worn by Speke. Then he and his wife advanced alone to meet Kamrasi's people, who recognized the similarity of his beard, and at once greeted him with a most extravagant welcome, dancing and waving their lances and shields, shouting and singing most excitedly.

who had been impersonating him. When Baker went to meet the real Kamrasi he managed somehow to produce from the remnants of his baggage a Scottish highlander's kilt, sporran, and bonnet. There was little left for Kamrasi to demand but sure enough he demanded it, and the Bakers hid their last possessions under their beds. Kamrasi kept them prisoners in his camp, and there they might have perished had not Ibrahim arrived from Gondokoro bringing letters, ammunition, and cloth to make some clothes. Baker rigged up a still and made a raw spirit from sweet potatoes which almost dispelled his chronic fever.

In November, 1864, Ibrahim was ready to leave, and the caravan, over 1,000 strong, with 700 loads of ivory, set out for Gondokoro. Two months later, as they approached their destination, the Bakers rode ahead on oxen, unfurled a Union Jack and fired their muskets. Some of the Egyptian garrison came out to greet them, firing in return. The journey from Gondokoro to Lake Albert and back again—an overland distance of not quite five hundred miles—had taken nearly two years.

There was a final disappointment. No boats were waiting at Gondokoro as the Bakers had expected—no letters, no supplies. They had been given up for dead long ago. Baker felt "almost choked." He had neither goods nor resources and a thousand miles to go to reach Khartoum. He sat down under a tree and recalled the words of an African chief: "Suppose you get to the great lake, what will you do with it? What will be the good of it?" And he asked himself: "Had I wasted some of the best years of my life to obtain a shadow?"

With Baker, dark moods quickly gave way to action. There was a boat on the river that had carried slaves who had mostly died on board from bubonic plague. He hired the vessel for £40 ($100) to be paid in Khartoum, had it scrubbed and fumigated with tobacco, put his men on board, hoisted the flag and "amid the rattle of musketry glided rapidly down the river." Despite his precautions, plague broke out and one of the Bakers' two faithful servants died almost within sight of Khartoum, which they reached on May 5, 1865. Five months later they were in Cairo. They had been in Africa nearly five years. The Bakers found a job at Shepherd's Hotel for their last remaining servant and, "with a heart too full to say goodbye," left for home.

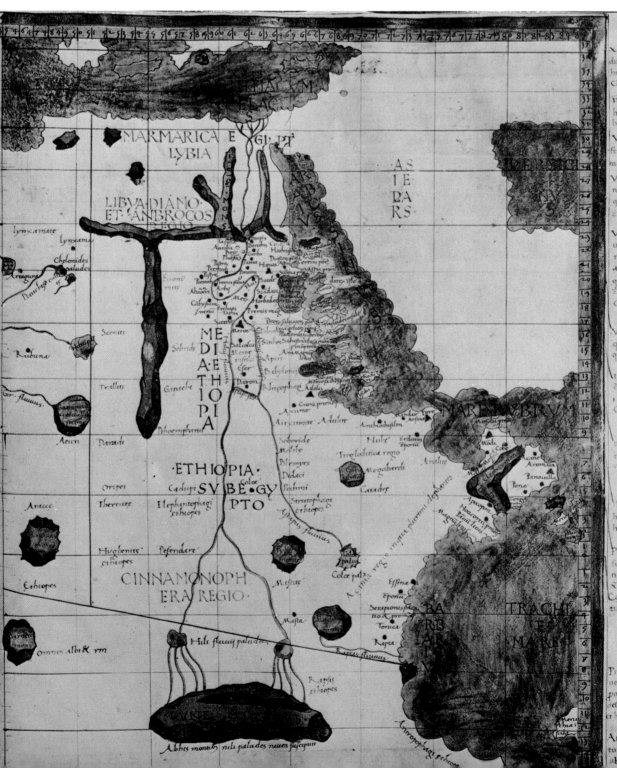

The White Nile and the Congo

10

Above left: Ayao villagers walking on a path near Fort Johnston on the Shire River. After his hard struggle up the Ruvuma River, David Livingstone once more reached the Shire River on October 13, 1866.

Left: Ptolemy's map showing the sources of the Nile River. His famous *Geography* dates from about A.D. 150, but hundreds of years later European cartographers were still showing the twin lakes he described as fed from the Mountains of the Moon to be the sources of the Nile. It was not until explorers began to penetrate inland that the maps started reflecting more accurate information.

Burton, Speke, Baker. Each in his turn believed that he had "settled" the question of the White Nile. But none of them had mapped its whole course. Each had found a lake, and Speke and Baker had seen stretches of the Nile, but neither had followed it down to the Sudan. No one could yet be certain that the explorers were talking about the same river. No European had circumnavigated any of these great central lakes either. Until that was done, no one could be sure what rivers ran in or out, and what became of them.

There was the vexing question too of Ptolemy's Mountains of the Moon. The ancients said they were the true source of the Nile. But where were they? Burton thought they were in Tanganyika northwest of his lake. Speke firmly believed that he had seen them, they were the Virunga chain of volcanoes west of *his* lake, in what is now Rwanda. Krapf and Rebmann had seen snow-capped peaks, but their mountains were in the wrong place. Livingstone had a different theory altogether. He thought the Nile rose much farther south, and perhaps flowed through Burton's or Speke's lake on its way north. There was plenty of room for argument, and argument there was. The whole river system of central Africa had to be sorted out.

In the opinion of Roderick Murchison, the best man to tackle this task was David Livingstone. After the doctor's return from the Zambezi in 1864, Murchison wrote: "There is at the moment a matter of intense geographical interest to be settled: namely, the watershed, or watersheds, of South Africa." To carry out this task, he suggested, "would be the completion of your remarkable career."

"I would not consent to go simply as a geographer," Livingstone replied, "but as a missionary, to do geography by the way." On these terms Livingstone was commissioned to return to Africa as leader of the next expedition.

On his 53rd birthday, March 19, 1866, he sailed from Zanzibar to the mainland with 60 men, including 3 who had marched with Speke and Grant and some Indian troops from Bombay. The pack train consisted of a weird assortment of Indian buffaloes, camels, mules, and donkeys. For company Livingstone had brought his poodle.

He planned to start inland from a spot near the mouth of the Ruvuma River. It was good to be back again in Africa, "the mere animal pleasure of travelling in a wild unexplored country is very great." But Livingstone's Indian soldiers were idle, disobedient, and horribly cruel to the pack animals. They fell sick, and died or deserted, as did most of the porters. Soon the expedition began to pass through country despoiled by Arab slavers. Livingstone found "village after village all deserted and strewn with corpses and skulls." There was, of course, little food to be had in the ravaged land. By the time Livingstone's party reached the Shire River south of Lake Nyasa, it had shrunk to 11 nearly starved men.

Left: slave chains Livingstone brought back to London after his Zambezi expedition. They are immensely heavy, and could not have been worn on the march. They were probably used to tether slaves on the coast, where they were herded like animals, awaiting shipment to their final destination.

They struck northwestward toward Lake Tanganyika through trackless bush, without guides or provisions, dependent on gun and compass, and in constant peril from the slaving bands. "Hunger sent us on," wrote Livingstone. On Christmas Day, 1866, he dreamed of butter. Because of raids by the slavers "there are no people here now in these lovely wild valleys." The village gardens and herds they had counted on for food had long disappeared. "An incessant hunger teases us—real biting hunger and faintness." For a while they existed on boiled mushrooms, which, Livingstone noted, are "good only for producing dreams of roast beef."

While they were wading through some forest rivers, the poodle drowned. Then two more porters ran away, taking with them the medicine chest on which Livingstone so greatly depended. "I feel as if I had now received a sentence of death," he wrote in his journal.

Nearly a year after his departure from Zanzibar Livingstone struggled up to the southern end of Lake Tanganyika. Weakened by rheumatic fever, dysentery, and starvation, the missionary had a constant singing in the head and "fits of insensibility." He was rescued from this unfortunate condition by Arab slavers, the very people he was trying to destroy. A party of them fed and nursed him, gave him clothing, and resupplied him with beads. When the slavers struck out to journey westward Livingstone went with them toward a large lake of which they spoke. On November 8, 1867, he added Lake Mweru to the map of central Africa. The Portuguese traveler Lacerda had seen it 70 years before but he had died near its shores. Livingstone was the first to chart and describe Mweru, and rule it out as part of the Nile drainage.

The Arabs turned back for their base at Ujiji. But Livingstone had heard of yet another lake. In spite of sickness and a mutiny among his men, he decided to continue southeast in search of it. Only four men agreed to go with him. Once more they set forth into the unknown.

Here was Darkest Africa indeed. Their way took them wading through swamps waist-deep in leech-infested water. On the high lands thick matted grasses reached far above their heads. And everywhere, "an abundance of wild beasts," incessant rains, chronic dysentery, and malaria. On July 18, 1868, they reached Lake Bangweulu, a lake surrounded by swamps which flood in the rainy season changing the shape of the lake. Livingstone persuaded some canoemen to paddle him to an island where he slept the night. But he could find no canoemen to take him farther. He had no goods to offer, and there was no alternative but to turn north again and rejoin the Arabs. Again they fed and nursed him. On March 14, 1869, three years after leaving Zanzibar, he reached Ujiji as a "mere ruckle of bones." He had expected to find medicines, letters, and stores sent after him. He found nothing, not even quinine which would have been particularly helpful to him. Despite this blow he thought more and more about the central puzzle: where lay the ultimate sources of both Congo and Nile? Did both issue from the heartland "sponge" of central Africa's complicated river system? He must go in search of "an unvisited lake, west or southwest of this," whose overflow, "whether of Congo or Nile, I have to ascertain."

So Livingstone went off again on July 12, 1869, with an Arab companion and five porters. Although his health was failing, he recorded in his journal every detail of the long, laborious route: plants, trees, beasts, insects, climate, longitude, and latitude. Caught in a drenching rainstorm, he was able to sit calmly on a fallen log and note how "a little tree frog, about half an inch long, leaped on a grassy leaf, and began a tune as loud as that of many birds, and very sweet; it was surprising to hear so much music out of so small a musician."

"I am nearly toothless, and in my second childhood," he wrote. Yet despite constant sickness and hunger, the doctor went on. His careful notes reveal that "slowly and surely I saw the problems of

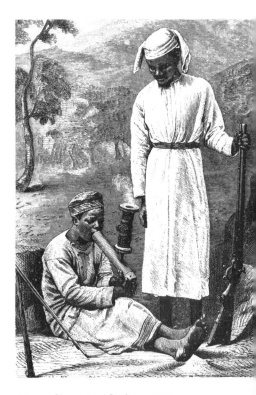

Above: Chuma and Susi, two men who served Livingstone faithfully for many years. Chuma was liberated from slavers in 1861, and Susi was originally hired at about the same time to cut wood for the boat on the Zambezi expedition. They went with him on all his later journeys, and his diary shows his growing dependence on them in the last two difficult years of his life.

Above: Livingstone reading the Bible.
It was the cornerstone of his life, and
he read it constantly for comfort and
inspiration, often comparing his own
difficulties and their solution with
those he found in the Biblical stories.

the fountains of the Nile developing before my eyes." Two of his
attendants deserted him, and on June 26, 1870 "with only three
attendants, Susi, Chuma, and Gardner," he started off to the
northwest. On this march he suffered seriously from the explorers'
old complaint, foot ulcers. In a district called Bamberre, Livingstone
was marooned for eight months, sick with malaria and dysentery.
He read the whole Bible four times and longed for home, yet "I
cannot give up making a complete work of the exploration."

On March 29, 1871, the small party reached the Lualaba River.
At first Livingstone believed it to be the Nile. Actually the Lualaba
is the Upper Congo. At Kisangani now in the Republic of Congo
(Kinshasa), some 500 miles or so north of where Livingstone saw
the river, it swings west toward the Atlantic. This was one discovery
Livingstone would not make.

The Arabs had established a post on the banks of the Lualaba

at Nyangwe. Here Livingstone found a large market at which slaves from the Congo forests were collected to be driven east to Ujiji and the coast beyond. On July 15, some of the Arabs' armed men went berserk and fired into the people at the market where many women and children were peacefully going about their business. Panic-stricken Africans jumped into the river and were drowned. Almost 400 people perished.

Sickened by this senseless cruelty Livingstone determined to send out pleas for the end of the brutal trade in human beings. He and his three faithful companions turned back for a 350-mile walk to Ujiji, "almost every step in pain." It was an incredible journey. He was certain that this time he would find at Ujiji a good supply of stores with which, after a rest, he could start off again. He found nothing. Supplies had been sent, but all had been plundered by the headman of the caravan on the way from Zanzibar to Ujiji. Living-

Above: a massacre of Africans by Arabs. Livingstone saw many such senseless killings, but the worst took place one hot, sultry day when nerves were taut and tempers easily roused. Three men carrying guns in a crowded market haggled about the price of a chicken, two guns went off and the slaughter began. Panicking people ran, jumping into the river and drowning, while shot after shot cracked out into the helpless mob.

Above: the hat that Henry Stanley wore at the famous meeting with Livingstone, in the remote African town of Ujiji.

stone was destitute. He had to decide whether to starve or beg from the Arabs.

At the lowest point in his fortunes "Susi came running at the top of his speed and gasped out: 'An Englishman! I see him!' and off he darted to meet him. The American flag at the head of the caravan told me the nationality of the stranger." Henry Stanley had arrived.

This famous meeting at Ujiji on October 28, 1871, is one of the great moments in the history of Western exploration of Africa. The contrast between the principals could not have been greater. The aging missionary still had his humility and unshaken faith, his gentle resolution, his humor, and love of nature. His inflexible purpose and his total dedication to the will of God and to the needs, as he saw them, of humanity had not been shaken. The tough, self-confident Stanley, an ambitious New World journalist born in Wales, was as ruthless as Livingstone was gentle, and as worldly as the other was spiritual. He had his way to make and his newspaper to serve. Yet in the five months they spent together, the journalist developed a respect for the missionary amounting to hero worship. For Stanley the meeting was a turning-point of his life.

Above: Livingstone's battered blue cap with its tarnished gold band. After his death it was listed as part of his personal possessions: "In the chest was found a shilling and a half [about 18c], and in the other his hat."

Good food, medicine, and rest brought about the last of Livingstone's astonishing recoveries. Together the two men explored the northerly end of Lake Tanganyika and finally settled the question of the Ruzizi. The river flows into Lake Tanganyika, not out of it. This, however, confirmed Livingstone's belief in his error that the Lualaba was the Nile. But to make sure he needed to explore the river. He went with Stanley to Kazé where he found the remnants of his rifled stores. Stanley tried hard to persuade him to return to the coast to get supplies and a new set of dentures, but the doctor adamantly refused. "I feel as if appointed to this work and no other."

On March 14, 1872, Stanley left for Zanzibar, and Livingstone had to wait five weary months for supplies and porters to arrive. On August 25, he set out again for the region of Lake Bangweulu and the "fountains of Katanga" beyond—as he believed, the fountains of the Nile. But he could not be sure. "I am oppressed with the apprehension that after all it may turn out that I have been following the Congo, and who would risk being put into a cannibal pot and converted into a black man for it?" Fever and dysentery plagued him and would not yield to medicine. He lost blood constantly—

277

Above: a white sedge-flower, which grows in the marshy areas of Zambia and Angola, where Livingstone spent so much of his time.

Right: Livingstone's diary entry of April 19, 11 days before his death. Until then, he had kept up his scientific notes, in spite of severe pain. That day, although he was still riding the donkey, he wrote, "No observations now...I can scarcely hold the pencil."

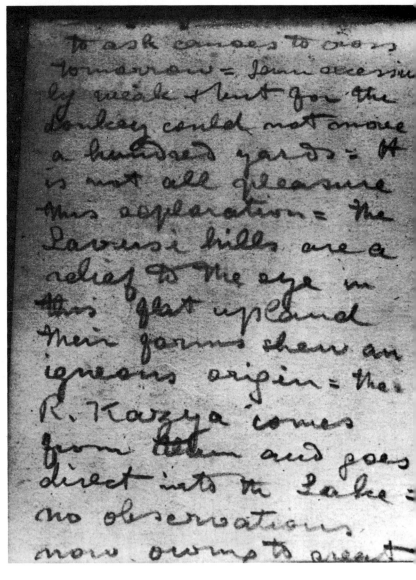

"a safety-valve for me." Sometimes they were neck-deep in bogs and feasted on by leeches. "Storm-sprayed by rain and cold," Livingstone could still catalog the flowers in bloom: "marigolds, a white jonquil-looking flower without smell, many orchids, white, yellow and pink ascelpias, clematis, gladiolus. . . ."

Marooned by floods, the little band killed their last goat on whose milk Livingstone's life depended. When swamps became too deep for wading they hired canoes and paddled on through reeds and rivulets, exposed to constant rain. Whatever the hardship, observation never ceased. "A lion roared mightily. The fish-hawk utters his weird voice in the morning." Livingstone grew weaker and weaker from loss of blood but "nothing earthly will make me give up my work in despair."

When he could walk no longer, his men carried him in a hammock. In one of the understatements of all time he noted: "It is not

Above: Livingstone's grave, where his body—carried by his devoted men from the African village where he died—lies in London's Westminster Abbey.

all pleasure, this exploration." At a village called Chitambo's in the district of Ulala, he made his last entry in his diary on April 27, 1873. Too weak to turn the key himself, he signaled to Susi to wind up his chronometer. On April 30, 1873, Livingstone died.

The sequel is unique in African exploration. Livingstone's men, directed by Susi and Chuma, cut out his heart and viscera and buried them under a tree. They embalmed his body with raw salt, dried it in the sun, and lashed it to a pole, wrapped in cloth and bark. For eight months they carried it through swamp and forest, over lake and mountain, to deliver it to the Zanzibar authorities. With Livingstone's body they carried all his precious journals, notes, and scientific observations. David Livingstone was buried on April 18, 1874 among many of the national heroes of Britain in Westminster Abbey, London. It seems fitting that his heart remained in Africa.

Three Great Problems Solved 11

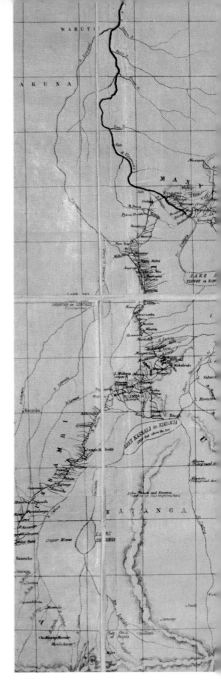

On their way through Kazé to the coast, Livingstone's faithful servants had found two malaria-stricken Europeans en route with supplies for their master who no longer needed succor. Commander Verney Lovett Cameron and Assistant Surgeon W. E. Dillon, both of the Royal Navy, had been sent to Africa by the Royal Geographical Society to help Livingstone wherever he might be.

"Young, stouthearted, eager, and brave" was Stanley's description of the 28-year-old Cameron. In Zanzibar he had engaged Bombay, the servant of Burton and Speke—who proved to be a sad disappointment—and a rascally and reluctant set of porters. The two naval officers had left the coast on March 28, 1873, one month before Livingstone's death. Now the original purpose of the journey had gone Cameron decided to continue, and "follow up the Doctor's explorations." He had already decided that Livingstone had been wrong about the Lualaba. He believed that it was an arm of the Congo and not the Nile. His plan was to pick up canoes at Nyangwe and float down the unknown waters of the Congo. Dillon was too ill to leave Kazé, and soon after his companion's departure shot himself in a fit of delirium brought on by malaria.

Cameron headed for Lake Tanganyika and, on February 18, 1874, suffering from crippling ulcers of the feet, he and his men reached Ujiji. His first task was to find the lake's outlet. With so many rivers flowing in, he argued, at least one must flow out, but no one had yet found it. Cameron sailed up to the Lukuga, one of the rivers on the lake's western shore. He was uncertain, however, whether he had found the river's mouth or its source. What he had found was a grassy channel without a perceptible current. One set of guides told him that it flowed into the lake but the local chief disagreed. He assured Cameron that there was a current, and that it moved westward toward the Lualaba. The only way to prove this would be to cut a channel through miles of matted reed to make the river navigable, but this was too much of a task for Cameron. He was inclined to accept the chief's word and left the Lukuga with a firm belief, but no proof, that he had become the first European to see this headwater of the Lualaba and hence of the Congo. In his journal he noted 96 rivers flowing into the lake and "one, the Lukuga, going out."

On August 3, 1874, he reached the Lualaba and found it to be

Above: part of the general map of Africa which was compiled under the direction of Cameron, based on his personal observations and surveys during his time in Africa, and on the other information he obtained.

Right: Verney Lovett Cameron, who set out to bring help to Livingstone. After his transcontinental African journey he became convinced that the greatest help to Africans would come from the commercial companies being formed to develop central Africa, and he devoted himself to their interests.

a mile wide and running at three or four knots (nautical miles) an hour. It would surely be possible to navigate such a noble water to the sea. But he could not buy or hire any canoes. The only acceptable tokens of currency at Nyangwe were slaves and cowrie shells, and Cameron had neither. He failed to get a single canoe. After taking altitude readings he was convinced that "the Lualaba could have no connection whatever with the Nile system, the river at Nyangwe being lower than the Nile at Gondokoro. . . . This great stream must be one of the headwaters of the Congo."

Cameron had to leave the proving of his claim to Stanley, and on August 26, 1874, left Nyangwe to find a lake called Sankorra, reported to lie to the south, which he believed might be the source of another arm of the Congo. Here, perhaps, he would be able to get his canoes. The people he encountered had never seen a white man. At one village about 500 crowded round to watch him eat a meal. Not all villages proved so friendly, and a few days later he was under attack and forced to retaliate. But Cameron, unlike Stanley who believed in using force, "felt that the merit of any geographical discovery would be irretrievably marred by shedding a drop of native blood except in self-defence."

Lake Sankorra receded like a mirage. Everyone had heard of it, no one had been there. Several months later Cameron was camped at the village of a powerful despot named Kasongo, and experiencing the usual maddening delays in getting promised guides and supplies. Kasongo's retinue included men whose hands, lips, noses, and ears had been cut off as a result of his bad temper. Despite this, the mutilated subjects followed him around like faithful dogs. Although he demanded everything Cameron had, from watch and rifle to books and boots, he refused to supply guides or help to reach Lake Sankorra. Cameron reluctantly abandoned his hopes of finding the lake and floating down the Congo to the sea, and began to consider the problem of getting away from his grasping host. His rescuer was "an old and ugly Negro," a slave trader called Alvez, who arrived at Kasongo's village riding in a litter born by his porters. Alvez was on his way to Angola with his caravan of slaves and ivory. Cameron, with reluctance, decided to travel in his company. They moved off following the Lualaba upstream on June 10, 1875, with 1,500 yoked slaves.

Alvez' men plundered the countryside like a swarm of locusts, digging up sweet potatoes, stripping the bananas, and destroying unripe crops. Meanwhile they continued their slave raiding. Cameron was shocked to see a "bag" of 52 women brought in, tied in lots of 17 or 18, some with babes in arms and some far advanced in pregnancy, all covered with weals from brutal beatings. To procure those 52 women, he reckoned, at least 10 villages, each with a

Above: the entrance to the Lukuga outlet of Lake Tanganyika, which Cameron sketched in May, 1874.

Below: Walking through the grass in northwest Zambia. The whole of Africa is seamed with paths like this, running through bush or forest, so narrow that it is only possible to walk in single file.

population of 100 or 200, had been destroyed and the people left to starve in the bush. "Africa is bleeding out her life blood at every pore." The brutal treatment of the slaves appalled Cameron. But, with a handful of men and no guides or supplies, there was nothing he could do to help Alvez' victims.

In a region called Ulunda, they left the Congo's headwaters behind and headed a little south of due west, to those of the Zambezi. These two great systems interlocked so closely, Cameron observed, that a 20-mile-long canal could probably connect them. The route now lay over enormous flooded plains, and fish appeared on a menu that otherwise grew increasingly meager. Cameron's goods were all but exhausted and he was reduced to offering his bedding for a dying pig, and tearing up his overcoat to barter away piece by piece. Alvez refused help and obliged Cameron to pay with his last remaining beads for a chunk of rotting elephant's trunk.

When the miserable retinue reached Portuguese territory, the usual signs of civilization appeared—high prices and strong liquor. They were still far from the Portuguese cities and the coast when Alvez reached home. He was greeted by a mob of women who pelted him with flour as a sign of honor. After the festivities he paid off his men —each got 20 yards of cloth and a little gunpowder in reward for nearly two years on the march. They seemed satisfied.

Cameron went on toward the Atlantic coast with Bombay and his few remaining men, soaked in perpetual rain and short of food. Most of the porters were too weak to carry loads any longer and lay down in despair. There was only one chance to save their lives: to make a forced march to the west coast and send back supplies. Cameron started off with 5 men and a single load weighing 20 pounds, half a chicken and 2 yards of cloth. There were 130 miles to go across a mountain range rising to 8,595 feet. The group marched at top speed for 12 or 13 hours a day, scrambling on hands and knees over crags, and sleeping in the open. Every night, no matter how exhausted, Cameron fixed his position by the stars, recorded his altitude by noting the temperature of boiling water, and entered his findings in his journal. At sea level, water boils at 212°F. For every 550 foot increase of altitude the boiling point drops approximately 1°F. In the days before handy aneroid altimeters were available, this simple method gave a fair approximation of altitude. It was by "boiling his thermometer" that Cameron estimated that the Lualaba was lower than the Nile and could not drain into it.

There was precious little to eat. When they were almost in sight of the sea, Cameron was seized by an attack of acute scurvy. On the last range of hills, when he was scarcely able to stagger, a man met them with a basket of food, sent by a Portuguese trader who had heard of their approach from local tribesmen. As he neared Benguela on November 7, 1875, Cameron unfurled his flag and marched into town to be greeted by a Frenchman who sprang from a hammock, uncorked a bottle of wine, and drank to "the first European who

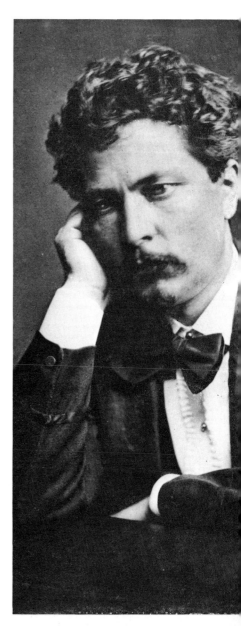

Above: a photograph of Henry Morton Stanley, taken when he left on his search for Livingstone. His stormy, insecure childhood formed an often ruthless, passionate character for life.

Below: Edward Pocock. Stanley warned their family that Africa could be cruel, but permitted himself "to be overborne by the eager courage and devotion of these adventurous lads."

Below: Frank Pocock, a fisherman's son who, with his brother, accompanied Stanley on his expedition in 1874.

had ever succeeded in crossing tropical Africa from east to west."

As a geographer, Cameron was accurate and perceptive. He was right about the Lukuga, right about the Lualaba. His charts of the unknown country between the Lualaba and the Kasai rivers, in modern Katanga, filled in an important gap on the map. His outlook on African character and society was more attuned to Livingstone's than to that of Stanley, Speke, or Baker. He made one more expedition on the west coast of Africa, with Sir Richard Burton. Cameron was killed in a hunting accident in England in 1894.

Fourteen months after Cameron left Nyangwe, Henry Morton Stanley arrived. Where Cameron had failed to get canoes, the "breaker of stones" succeeded by the simple and direct method of using force and threats. At this village beside the majestic pale-gray Lualaba, Stanley embarked upon the last lap of his epic journey across the continent from coast to coast.

His was a very different kind of expedition from Cameron's, and he was a very different man. Yet both had been set upon the path of exploration by a deep love and admiration for David Livingstone. Both wanted to complete Livingstone's work, and Stanley did so. He really did settle for once and all not only the question of the Nile, but also that of the Congo and the great African watershed of which Sir Roderick Murchison had written to Livingstone so many years before. After Stanley, there were plenty of pieces to be fitted into the jigsaw, but the pattern was clear.

The story of Henry Morton Stanley has often been told. Born in 1841, the illegitimate son of a Welsh farmer, brought up in a workhouse without love or kindness, he reached New Orleans as a cabinboy, took the name of his American benefactor, and became a successful roving reporter for the *New York Herald*. The *Herald*'s famous editor, James Gordon Bennett, Jr., sent him on the expedi-

Above: Lake Victoria. Stanley first saw the lake on February 27, 1875. He reached the brow of a hill, and the first quick view revealed a long, broad arm of water stretching eastward.

Above right: Mutesa's palace. The old palace of the Kabaka, or king, of Buganda, where Mutesa gave audience to Speke, Grant, and Stanley, still stands on the hill at Rubaga, and is preserved today as a national monument. It closely resembles the descriptions made in the 1800's.

tion of 1871 to find Livingstone at Ujiji. Until that encounter, journalism was Stanley's life and he had no thought of exploration. "I detest the land most heartily," he had written of Africa in his journal. "I am seldom well except for a day or two when steeped in quinine." Three years later he heard of the death of his hero. "May I be selected to succeed him in the opening up of Africa to the shining light of Christianity!"—adding significantly, "but not after his method." Livingstone had been almost a saint, but in Stanley's opinion "the selfish wooden-headed world requires promptings other than the Gospel."

In London, Stanley bought and read 130 books on Africa, and planned the most ambitious journey ever made in that continent. He persuaded the London *Daily Telegraph* to back the exploits, and Bennett to share the expense. For his companions he chose, almost at random, the two young Pocock brothers, Frank and Edward, sons of an English fisherman, and a London hotel clerk, Frederick Barker.

Stanley had three clear objectives. The first was to sail all around Lake Victoria. He would find out once and for all whether it was one lake, as Speke had believed, or several smaller ones as maintained by Burton and others, and whether other rivers flowed out of it as well as Speke's. The second was to do the same on Lake Tanganyika, to check Cameron's discovery of the Lukuga creek and find out whether the lake had any other outlets. He would make these lake voyages in a barge (the *Lady Alice*), that could be taken apart in five pieces, carried to the lakes and reassembled. The third objective was to reach the Lualaba where Livingstone had abandoned it and follow it down to wherever it led.

In Zanzibar, Stanley packed more than 8 tons of baggage into 60-pound loads, and assembled 356 men plus donkeys and dogs. The expedition set out from Bagamoyo on November 17, 1874. The

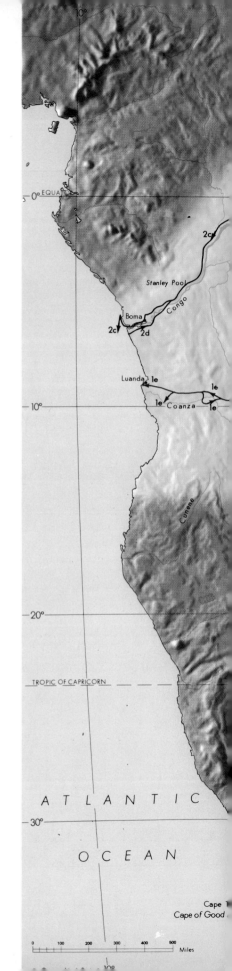

big caravan offered a tempting prize and was attacked in earnest by
2,000 warriors who were beaten off with rifle-fire but at a cost of
26 of Stanley's men killed and others wounded. Disease and
starvation killed many others. By the end of January, 1875, Stanley
had lost one quarter of his men, including Edward Pocock, and had
had to burn valuable stores. On February 27 they reached Mwanza
on the southern shore of Lake Victoria.

Stanley launched the *Lady Alice* and, with 11 men, set sail up
the lake accompanied by a flotilla of canoes. The hazards now were
violent storms, hippopotamuses that tried to overturn the boats, and
tribesmen in canoes who attacked them. But at the northern end of
the lake the "pleasing civility" of Mutesa's well-ordered kingdom
rewarded them. Six beautiful canoes paddled out to greet them.
Their commander, a handsome young man clad in a headdress of
beads and feathers and a robe of red and white goatskin, conducted
them to a ceremonial reception by thousands of people dressed in
bark robes. Mutesa ordered a salute of between 200 and 300
muskets and innumerable drums that boomed like thunder.

Stanley's impressions of Mutesa were very different from Speke's.
The king was 13 years older and a "large-eyed, nervous looking,
thin man" whom Stanley found intelligent and distinguished.
"Either Mutesa is a very admirable man, or I am a very impression-
able traveler, or Mutesa is so perfect in the art of duplicity
. . . that I became his dupe." This was possible. For Stanley's benefit
he laid on a naval review of 40 war canoes and about 1,200 men
commanded by an admiral in a crimson, gold-braided jacket.

Impressed by the king's interest in Christianity, Stanley wrote a
letter to his newspapers appealing for missionaries, and entrusted it
to a Belgian explorer, Colonel Linant de Bellefonds, who turned up
at Mutesa's. The colonel was murdered in the Sudan on his way home
and the letter was found in his boot. When it reached England in
November, 1875, the letter created a sensation. Within weeks
£25,000 ($60,000) was subscribed for the dispatch of a mission to
Buganda the following year. This was the start of the British pene-
tration that was to lead to the incorporation of most of eastern Africa
into the British Empire.

After a 12-day visit at the Buganda court, Stanley and his men
headed the *Lady Alice* south toward their base. En route they
narrowly escaped death on Bumbire Island where they were

20°　　　　　　　　　30°　　　　　　　　　40°　　　　　　　　　50°

Ubangi

2c

Congo　　　　Yambuya

2e

d　　Stanley Falls　2d　　2e

2d　　2c

2c

1h　1h

Nyangwe　　1h

2c　2c　　1h

Luama　　2b　1h　1g

Ujiji　1g

1h　1g

2a　Lake

1g　2b

Lualaba　1h

Lake

Tanganyika

1g　2b

1g　2b

L. Mweru　1g　1h

1g　1h

1e　1g

L. Bangweulu

1e　1g

MUCHINGA MTS.

1e

Zambezi　1e

1e

1e

1e

1e

1d　1e

Linyanti　1f

Victoria　1d

Falls

Zouga　1e

1c　1d

1d

1c

Lake Ngami　1c

1e

1c

Kalahari　1b

Desert　1e

Kolobeng　1b

1b

1b e

1a

Kuruman

1a

Vaal

1d

1e

Orange　DRAKENSBERG

1a

1e

Port Elizabeth

MITUMBA MTS.

Lake Albert　2e

2e

RUWENZORI RA.　Ripon Falls
16,763　2b

Lake Edward　2b

2e

Lake　2b

2e　Victoria　2b

2b

1h & 2a

2e

2e

2b

2e

2b

1h　Tabora

2a　1h

MT KENYA
2a

KILIMANJARO
19,340

2b

2a

Bagamoyo　Zanzibar

1g

Lake
Nyasa

1f

(L. Malawi)

1f

Luangwa　1g

1g

1f

1g

Rovuma
1f

L. Shirwa

1f

MLANJE PEAK
9843

Quebrabasa　1f

Rapids　Tete　1f

Shire

Zambezi

Quelimane

1f

Shupanga　1e

1e　1f

Limpopo

1f

COMORO IS.

ANJOUAN I.

1f

I N D I A N

O C E A N

EQUATOR　0°

10°

MOZAMBIQUE CHANNEL

MADAGASCAR

TROPIC OF CAPRICORN

20°

30°

Livingstone	1a	1841
Livingstone	1b	1842
Livingstone	1c	1849
(with Oswell & Murray)		
Livingstone	1d	1850-2
(with Oswell)		
Livingstone	1e	1852-6
Livingstone	1f	1858-63
(with Charles Livingstone & Kirk)		
Livingstone	1g	1866-9
Livingstone	1h	1869-73
Stanley	2a	1871-2
Stanley	2b	1874-6
Stanley	2c	1876-7
Stanley	2d	1879-84
Stanley	2e	1888-9
(relief of Emin Pasha)		

Above: Tippu Tib was born in Zanzibar of mixed Arab/Negro parentage. He was intelligent, probably not as brutal as many slave traders, had some idea of organized administration, and was always friendly to Europeans.

Below: the Congo forest. When Stanley fought his way through, he was plagued by ticks that buried themselves in his nostrils, snakes, spiders, and lice, as well as armies of ants, wasps, and hornets.

attacked by a mob of angry warriors. They escaped without their oars but pulled up the duckboards and paddled on with only 4 bananas to sustain 12 hungry men. After an absence of 57 days they reached camp to find that Frederick Barker had died. The cost of discovery was great, but Stanley was able to write: "I can state positively that there is but one outlet from the lake, viz: the Ripon Falls."

The whole expedition now crossed the lake to Mutesa's in hired canoes, intending to proceed to Lake Albert. Mutesa was at war with one of his subject tribes and encamped with 150,000 warriors plus 50,000 women near the Ripon Falls. He told Stanley that he must wait until the war was over for guides and an escort to Lake Albert. During the three-month wait, the explorer read to the king from the Bible and, he believed, began Mutesa's conversion to Christianity. The "good, brave, excellent" king kept his word and provided Stanley with an escort of 2,300 men to take him to Lake Albert, but the people living on its shores refused to let this army pass, and Stanley had to give up his idea.

Having proved that "Speke . . . discovered the largest inland sea in Africa . . . as well as its principal outlet" Stanley could mark *completed* on task number one. Now he was ready to tackle the second. Early in 1876 he led his men from the "land of bananas and free entertainment" southwest to Lake Tanganyika, where his objective was to make the first complete exploration and determine what connection, if any, Burton's lake had with the Nile drainage. At Ujiji the *Lady Alice* was put together and Stanley once more took to the water in June, 1876. He sailed completely around the lake, re-examined the Ruzizi and took a look at the reed-choked mouth of Cameron's Lukuga creek. Stanley's tests showed no current flowing one way or the other. The local chiefs told him that it was a two-way river, flowing in during the dry season and out during the wet. Stanley believed that the lake was slowly rising and would soon push away the silt and debris choking the creek, and establish the Lukuga as a regular tributary of the Lualaba, which he called the Livingstone.

By August 25, 1876, when the expedition set out again from Ujiji to complete Livingstone's exploration of the Lualaba, death and disease had reduced its strength to 130 men of whom only 30 were armed. They recrossed Lake Tanganyika and headed for Nyangwe on a path that took them, much to the porters' dread, up steep mountains through Manyuema, a country whose inhabitants were known to be cannibals. At Nyangwe Stanley found the camp of a famous Arab slave trader, Tippu Tib, who had made himself the richest and most powerful individual in central Africa. His real name was Hamed bin Mohammed—a "tall, black-bearded man of negroid complexion, in the prime of life, straight, and quick in his movements, a picture of energy and strength." He had a fine intelligent face, with a nervous twitching of the eyes, and gleaming white and perfectly formed teeth.

Nyangwe stood on the edge of a vast tropical rain forest that stretched no one knew how far to the north, and was believed to be the haunt of cannibals and dwarfs, full of snakes hanging from branches, and gorillas. Stanley wanted the Arab to go with him at least part of the way down the Lualaba into this unknown jungle. After much persuasion, Tippu Tib agreed to accompany Stanley for 60 marches, on payment of 5,000 Spanish dollars.

The combined expedition under the two leaders left Nyangwe on November 5, 1876, Stanley and Frank Pocock with a force of 154 and Tippu Tib with about 700. Both parties included women and children. The journalist called the jungle a Turkish bath. Getting through was like struggling always in a "feeble solemn twilight" with hardly a glimpse of the sun. Everything was drenched in moisture and deep in mold and decaying vegetation. They stumbled through "crawling, obstructing lengths of wild vines." Progress was dreadfully slow and the expedition became "utterly demoralized." Tippu Tib asked to be released from his contract. "The air is killing my people," he said. Stanley managed to talk him out of it. A few days later they came to a village with a street 500 yards long flanked on each side by skulls, 186 in number. The chief said they were skulls of *sokos,* chimpanzees, but Stanley bought two which he took back to England and had identified. They were human.

At this point Stanley had the *Lady Alice* put together and paddled down the river in her with 36 men, everyone else following on foot. Starvation, smallpox, dysentery, and ulcers attacked the land party and every day two or three bodies had to be tossed into the river. On December 2, 1876, Tippu Tib said that he had had enough and this time Stanley agreed.

"We shall go on," he told his own people, "all I ask of you is perfect trust in whatever I say. As a father looks after his children, I

Below: Stanley entitled this sketch he drew "One Foot in the Grave." A man named Zaidi was caught among broken rocks, from where he could "contemplate with horror the almost utter impossibility of rescue." However, on this occasion, Zaidi *was* saved.

will look after you. Many of our party have already died, but death is the end of all; it was the will of God, and who shall rebel against His will?"

On Christmas Day, 1876, there was a regatta followed by sports. Tippu Tib beat Frank Pocock by 15 yards in a sprint and won a silver goblet Stanley had brought along. The porters gave a war-dance, clad in feathers, and Tippu Tib provided a banquet of rice and roast mutton. Next day the parties split up. Stanley embarked 149 men, women, and children, plus some donkeys, in canoes, each of which was named after a British cruiser. He showed Pocock a blank chart of where they were going. "I assure you, Frank, this enormous void is about to be filled up." They set off "down the river for the ocean—or death." It was death for a great many.

Stanley's flotilla led by the *Lady Alice* was constantly attacked by the war canoes of the river tribesmen, many of whom were cannibals and regarded the intruders as meat. They came to a chain of seven cataracts and had to unload all the stores, dismantle the *Lady Alice*, and carry everything, including the canoes, through thick jungle and over rocks and cliffs. Nearly all the way they were under attack from cannibals whose "fierce yells came pealing to our ears, even above the roar and tremendous crack of the cataract." Back on the river a few days later they had to fight off an attack by 54 enormous war canoes, the 28th and most ferocious of all their battles. The attackers' village was ornamented with human skulls and had a fetish temple made of ivory.

Day after day "we are stunned with the dreadful drumming which announces our arrival and presence on their waters." The river was by now four miles wide, and so broad that, when storms blew up, shipwreck was added to their perils. Food was always scarce and sometimes nonexistent. "It is a bad world, master, and you have lost your way in it," said the dying wife of one of his men. At last, beyond the cataracts and cannibals, they came to a reach whose inhabitants were friendly. Stanley asked their chief the river's name. "Ikuta ya Kongo," he replied. The question Livingstone had died trying to answer was resolved.

When they had paddled and hauled for over 1,000 miles, the river broadened out beneath white cliffs that reminded them of Dover. "I feel that we are nearing home," Frank Pocock said, and suggested naming the spot Stanley Pool. But Frank's hope had no basis in fact. Not far beyond Stanley Pool another series of cataracts compressed the river's flow into the wildest stretch of water Stanley had yet seen. Once again they had to haul the *Lady Alice*, their 17 surviving canoes, and all the stores down precipices, making for the purpose a tramway with wooden rollers. Then more cataracts, where 9 out of the 17 canoes were lost and Stanley himself nearly drowned.

Pocock was so crippled by ulcers on the feet that he could only crawl. Yet he remained "joyous and light-hearted as a linnet" and fond of singing hymns. "The servant had long ago merged into the

Above: tribes in the remote areas of the Congo still hold to their old beliefs. During droughts in the upland savannah regions, the Rainmaker uses his occult powers to call upon the gods to bring rain. Here a herdsman is watering his cattle at one of the remaining small pools of muddy water, while waiting for the Rainmaker's traditional ritual to bring results.

companion; the companion soon became a friend." On June 3, 1877, this faithful, uncomplaining young man was drowned while trying to shoot the Massassa Rapids. "Alas, my brave, honest, kindly-natured, good Frank," wrote his grieving companion, "I am weary, oh so weary, of this constant tale of woes and death . . . I shall weep for my dear lost friend."

The river seemed to go on for ever and with each mile Stanley's troubles increased. His men were mutinous and sullen with exhaustion and hunger. Another canoe was lost. Three miles of rapids took 30 days to cover with the loss of 4 more men. Even the leader began to doubt—"the full story of the sufferings I have undergone cannot be written."

Early in July, 1877, after five months of torture, came the first whiff of civilization—rising prices. They were asked four yards of cloth for one scrawny rooster. By now "my people were groaning

Above: the *Lady Alice*. Stanley designed
the barge, made of Spanish cedar, so
that it could be dismantled into five
sections (shown right) which could be
carried if the river was impassable.

aloud; their sunken eyes and unfleshed bodies were a living reproach
to me." One man went mad. Others, caught stealing from the villagers, were abandoned to slavery. Toward the end of the month,
they reached a point where Stanley heard that Boma, the European
trading post farthest inland from the coast, was only five days'
journey. The decision was made to save time by striking overland.
The men hauled the *Lady Alice* to a cliff-top and abandoned her. She
had journeyed nearly 7,000 miles, 2,000 miles of it on the heads of
porters.

On August 1, 1877, the expedition, now numbering in all 115
people, including 3 mothers with newborn babies, set out overland. After a dinner of 3 fried bananas, 20 peanuts, and a cup
of muddy water, Stanley wrote a letter appealing for aid from "any
gentleman who speaks English at Embomma" and persuaded a
chief to send it on ahead. Three days later the bearers returned with
"long springing strides" and a letter signed by the agents of an
English company, Hatton & Cookson. Supplies followed close
behind. Stanley's surviving men and women fell upon the provisions
with a "glorious loud-swelling chant of triumph and success," telling
of cannibals, cataracts, great inland seas, ambushes, battles, victories,
and hunger all behind them. For the leader there was pale ale, sherry,
and champagne, tea and coffee, plum pudding, and gooseberry jam.
"The gracious God be praised forever!"

On August 9, 1877, exactly 999 days after the departure from
Zanzibar, Stanley led the expedition into the trading outpost to be
greeted by a group of men whose "pale color, after so long on
gazing on rich black and richer brown, had something of an un-
accountable ghastliness." The Europeans had brought a hammock,
and made Stanley get into it: "I yielded, though it appeared very
effeminate." Three days later he reached the mouth of the Congo and
the blue Atlantic. "The three great problems of the Dark Continent
had been fairly solved."

The Portuguese governor general of Angola offered to send
Stanley to Lisbon in a gunboat, but he refused in order to accompany
his people to Zanzibar. They reached the island in a British naval
vessel on November 27, 1877, just over three years after their
departure. With the death of one of the women the day after their
arrival, the number of survivors was reduced to 114, including
13 women. Of the 4 Europeans only Stanley, "the breaker of
rocks," survived.

Left: view across the Congo River near
Yangambi, Congo (Kinshasa). Before
Stanley, no European had succeeded in
navigating the Congo down its length.
It was shrouded in mystery and fear.
Today its main stream and the tributaries
are valuable commercial waterways,
and the non-navigable sections
have been bypassed by railroads.

The River of Gazelles

12

Left: a tributary of the Zambezi winds its way through miles of matted grass and reeds. All the explorers, whether trying to trace the source of the Nile, the Zambezi, or the Congo, had to fight their way up rivers whose course was blocked by thick mats of plants such as rushes, papyrus, and grass. They often speak of hours of rowing and punting through vegetation, until their men were exhausted.

Above: Alexandrine Tinné, one of the few women who faced the difficulties of African exploration, with its ever-present chance of sudden, violent death at the hands of hostile tribesmen.

The discoveries of Speke, Baker, and Stanley settled the origins of the White Nile. The Blue Nile had been settled by Bruce. One major tributary of the Nile remained to be explored. This was the Bahr el Ghazal, the river of gazelles, a system of rivers rather than a single stream. The Bahr el Ghazal joins the White Nile between 500 and 600 miles above Khartoum. It drains a basin that lies between the hills of Darfur in the northwest Sudan and the watershed between the Nile and the Congo to the southwest. Some thousands of square miles of sudd block the lower reaches of this system, which fans out like strands of hair spread across a basin some 800 miles wide.

One of the first Europeans on the Bahr el Ghazal was John Petherick, the Welsh hunter and trader who failed to meet Speke and Grant at Gondokoro. Petherick went to Egypt in 1845 in the service of Mehemet Ali to search for coal in the Kordofan province of the Sudan. Eight years later, he moved into the Bahr el Ghazal area to purchase ivory and possibly—as some people later hinted—slaves. He explored the Jur River and several other tributaries of the system. Then, pushing on to the southwest, he became the first European to enter the Niam-Niam (Azande) territory of the northern Congo. Besides maps of the river, Petherick's discoveries added to the list of African wildlife. He was the first to see the whale-headed stork and the waterbuck, a rare species of antelope that lives in the wet lands of rivers and marshes.

The only woman to explore Africa in her own right was Alexandrine Tinné, said to be the richest heiress in The Netherlands. In 1863 she appeared on the Sudanese scene with her mother, an aunt, and five scientists, and made her way up the shallow channel of the Bahr el Ghazal. From Khartoum her party were paddled upstream in barges as far as they could go. Then they went overland to the Jur and Kosango rivers and beyond to the borders of Niam-Niam. Alexandrine's mother and one of the scientists died from fever and one scientist was killed by a charging buffalo. Miss Tinné's aunt died soon after their return to Khartoum in July, 1864. The survivors brought back much valuable material relating to the plants, animals, geology, and climate of a region only partially explored.

Alexandrine Tinné inspired biographers to use such adjectives as "young and beautiful, remarkably accomplished, a daring horsewoman, mistress of many tongues including Arabic." After the Bahr el Ghazal expedition, she made her base in Cairo and traveled in

Algeria and Tunisia. In 1869, she recruited two Dutch sailors in Tripoli to join her on a caravan bound for Lake Chad. Knowing the hazards of desert travel she took two iron water tanks carried by camels. A rumor spread that the tanks were full of golden coins. At a camp in the Sahara the guides slew her Dutch sailors, slashed Alexandrine with sabers, and left her lying in the blazing sunshine crying for water, to bleed slowly to death. She was only 30 years old.

Early that same year, a German botanist, Georg August Schweinfurth, born in 1836 in Riga, Latvia, arrived in Khartoum to explore in the equatorial districts southwest of the Nile. He later wrote that "the blameless avarice of the plant-hunter," was the main reason for his journey. But Schweinfurth also wanted to explore the watershed between the Nile and the Congo, where the Niam-Niam cannibals lived. Although most of the country in the Bahr el Ghazal region was still unknown to Europeans, it had been deeply penetrated by Khartoum-based Arab slave and ivory traders. They had set up a system of interior trading posts, or *zaribas,* where their agents kept trade goods and assembled ivory and slaves. At intervals, armed men from the zaribas raided surrounding tribesmen for cattle, keeping the country in constant ferment. The only safe way to travel in the Bahr el Ghazal area was in company with one of the well-armed parties of Khartoum traders.

In January, 1869, Schweinfurth attached himself to a trader's party and left Khartoum for the interior. They sailed as far as possible up the Bahr el Ghazal, and then went on foot to the zaribas. The botanist, a great walker, tramped most of the way and settled in at one of the zaribas in considerable comfort.

Schweinfurth possessed in full measure all the thorough, meticulous, and patient qualities associated with German scholars. He collected all day and classified far into the night. His interests extended to birds, insects, trees, and rocks, and to the customs and skills of the Africans. He was one of the healthiest and happiest travelers who ever set foot in Africa. His record of superb health was broken only once or twice by ulcers and scurvy, never by malaria or dysentery. He looked after himself very carefully, never forgetting to take his antimalarial quinine or to wear his hat. A fair share of travelers' troubles came his way: unpalatable food and, sometimes, hardly any at all; he got soaked on exhausting marches and lost his stores; on one occasion he ran out of ink, but made do

Right: East Africa, showing exploration carried out in the region between the 1840's and the 1890's.

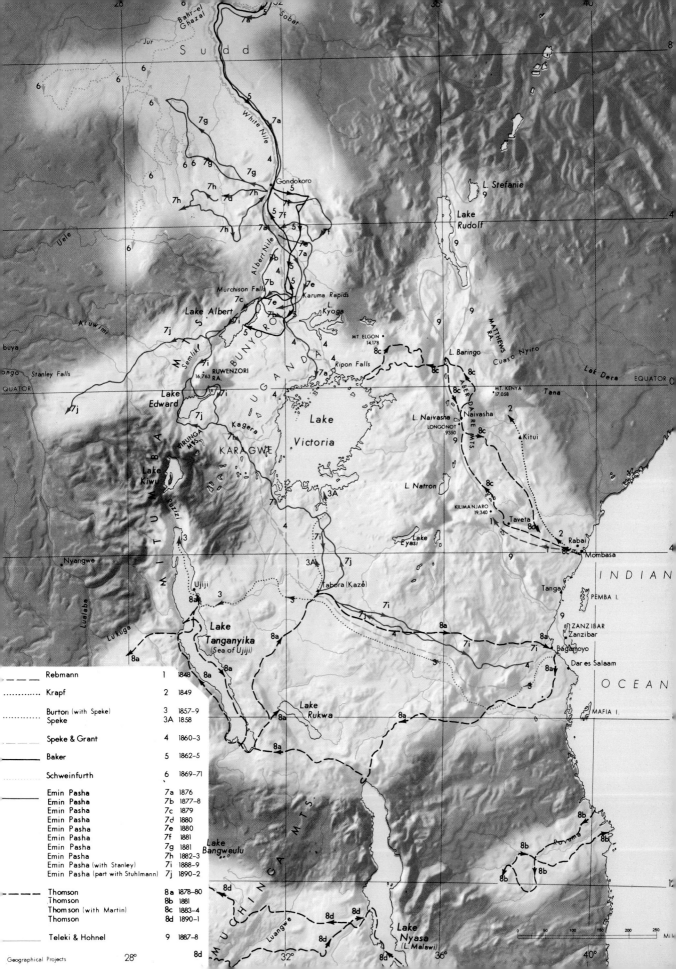

Right: *Cucumis Tinneanus,* a plant which was collected by Alexandrine Tinné and her mother in January, 1864, near the source of the Bahr el Ghazal.

Above: a Schweinfurth drawing of a Niam-Niam hut. Niam-Niam means great eaters, the name given to the tribe because of its cannibal tastes. Schweinfurth reported they were "men of like passions with ourselves, equally subject to . . . grief and joy."

with hen's blood. Schweinfurth spent two-and-a-half years among the western tributaries of the Nile. Later he described the glories of the great tropical forests, mountains, and river valleys in vivid and enthusiastic prose in his book *The Heart of Africa.*

Early in 1870, his company of Khartoumers set out for the dangerous but ivory-rich Niam-Niam cannibal country. Their caravan numbered over 800 men, women, and children, and a large herd of cattle looted from the natives of the region. Following a northward-flowing stream, they came to a stream that flowed the other way. "I was the first European coming from the North," Schweinfurth wrote with satisfaction, "who ever traversed the watershed of the Nile." On March 19, he stood on the banks of the Uele. This was "a thrilling moment that can never fade from the memory. . . . Westerly was the direction of the stream which did not belong to the Nile at all." It "belonged" to the Congo, which it reached by way of the Ubangi River to the west.

Crossing the Uele, the caravan entered the country of the resplendent and despotic King Manzu who ruled much in the style of Mutesa or Kamrasi. His village was made up of thatched reed houses and contained a hall 150 feet long and 50 feet wide. There King Manzu himself, attired in a black baboon headdress adorned with red feathers, with the tails of genets, civet cats, and giraffes dangling from his knees and elbows, and a necklace of lions' fangs, danced "furiously" in a circle of 80 selected wives and massed ranks of armed warriors. Schweinfurth dressed in his best clothes for the occasion—a long black frock coat and polished boots. Manzu was "slight and stiff," with a Nero-like expression of "total ennui and satiety." Schweinfurth thought he looked cruel and avaricious, and "in his eyes gleamed the wild light of animal sensuality."

The German visitor presented Manzu with a telescope, a silver platter, a book with gold edges, a distorting mirror, and over a thousand beads. Manzu reciprocated with a drum concert and a performance by jesters and clowns. He also gave the visitor a portable house made of reeds, and asked for Schweinfurth's dog in return. Schweinfurth countered by asking for a forest-hog and a chimpanzee. He did not get either. Manzu finally persuaded the German to part with his dog by offering him a Pygmy in exchange. The botanist hoped to take the Pygmy, whom he called Tikkitikki, back to Germany. But Tikkitikki died from overeating before he could reach Schweinfurth's homeland.

Manzu's tribe were cannibals. When Schweinfurth let it be known that he was looking for human skulls and bones, they poured in. Most had been boiled and scraped with knives. Some were still warm from the cooking pot. But out of 200 skulls, only 40 were intact. The rest, Schweinfurth noted regretfully, had been smashed to get at the brains. He packed up the skulls, labeled them, and sent them back to Berlin via Khartoum.

Schweinfurth's heart was set on going south from the Uele to look for the source of the Ubangi River, but Manzu refused to give him permission. So with his Pygmy, a wealth of pressed plants, native ornaments, and weapons, Schweinfurth turned back with the ivory traders on April 12, 1871. His stay in the Bahr el Ghazal country had been "one of the most pleasant and successful journeys that has ever been undertaken in so remote a part of the continent."

The return journey was a great deal less successful. A fire swept through one of the zaribas and destroyed all his notes, records, observations, and specimens. He lost his stores and personal possessions in the flames—even his hat and his quinine. For the remaining months of the journey, lacking a chronometer, Schweinfurth literally counted every step of the way. There were $1\frac{1}{4}$ million steps to Khartoum which he reached on July 12. Travels through the malarial swamps so often fatal to Europeans had not impaired Schweinfurth's health in the least. He lived for some time in Cairo, traveling every winter and forwarding his collections to museums. He died, in his 90th year, in Berlin.

During his Cairo years, Schweinfurth had received a visit in 1882 from Joseph Thomson, a young Scottish geologist en route for Zanzibar to start his third African journey. Thomson had begun his African career at the age of 20 by joining an expedition to Lake Tanganyika. On the death of the appointed leader, he took command

Above: Georg August Schweinfurth. He devoted most of his life to Africa. His interest in anthropology, botany, geology, and archaeology carried him for thousands of miles, from the Congo to Lebanon and the Yemen. He continued his journeys until he was 78.

and led the expedition to the northern tip of Lake Nyasa, on to Tanganyika and safely back to Zanzibar in 1880. His second journey took him to the Ruvuma Valley to prospect for coal on behalf of the Sultan of Zanzibar. Thomson had proved himself to be an enterprising, determined, and resourceful explorer and had now been appointed by the Royal Geographical Society to head an expedition of his own. The task was to "ascertain if a practical direct route for European travellers exists through the Masai country from any one of the East African ports to Victoria Nyanza." He was also instructed to explore the Mount Kenya area and to make a general scientific survey of the region—one of the last to be explored. Little had been learned about the region since Krapf had been there.

The Masai are a nomadic, cattle-owning tribe whose homelands lie athwart the Tanzania-Kenya border. In the 1800's their red-ocher-painted warriors were trained and disciplined for nothing but war. The rolling steppes of Masai country lay across the most direct route from the coast to Lake Victoria. Those who followed it did so in peril. Several caravans of Swahili traders had suffered heavy casualties from the hostile Masai. In 1880 no European had yet traversed the route, but Gustav Adolf Fischer, sent out by the German African Society of Berlin, was planning to try it. His was a large, well-equipped expedition which aimed to reach a distant and unmapped lake, Baringo.

In Zanzibar, Thomson took on a young Maltese sailor, James Martin. He could speak 10 languages "sailor-fashion" but could not read or write. Martin "never presumed upon the favour with which I regarded him and had no opinions of his own." He proved an ideal companion for Thomson, who liked his own way. They left the coast on March 15, 1883, with 3 donkeys and 113 men. At Taveta, about 150 miles inland and practically in sight of Kilimanjaro, they found "an African arcadia" rich in crops, shade, and food.

Above: a Masai manyatta, or hut of skins and mud stretched over a wooden frame. A nomadic people, the Masai do not build permanent settlements or villages, but each family lives in its own manyatta. When they move on, they can quickly build a similar structure at the next place where they stop.
Left: scimitars and daggers from the Uele River. King Manzu ruled over a people called the Monbuttu, widely famed for their skill in making iron and copper ornaments and weapons.

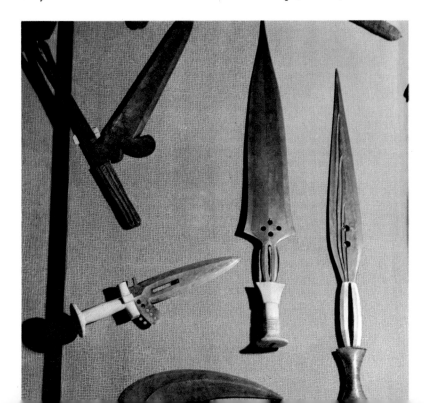

The expedition paused there to restring 60,000 beads, the better, they hoped, to please Masai taste. Pestered by the Taveta people for a charm to keep off the Masai, Thomson dropped some fruit salts into a glass of water. The effervescence proved so impressive that he repeated the trick at almost every camp. He also created much wide-eyed astonishment by removing his two false teeth and putting them in again.

From Taveta, the Thomson caravan marched due west past Kilimanjaro into the Masai country to find that Fischer had passed

Left: Suk boys. The Suk are a primitive tribe, living in Kenya, north of Lake Baringo. As well as the usual cattle, sheep, and goats, they keep camels, and these are camel herdboys.

through a short while before. There had been a brush between his caravan and the Masai, the country was in a state of turmoil, and Thomson's party had an anxious moment when a deputation of Masai warriors appeared. The warriors, thickly smeared with sheep's fat and red ocher, their hair twisted into dangling pigtails, were carrying long, broad-bladed spears. They occupied the explorer's camp as if they owned it. Thomson felt like a freak in a circus side show as they crowded around him, prodded, and pinched, fingered his hair, and tried to pull off his trousers. Next day he heard that the *moran* (warriors) were mobilizing to attack in force, so he retreated to Taveta. Before setting out for a second time on July 16, 1883, he joined forces with a considerably stronger Swahili caravan.

This time the Masai did not molest them. They marched past Kilimanjaro and north into the Great Rift Valley. Some 50 miles northwest of Nairobi in present-day Kenya, Thomson climbed the extinct volcano Longonot and was the first European to look down into its deep cauldron. Just to the north of Longonot and almost in its shadow lay Lake Naivasha, which Thomson found to be "one moving mass of ducks, with ibises, pelicans, and other aquatic birds." Fischer had passed through earlier that year and so became the European discoverer of this lovely lake on the floor of the Great Rift Valley. The Masai had forced him to turn back, and he did not reach Lake Baringo.

The arrogant Masai again invaded Thomson's camp, and "treated us as if we were so many slaves." They made the Europeans take off their boots to show their toes, demanded beads, and behaved in a threatening manner. At Gilgil in the Naivasha area the expedition came upon a camp of 3,000 moran who were preparing to attack another Masai clan. Probably it was their chief preoccupation with internal warfare that allowed the travelers to go through.

On October 6, Thomson left Martin and the caravan and, with 30 picked men, made a dash east to Mount Kenya. They crossed a range of mountains rising to 8,000 feet which Thomson named after Lord Aberdare, who in 1886 became president of the Royal Geographical Society. Later the party camped beside a spectacular waterfall which Thomson named for himself. On the cold and windswept plains below Mount Kenya, cattle were dying in thousands of the disease rinderpest. There was no food to be bought and the Masai would not let the expedition shoot game. Thomson and his men had

to overcome nausea and eat the stinking flesh of the dead cattle.

They pressed on to reach the forested base of the mountain near the headwaters of the Ngiro River. That evening "a dazzling white pinnacle caught the last rays of the sun, and shone with a beauty marvellous, spirit-like, and divine." Thomson's hope of climbing it had to be abandoned. The party's supplies were exhausted. The Masai were menacing them, "fruit salts and a couple of artificial teeth were no longer novelties." The explorers decamped by night and headed northwest in soaking rain over forested hills until they reached the lip of a trough 3,300 feet deep. There they looked down on "a dazzling expanse of water glittering like a mirror in the fierce rays of the tropical sun." One more lake had been discovered. Next evening, the party camped by Lake Baringo, reunited with their caravan, feasting on millet porridge and fish. The following day Thomson made friends with the local Njemps whose young ladies sat on his knee and "lolled about the floor like young puppies"—a pleasant change from the overbearing moran. From Baringo, they marched due west and early on December 10, 1883, reached the northeast border of Lake Victoria, 45 miles from the Ripon Falls. The exuberant Thomson danced a Scottish reel to entertain the Kavirondo people of the lake shore.

Thomson's homeward journey started on December 13, 1883, and soon led him to the discovery and naming of another mountain, Mount Elgon, 14,178 feet high. Here he was badly gored by a wounded buffalo and had to be carried on a hammock—"the first time I had ever sunk so low." But not the last. Dysentery so weakened him that at Naivasha he collapsed and had to be carried over an escarpment 9,000 feet high through biting cold and almost continuous rain or hail. For six weeks Thomson lay semiconscious in a damp, cold, and windowless grass hut. Then he decided he might as well die on the road, and set off in a hammock. Instead of dying he began to mend. He passed through Ulu with "rising hopes of life" and reached the coast on May 24, 1884. In Zanzibar, good nursing and his own youth and strength combined to bring about a complete recovery.

Like other explorers, Thomson went back for more, despite the rough treatment Africa had given him. He made three more journeys. The first, in 1890–1891, in the service of the British South Africa Company, was to the regions where Livingstone had wandered, north of the Zambezi between lakes Nyasa and Bangweulu.. He covered around 1,000 miles of still unmapped territory, making contact with the native peoples and drawing up trade agreements with their chiefs. It was said of Thomson that he had "the high and glorious distinction of never having caused the death of a native." But African travel caused his own death. The final journey, his sixth, broke his health, and he died in London in 1895 at the age of 37. By nature energetic and forward-thrusting, he had schooled himself in patience and restraint and was guided by the Italian saying: "who goes slowly, goes safely: who goes safely, goes far."

Above: a flowering cork tree. In the background is Mount Elgon, a huge, extinct volcano straddling the borders of Kenya and Uganda.

Left: Thomson's Falls, which he named for himself. They lie at the northern end of the Aberdare Range, where it drops steeply to the Great Rift Valley.

Completing the Puzzle

13

The England to which Joseph Thomson returned in 1884 was preoccupied with the fate of one of its national heroes, General Gordon. The general was besieged in Khartoum by the forces of a Moslem religious fanatic. From this situation arose the last of the great African expeditions, the last major geographical discoveries, and the final solution of the Nile puzzle.

In 1869, the Khedive (ruler) Ismail of Egypt had resolved at last to tackle the open scandal of the slave trade in the Sudan. He commissioned Samuel Baker—Sir Samuel by then—to bring under control the Upper Nile regions between Khartoum and Bunyoro. When Baker's four-year term of office as governor general was completed in 1873, Ismail appointed the British colonel, later general, Charles Gordon of the Royal Engineers to succeed him.

Among Gordon's aides were the men who completed the exploration of the Nile between the Ripon Falls and Gondokoro (near

modern Jūbā). One was an Italian, Romolo Gessi. Gordon brought two steel boats up the river as far as the rapids above Gondokoro. Gessi had the boats taken apart, carried up the rapids in sections, and reassembled. Then in 1876, with a compatriot, Carlo Piaggia, Gessi sailed up the river and around Lake Albert, finding it to be considerably smaller than Baker had believed.

Gordon sent another of his officers, an American, Colonel Charles Chaillé-Long, to Buganda to make contact with King Mutesa. Mutesa welcomed his guest with traditional honors by the sacrifice of 30 human victims. On his way back Chaillé-Long, following the Nile down from the Ripon Falls to the Karuma Falls, filled in the last remaining blank and discovered Lake Kyoga.

Another of Gordon's men was a German explorer and surgeon, Eduard Schnitzer. In 1876 Gordon engaged Schnitzer as a medical officer and sent him up the river to a post at Lado. Here he was so

Above: Lake Albert. Although it is not as large as Baker thought, it is a sizable lake, 100 miles long with an average width of about 20 miles.
Below: General Charles Gordon, who was killed at the capture of Khartoum.

Below: The Congo forest. The first stage of Stanley's journey from the mouth of the Congo could be done by boat. But after reaching Yambuya, he had to cover hundreds of miles on foot.

successful that in 1878 Gordon appointed him governor of Equatoria, the southern part of present-day Sudan. Emin Pasha, as Schnitzer now called himself, was a scholar rather than a soldier. Short-sighted, shy, mild of manner, the master of 8 or 10 languages, he made valuable observations of the plants, insects, birds, beasts, and peoples of the Sudan. Many of his specimens were sent to European museums. His main geographical discovery was the Semliki River which flows into Lake Albert from the south.

Between 1881 and 1885, a Moslem leader, Mohammed Ahmed, who called himself the Mahdi, raised the Sudanese Arab tribes in revolt against the rule of Egypt. Egyptian garrisons in the Sudan were overrun or cut off and the capital, Khartoum, was threatened. In this emergency the Khedive appealed to Gordon, who had by then resigned his governor generalship, to return to Khartoum to evacuate the garrison. Gordon agreed. In March, 1884, he entered Khartoum and for 10 months he succeeded in holding off the Mahdi's forces. But by the beginning of 1885 he could hold out no longer. On January 26, the Moslem forces burst into the city and slew Gordon and most of the Egyptians. For six months the Mahdi became the undisputed master of the Sudan. Then he died, and the country fell into chaos.

At Lado on the Upper Nile, Emin Pasha, his Egyptian and Sudanese soldiers, and two Europeans, Wilhelm Junker and Gaetani Casati, were now cut off from all contact with the outside world. They retreated stage by stage to Wadelai, a little way north of Lake Albert. Their very existence was forgotten until Junker emerged by way of Buganda and brought news of his companions' predicament to Cairo in 1886. Public concern in Britain led to the raising of a fund to equip an expedition to take supplies to Emin Pasha and his companions and to bring them back to civilization. Henry Stanley was placed in charge.

Stanley decided to start from the mouth of the Congo, cross the tropical rain forests in the center of Africa to Lake Albert, and sail up to Wadelai and the beleaguered Emin. He took 10 Europeans, 697 porters recruited in Zanzibar, and a contingent of 97 men under the trader Tippu Tib, who now controlled all the regions on the Upper Congo between Nyangwe and Stanley Falls. Tippu Tib undertook to provide a further 600 men to carry stores to Emin from Stanley Pool.

On June 15, 1887, the expedition reached the limit of river navigation at Yambuya. Here Stanley was obliged to leave more than half of his men and stores under his second-in-command, Major Barttelot. They were to follow on as soon as Tippu Tib's promised porters arrived. Stanley set out on June 28 with 4 Europeans and 384 carriers. The march was estimated at about 550 miles, all through unknown country.

The Ituri forest of the central Congo remains, even today, second only to that of the Amazon basin as the densest, darkest, wettest, most impenetrable tropical forest on earth. No sunlight penetrated the canopy of foliage overhead, and rain sometimes fell for several days and nights on end. Stanley's men had to hack a path through creepers and tangled undergrowth. Pygmies discharged poisoned arrows at the intruders and planted poisoned skewers in their path. Hornet stings and cuts developed into terrible ulcers. The marchers' route took them through a region depopulated by slavers, where no food whatever was to be found.

It took five months to get through the forest. In the last 70 days the expedition lost 180 men. When they staggered into a village that had escaped being plundered, they gorged themselves for 13 days. Another 12 days and they emerged suddenly into open air and sunlight where the sight of green plains, cattle, and "a brand-new sky of intense blue" transfigured everyone. Skeletons as they were, they

Above: one of Stanley's many problems was the known hostility of the Arabs to Europeans. He solved this by the brilliant idea of enlisting Tippu Tib's cooperation, but realized that absolute reliance could not be placed on his assistance. His forebodings proved justified when the Arab's carriers would not go beyond the Aruwimi River.

Below: Stanley's boots. He wore these all the way down the Congo. The repairs are all his own work, part of the skill he had to develop in maintaining his own clothing and equipment.

Left: Stanley's grueling "rescue" of Emin Pasha turned out to be an anticlimax. Emin was perfectly well, and his first thought was to present his rescuer with a new pair of shoes.

danced in the sun. But not for long. Soon they were under attack and had to fight their way to the shores of Lake Albert. They got there on December 13, 1887, after 169 days.

In the forest, Stanley had been forced to abandon the boat he was carrying in sections to launch on the lake. Now he had to turn back to fetch it, and to find out what had happened to Major Barttelot's contingent. Stanley collected the boat and, sick with acute gastritis, was carried back to Lake Albert in a hammock, still without any news of Barttelot's men. A few days afterward Emin Pasha arrived.

The German turned out to be in the best of health. Smartly clad in a neat white uniform, he seemed to lack for nothing. In his years of exile he had planted crops and built comfortable quarters. He had established a small cotton ginnery (a gin is a machine for separating cotton fiber from seeds and waste material) and a dockyard, added to his collection of skins of birds and other animals, and studied ethnology and bird migration. He had also, it was said, amassed £60,000 ($144,000) worth of ivory. Emin lived in considerable style, and most of his men had taken native wives. Far from wanting to be rescued, he wanted to stay where he was. He did, however, want supplies and ammunition, but Stanley convinced him that these could not be sent to Wadelai. Besides, Mahdist forces were advancing up the Nile. Emin shilly-shallied for three weeks. He then reluctantly agreed to accompany Stanley—taking his men and their families and possessions—to the coast by way of lakes Victoria and Tanganyika.

Stanley had first to find the missing Barttelot and the rear column. By forced marches he retraced his footsteps through the forest in 62 days, with further losses among his men. Ninety miles short of Yambuya, on August 17, 1888, he came upon the remnants of his column. They had a terrible tale of disaster to tell. Major Barttelot had been murdered, and another officer had died. Of the large contingent Stanley had left at Yambuya, only 60 service-able porters and 1 European remained. Tippu Tib had failed to send the promised porters and had continued to make excuses for over a year while the column melted away as a result of death and desertion. The Arab's plan was to plunder the stores when the column had become sufficiently weakened.

Within two weeks, Stanley got together 500 men and started through the forest for the third time, taking all his stores. Beside Lake Albert he had to wait for three months while the indecisive Emin gathered together those of his men and their families who were willing to be rescued. On April 10, 1889, a crowd of over 1,500 men, women, and children, with their household goods including bedsteads and grindstones, set out to walk the 1,300 miles to the coast at Bagamoyo. They reached there on December 4.

On the way, Stanley made his last two geographical discoveries. Leaving the southern end of Lake Albert, the crowd descended into the valley of the Semliki River and found that it issued from an unmapped lake, 70 miles to the southwest. This Stanley named Albert Edward Nyanza after Britain's Prince of Wales. It is now called Lake Edward. A great range of mountains could be seen on the farther, eastern side of the lake. The clouds that at first hid the range drew aside to reveal peaks white with snow, rising to nearly 17,000 feet. This was the Ruwenzori range—the legendary Mountains of the Moon drawn on Ptolemy's map, and believed by the early Greeks and Romans to be the ultimate source of the Nile. The Bakers, Emin Pasha, Gessi, Casati, and Stanley himself on his

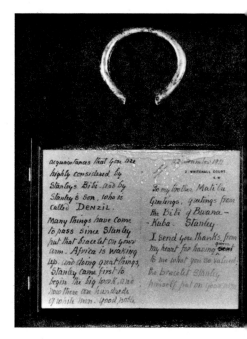

Above: this letter was written by Lady Dorothy Stanley to Chief Kavali Matibu, an old Congo friend of her husband's, thanking him for sending her the bracelet shown. The bracelet had been placed on Kavali's wrist by Stanley, and preserved by his son.

Above: Karamoja dancers. When Karamoja Bell entered their country, the tribes were fighting one another. Now it is peaceful, with three administrative districts, each with a chief.

previous journey, had all been near the mountains at one time or another. All had missed them. The Ruwenzori range was scaled and charted by the Duke of the Abruzzi in 1906.

As it turns out, the Greeks and Romans were proved nearly correct. Water from snows melting on the Ruwenzori range finds its way to Lake Edward and then through Lake Albert to the White Nile. But the ultimate source of the Nile is some way to the south of the Ruwenzori range. The Kagera River flows into Lake Victoria on its western side. At flood the Kagera's flow can be traced through Lake Victoria to its issue as the Victoria Nile. But the Luvironza River in Burundi is the Nile's most remote headstream. It flows into the Ruvura River, which is a headstream of the Kagera River.

After Stanley's important discovery came a long, depressing tramp to the coast with Emin's raggle-taggle caravan. Stanley tired of "the continual rising in the morning with a hundred moaning and despairing invalids wailing their helplessness and imploring for help, of those daily scenes of disease, suffering, and unmitigatable misery. . . ."

By this time the colonial era was getting under way in Africa. At Bagamoyo, Stanley, Emin, and their men were greeted by the German commandant and given a banquet. The party ended suddenly with Emin falling off a balcony and suffering concussion. Emin however recovered and later returned to Africa where he took service with the government of German East Africa (now Tanzania). Soon afterwards, in 1892, he was murdered by tribesmen at Stanley Falls.

When Stanley reached London in 1890, he gave up his American citizenship and once more became British. The public acclaimed his exploits, and European kings and queens rained congratulations on him. He was 49 years old and had done with African travel, but was ready for exploration in the new field of marriage. The following year his wedding took place with pomp and ceremony in West-

Above: The twin summits of Margherita Peak and Alexandra Peak, the highest peaks of the Ruwenzori Range. Ruwenzori is the local word for rainmaker. But the local people called the mountains *Gambalagala,* literally "my eyes smart," referring to the sun glistening on the snow at the top.

Left: Stanley lecturing in the Albert Hall after his return to London, with the Prince of Wales in the chair. Stanley had to face some hostile comment on his handling of the Emin expedition, but the magnitude of his achievements was still recognized by the general public.

minster Abbey. His bride, Dorothy Tennant, was the talented daughter of a Member of Parliament. Stanley himself was elected to Parliament, and bought a small country estate in Surrey. In 1899, he was knighted. He died in 1904.

By the end of the 1800's, no major geographical discoveries in eastern and central Africa remained to be made. The few blanks left on the maps had been gradually filled in. One of these was the semidesert area north of Thomson's route to Lake Victoria, in the extreme northwest of present-day Kenya. It is a hard, waterless region of rock, scrub, and volcanic mountain, sparsely inhabited by nomadic Somalis with flocks of camels, and by Galla tribes. Here, rumor said, lay the largest unmapped lake in eastern Africa. About 185 miles long, it was larger even than Lake Albert. This prize fell to two Hungarian noblemen, Count Teleki and Lieutenant Ludwig von Höhnel. Leaving Zanzibar on January 23, 1887, they followed Thomson's route through the dangerous country of the Masai and Kikuyu, sending up rockets every night to impress the tribes. They shouldered their way through armed warriors, sometimes showered by arrows and retaliating with guns. The Hungarians were the first to climb above the snowline on Mount Kenya, reaching a height of 15,355 feet.

Marching northward, they passed and named the Matthews range of mountains. On March 4, 1888, Count Teleki wrote they were "rewarded for all our arduous struggles and terrible privations by coming in sight of the long-sought lake gleaming away in the far distance." He named it after Crown Prince Rudolf of Austria. Although short of food the party marched up the eastern side and found another, smaller lake which they named after Rudolf's wife, the Archduchess Stefanie. Their return journey ended at the coast on October 24, 1888.

The last lake had been fixed in its correct position, labeled, and described. But there was much still to be discovered about the plants and trees, birds and beasts, minerals and hydrology of Africa. Further discoveries of this kind were to be made by geologists, naturalists, scientists, and surveyors. In 1883, the German explorer Fischer first described the Great Rift Valley, that trough which cuts through eastern Africa and the Middle East from Mozambique to Syria. Ten years later, a geologist, John Walter Gregory, studied and described it scientifically, and explained its origins. On Mount Kenya Gregory mapped and named many lakes, rivers, glaciers, and cols, including the Teleki Valley.

Big game hunters also filled important gaps. The elephant hunter "Karamoja" Bell was the first European to explore the region along the present Uganda-Kenya border, the district from which he took his name. Frederick Courtney Selous, the most famous of all South African hunters, explored much of what is now Rhodesia between 1872 and 1892. By the end of the 1800's the era of the explorer was over. The era of the colonist, administrator, and surveyor had begun.

Past, Present, and Future

14

Left: Jomo Kenyatta, president of Kenya. For over 40 years he has been a leading spokesman for African nationalism. Since 1928 he has worked for the restoration of African government to Africans. He believes in democracy based on African tradition.

Left: Kenneth David Kaunda, president of Zambia. His political creed—faith in the common man and belief in non-violence—owes much to India's Gandhi. In 1958 he formed the Zambia National Congress. In 1959 he was jailed for nine months. His passive resistance succeeded, and in 1964 Zambia became independent.

Left: Julius Kambarage Nyerere, the president of Tanzania, formerly the countries of Tanganyika and Zanzibar. His Roman Catholic faith was formed at school, and in 1949 the missionaries sent him to Edinburgh University. He has said, "I formed the whole of my political philosophy while I was there."

The European explorers were like sappers who lay their charges, light the fuse, and blow up a dam. They broke the long, tribal isolation of Africa and, when they had finished, the ideas, beliefs, and inventions of Europe and America came in with a rush, like liberated waters. Within the next half-century, the fabric of African society was to be drastically and irreversibly changed.

The first and most immediate effect of European exploration was to end the slave trade. It could not be stamped out without the active intervention of European governments which were drawn in, sometimes against their will, to stop slave raids and protect Christian missionaries. So the seeds of colonialism were, in part, humanitarian, germinated by the desire to suppress slavery.

From 1890 onwards, France, Belgium, Britain, Italy, Spain, and Germany established in Africa the shortest-lived empires the world has ever known. Within 75 years their colonies were founded, consolidated, partially developed, and lost. By 1965, European political control had been withdrawn from virtually the whole of Africa north of the Zambezi River, except in the Portuguese provinces of Mozambique, Angola, and Portuguese Guinea. The Spanish still cling on in the Spanish Sahara and the French exercise nominal control over a bit of Somaliland called the French Territory of Afars and Issas, but these are little in comparison with the vast area of newly independent territories.

South of the Zambezi, European, or at least white, control remains. The reasons for this are climatic and historical. The Dutch and the British sent settlers to the Cape, and the climate of the Cape and the country north to the Zambezi Valley allowed them to thrive and raise their families. So European settlement took root and, like a transplanted cutting, grew up to an existence independent of its parent stock. Between the Zambezi and the Sudan, the climate was in the main unhealthy to Europeans. The only places with climates similar to those of Europe were in the highlands of Kenya and present-day Tanzania.

By 1965, all those parts of eastern and central Africa which had been parceled out among European powers as colonies or protectorates had reverted to African rule. One, alone, had never departed from it. Except for a very brief interlude from 1935 to 1941 when Italy occupied the country, Ethiopia remained independent as it has been since the dawn of history. In 1970 the part of Africa with

MADEIRA
(PORT.)

CANARY IS
(SP.)
IFNI

MOROCCO

TANGIER
SP. MOROCCO

TUNISIA

RIO
DE
ORO

ALGERIA
(FR.)

LIBYA

EGYPT

A S I A

FRENCH WEST AFRICA

ANGLO-EGYPTIAN
SUDAN

ERITREA

SOCOTRA
(BR.)

GAMBIA

PORT
GUINEA

SIERRA
LEONE

LIBERIA

GOLD
COAST

NIGERIA

1

2

1

CAMEROON
(FR. MANDATE)

1

FERNANDO PÓO
(SP.)

PRINCIPE
(PORT.)

RIO
MUNI

SÃO TOMÉ
(PORT.)

ANNOBÓN
(SP.)

FRENCH EQUATORIAL AFRICA

CABINDA

ASCENSION I.
(BR.)

ST. HELENA
(BR.)

BELGIAN
CONGO

ANGOLA
(PORT.)

UGANDA

3

PR.
SOMALILAND

PEMBA I.
(BR.)

BR. SOMALILAND

ABYSSINIA
(ETHIOPIA)

ITALIAN SOMALILAND

KENYA

TANGANYIKA
TERRITORY
(BR. MANDATE)

PEMBA I. (BR.)

ZANZIBAR
(BR.)

ALDABRA IS.
(BR.)

COMORO IS.
(FR.)

PROVIDENCE
IS. (BR.)

NORTHERN RHODESIA

NYASALAND

MOZAMBIQUE
(PORT.)

SOUTH WEST
AFRICA
(UNION OF
S. AFRICA
MANDATE)

WALVIS BAY
(UNION OF S. AFRICA)

BECHUANALAND

SOUTHERN
RHODESIA

BASSAS DA
INDIA
(FR.)

EUROPA
(BR.)

MADAGASCAR

RÉUNION
(FR.)

SWAZILAND

UNION OF
SOUTH AFRICA

BASUTOLAND

1 British Mandate

2 French Mandate

3 Belgian Mandate of Ruanda Urundi

© Geographical Projects

0 200 400 600 800 1000
Miles

Above: Africa in 1950. At that time a very large part of the continent remained under European control.

which we have been dealing is divided between one republic controlled by a minority of European stock, South Africa; one province controlled, as it has been for more than 400 years, by Portugal, namely Mozambique; the French Territory of Afars and Issas; the self-governing British ex-colony of Rhodesia, which declared independence in 1965; and 16 fully independent African states: Egypt (United Arab Republic); Sudan; Ethiopia; Somalia; Kenya; Uganda; Zambia; Malawi; Tanzania; Congo (Brazzaville); Congo (Kinshasa); Rwanda; Burundi; Botswana; Lesotho; and Swaziland.

While Europeans have withdrawn politically, European cultural and economic influence remains. Primarily, this influence is technological. Superior skills in the control of the environment put

© Geographical Projects

Above: Africa in 1970. By this date almost all the countries in Africa had gained their independence.

Western man in the lead. These skills do not consist only in the invention and use of devices like plows and tractors, automobiles and aircraft, telephones and computers, and explosives and chemicals. They include basic techniques such as literacy, mathematics, and scientific research. Science based on strict inquiry and experiment, unblinkered by tradition and superstition, came in with a rush under European influence and began to reshape African society at the deepest level, that of ideas. The world-wide technological revolution which has resulted from the pursuit of scientific knowledge came late to Africa, but in Africa, as elsewhere, it has come to stay.

The effects of introducing an advanced technology into societies whose members are predominantly small farmers and nomads living at the subsistence stage of a primitive economy are many. Two in particular may be singled out for mention. One is literacy. It was not unknown in Africa before the European incursion. Arabs had introduced it on the East African coast and Ethiopians had had their Amharic script, but it was patchy and rare. Among the great majority of farmers and cattle herders, literacy was entirely unknown. When introduced by Europeans—at first by missionaries —it brought with it a large and random assortment of the ideas, beliefs, experiences, and aspirations of the Western Christian world. There was a great pouring of new wine into old bottles, and many of the old tribal bottles burst. This is not to say that all traditional African concepts of society have been swept away before a flood of Westernism. They have not. They are still there, and the basis of the post-colonial African societies that are now evolving will be a mixture of the two sets of ideas. The culture of new Africa will be neither a mere reflection of Western values, nor a straight continuation of former African ones, but a balance struck between the two.

The second influence of Western technology on African societies —and some would say the most profound of all—is that of medicine. Western medical techniques keep alive millions of people who would formerly have died, especially millions of children. Under tribal conditions infant mortality was very high, probably in the order of 70 per cent. It is shrinking rapidly to a level of perhaps one-tenth of this. Epidemics such as bubonic plague, smallpox, yellow fever, typhoid, and typhus have been almost wholly brought under control. Malaria and dysentery, the two great endemic killers, have lost their terrors. These spectacular and speedy medical triumphs, allied to the abolition of the slave trade, have resulted in a rapid population growth like that in all parts of the world, but nowhere has this been more explosive than in Africa. In many countries populations are doubling about every 25 years. The process is cumulative. There is no end in sight. Africa is filling up with people as a reservoir fills with water when the floodgates are closed and the rivers in spate. One day the once empty continent must overflow.

Such sudden population rises have consequences which are numerous, far-reaching, and hard to foresee. The most obvious and immediate concerns food production: how to feed all these extra mouths? Output of crops and livestock needs to be quadrupled or more and then quadrupled again. Methods of subsistence farming followed for centuries will no longer suffice. Agriculture has to be retooled to fit the new demands.

All tribal societies were based upon the ownership and use of land and cattle. In changing these, the foundations of African societies must crumble and new ones be laid. The woman with a hand-hoe in a patch of mealies has to give way to the tractor and plow. So little patches of garden scattered around in the bush must give way to large fields workable by machinery and convenient for the use of fertilizers, crop sprays, and plant-breeding techniques. This in turn demands far-reaching changes in systems of land

Above: a baby being weighed by a young medical officer, one of many African men and women who have been learning to care for their own people as nurses, doctors, and social workers. There are now widespread systems of clinics, with mobile health teams touring the remote villages, bringing regular medical care.

Right: an African delegate to the United Nations, concentrating on a debate. With independence the countries of modern Africa now form an important force in world affairs, playing a full part in solving international problems.

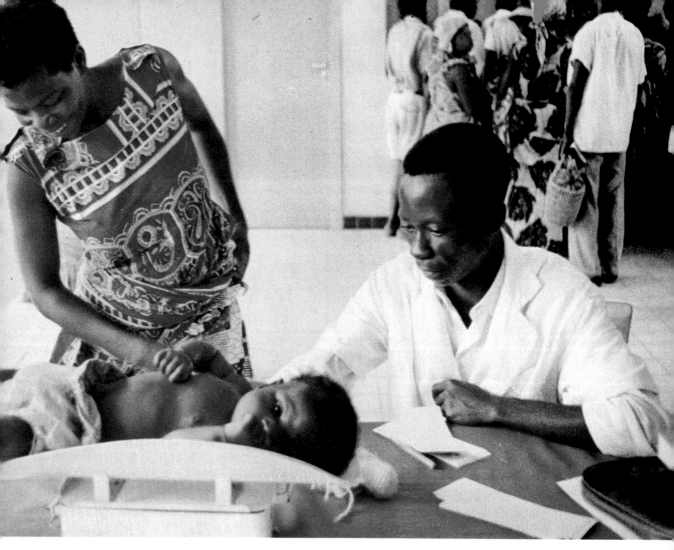

tenure, village economy, and the exercise of authority. The village elder disappears and perhaps divides his former functions among the secretary of a cooperative, chairman of an elected council, magistrate, clergyman, and registrar of lands.

Changes called for in the lives of cattle-owning nomads are even more profound. There is no longer space for flocks and herds to roam at will over vast stretches of unoccupied countryside. Bush and forest—and wildlife with them—are melting away, and plains have become eroded by over-grazing. In order that their children may go to school, families must settle permanently in villages instead of moving around. Animals must be confined in fenced enclosures where modern methods of grassland control can be applied. To most cattle-owning tribesmen, cattle are currency. As a token, one animal is as valuable as another, and people will no more cull a barren cow from the herd than they will tear up a worn currency bill. But culling is essential to good husbandry. In order to practice it, the tribesmen must first change their whole set of values, together with some of their deepest religious and social beliefs. In the past such changes have come gradually, allowing time

for each new generation to adjust. Now they are coming not even in a single lifetime, but in a few years.

"After the work of exploration," Livingstone wrote, "comes the harder task of civilization." Except in Rhodesia and South Africa this has been taken over mainly by Africans themselves. This is not to say that African peoples and governments do not seek, and sometimes welcome, European help. But they do not need, and never welcome, patronage. They seek advice when they consider it disinterested, and aid when they can get it on their own terms.

In the Republic of South Africa the problem of how to build and operate a just and healthy multiracial society has yet to be solved. There are human problems that have no solution, and at times this looks like one of them. There is a solution now under trial which so far has commanded little sympathy in the world at large and none at all in other African states. South Africa has become one of the testing grounds and danger spots of today's world. History cannot be unwritten, nor people tidily returned to the areas they came from.

In settling Africa's geography, the explorers unsettled its societies by exposing them to the disruptive influence of a self-confident, aggressive Western world then in the full flush of enthusiasm for its own technological triumphs. It remains now for their African successors to follow paths they opened toward, as they believed, the development of civilized ways of living. Above all it remains for modern pathfinders of all races to make a way through the jungle of human fears, greeds, and hates, as those determined explorers found a way, with inflexible purpose and unrelenting will, through the dark and dangerous jungles of the heart of Africa.

Above: Kampala, capital of Uganda. Among the modern capital cities of Africa, Kampala, built on a series of hills, is one of the most beautiful. It has combined very fine modern buildings with an individual, and strongly African, atmosphere.

Acknowledgments

Aldus Archives 178(L), 191, 193, 197, 201, 206, 211(T), 212(T), 215(B), 217, 218, 219, 236(T), 237(B), 242, 245, 250(R), 263, 273, 298(B); Black Star, London 176; Reproduced by courtesy of the Trustees of the British Museum 183, 231; British Museum/Photo R.B. Fleming © Aldus Books 281(T); British Museum/John Freeman © Aldus Books 179, 208, 270(L); British Museum/Photo Michael Holford © Aldus Books 300; Photo Mike Busselle © Aldus Books 178(R), 259; Camera Press 175(L), 187, 301, 314(T)(C)(B); Photo by J. Allan Cash 172, 195, 311(B); Bruce Coleman Ltd./Photo Jen & Des Bartlett 221; Mary Evans Picture Library 258, 268, 274, 281(B); Christian Simonpietri of Gamma 241; Geographical Projects Limited, London 168, 200, 226, 287, 297, 316, 317; Photo Alfred Gregory, Blackpool 312-13(T); R.J. Griffith 198, 212(B), 261, 278(L), 282(R), 294; Robin Hallett 189(T), 254(R), 284(T); Desmond Harney 170(T), 247(T), 252, 302; Desmond Harney (*Daily Telegraph* Colour Library) 304, 305; Supplied by Dr. H.J. Hienz, University of Witwatersrand, Johannesburg 223; Peter Hill, A.R.P.S. 189(B), 244; By courtesy of the David Livingstone Memorial, Blantyre, Scotland 220, 222, 234, 237(T), 278(R); Courtesy London Borough of Richmond upon Thames 248, 249, 253(B); Ian Berry of Magnum 170(B); Sergio Larrain of Magnum 319(B); Malawi Department of Information 232, 235, 270(R); Mansell Collection 255, 262, 275, 282(L), 284(C)(B), 289(L), 293, 299, 309(T), 312(B); Courtesy Matter & Weich (PTY) Ltd., Cape Town 207; Courtesy Alice Mertens 175(L), 204; National Portrait Gallery, London 190, 254(L), 307(B); Photo Klaus Paysan 233; Picturepoint, London 205; Pitt-Rivers Museum, Oxford 215(T); Popperfoto 174, 177, 180, 184, 185, 211(B), 289(R), 291; Radio Times Hulton Picture Library 209, 214, 216, 238, 276-77(C), 283, 288, 310; Reproduced by permission of the Royal Geographical Society 250(L), 311(T); Photo Mike Busselle © Aldus Books, reproduced by permission of the Royal Geographical Society 166, 224, 228, 229, 230, 236(B), 247(B), 253(T), 256-57, 257(T), 264, 265, 272, 276(L), 277(R), 295, 298(T), 309(B); Photo supplied by SATOUR 173; Scala, Florence 186; Photo Emil Schulthess 260, 292, 308; South African Library, Cape Town 202; Crispin Tickell 192, 196; Lancelot Tickell 182, 266, 267, 285, 306-07(T), 320; United Nations 319(T); James Wellard (c/o Curtis Brown, London) 239; Westminster Abbey/Photo Mike Busselle © Aldus Books 279; Roger Wood, London 240.

PART THREE

Seas of Sand

Below: a watercolor painting of a sandstorm by Lady Anne Blunt, who explored the central part of Arabia with her husband in the late 1800's. Phenomena such as sandstorms, added to the harsh climate of the desert, made exploration of it especially hard.

PART THREE

Seas of Sand
BY PAUL HAMILTON

Right: one of the gracefully curving sand dunes in the vast Sahara. The dune areas of the Sahara are called *ergs,* and make up one-third of the area of the desert. The dunes are formed by the desert winds. They can move across the surface of the desert as the wind blows sand away from one side, and stacks it up on the other side.

Foreword

Deserts, like the sea, seem to have a special appeal for a special sort of person. The endless miles of emptiness, the harsh necessity for self-sufficiency when sources of supply on a journey are few or nonexistent, the tight interdependence of a group of travelers who must support one another to survive in the trackless waste—life in the arid wastes of Arabia and Africa captured and held the imaginations of many explorers, bringing them back again and again to the challenge and serenity of the desert.

Like the explorers of other parts of Africa, the men who mapped the deserts wrote long accounts of their travels and published them faithfully upon their return. Their activities, too, were frequently sponsored by learned societies in Europe, made up of sensible men in business suits who had little sense of the anguish or the satisfactions inherent in desert life. Like those before them, they were completely dependent on the local tribesmen who guided and surrounded them: but in the desert these local tribesmen were fierce and haughty men whose traditional way of life depended on exclusive knowledge and control of the life-saving oases along the desert routes. Many travelers disappeared, never to be seen again. Even today, travel in the desert could not be described as safe.

The story in this part of the book is one of vivid and memorable personalities. Each traveler left a curiously personal mark. Many of them seemed to be haunted men, who found their peace in challenging their endurance to the uttermost limits. They were frequently hungry, usually thirsty, often exhausted, and yet they went on—and most of them came back to repeat the experience. The emptiness was their fulfillment.

Arabia

1

Nearly a fifth of the earth's land surface is made up of desert. This does not mean that it is covered by mile after mile of sand. But it does mean that a fifth of the land is dry and barren. Some deserts are, indeed, sandy wastes. But others may be gravelly plains or rocky, mountainous areas. Deserts are not always hot either. Some are burning hot in summer and freezing cold in winter. And the wastes of Siberia and the frozen Arctic regions of Europe and North America are often referred to as *cold deserts*.

The one characteristic of all desert regions is the lack of water. In the cold deserts, all the water is frozen. In the tropical regions, rain seldom falls. When it does, it comes in short torrential down-

Above: Arabia, from Ptolemy's *Geography*. In this work, Ptolemy, a scholar from Alexandria, Egypt, summed up what was known about the world's geography in the A.D. 100's. His theories were accepted by the European world for centuries. This map dates from some 1300 years later than the original *Geography*—it was made in about 1460.

pours which quickly sink through the surface to the water deposits beneath. These underground water supplies feed the *oases*—the desert springs where trees and plants grow, and where the thirsty traveler can replenish his water supply. But these "islands" in the desert may be hundreds of miles apart, with nothing between but empty waste.

Few plants are native to the desert, and few animals live there. What life there is has adapted itself to the hostile environment. The camel can go for days without water. Smaller animals burrow underground to escape the heat of the sun. Desert plants can store water for long periods and lose little through evaporation. The

329

animals and plants of the Arctic regions have similarly adapted themselves to their icy homeland.

The greatest desert area in the world stretches in a broad swath across northern Africa from the Atlantic coast to the Red Sea, on into Arabia and, beyond the Persian Gulf, into Iran and Afghanistan. It reaches from the Sahara, in Africa, through the An Nafūd and Rub' al Khali deserts in Arabia and the Dasht-i-Lut and the Dasht-i-Kavir deserts in Iran, to the Dasht-i-Mārgo and the Registan deserts in Afghanistan. In Africa, the Sahara cuts off the Arab nations along the coast of the Mediterranean Sea from the Negro countries of central Africa, and is broken only by the fertile lands of the Nile Valley and a few scattered oases. The Arabian Peninsula, apart from a narrow coastal strip, is nearly all barren. For centuries, these desert lands presented an almost unanswerable challenge to travelers. The harsh climate, the lack of water, and the fierce and often fanatical tribesmen combined to make the deserts some of the most impenetrable regions of the world. Yet, despite the huge difficulties, travelers did venture into these fearsome, desolate lands. And it was to the Arabian Peninsula that they turned first.

When the first European explorers reached Arabia, there were no clear-cut political divisions because most of the peninsula was under Turkish rule. They found, however, a number of sharply defined and widely contrasting geographical regions. The Hejaz, the coastal region along the Red Sea including the holy cities of Mecca and Medina, consists of a narrow, infertile coastal plain and, inland, a high mountain range. In the south of the peninsula, in what is now Yemen, lies the Wadi Hadhramaut, a long fertile valley some 300 miles long, with walls often as much as 1,000 feet high in places. The Nejd, in the center of the peninsula, is a relatively fertile region, with towns and settlements, wadis and oases. The largest part of Arabia is, however, true desert. The rolling sand dunes of the An Nufūd and the Rub' al Khali—the Empty Quarter—stretch for mile upon mile. These arid wastes presented an irresistible challenge to European explorers.

Left: an Arabian pottery camel, from the Roman era. Models like this have been found in both the Sahara and the Arabian deserts, along the age-old caravan routes that cross the wastes.

To the early explorer, jogging along on the back of a camel at a monotonous few miles an hour, the Arabian Desert seemed like hell itself. On all sides, the sands stretch away to the distant horizon. Day after day the sun blazes down from a cloudless sky. In the three-month summer, the heat is intense, with the temperature rising in some places to 130°F, but in winter the temperature can drop to freezing point (32°F). What winds there are bring no refreshing air, but are made red hot by the sands over which they have come. All around is emptiness and silence, broken only by the sound of camels' feet plodding through the soft sand. Nor can the thirsty traveler be sure of finding water. When he reaches the scattered water holes, he may well find that they are dried up or foul.

Until the advent of the tracked automobile, the only way to cross the desert was on the back of a camel. Without the camel, life in

Above: camels in Arabia. These odd-looking animals are superbly adapted for life in the desert, and provide their masters with transportation, food, clothing, and a visible measure of their wealth and social standing. For centuries, camel caravans using traditional routes were the only way for men and goods to cross the deserts.

the desert would have been impossible for the wandering desert tribes of Arabia—it provides transportation, food, drink, and clothing. Its large soft feet enable it to travel over the sand with 200 pounds of baggage on each side of its saddle. Fully loaded, a camel can cover some 25 miles a day, but without packs it can go much farther—sometimes up to 100 miles in a single day.

The camel is remarkably well adapted in other ways to life in the desert. It can go for as much as five days without water, although the nomads do try to give their camels water to drink every day. Camels get some moisture from their food, and they retain most of the water they drink, because they sweat very little. Besides, they can eat even the driest and most prickly brushwood. And, if there is no food at all available, the camel can live on the fat stored in the hump on its back. As it uses up the fat, the hump will shrink, but as soon as it is fed properly again, the hump returns to its normal size.

As a means of travel, however, camels have their limitations. They are obstinate and bad-tempered, and will never obey commands willingly. Their unusual gait produces a strange swaying motion, which can make the traveler feel "seasick"—a fact which could have earned the camel the name "ship of the desert."

Despite the harsh desert climate, and the difficulties of travel, it is possible that the early explorers found the hostility of the nomads the greatest obstacle to their journeys. These nomads were Bedouins, a desert people who today live in much the same way as their ancient forebears. Bedouin society is divided into several classes, and throughout the class structure it is the camel that separates the superior tribesmen from the inferior. At the bottom of the Bedouin social scale are the people who live in permanent houses of mud or stone. The desert nomads despise them as being

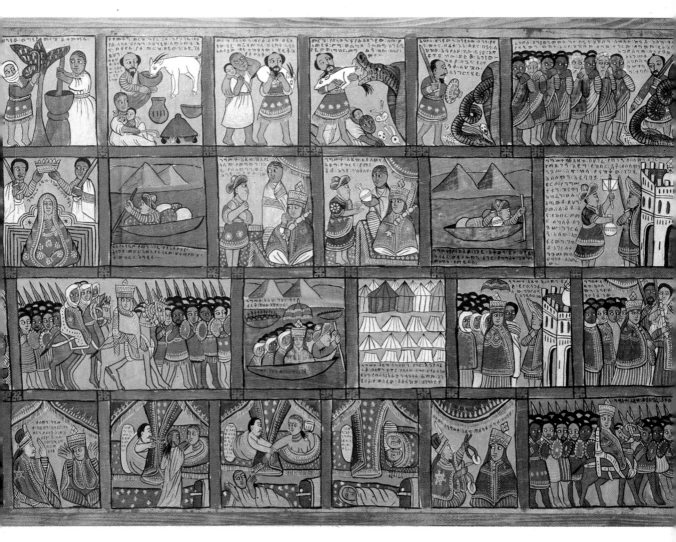

Above: more than one land has claimed the Queen of Sheba for its own. Here is an Ethiopian portrayal of their tradition of the queen, believed to have been the ancestress of their own royal line. The last two rows show the queen's visit to King Solomon.

Left: the entrance hall of the Temple of the Moon God at Marib in Yemen. In Yemenite folklore this was the palace of the Queen of Sheba. The Bible reports that she came to Solomon "with a ... great train, with camels that bore spices and ... gold and precious stone."

merchants of the land, and not true men of the desert. Then come the seminomads, the Aradbar tribes, who live part of the year in towns and are therefore considered to be soft by the men of the desert. The shepherds, who look after sheep and goats, are also considered inferior because sheep cannot travel as far as camels.

The aristocrats of the desert are the tribes who live in black tents made of goat's hair and sheep's wool, and spend nine months of the year—including the cooler winter months—in the heart of the desert. They raise only camels as livestock, and depend on them for all the necessities of their life. It is logical, therefore, that the Bedouins reckon their wealth by the number of camels they own.

To their natural dislike of the European intruders, the Bedouin tribesmen added extreme religious fanaticism. Their religion was Islam, and they regarded the Christian travelers as *infidels* (unbelievers) to be converted or destroyed.

The Islamic religion was founded in Arabia in the early 600's. At that time, Arabia was a primitive land where the various tribes warred constantly among themselves in an endless succession of blood feuds or intertribal quarrels. Throughout Arab society, a state of lawlessness prevailed. The Arabs worshiped idols, and the code that governed their behavior was a primitive one. Among the people of Mecca, poverty and suffering were rife. The position of women was intolerable—Arab men could marry as many wives as they chose, and divorce was commonplace. Unwanted baby girls were killed. This state of affairs would probably have continued for hundreds of years had it not been for the birth in Mecca in about 570 of one of the most remarkable men the world has ever known. That man was Mohammed.

At first, Mohammed's life was little different from that of other Arabians of his time. Then, when he was about 40 years old, he saw a vision of the angel Gabriel. Gabriel called on Mohammed to become a prophet, and to preach God's word among his fellow countrymen. This first vision was followed by others. To begin with, Mohammed told only his family and a few friends what he had seen. Then he began to preach to the people of Mecca, attacking Arab society of the time. He taught that there was only one God (Allah), and that he, Mohammed, was God's prophet. Many who heard him scoffed at his words. Others listened, and began to follow his teachings.

Mohammed's attacks on Arabian society aroused the hatred of the people of Mecca. In 622, he was forced to flee the city. His flight to Medina is called the *Hegira,* and it is from the year of the Hegira that the Moslem calendar dates. In Medina, Mohammed was welcomed as a prophet, and soon most of the people there followed his teachings. Secure, and at the head of an established religious community, Mohammed could now turn his teaching into law. He abolished idol worship, and the killing of baby girls. He limited polygamy so that Moslem men could marry no more than four wives, and he restricted the practice of divorce. Gambling and drinking intoxicating liquors were also prohibited. But perhaps Mohammed's most important reform was a ban on violence and war—except in self-defense and for the Islamic cause. This latter exception—"for the Islamic cause"—was to have far-reaching effects through the ages, and was responsible for the difficulties of many of the early explorers.

By the time Mohammed died in 632, he had been accepted as the Prophet of God by the Meccans as well as the Medinans. He was succeeded by one of his disciples, Abu Bakr, who became the first *caliph* (leader) of the Moslems. Not content merely to protect the Moslem faith in Arabia, Abu Bakr organized a *jihad* (holy war) to conquer the infidels and establish Islam throughout the world. His plans came very near to succeeding. Within a hundred years, the Islamic Empire was more widespread than that of Rome. It reached to the Pyrenees Mountains in northern Spain, throughout Arabia and Syria into present-day Afghanistan and India, and right across northern Africa. Later, it spread down into the Negro lands of east and central Africa. The Moslem invaders did afford a degree of

Below: northern Africa and the Arabian Peninsula, showing the main geographical features. For centuries, these desert regions offered little more than an exciting challenge to explorers. Today, however, vast resources of oil and minerals have been discovered under the sand, and this new wealth is bringing prosperity to the desert lands.

religious tolerance to the people they conquered, but all non-Moslems had to pay a special tax to gain exemption from army service. And, as time passed, Islam became the main religion in the conquered lands.

But in Arabia, the birthplace of Islam, religious tolerance was limited. Moslem law barred non-Moslems from entering the holy cities of Mecca and Medina on pain of death, and Christians traveling anywhere in the Arabian Peninsula did so at great risk. Yet despite the dangers which awaited them in Arabia, explorers were still

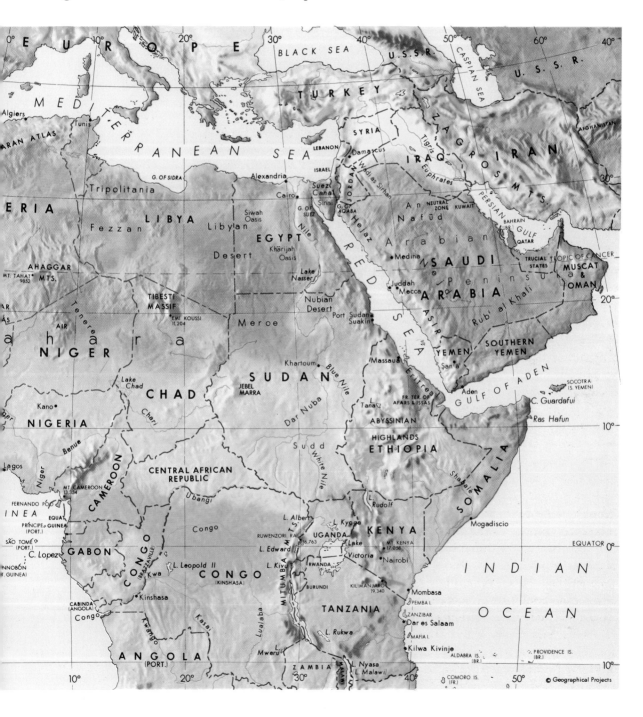

Left: a Turkish miniature of the 1500's. It shows the black tent of the aristocratic Bedouins, and a well— both sights as familiar in the desert world now as when it was painted.

willing to risk their lives to penetrate the unknown interior of the peninsula. What was it that drove them on?

First, to the natural attraction of the unknown was added the even greater lure of the forbidden—the excitement of doing something that was not permitted, at no matter what risk. So great was this lure that a few European adventurers even disguised themselves as Moslems and took part in the pilgrimage to Mecca—the *hajj*, which all Moslems must make at least once in their lives. These adventurers took part even though, had they been discovered, they would probably have been killed. The second great reason for the European interest in Arabia lay in the rumors of wealth which, for thousands of years, had circulated in Europe. The people of Yemen claim that the fabulously wealthy Queen of Sheba was their ruler, and believe that the Temple of the Moon God at Marib was her palace. Certainly, caravans used to pass through Arabia, carrying such treasures as frankincense, myrrh, cinnamon, gold, pearls, and precious stones. The legends of riches aroused the interest of European explorers and merchants alike, who determined to discover whether or not they were true.

But when the first European explorers reached Arabia, they saw little sign of this fabled wealth. The difficulties of travel were, however, ever present. And the character of the peninsula changed little as the centuries passed. A hot, dry, inhospitable land of extreme temperatures, it was inhabited by men whose hostility to travelers who did not share their faith was often fierce. It is not surprising, therefore, that it took until the 1930's for European explorers to fit together the last few pieces of the Arabian jigsaw.

Below: Arabia, showing the principal routes of the trade caravans, together with those followed by pilgrims to the holy cities of Mecca and Medina. These routes existed long before there were proper maps and, for much of their length, led through empty desert. The camel caravans, however, managed to follow the same route year after year in their journeys across Arabia.

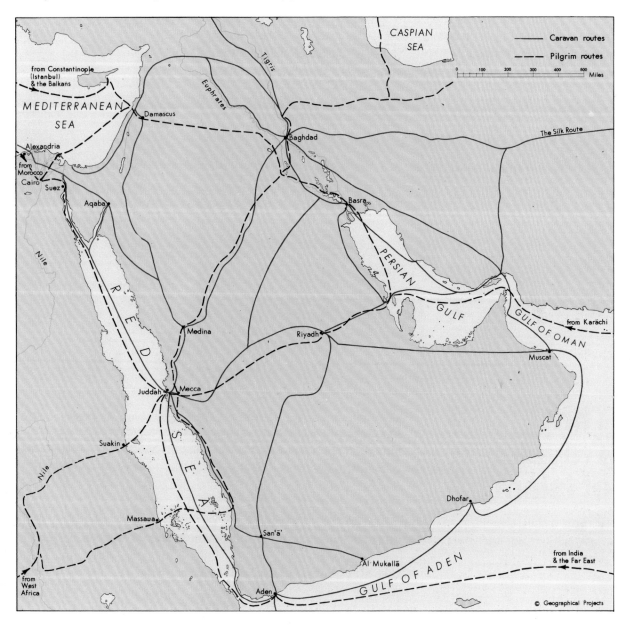

337

The
Traveler
of Islam
2

The first travelers in Arabia to leave any record of their journeys were Moslems making the pilgrimage to the holy cities of Mecca and Medina. Their accounts of the hajj fascinated Western readers who, as non-Moslems, were forbidden to take part in the Moslem ceremonies. They also inspired Europeans to try to see the forbidden cities for themselves.

One of the most remarkable of the Moslem travelers was Sheik Mohammed ibn Abdulla Ibn-Batuta, who was born in Tangier in 1304. Ibn-Batuta came from a family of religious judges, and he had studied theology and law in Tangier before he decided to make the pilgrimage. Although the pilgrimage was above all a religious duty, it also provided Ibn-Batuta with an opportunity to broaden his

وَكَادَ مِنْ عَرَفِ الجِمَالِ الشَّرِّ وَأَنْشَدَ
مَا الحُجُّ سَيْرَكَ تَأُوبَاً وَإِدْلاَجَاً وَلاَ إِعْيَاءُ مِثْلَ جِمَالاً وَأَجْدَالاً

الحَجُّ أَنْ تَقْصِدَ البَيْتَ الحَرَامَ عَلَى تَحْرِيدٍ كُلِّ الحَجِّ لاَ يَعْنِي بِهِ بَاجَا
وَأَسَطَّى كَاِبلُ الإِنْصَافِ مُتَّخِذَاً رَدْعَ الهَوَى هَادِياً وَالجَوْنَ مِنْهَاجَا

education. By talking and studying with the scholars he met on his journey, he would fit himself to assume the duties of a magistrate when he returned to Tangier. In June, 1325, the 21-year-old pilgrim said good-by to his parents and set off for Arabia.

Money seems to have been no problem for Ibn-Batuta. Apparently, his family was well enough known in the Arab world to ensure that he would be introduced not only to scholars but also to the powerful rulers who could help to make his journey easier. And he himself soon seems to have become an experienced traveler. He did, of course, have the advantage of being an educated young man from the "Far West." As such, he was an object of curiosity and interest, and someone to be welcomed and entertained.

Above left: the color and splendor of life in the Moslem world, remarkable to European travelers, would have seemed normal to Ibn-Batuta. Here, an Arabian miniature shows a group of Middle Eastern horsemen.

Above: another illustration from the same manuscript, dated 1237. Some of the riders are mounted on camels—the most usual form of transport in Arabia.

From his lively *Travels* we do not only learn about the religious ceremonies of the hajj. Ibn-Batuta also includes his impressions of the people he met and of the towns and cities he visited. He gives details about food and traveling conditions and the different kinds of trade and business carried on throughout Arabia.

When Ibn-Batuta first set out from Tangier in 1325, he traveled along the North African coast road to Alexandria. From there, he went south to Cairo and Upper Egypt where he hoped he would be able to board a boat to cross the Red Sea. But because of a local war in that part of Egypt, he had to return down the Nile River and make his way to Damascus. There he could join a pilgrim caravan for the journey to the holy cities.

It was early August, 1326, by the time Ibn-Batuta actually reached Damascus, a city which, like many other travelers, he found more beautiful than any other he visited. Perhaps his enthusiasm may have been partly due to the fact that he got married there. It must have been a whirlwind courtship because on September 1 the pilgrim caravan left the city for the hajj.

Above: a water hole in the wastes of Arabia. Desert travel can still be hazardous—note the cartridge belts worn by the men. The woman, like all nomads, has her wealth in portable form—her beautiful silver ornaments.

Right: a group of camels with their herder, a woman. Among the nomads of the desert, it is the women who do all the heavy work, even to taking down and putting up the tents when the nomads strike camp, and move on.

This army of thousands of pilgrims made its way southeastward behind the coastal mountains of present-day Syria and Jordan. South of Damascus the caravan stopped for four days at Al Karak so that the travelers could rest and prepare themselves for the terrible heat of the desert. At Tabūk, 200 miles farther south, the caravan started to make forced marches, traveling night and day to reduce the time from one water hole to the next. At the Wadi al Ukhaydir, Ibn-Batuta was told a frightening story about a caravan which had passed through the valley in a previous year. Apparently a particularly dry wind had dried up the water supplies in the oases, and hundreds of people had died of thirst.

Five days' journey from the Wadi al Ukhaydir, which Ibn-Batuta appropriately referred to as the valley of hell, the caravan reached Medā'in Sālih. At Medā'in Sālih, there was an abundant supply of water, yet the pilgrims would not drink. They believed that Mohammed had once ridden his camel through Medā'in Sālih without stopping and had forbidden his followers to waste time by stopping to drink there. Ibn Batuta was amazed at this strange custom on the part of the pilgrims, though other travelers do not mention it.

From Medā'in Sālih it was another half day's journey through the

Above: a plan of the Kaaba enclosure in Mecca, painted on a Turkish tile in the 1600's. The Kaaba, or Cubical House, is the central point of the whole Moslem pilgrimage. It is Moslem belief that Abraham and his son Ishmael built the Kaaba on the site of the house where Hagar and Ishmael lived after their flight into the desert.

desert to the oasis of Al 'Ula where the pilgrims were allowed to drink and rest. The caravan remained several days there, while everyone washed their clothes and replenished their meager supplies. Three days later they arrived at Medina, where they worshiped at the mosque where Mohammed is buried.

Shortly after leaving Medina, the caravan stopped for the pilgrims to change into the *ihram,* the special garment worn by all Moslems making the pilgrimage. The ihram consists of two pieces of white cotton cloth which are wrapped around the body. When they had put on the ihram, the pilgrims were ready to begin the final stage of the journey to Mecca. Although Ibn-Batuta writes in great detail about the various rituals of the hajj, he also found time to observe the people of Mecca. He was greatly impressed by the elegance of the merchants in the holy city, and he thought the women were beautiful, chaste, and pious. He was overwhelmed by the sweet scent they left behind them as they moved about, and explains that these women would go without food in order to save money to buy perfumes. Then every Thursday night—the eve of the Moslem

Above: a frankincense tree in Dhofar, in the south of the Arabian Peninsula. Left: a closer view of a branch showing how the bark is cut away to let the resin seep out. The resin is milky at first, and hardens into pale drops (called *tears*) after two to three months' exposure to the air. These tears are burned as incense.

343

Sabbath—they would come to the mosque wearing their finest clothes and saturated with exotic perfume.

By mid-November, 1326, Ibn-Batuta was ready to leave Mecca. He had already made friends with the commander of the caravan which would go northeast to Baghdad, and was therefore able to travel under his protection. A vast number of pilgrims traveled with the Baghdad caravan. Groups of peddlars accompanied the caravan, so that the pilgrims could buy food and the few necessities they needed along the way. When the caravan entered the Nejd, it stopped at a *birka*—a reservoir—that had been built for the use of pilgrims in the early 800's. Even today this reservoir is used by the Bedouin tribesmen to water their camels.

When the caravan arrived in Baghdad, Ibn-Batuta decided that he would continue his travels through the Middle East. From then on it is more difficult to follow his exact route. According to his journal, in 1327 he was back again in Mecca where he stayed for three years. He also made a short trip to East Africa and then returned again to Arabia to visit Yemen. Ibn-Batuta got as far up into the mountains of this region as the ancient city of Şan'ā'. He then returned to the coast at Aden.

From Aden, Ibn-Batuta made his way to eastern Africa but he later returned to Arabia and traveled along the south coast to Dhofar. Like many other travelers in the area he commented on the incense trade. At the port of Hasik there were a great number of frankincense trees. Ibn Batuta explains that these trees have "thin leaves out of which drips, when they are slashed, sap like milk. This turns into a gum, which is the frankincense." Another thing which impressed him at Hasik was the dependence of the local people on the fish they caught. These were called *lukham* and were like a dogfish. When these fish had been sliced open and dried in the sun they were eaten. The bones were saved, and used by the people to weave flimsy coverings for the walls of their primitive huts.

Ibn-Batuta continued following the Arabian coast to Oman and then around into the Persian Gulf. At Bahrain, he prepared for his third journey to Mecca, this time traveling westward across the peninsula. At Mecca, this restless and inquisitive young man decided to prolong his travels. He visited central Asia, India and even China before, some 15 years later, he made his way home to Tangier.

Ibn-Batuta's journal reflects in great detail the Arab world of the mid-1300's. It was, for him, an ordered world, where an educated young man could move about with great freedom and in safety. The explorers who followed him into the Arabian Peninsula found it a far more hazardous place.

Right: in the Persian Gulf, on the island of Bahrain, a fisherman casts his net. More than 600 years ago, Ibn-Batuta would have seen fishermen casting their nets just like this.

Visitors to Mecca

3

Left: the prophet Mohammed,
ascending to a welcoming heaven on
his donkey al-Burak. The picture comes
from a Persian manuscript of about 1540.

Above: Di Varthema presenting his
book to the Countess of Albi, to
whom it is dedicated, from the German edition of 1515. It is possible
that the artist of the woodcuts in
this edition had seen Di Varthema,
as in each he is recognizably the
same person, wearing a goatee beard.

Since the time of Mohammed, no non-Moslem has been permitted to
enter the holy cities of Mecca and Medina. Even today, only the
followers of Islam are permitted to pass the stone gateposts 15 miles
outside the city of Mecca. The sacred territory around the holy
cities, which comprises a large section of the Hejaz, has therefore
remained officially closed to curious non-believers. In spite of this
ban, a few adventurers have been willing to risk their lives to observe
and record the religious fervor of the hajj. These travelers have left
records not only of the pilgrimage, but of the routes leading to and
from Mecca and Medina, the countryside around the cities, and the
Bedouin tribesmen who roam the area.

The first non-Moslem known to have visited the holy cities was
an Italian, Ludovico di Varthema. He wrote a book about his travels,
which was published in Rome in 1510. In it, he recounts his adventures in Egypt, Syria, the Hejaz, and Yemen. He also describes his
subsequent journeys in India, and eastward as far as the Spice
Islands (the Moluccas).

Like Ibn-Batuta's story, Di Varthema's book has the liveliness and
fascination of an adventure novel. In it he writes little about his
family or early life. All we know is that he lived in Bologna and
had probably been a soldier before deciding to become a traveler.
He was obviously a man of spirit and boldness, who wanted to see
faraway lands, and win the kind of fame which explorers could
achieve at that time. Unlike Ibn Batuta, Di Varthema was not a
learned man. He describes himself as "of very slender understanding"
and not given to study. In his own words, he resolved to see things
"personally and with my own eyes, to endeavor to ascertain the
situation of places, the qualities of people, the diversities of animals,
the varieties of the fruit-bearing and odoriferous trees—remembering
well that the testimony of one eyewitness is worth more than ten
thousand hearsays."

Early in 1503, Di Varthema arrived in Alexandria in Egypt and
from there went on to Cairo. He then made his way to Beirut and
Damascus, where he seems to have picked up a working knowledge
of Arabic. It was April, 1503, when he arrived at Damascus, and
the hajj caravan was preparing for the annual pilgrimage. In the
early 1500's, a tough and well-armed escort was necessary to protect
the pilgrims from the Bedouin raiders who followed the caravan.
The Bedouins would often attack the pilgrims and camels when they

Above: Mamelukes exercising in front of a palace in Cairo. The Mamelukes first came to Egypt as prisoners of war. Originally from Europe and Circassia, they were converted to Islam, and became enormously powerful. In 1250, they seized control of Egypt, and they ruled the country until 1517.

stopped at an oasis to refresh themselves. Ibn-Batuta had not mentioned this particular danger, which suggests that the Bedouins had become more hostile toward strangers in the 200 years since he traveled on the same road. Di Varthema made friends with the captain of the Mameluke escort which was to accompany the caravan to Mecca. Using his wits, and perhaps some money in the form of bribes, he managed to persuade the Mamelukes to allow him to enrol as one of them.

In Di Varthema's time, the Mamelukes, from whose ranks the escorts for the pilgrim caravans were drawn, ruled over the lands of Egypt and Syria. Originally, however, they had come to Egypt as prisoners of war from Europe and Circassia (the southern part of Russia). Converted to Islam, the Mamelukes gradually rose to power in the government service, and in A.D. 1250, they seized control of Egypt. From Di Varthema's point of view, one of their most important characteristics was that, although as Moslems they could make the pilgrimage, they did not necessarily look like Arabs. In the

Mameluke guard, Di Varthema could join the hajj with little fear of detection.

When he enrolled in the guard, Di Varthema took the Arabic name of Yunos, and obtained a uniform and a horse. It was an enormous caravan that started on the 40-day march to the holy cities—according to Di Varthema, there were 40,000 pilgrims, 35,000 camels, and a Mameluke escort of 60.

One of the most interesting parts of Di Varthema's journal is an account of the caravan's first stopping place inside the Hejaz region, at the oasis of Khaybar. For many centuries, there had been a Jewish colony there, perhaps founded after the destruction of Judea by Nebuchadnezzar II in the 500's B.C., and colonized by refugees from subsequent disasters.

Di Varthema describes the mountainous oasis as being 10 or 12 miles in circumference with a community of between 4,000 and 5,000 people "who go naked and are in height five or six spans [about four feet], and have a feminine voice and are more black than any other color. They live entirely on the flesh of sheep and eat nothing else. They are circumcised and confess that they are Jews; and if they can get a Moor [Arab] into their hands they skin him alive."

At Khaybar, Di Varthema was also impressed by seeing eight

Right: the battle for a water hole in which Di Varthema reports that 1,600 Bedouins were killed by the caravan's Mameluke guard. Di Varthema says that the water hole was in the valley of Sodom and Gomorrah, which he describes as truly desert and barren. According to the Bible, the cities were destroyed because of the wickedness of their inhabitants.

349

Above: Di Varthema's caravan on
its way to Mecca. Di Varthema says
of the group: "The pilgrims travel
with wives and children and houses
like a Turkish tent made from wool. . . .
The caravan was going in two groups . . .
60 of them Mamelukes for saving the
people. One part of the Mamelukes
were going first, another one in the
middle and the third part behind the
group. We traveled night and day."

beautiful thornbushes, and two turtledoves fluttering above them.
This was like a miracle, he says, because the caravan had traveled for
16 days and nights without having seen a single animal or bird.

Eventually, the caravan reached Medina. There, the pilgrims
prayed at Mohammed's tomb—a substantial building which Di
Varthema carefully described in order to disprove the medieval
legend that Mohammed's coffin was suspended in the air by giant
magnets. Soon after leaving the city, the caravan stopped for a day
to give the pilgrims time to bathe and put on the ihram, just as
Ibn-Batuta had described.

Di Varthema traveled on with the hajj to Mecca. There he was
careful to write down all sorts of details, not only of the religious
ceremonies, but of the city itself and the trade which went on there.
Moslems from many Eastern countries were gathered in Mecca in
that May of 1503—Indians, Persians, Syrians, Ethiopians. All of
them had come as pilgrims on the hajj, but some were more interested
in the possibilities of trade than in the religious festivities.

About 10 miles east of Mecca is the sacred Mount Arafat where
part of the Moslem ceremonies took place. At the foot of the
mountain were two reservoirs, one for the caravan from Cairo and
the other for the one from Damascus. The Cairo caravan was far
larger than the Damascus one, with 64,000 camels accompanying
the pilgrims and an escort of 100 Mamelukes. The ceremonies at

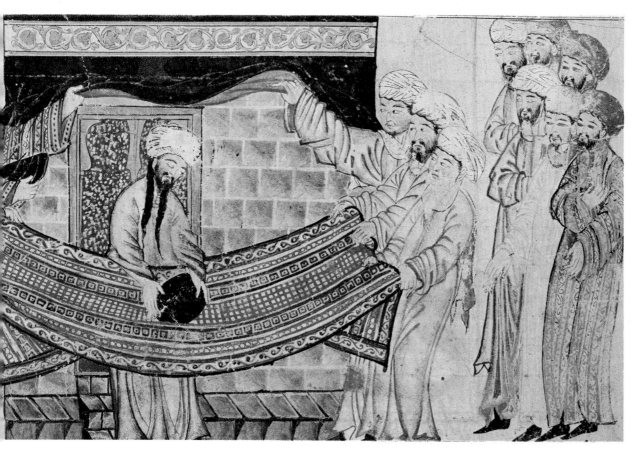

the mountain included the sacrifice of at least two sheep for every pilgrim. The meat was given to the poor, and Di Varthema thought that more people came because they were hungry, than wanted to take part in the ceremonies.

When the caravan returned north to Damascus, Di Varthema decided to desert the Mameluke guard. This was a dangerous move and could be punishable by death. The Mameluke officers had no intention of allowing deserters from the escort to wander about in Arabia as they wished. Besides, Di Varthema was in danger of being killed as a non-Moslem in the holy city. However, he soon thought of a way to extricate himself from this tight corner. The Arabs were at that time badly in need of guns to use against the Portuguese, whose ships were beginning to divert the profitable trade between India and Europe around Africa and away from Arabia. Di Varthema managed to convince a merchant that he was a skilfull maker of cannon, and was allowed to hide in his house.

When the pilgrim caravans and the Mamelukes had left Mecca, Di Varthema ventured on to Juddah, the port of Mecca. Juddah too was a dangerous place for a Mameluke deserter. There the Italian hid himself in a mosque. He pretended to be very ill and lay groaning among the large group of beggars who had also found shelter there. In the evening he would steal out to buy food and observe the goings on in the busy port.

Above left: the Mosque of Mohammed in Medina, where Mohammed is buried. The visit to Medina is part of the Moslem pilgrimage and, as in Mecca, the prayers to be performed are very precisely defined, and pilgrims need guides to help accomplish the ritual.

Above: Mohammed blessing the Black Stone, which is now situated on the south wall of the Kaaba. To kiss the stone is part of the ritual at Mecca.

After three weeks in hiding, Di Varthema managed to get a place on a ship bound for Persia that stopped along the coast of Yemen and docked at Aden. There, Di Varthema experienced his first real misfortune. The Arabs of Yemen were suspicious of any outsider whom they thought might be a spy for the Portuguese traders. Perhaps because his disguise seemed less credible than in Mecca, the Italian spent several months in jail. But afterwards he managed to travel inland in Yemen and reached as far up in the mountains as Ṣanʿāʾ.

After his visit to Ṣanʿāʾ, Di Varthema returned to Aden where he was again forced to hide in a mosque during the day. He nevertheless managed to get himself a place on a ship which was going to Persia and then on to India. By 1510, he had apparently made his way home to Italy, because in that year the book of his travels was published.

Nearly 200 years passed before the next recorded visit of a European to Mecca. This was made by Joseph Pitts, an English

Below: a lone rider on the coastal plain north of Juddah. Di Varthema would have made this part of his journey equally alone—he deserted the Mameluke guard in Mecca and traveled on to Juddah by himself.

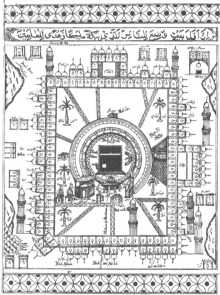
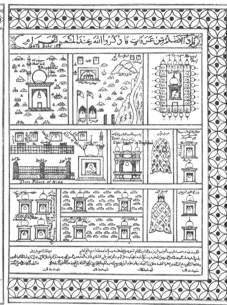

seaman who, in 1678, was captured by Barbary pirates off the north coast of Africa. Pirates in those days often kept their prisoners for years. Pitts, who was later sold as a slave to a Moslem cavalry officer, did not make the pilgrimage until 1685. By the time he accompanied his master to Mecca, he could speak both Arabic and Turkish. He had also been forced to become a Moslem. Having observed and recorded the various stages of the pilgrimage, Pitts managed to escape and eventually returned home. Once back in England, he wrote a book about his adventures.

The next known European visitor to Mecca was a mysterious Spaniard, who called himself Ali Bey. He made the pilgrimage in 1801. Ali Bey not only knew Arabic, but was also trained in geology and botany. He took scientific instruments on his journey and, surprisingly, he managed to use them without arousing the suspicions of the inhabitants of Mecca. His principal contribution to exploration was that he fixed the position of Mecca by astronomical observation.

Eight years later, in 1809, Ulrich Jaspar Seetzen, a German botanist, made a journey to Mecca disguised as a Moslem. He had already spent some years traveling in the Middle East, and had a thorough knowledge of Arabic. From Mecca, Seetzen went on to Medina, and then to Al Mukhā. Unfortunately, soon afterward his disguise must have aroused suspicion and, in 1811, he was murdered somewhere near Ta'izz.

During the 300 years between Di Varthema's visit to Mecca and Seetzen's travels in Arabia, the political situation in and around the Arabian Peninsula had altered greatly. The Turks had extended the Ottoman Empire to include Iraq, Syria, Palestine, Egypt, the north coast of Africa, and the Hejaz, but they did not penetrate the heart of Arabia. In the 1500's, the Portuguese seized the island of

Above: the Mecca certificate, given to pilgrims to the sacred city. It shows the landmarks of the pilgrimage. As every true Moslem is commanded to make at least one pilgrimage to Mecca during his life, if it is at all possible, this certificate is looked on almost as a passport to heaven. Below: Ali Bey, said to have been a Moslem prince, son of Othman Bey.

Above: Ulrich Jaspar Seetzen, a German botanist. Seetzen visited Mecca, but was later murdered near Ta'izz.

Socotra off the southern coast of Arabia, and established a base at Muscat, and one farther east at Hormuz on the Persian Gulf.

By the end of the 1500's, Portuguese power had begun to decline. The Dutch, the British, and the French began to push eastward into the Indian Ocean and the Pacific to acquire new territory and build up overseas empires. The Red Sea and the Persian Gulf were frequently visited by ships of the British, Dutch, and French East India companies, which used to call at the major ports in Arabia. But few of the men on these ships ventured farther inland than the warehouse areas in the ports.

Inside Arabia itself, important religious and political developments had taken place. These developments had their root in a reformation of Islam, which involved a return to the simple practices and teachings of Mohammed. The movement was led by Abd al-Wahhab and sprang up in the district of al-Ared (in the southern part of the Nejd in which lies the present-day town of Riyadh).

In the mid-1700's, Abd al-Wahhab had been taken under the protection and patronage of Mohammed al-Saud, head of the Saudi family, which ruled the area around Dar'iyah. In 1745, he founded the Wahhabi sect, and preached the reformation of Islam. His religious message strengthened the Saudis in their rivalry with neighboring chiefs. Every campaign fought by the recently converted tribesmen against a rival state became a holy war.

Through Mohammed al-Saud, the Wahhabis became the masters of the Nejd. His son, Saud bin Abdelaziz al Saud, also played a part in enlarging the Wahhabi empire, entering and capturing the Hejaz in 1802. The Wahhabis subsequently expanded their authority up to Damascus and even seized Mecca and Medina. At this point the Sultan of Turkey became alarmed about the Wahhabi movement, which threatened both the Ottoman Empire and his own religious position as Caliph of Islam. He ordered the governor of Egypt, Mohammed Ali Pasha, to deal with the situation.

In 1812, an Egyptian army drove the Wahhabis out of Mecca and Medina. Six years later the Egyptians heavily defeated the Wahhabis at Dar'iyah, and then reduced the Saudi capital to a state of ruin. The power of the Saudi family was broken and the Wahhabi empire ceased to exist. But the religious fervor of the Wahhabi religion survived among some of the tribes. It was to be a factor in the eventual revival of the powerful Saudi family in the late 1800's.

LIBEDIA·

While the Egyptian campaign against the Wahhabis was at its height, a Swiss explorer, John Lewis Burckhardt, arrived in Juddah, the port of Mecca. His aim was to make the pilgrimage to Mecca. Burckhardt traveled disguised as a Turk, calling himself Ibrahim ibn Abdullah. He spoke excellent Arabic, knew the teachings of the Koran (the Moslem holy book), and, as a last resort, could claim to be a convert to Islam, though it is not clear if indeed he was.

Burckhardt had been employed to seek the sources of the Niger River by a society in London called the Association for Promoting the Discovery of the Interior Parts of Africa. But, while waiting for a caravan at Cairo, he had decided to explore further in the Middle East before resuming his mission.

Burckhardt traveled about in the Hejaz and made a detailed account of everything he saw and heard in Arabia. He was a careful man, little impressed by the kind of adventures which had carried Di Varthema from place to place, and was content to go about unnoticed while he made notes for his journal. Burckhardt was the supreme observer not only of the hajj, but of all aspects of the religious and secular world he visited. His journal is among the most complex documents about the holy cities. Long after it was

Above: one of the Portuguese forts along the Arabian coast. When Portuguese ships sailed regularly to India by the sea route round the Cape of Good Hope, the Portuguese built forts to safeguard the route in strategic places along the coast. But the Portuguese never settled inland.

Below: Selim III, Sultan of Turkey 1789–1807. It was during his reign that the fanatical Wahhabis began to take over much of Arabia.

Left: the last battle against the Wahhabis, the capture of Dar'iyah. It was taken only after a siege lasting five months, during which both Egyptians and Wahhabis suffered in the merciless heat of the desert.

published, explorers, students of religion, and anyone interested in the Arabian country and in the politics, history, and commercial life of the area during this period found it essential reading.

After spending a year in Arabia, Burckhardt returned to Cairo, hoping this time to meet up with a caravan to take him into the Sahara. There he rested and made some final notes about his Arabian travels. He was also convalescing from dysentery, which he had caught during his stay in Medina. And, before the next caravan was ready to depart for the interior, Burckhardt died from another bout of this deadly disease. It was characteristic of him that before his death he had mailed the manuscript of his journal to his patrons in London.

The next European visitor to Mecca and Medina had read and been fascinated by Burckhardt's journal. This was an Englishman, Richard Burton, who made the pilgrimage in 1853. He traveled disguised not as a convert to Islam but as a born Moslem. Burton had an extraordinary facility for learning languages. At the age of 21

Above: Abdul ibn Saud, the chief of the Wahhabis. Accepting a promise that his family and city would be saved from destruction, he surrendered to the Egyptians. He was sent to Constantinople where, after being paraded for three days, he was publicly beheaded.

357

Above: John Lewis Burckhardt, the Swiss explorer, in the Moslem dress in which he disguised himself for the journey to Mecca. He was a careful observer and kept a detailed journal.

Above right: Petra, an ancient ruined city in what is now Jordan. David Roberts based this picture on drawings that Burckhardt himself had made.

he had landed in Bombay, India, as an army lieutenant and spent the next seven years there learning Persian and Arabic, as well as various local Indian dialects. It was during this period that he first decided upon his scheme for making the pilgrimage. In the autumn of 1852, Burton returned to London and secured a year's leave from the army and the promise of some money for his exploration from the Royal Geographical Society.

In April, 1853, Burton was ready to start for Mecca, pretending to be an Afghan pilgrim and doctor. He hoped that as a doctor he would be able to observe the details of Arab family life.

Some of Burton's trickiest moments came at the start of the

journey. At Suez, for instance, his companions found a sextant among his belongings, not the kind of thing that a genuine pilgrim was likely to be carrying. A boy in the group accused Burton of being an infidel. Burton ruefully threw away his sextant and, to restore the confidence of his Moslem companions, "prayed five times a day for nearly a week." It seems fairly clear that the Moslems who were suspicious of Burton were also aware that he was carrying with him a good deal of money, and they hoped to benefit from some of it. "The scene ended," reports Burton, "with a general abuse of the acute youth."

At Al Wajh on the Red Sea coast, Burton's identity was again

Above: the temples and rock tombs at Petra today. The carvings now seem somewhat more eroded, but they still show the amazing accuracy of Burckhardt's thorough reports on the places he visited. The city of Petra was once a flourishing trading center, but the area around the ruins is now inhabited mainly by bands of nomads.

Left: the fez that Burton wore. He was particularly fond of assuming native costumes and took great care to make himself as indistinguishable as possible from the local people.

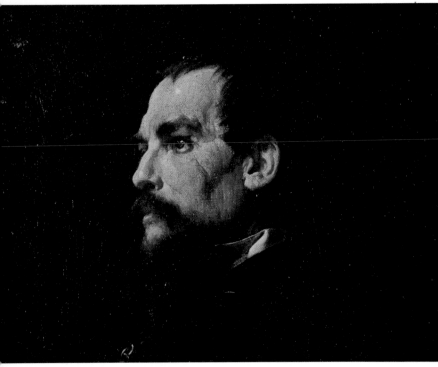

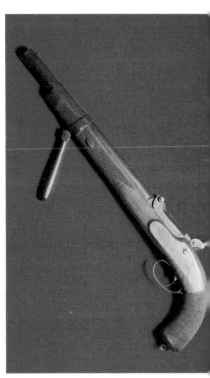

Above: Richard Burton (1821-1890). painted by Frederic Leighton in 1876. With his flair for languages and his enthusiasm for blending into an exotic background, Burton was one of the most flamboyant of the Arabian explorers.

Above right: Burton's pistol. Had Burton carried such a weapon openly when he made the pilgrimage to Mecca, his companions would certainly have suspected that he was not a dervish.

questioned. A number of Moslems were lounging about at a coffee house—"lying down, smoking, drinking water, bathing, and picking their teeth with their daggers." Among them was an inquisitive man who called himself a Pathan (a person of Afghan stock, living on the borders of Pakistan and Afghanistan). "He could speak five or six languages, he knew a number of people everywhere, and he had traveled far and wide over Central Asia. These fellows are always good detectors of an incognito. I avoided answering his questions about my native place . . . I asked him, when he insisted upon my having been born somewhere, to guess for himself. To my joy he claimed me for a brother Pathan. . . . We then sat smoking with 'effusion' . . ."

Burton gives a particularly vivid account of the pilgrim ship that carried them from Suez to Yanbu', the port of Medina. Named the *Silk al-Zahab* (golden wire) the ship had two masts—but only one with a sail—and no deck, except at the stern which was high enough to act as a sail in a gale of wind. "She had no means of reefing, no compass, no log, no sounding lines, no spare ropes, nor even the suspicion of a chart." On boarding her, Burton explains, the first thing to be done after gaining standing room was to fight for greater comfort. "In a few minutes nothing was to be seen but a confused mass of humanity, each item indiscriminately punching and pulling, scratching and biting, butting and trampling, with cries of rage and all the accompaniments of a proper fray." Burton and his companions eventually triumphed over the opposition, composed mainly of North African pilgrims, and arranged themselves reasonably comfortably.

During the journey down the Red Sea the *Silk al-Zahab* kept close to the coast. Every night the ship anchored to allow the pilgrims to sleep on dry land. One evening, while wading to the shore, Burton felt the acute pain of something running into his toe. He extracted what seemed to be a piece of thorn, but, by the time the ship reached Yanbu', he could hardly put his foot to the ground. This accident meant that he had to make the long, slow, bandit-threatened trip to Medina and Mecca in a *shugduf,* a sort of cot slung along the side of a camel like a pannier. What Burton thought was a thorn turned out to be the spine of a sea urchin, a type of small sea animal. This unfortunate accident put an end to Burton's ambitious plan of

Above: the ihram, the costume worn by the pilgrims to Mecca. While wearing the ihram, the pilgrim must follow strict rules of ritual purification.
Below: boats like those the pilgrims would use to reach the Arabian coast.

crossing Arabia after he had made the pilgrimage to the holy cities.

Burton's journey from Medina to Mecca was by an inland route not previously reported by a European. But there was nothing geographically new about it. From the point of view of exploration, this great adventurer's Arabian travels were one of his lesser achievements. The brilliance of Burton's journey to Mecca was his faultless disguise and his journal, *Personal Narrative of a Pilgrimage to Al-Medinah and Meccah*. His account, for instance, of his first sight of the Kaaba, housing the sacred Black Stone, shrouded in the black cloth *kiswah*, conveys with conviction one of the supreme moments of his pilgrimage. "There at last it lay, the bourn [object] of my long and weary pilgrimage ... I may truly say that, of all the worshippers who clung weeping to the curtain, or who pressed their beating hearts to the stone, none felt for the moment a deeper emotion than did the Haji [pilgrim] from the far-north. It was as if the legends of the Arabs spoke truth, and that the waving wings of Angels, not the sweet breeze of morning, were agitating and swelling the black covering of the shrine. But, to confess the humbling truth, theirs was the high feeling of religious enthusiasm, mine was the ecstasy of gratified pride."

In 1908–1909, another Englishman, A. J. B. Wavell, repeated Burton's feat of making the journey to Mecca and Medina in disguise. Wavell traveled as a Zanzibari pilgrim. Perhaps the unique aspect of his journey was that he traveled on the recently completed Hejaz Railway from Damascus to Medina. The building of a railroad for the pilgrims had been sponsored by the Ottoman sultan, Abdul-Hamid II and had been financed by subscriptions from every part of the Moslem world. Although it was intended to make the pilgrimage safer and easier, the railroad was at the same time strategically useful to the Ottoman Empire. The Ottoman Turks were at that time having to defend Syria and the Hejaz against the advances of the British. Besides, they were constantly harassed by the Bedouins of Arabia who never ceased their opposition to Turkish rule.

The rail distance between Damascus and Medina was over 1,000 miles. It took four days—a remarkably short time when compared with the 30 or 40 days it took for the journey by caravan. The train was extremely crowded, and many pilgrims who did not try to board it until the last minute were turned away. Sitting opposite

Above: a cartoon of Burton in 1882, captioned "Captain Burton, our commercial traveller." Behind him are Baedeker and Murray—both of whom wrote notable guidebooks in the 1800's —lamenting that Burton got there first.

Wavell and his traveling friends in the train were two Turks, father and son, whose only luggage appeared to consist of a phonograph. This was apparently a popular innovation to the other passengers in the car who were eager to listen to recordings of passages from the Koran.

Added to the unpleasantness of overcrowded conditions in the train was the danger of attack by Bedouins. The tribesmen resented the railroad because of their vested interest in camel transportation and the old pilgrim caravans. From Medā'in Sālih onward the railroad stations had to be guarded by Turkish garrisons. But the crowded train carrying Wavell's party arrived safely at Medina.

From Medina to Yanbu', Wavell and his companions traveled in the traditional way, with a camel caravan. At Yanbu' they boarded a steamer, another innovation, which conveyed them south to Juddah. At Mecca they began the pilgrimage, which in all took five days. As usual this involved a trek to Mount Arafat, and like almost all the Europeans who preceded him, Wavell was particularly impressed by this part of the hajj: "At least half a million people are traversing these nine miles of road between sunrise and ten o'clock this day; about half of them are mounted, and many of them possess baggage-animals as well. The roar of this great column is like a breaking sea, and the dust spreads for miles over the surrounding country. When, passing through the second defile, we came

Above: a picture of a *takhtrawan*, a grandee's litter, from Burton's book, *Personal Narrative of a Pilgrimage to Al-Medinah and Meccah*. Burton reported that the pilgrims traveled on foot or on camel. The wealthy were borne in these splendid litters, with a horse saddled ready for the grandee should he decide to leave his litter.

Right: a station under construction on the Hejaz Railway. The Pilgrimage was a difficult and often dangerous journey, and the railroad was built to make it easier for the pilgrims. However, the Bedouin tribesmen who had an interest in the camel caravans resented the railroad, and they often used to attack the passing trains.

Below: Kasim Pasha, director in chief of the construction of the railroad.

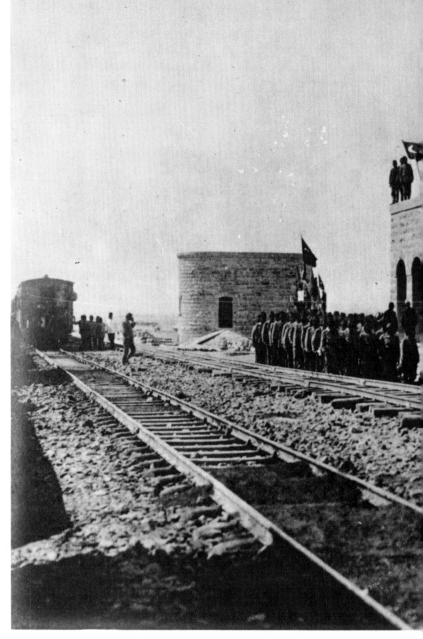

in sight of Arafat itself, the spectacle was stranger still. The hill was literally black with people, and tents were springing up round it, hundreds to the minute, in an ever-widening circle. As we approached, the dull murmur caused by thousands of people shouting the formula, 'Lebeka lebeka, Allohooma lebeka,' which had long been audible, became so loud that it dominated every other sound. In the distance it had sounded rather ominous, suggestive of some deep disturbance of great power, like the rumble of an earthquake."

In spite of the innovations of railroad and steamer, the pilgrimage to Mecca changed little between the time Di Varthema joined the

Above: A. J. B. Wavell in Damascus in 1908. Like Burton, he made the trip to Mecca disguised as a pilgrim.

hajj and Wavell's visit to the holy cities 400 years later. Travel was perhaps easier, but the dangers of discovery were just as great, and each of the travelers was aware that his life was staked on the effectiveness of his disguise. But, far from deterring travelers, the dangers of visiting the forbidden cities actually attracted adventurers to Arabia—their stories of the hajj, of the holy cities, and of Arabian life fascinated Europeans and gave them a glimpse of the beliefs and customs of the Moslem world. And in their attempts to follow routes previously known only to the Moslem pilgrims, these bold men carried out the first exploration of the Hejaz.

Arabia Felix
4

Many explorers have found the southwest corner of Arabia the most fascinating part of the whole country. This mountainous region consists of two main areas—Yemen, facing the Red Sea in the west, and the Hadhramaut country, which faces the Gulf of Aden in the south. It is an area of extraordinary natural beauty, from the high mountains of Yemen to the deep gorge of the Wadi Hadhramaut. But much of its appeal for travelers lies in its ancient history.

From about 1400 B.C., a flourishing civilization existed in Yemen. The country's first capital was at Main. Then, in 950 B.C., a tribe called the Sabaeans invaded the fertile Yemen uplands and established their capital city at Marib, the legendary capital of the Queen of Sheba. The Sabaeans were succeeded by the Himyarites who moved the capital to Zafar, south of the modern city of Şan'ā'. The three ancient kingdoms are usually referred to collectively as the Sabaeans, and their language as Himyaritic.

At the time of the Sabaean kingdoms, Yemen was immensely rich in agriculture and natural resources, adorned with fine temples and palaces. But above all, the Sabaeans traded in myrrh, frankincense, cinnamon, and numerous other aromatic herbs. These spices and herbs were in great demand in the Middle East and Europe for making perfumes and ointments and for burning as incense at religious ceremonies. The route by which they were exported became known as the Incense Trail, and the rich trade in these treasures led European writers to call the southwestern part of Arabia, and Yemen in particular, *Arabia Felix*—which in Latin means happy, or fortunate, Arabia.

In the mid-1700's, however, little was yet known about the history of Yemen. For centuries, geographers, explorers, and scholars had speculated about the country. They knew something about it from references in the Old Testament and classical literature. But it was not until 1759 that an expedition was organized to visit Arabia—and in particular Yemen—with the hope of learning more about its history, and about the land itself.

Left: a hill tribesman, from the Hadhramaut region in southern Arabia, sits on a barren ledge overlooking the vast natural chasm of a wadi spread far beneath his feet.

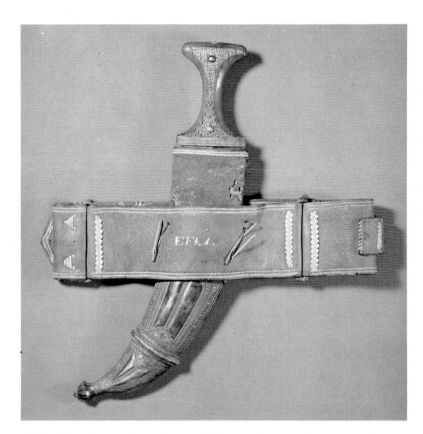

Above: Carsten Niebuhr, the German explorer who was the only member of the Danish expedition of 1761 to return to Europe. Although there was no official leader of the group, Niebuhr's force of character and his methodical scholarship—as well as the fact that he survived to report the group's findings —made him outstanding among the expedition members.

Above right: a dagger and sheath that Niebuhr brought back from his travels.

The idea for a scientific expedition to increase European knowledge of pre-Islamic Arabia was suggested to King Frederik of Denmark by a Hebrew scholar called Johann David Michaelis from Göttingen in Germany. The king showed his interest in the scheme by drawing up a list of instructions for the explorers. He also made arrangements for a ship to be fitted out. Five scholars, each one an expert in his particular field, were selected for the expedition. The project was patronized and financed by King Frederik, but the men who made up the party came from Germany, Sweden, and Denmark. Carsten Niebuhr, the mathematician and surveyor, was from northern Germany; William Baurenfeind, the artist, was from southern Germany. Peter Forskål, the botanist, and Berggren, their European servant, were Swedes. The two Danes were Friedrich Christian von Haven, a philologist and Oriental scholar, and Christian Carl Kramer, a surgeon and zoologist.

Below: a farmer from the Yemen highlands, with a dagger and sheath very similar to the one that Niebuhr brought back from Arabia over 200 years ago.

Above: William Baurenfeind, the artist on the Danish expedition, in an engraving taken from a self-portrait. Baurenfeind died on board the ship taking the party to India.

There was to be no official leader of King Frederik's expedition—each man was to pursue the area of inquiry for which he was best qualified. It is difficult, however, not to think of the Danish expedition as Carsten Niebuhr's. Niebuhr proved himself a man of quite exceptional intelligence and character. And he was the only member of the party to return safely to Europe.

The expedition sailed from Copenhagen for the Mediterranean Sea in January, 1761. The party then made a short trip through Alexandria and Suez to Mount Sinai, later returning to Suez. From Suez, they sailed to Juddah where they arrived in October, 1762.

After remaining there for six weeks, the men boarded another ship to take them on to Al Luhayyah, the northernmost port of Yemen. During the 1700's, Moslem fanaticism in Yemen was at a low ebb and the members of the expedition were unmolested. They wore Arab dress, but were never required to prove that they were Moslems.

The party traveled along the coastal strip to Bayt al Faqīh, the center of the coffee trade. There, Europeans were already well known and accepted as buyers of this important Yemen product. Bayt al Faqīh was the inland depot for coffee on its way from the Yemen hills to the big ports such as Al Mukhā. Because travel was so safe, some of the members of the team ventured to go on short expeditions of their own. Forskål went up into the hills to collect herbs. Niebuhr hired a donkey to explore the Tihama—the narrow, infertile coastal plain bordering the Red Sea. On his excursions, Niebuhr was careful to dress as a poor man so as to discourage the numerous robbers who roamed the area.

"A turban, a greatcoat wanting the sleeves, a shirt, linen drawers and a pair of slippers were all the dress I wore. It being the fashion of the country to carry arms when traveling, I had a saber and pistols at my girdle. A piece of an old carpet was my saddle, and served

Above: the terraced fields of Yemen still closely resemble Niebuhr's description of them. Agricultural methods in the Yemen highlands have changed little for hundreds of years.

Above: Peter Forskål, the Swedish botanist on the Danish expedition. Below: a woman of Juddah selling bread, a drawing by the German artist, Baurenfeind. Niebuhr published this in his account of the expedition.

me likewise for a seat at table and various other purposes. To cover me at night I had the linen cloak which the Arabs wrap about their shoulders, to shelter me from the sun and rain. A bucket of water, an article of indispensable necessity to a traveler in these arid regions, hung by my saddle. I had for some time endeavored to suit myself to the Arabian manner of living, and now could spare many conveniences to which I had become accustomed in Europe, and could content myself with bad bread, the only article to be obtained in most of the inns."

As members of the party—sometimes traveling alone and sometimes as a group—went up into the highlands of Yemen, they observed that the villages were built of stone, in contrast to the mud villages in the lowlands. They wrote, too, of the life of the industrious farmers. Niebuhr reflects upon the countryside in his account of a visit to a village called Bulgosa. "Neither asses nor mules can be used here; the hills are to be climbed by narrow and steep paths: yet, in comparison with the parched plains of Tihama, the scenery seemed to me charming. . . . The coffee trees were all in flower at Bulgosa, and exhaled an exquisitely agreeable perfume. They are planted upon terraces in the form of an amphitheater. Most of them are only watered by the rains that fall; but some, indeed, from large reservoirs upon the heights; in which spring water is collected, in order to be sprinkled upon the terraces; where the trees grow so thick together that the rays of the sun can hardly enter among their branches. We were told that those trees, thus artificially watered, yielded ripe fruit twice in the year. . . ."

Nevertheless, travel in the mountains, where the mean temperature in summer is 85–90°F, and in the Tihama, where it can get as hot as 130°F, had already begun to affect the members of the expedition. Niebuhr caught "cold"—malaria—and Von Haven was so ill that he died before they reached Al Mukhā in April, 1763. Forskål wrote uncharitably that Von Haven "by his demise" had "made the expedition incomparably easier for the rest of us. He was of a very difficult disposition."

Left: the ruins of the great dam at Marib. Only the northern and southern ends, which were fixed to the wadi wall, have survived. The northern part is flanked by a fortress, now in ruins.

The party, now reduced to five men, set out for Ṣan'ā', the capital of Yemen. They struggled through the fierce summer heat of the Tihama up to cool and pleasant Ta'izz. But by the time they were ready to leave and go on to Ṣan'ā', Forskål himself was weak with fever and had to be lifted onto his donkey. Though the journey was through beautiful mountain country, it was an unbearable experience for them all. For Forskål in particular, the last and most terrible part of the journey was from Menzil to Yarīm. Suffering agonies of pain, he had to be lashed to the back of a baggage camel.

Forskål died at Yarīm on July 11, 1763. He was 32 years old, a man of great brilliance and promise. Niebuhr described him as the most learned man in the whole group.

The road from Menzil to Yarīm crossed a shoulder of Jebel

Above: Bab el-Yemen, the main gate of the city of Ṣan'ā', the capital of Yemen. It was on the grueling trip to Ṣan'ā' through the Yemen mountains that Peter Forskål died in 1763.

Right: a stele—a carved stone slab— the work of Sabaean artisans, dating from the A.D. 200's. It pictures worshipers before a goddess in a temple (above), and a woman reclining on a couch, attended by her servant (below).

374

Summara at a height of 9,000 feet, and the landscape changed suddenly as they entered the dried up plateau of central Yemen. From Ta'izz to Menzil there had been rain every day. Niebuhr says that the earth there was "covered with a charming verdure," but at Yarīm, "no rain had fallen for three months, although distant thunder had been heard almost every day. In this want of rain the locusts had multiplied prodigiously . . ."

Though ill himself, Niebuhr remained faithful to the scholarly goals of the expedition and took note of the existence of important remains near Yarīm. "At two miles distance ... stood a once famous city Dhafar, very little of the ruins of which now remain. The first magistrate of Yarīm, however, told me that a large stone is still to be seen there with an inscription, which neither Jews nor Mahometans [Moslems] can explain. . . ." Niebuhr thought that the city was probably once the seat of the Himyarites, and that it was likely to contain Himyaritic inscriptions.

Niebuhr also reports what he had heard about Marib—sometimes called Mariabba—the old Sabaean capital. At Marib other important ruins were to be found, the most noteworthy being a great dam which had fallen into disrepair. This was one of the immense dams which had been part of the advanced and prosperous civilization of the Sabaeans.

The four remaining members of the expedition, now all suffering from fever, stumbled on to Ṣan'ā'. They had two days' enforced rest waiting for an audience with the *imam* (ruler), and spent them admiring the beauty of the neighborhood, where, among other things, 20 different kinds of grapes were grown. The men were well received by the imam, who urged them to stay as long as they liked. They were, however, worried by their poor health and their nerves had been shaken by the deaths of Von Haven and Forskål. They remained at Ṣan'ā' for only 10 days.

Nevertheless, before leaving the capital, Niebuhr took care to note down as much as he could about the plan of the city and the life of its inhabitants. One of the things which interested him most was the Jewish community of about 2,000 which had a village outside the walls of Ṣan'ā'. Although they were fine artisans and kept shops in Ṣan'ā', the Jews returned to their district at night and were generally badly treated. Niebuhr also noted that, when one Jew was found guilty of a serious crime, the whole Jewish community suffered punishment for it. On one occasion all synagogues and houses above a certain height were demolished.

It took Niebuhr and the depleted party nine grueling days to travel from Ṣanʻāʼ down into the tropical heat of Al Mukhā. In Al Mukhā all four collapsed with fever, and Kramer, Baurenfeind, and Berggren had to be carried aboard the ship which was to take them on to Bombay on the west coast of India. But a few days after sailing, Baurenfeind and Berggren died. And in February, 1764, Kramer died in Bombay.

Niebuhr was now alone. During his 14-month stay in India, he gradually regained his strength, and decided to carry out the king's instructions to return to Europe by way of Muscat, the Persian Gulf, Iraq, and Aleppo, rather than by the temptingly easy voyage around the Cape of Good Hope. On his return journey, he was the

Below: an illustration from Harris's book about his journey to Yemen. Harris was one of the few travelers to reach Ṣanʻāʼ. Here, he is being interrogated by Ahmed Feizi Pasha, the Turkish governor general at the time of Harris' visit in the 1890's.

Above: Hermann Burchardt with a coffee merchant, Caprotti, in Ṣanʿāʾ, one of a group of photographs taken before Burchardt's murder in the hazardous country surrounding the city.

only European among his traveling companions. On November 20, 1767, he rode into Copenhagen again, having been away for very nearly seven years. He was only 34 years old.

Niebuhr then set to work to make the official report on the expedition. This involved studying the observations of his dead companions and combining them with his own. His book, first published in 1772, tells of the expedition's journeys in Yemen and of Arab manners and customs. It also covers those parts of the peninsula which none of the party had visited. This section of the book is based upon information Niebuhr had gathered by talking to educated Arabs and merchants.

Although the expedition had spent less than two years in Arabia, and had not penetrated the vast unexplored interior, it had carried out King Frederik's instructions. The six men had thoroughly explored the Yemen Tihama and had gone into the lower foothills. Niebuhr had collected the most reliable information possible about the rest of the peninsula. He was the first man to observe Arabia from a scientific point of view.

Above: the Englishman G. Wyman Bury. Below: Bury pictured in Arab dress. Bury was thoroughly at home in Arabia, and took the Arab name of Abdulla Mansur, which he later used as a pseudonym for his books about Arabia.

Right: an elaborately decorated house at Ṣan'ā', typical of the Yemenite houses of the city. Ṣan'ā' was first established as capital by an Abyssinian viceroy, around the middle of the A.D. 500's. It was probably a house like this in which Bury spent his honeymoon in Ṣan'ā' in 1913.

During the years that followed Niebuhr's journey, Moslem fanaticism in Yemen increased, and travel there became increasingly dangerous for non-Moslems. And, in fact, it was more than 70 years before the next European visited the area. The first explorers of the 1800's to brave Yemen's dangers were scholars and archaeologists, who hoped that the inscriptions and ruins Niebuhr had reported finding would throw light on the still-mysterious Sabaean-Ḥimyaritic civilization. Between 1843 and 1890, three travelers ..ched the Marib dam. The first was a Frenchman, Joseph Thomas Arnaud, who studied the inscriptions and carvings he found at Marib. The other two explorers—Joseph Halévy, a Frenchman, and Edward Glaser, an Austrian—traveled to Marib under the auspices of the Académie des Inscriptions et Belles Lettres in Paris. They both took copies of the inscriptions they found there. The inscriptions gathered together by these travelers added greatly to our knowledge about pre-Islamic Arabia.

Travel as far as Ṣan'ā' was, however, still dangerous. A. J. B. Wavell, who later made the pilgrimage to Mecca on the Hejaz Railway, managed to get to Ṣan'ā' in 1891, and W. B. Harris reached the city in 1892. Both were interested in the anti-Turkish revolt which flared up at that time. But Wavell was imprisoned and Harris only just escaped from ambush south of Ṣan'ā'. In 1909, the German Hermann Burchardt was murdered in the same area, exactly 98 years after Seetzen's murder near Ta'izz.

The next important explorer in Yemen was the Englishman G. Wyman Bury. Bury, who was known to the Arabs as Abdulla Mansur, had served with a British regiment in Arabia and had spent many years living with the Arabs along the coast of the Arabian Sea. Like other Englishmen who had been fascinated by Arabia, Bury preferred the wild tribesmen to the townspeople. He had an excellent knowledge of their language, and was willing to share all their hardships in order to live among them. In 1908, Bury planned an expedition to cross Yemen and proceed along the Rub' al Khali to southern Nejd, but this ambitious scheme was opposed by the Turks.

Southwestern Arabia was home to Bury, and in 1913, his English fiancée went out to Al Hudaydah for their wedding. Together the couple journeyed to Ṣan'ā' for their honeymoon. This trip, and Bury's other travels before World War I, are recorded in two books, *The Land of Uz* and *Arabia Infelix*. Bury's descriptions of the

Above: the East India Company's survey ship *Palinurus,* at anchor in the Gulf of Aqaba. The captain, Stafford Bettesworth Haines, was fascinated with the Arab world, and managed to share his enthusiasm with his officers, several of whom made journeys inland.

country still have an appealing humor. For example, when passing out of the coastal plain of Yemen and heading for the foothills, he comments: "While the morning is still grey you may hear the rapping shots of some tribal *fracas* [noisy quarrel] from the foothills, a cheery sound, denoting that the world is once more astir and taking an intelligent interest in its affairs."

No European of his time knew Yemen as Bury did. His knowledge of the Turkish administration and his understanding of the Arab tribesmen made him a most valuable intelligence officer in the Suez Canal area during World War I.

East of Yemen, along the south coast of Arabia, lie the countries that on modern maps are called Southern Yemen and Muscat and Oman. Until the 1800's, Europeans knew little about this region, known as the Hadhramaut. Burckhardt and Niebuhr had concluded that much of the interior was desert, and their theory was supported by the reports of Moslem geographers. Parts were certainly inhabited. But no one knew for certain just what the region hid.

Circumstances conspired to maintain the isolation of the Hadhramaut. As in other parts of Arabia, the Moslem tribesmen were acutely hostile toward European infidels. The Hadhramaut, too, was geographically isolated—it is cut off from the west by mountains, has few good harbors, and its northern boundary is tightly sealed

Below: an altar dating from near the time of Christ, with an inscription in Himyaritic script. This ancient alphabet is still used by the Ethiopians, but no longer by the Arabs. However, not even an Ethiopian could understand this inscription as, although he would know the letters, he would be unable to read the language.

by the uninhabited desert Rub' al Khali—the Empty Quarter.

For many years, the Arab pirates, who for centuries had operated with great success along the coasts of southern Arabia, also helped to preserve the Hadhramaut from European intrusion. At the beginning of the 1800's, however, their power on the seas began to decline. When Ibrahim Pasha of Egypt overthrew the Wahhabis in 1818, this greatly weakened the pirates as well. And when the wooden merchant vessels of former times were replaced by ironclad steamships, the pirates in their vulnerable wooden ships could no longer attack shipping with impunity. As the pirates' strength decreased, so the British government and the East India Company began to extend their influence to southern Arabia. In so doing, they paved the way for the first exploration of the Hadhramaut.

The East India Company's first move was to dispatch survey ships to the Arabian coast. The survey ships were to choose sites for coaling stations where the company's ships could refuel on their way from Suez to Bombay. One of the 50 ships was the *Palinurus*. Among its officers was James Wellsted, a pioneer of exploration in both the Hadhramaut and Oman.

Early in May, 1834, the *Palinurus* anchored near the little port of Bi'r 'Alī between a low island and a high dark cliff. Some ruins could be seen on top of the cliff, and Wellsted and a small party landed to have a look at them. They found plentiful remains of houses, walls, and towers along the shore, and a third of the way up the cliff they found inscriptions and more ruined houses. At the top of the precipice there was a massive stone tower, Husn Ghorab. This had once been an ancient port called Cana. Frankincense was brought by sea to Cana before it was taken inland to be stored at Sabbatha (now the remote village of Shabwa). In his book *Travels in Arabia,* Wellsted describes the tower as "a place of extraordinary strength . . . invaluable both as a place of safe retreat and as a magazine [storehouse] for trade."

The next year, on another surveying mission, the *Palinurus* called at Belhaf, a port a little to the west of Bi'r 'Alī. Wellsted heard that there were extensive ruins some way inland, and engaged a guide to direct him to the area. On the third day of his trek, Wellsted came to a well-watered valley in the center of which was an enormous

Below: broken pieces of stonework in the Hadhramaut. Many of these fragments have inscriptions on them. In the 1800's, such remains offered a new lure to explorers willing to brave the dangers of the country.

hill. "It is nearly 800 yards in length and about 350 yards at its extreme breadth. . . . About a third of the height from its base a massive wall . . . is carried completely around the eminence and flanked by square towers. . . ." Within the entrance, raised 10 feet above a platform, he found the inscriptions. Also within the massive walls were the ruins of a temple. This was Nakab al Hajar, one of the very few walled towns of southern Arabia, which dates back to about 1000 B.C.

This expedition was the first made by Europeans into the southern interior. The results thrilled explorers and archaeologists alike. The inscriptions found at Nakab al Hajar and Husn Ghorab furnished the first decisive proof to Europeans that Himyaritic records survived from the ancient Sabaean civilizations. Greatly encouraged by his finds at these two ancient sites, Wellsted wanted to explore farther in southern Arabia and, in particular, to reach the Wadi

Above: James Theodore Bent, who openly led a scientific expedition into the Hadhramaut in 1893. He was accompanied by his wife, who took photographs of the journey.

Right: exploration in Yemen, the Hejaz, and the Hadhramaut. In the Hejaz, exploration was made more difficult by the fact that the region around the holy cities was forbidden to non-Moslems, but all over Arabia explorers encountered the fierce religious fanaticism of Islam. Many of these explorers risked their lives to bring back reports of Arabia.

Hadhramaut. But when he tried to plan other journeys, he found his way barred by the hostility of the Arab population.

The Arabs of the Hadhramaut were among the fiercest opponents of European exploration. They had always been passionately concerned with their freedom, and their fury was aroused by the British seizure of Aden in January, 1839. Furthermore, the *sayids*—Moslem holy men who believe they are descended from Mohammed through his daughter Fatima—incited the Arab townspeople to attack any explorers foolhardy enough to try to penetrate the interior. The few travelers who did manage to penetrate as far inland as Tarīm had their clothing ripped off, their maps and notes stolen, and were soon terrified into retreat. It is only comparatively recently that the sayids' complete and exclusive control over religion, law, and learning in the Hadhramaut has been broken.

The ferocity of the sayids and their followers prevented further expeditions into the interior of the Hadhramaut for nearly 60 years. Then, at the end of 1893, an Englishman, James Theodore Bent, led an undisguised expedition into the interior. Despite the fears of the British officials at Aden, who were still opposed to the idea of provoking the tribesmen, Bent and his companions set out to explore inland from Al Mukallā. The Aden government derived some comfort from the fact that Theodore Bent had among his party a surveyor and mapmaker who might bring back some useful information about the inland regions. Also in the group were an Egyptian naturalist, a botanist from the Royal Botanical Gardens in London, and Mrs. Bent, who took photographs of the expedition.

On leaving Al Mukallā, the Bents' expedition climbed slowly and steadily to about 4,000 feet. There they found themselves on the broad level tableland which isolates the Wadi Hadhramaut from the south coast. After two more days of arduous travel, they began to approach the entrances of the wadis which lead on to the Wadi Hadhramaut. At first, they met with a hostile reception from the Bedouins, but when they entered the Wadi Hadhramaut the situation began to improve.

According to Mrs. Bent, as far as Shibām ". . . all was desert and sand, but suddenly the valley narrows and a long vista of cultivation was spread before us. Here miles of the valley are covered with palm groves. Bright green patches of lucerne called *kadhib,* almost dazzling to look upon after the arid waste. . . ."

Ibn-Batuta	1a	1325-32
	1b	1341-9
Di Varthema	2	1502-8
Niebuhr	3	1761-3
Burckhardt	4a	1812
	4b	1813-5
Wellsted	5a	1834
	5b	1834-5
	5c	1835
Burton	6a	1853-4
	6b	1854
	6c	1877
Bent, T. & H.	7a	1893-4
	7b	1894-5
	7c	1895-7
	7d	1897

© Geographical Projects

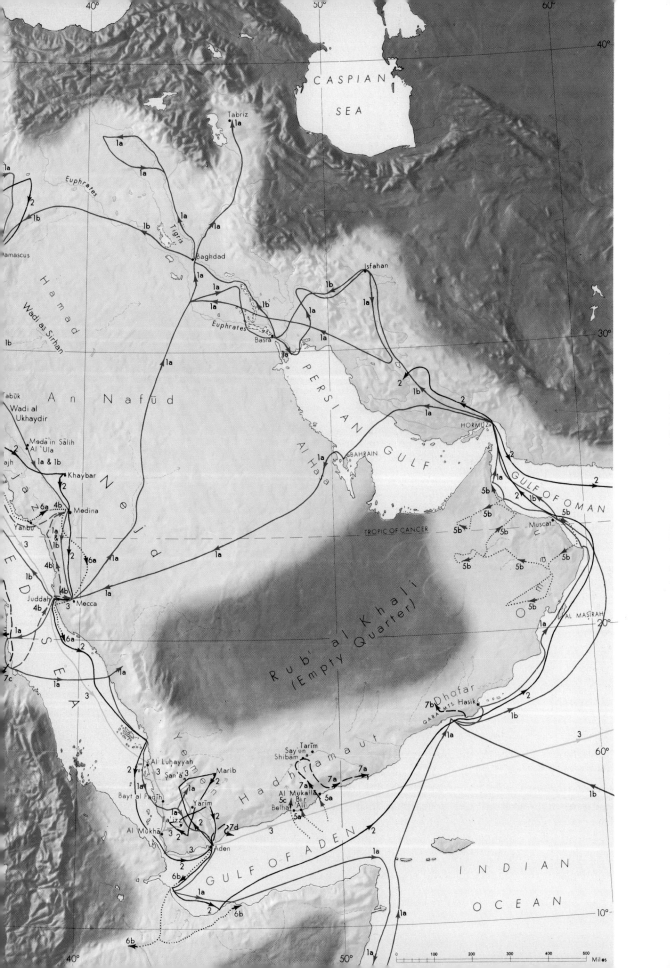

CASPIAN
SEA

Tabriz
1a

40°

50°

60°

40°

1a

1a

1a

1a

Euphrates

1a

Tigris

1b

1b

Damascus

Hamad

Wadi as Sirhan

1b

1a

1a

1a

1a

Baghdad

1a

1b

Euphrates

1b

Basra

1a

Isfahan

1b

1a

1a

30°

2

1b

2

1a

HORMUZ

2

GULF OF OMAN

2

Tabūk

Wadi al Ukhaydir

An Nafūd

Al Hasa

PERSIAN GULF

BAHRAIN

5b

2

1b

5b

Meda'in Sālih
Al 'Ula

1a & 1b

ajh

Khaybar

2

Medina

6a

4b

Yanbu

1a & 1b

1b

3

2

6a

4b

1a

1a

4b

Juddah

3

Mecca

4b

1a

1a

1a

TROPIC OF CANCER

5b

5b

5b

Muscat

5b

5b

5b

Rub' al Khali
(Empty Quarter)

5b

5b

5b

AL MAŞĪRAH

1a

20°

6a

2

R
E
D

S
E
A

1a

7c

3

1a

Dhofar

7b

QARA MTS. Hasik

2

1b

3

60°

1a

Al Luhayyah

Ṣanʿāʾ

3

Marib

Tarīm

Shibam

Say'un

Hadhramaut

7a

7a

7a

7a

2

1a

Bayt al Faqīh

Yarīm

1a

Al Mukallā

5a

Bir 'Ali

5c

Belhā 'Ali

5a

Al Mukhā

3

2

7d

Ta'izz

1a

2

3

2

Aden

7b

2

1a

GULF OF ADEN

1a

2

6b

INDIAN

OCEAN

10°

1a

1b

1a

40°

50°

6b

2

6b

0   100   200   300   400   500
Miles

The Bents managed to travel to Shibām despite a tribal feud in the area, but the Arabs' hostility soon forced them to leave the town. On their return, they received more insults and threats from the townspeople. In the safety of the sultan's palace, the Bents discussed their next move. They decided to make for the coast at Shihr, rather than Al Mukallā, using the Wadi Adim, a more easterly route than that by which they had come.

It was a hard and dangerous journey. The Hamumi tribe which dominated a long section of the route was involved in a war, and the Bents' party was attacked several times. When they reached the head of the wadi and emerged onto the surrounding plateau, it still proved to be difficult going. It was March, 1894, before they at last reached the safety of the coast.

Later that year, the Bents made another expedition, this time in Dhofar, farther along the southern Arabian coast toward Muscat. They found the ruins of seven ancient towns and ventured inland to the Qara Mountains. At the high point of the range, it was possible to stand looking northward into the Rub' al Khali, the Empty Quarter, and then to turn around and see the Arabian Sea. During this trip, as on their previous expeditions, the Bents collected lists of ancient words which they copied from inscriptions. They also took back samples of rare plants, shells, and insects.

Tribal quarrels had prevented the Bents from journeying along the Wadi Hadhramaut beyond Shibām to visit the ancient towns of Say'ūn and Tarīm. Nor were they able to see the tomb of the prophet Hud, or Bir Borhut, said by legend to be like a dark well or smoking volcano, where the souls of infidels could be heard moaning in agony. Forty years were to pass before these places were visited by a European.

In 1931, a Dutch Orientalist and former diplomat, Van der Meulen, and a German, Von Wissman, were sent by the Dutch government to explore the Hadhramaut. Thousands of Hadhramis had emigrated to the Dutch East Indies, where the prospects of making money were considerably better than in Arabia. This pattern of emigration had developed during World War I, and continued afterward. The Hadhramis remained in the Indies until they had made sufficient money, and then returned to spend the rest of their lives in Arabia. The Dutch government wanted to find out more about the country these immigrant workers came from.

As the Bents had done, Van der Meulen and Von Wissman started out from Al Mukallā. Although they had used an automobile for one or two local trips, when they set out to explore the Hadhramaut they traveled in the old way—on camels in the comparative safety of a caravan. The first place they visited was the Wadi Doan, which impressed them with its beauty. "The sun shines right into the wadi, where no life or movement are to be seen. Between patches of gay yellowish-green, formed by the fields of dhura, maize, and lucerne, lies unruffled the broad, shining, gray-green strip of date-groves. . . . This is the reward of weary travelers in the desert. . . . In spite of the heat, we cannot tear ourselves away from the spell cast by this valley full of fertility and beauty, in the midst of an endless desert of barren rock and stone."

Von Wissman and Van der Meulen traveled from the Wadi Doan to the Wadi Hadhramaut. The tribal quarrels which had prevented the Bents from visiting the ancient towns along the wadi were no longer an obstacle, and at both Say'ūn and Tarīm the travelers were received as honored guests. At Tarīm, the remotest and richest of the three towns of the wadi, the two men visited Sayid Abu-Bakr al-Kaf, the leading citizen of the area. Abu-Bakr had used his share of the income from the rich family fortune to build roads and schools, and to improve the living standard of the Bedouins. The explorers were greatly impressed by this man, whose name was to remain linked with the idea of a modern, peaceful Hadhramaut.

From Tarīm, Von Wissman and Van der Meulen made the two-day journey eastward to the tomb of Hud. According to the story, Hud had fled to this place pursued by his enemies. God opened the rock for him to escape, and his pursuers saw him no more. This important Moslem sanctuary was normally barred to non-Moslems,

Left: the high rocky hinterland of the Hadhramaut—the *jol*. The Bents were among the first explorers to reach this remote area of southern Arabia.

Right: Von Wissman and Van der Meulen (in the center) with Sayid Abu-Bakr al-Kaf and three of the sayid's aides. Abu-Bakr continued to work for a modern Hadhramaut until his death in 1967.

Below: the tomb of the prophet Hud, which Van der Meulen and Von Wissman visited under the protection of Abu-Bakr. According to the traditional belief, the dark rock in the picture is the petrified camel of the prophet.

but as Abu-Bakr's friends, Von Wissman and Van der Meulen were allowed to visit it. From Hud's tomb, the travelers passed through another wild and rocky wadi to visit the legendary volcano of Bir Borhut. It was something of an anticlimax. At Bir Borhut there was no volcano, and nothing to confirm the ancient legends of souls writhing in torment. Von Wissman and Van der Meulen simply found a deep cave, or series of caves, in the limestone rock, oppressively hot and eerily populated by bats.

Far left: Doreen Ingrams, who became famous to the secluded women and the children of the wadi villages. The men respected her for her endurance—she was able to ride a camel as untiringly as any of the desert patrols.

Left: Harold Ingrams. His success lay mainly in his ability to persuade the Hadhramaut people to abandon their intertribal struggles and work together for improvements in their life.

The next important explorer of the Hadhramaut was an Englishman, Harold Ingrams, who with his wife, Doreen, effectively opened up the area by establishing peace among the warring tribesmen. In the 1930's, the various states, towns, villages, and hamlets, were still constantly fighting among themselves, just as they had for over a century. When, in 1934, Ingrams was sent by the British government to be resident adviser at Al Mukallā, he set himself the task of trying to understand the people of the Hadhramaut region and their intertribal squabbles.

During the first three years of the Ingrams' stay in Al Mukallā, Doreen Ingrams worked among the women and children of the wadi villages. In this secluded region, women had for centuries been kept in complete subjugation to their husbands, and knew nothing about the world beyond their villages. Doreen Ingrams succeeded in making friends with them, and was even welcomed in the harems.

The Ingrams believed that progress could come to the region only through a long period of internal peace. The people wanted responsibility for their own way of life. In 1937, Harold Ingrams negotiated a treaty with the Sultan of Shihr and Al Mukalla. This established the idea of a resident adviser in the area, who would help organize a modern government and a scheme for constructing roads and schools. More important than this treaty, was the truce which Ingrams also arranged between the tribes—the *Sulh Ingrams,* or the Ingrams' truce—which at last brought a period of peace and

progress to the feuding, battle-weary people of the Hadhramaut.

In 1939, the Dutch explorer Van der Meulen made another trip to the Hadhramaut and was struck by the change from a land of war to one of peace. He writes: "The fortresses, the lookout towers, the trenches, all of which had been manned during our previous visit, were now deserted. Neglected gardens were irrigated again and the gates of walled villages and of fortified farm dwellings, in which men and women had lived as prisoners, were now wide open. Rifles and cartridges had lost their value and had disappeared from daily life. Women and children walked freely on roads and paths where one formerly met only men, well armed and in groups. A dying land with parched fields and date groves struggling against the sandblown wind, had put on a fresh garment of green, and with it life and happiness."

During the time they spent in the Hadhramaut, Harold and Doreen Ingrams also traveled in the inland regions which were still unknown to Europeans. They visited the Seiar Bedouins who lived in the area bordering the dreaded Rub' al Khali, and by talking to the Seiar chiefs tried to understand the way of life of this particularly wild tribe. They also ventured into the Mahra country of Tarīm. Their travels completed the exploration of the Wadi Hadhramaut, and helped to fill in the last blanks on the map of the region. When an aerial survey of the area was carried out, the exploration of the Hadhramaut was complete.

Above: three typical people of the tribes of the Hadhramaut, a photograph taken by Doreen Ingrams.

The Heart of Arabia

5

The heart of Arabia—the Nejd—was opened up to European explorers only after the Egyptian armies had heavily defeated the Wahhabis in 1818. Until this time, even the most carefully disguised traveler was in danger of being killed by the fanatical Wahhabis. For it was there, in the very middle of the Nejd, that Abd al-Wahhab, the founder of this extreme form of Islam, had been born in 1703. There the most fanatical supporters of his sect were found.

Geography as well as religious fanaticism kept the Nejd a closed area to European explorers until the mid-1800's. The traveler approaching from the north, east, or south has to cross vast stretches of sand desert before he reaches the cities and oases of this heartland of Arabia. To the west lie the Hejaz and the holy cities—a forbidden region to non-Moslem Europeans.

In the years between 1860 and 1880 a small band of explorers—most of them British—managed to penetrate this part of Arabia. Between them they investigated, described, and mapped great areas that on all earlier charts had been marked as unknown.

The first of these explorers was William Palgrave. In the summer of 1862, accompanied by a Syrian named Barakat, Palgrave crossed the An Nafūd, the desert north of the Nejd. Palgrave described it as

an immense ocean of loose reddish sand, heaped up into enormous ridges about 300 feet high. In the valleys between these great dunes, Palgrave and his companions felt imprisoned, hemmed in on all sides. Palgrave also experienced the *simoom,* the hot suffocating desert wind, when he and Barakat, accompanied by three Bedouins, were crossing the desert between Ma'ān and Wadi as Sirhan.

In his journal, Palgrave describes the first abrupt, burning gusts of wind. The horizon darkened to a deep violet. The Bedouins wrapped their cloaks around their heads and dropped to the ground to protect themselves from the burning wind and sand. Soon a stifling blast of hot air forced the camels to lie down on the sand. Everyone in the party lay covered up as much as possible for 10 minutes, while a still heat like a red-hot iron passed over them. Then came more gusts of wind, and the Bedouins unmuffled their faces. The worst was over. Palgrave and Barakat, however, both felt that their strength had been completely sapped by the heat. The camels lay flat as though dead from exhaustion. Then the sky, which had remained dark, began to grow lighter. At last it regained its dazzling clarity, the camels got up, and the small caravan remounted to resume its march across the desert.

Above: a pilgrim camp at Birkejemas-neh, sketched by Lady Anne Blunt who traveled through the Nejd with her husband between 1878 and 1879. The Nejd has often been referred to as the heart of Arabia.
Below: William Gifford Palgrave, the British traveler and author, who was the first European to enter the Nejd.

When they reached the Nejd itself, Palgrave and Barakat, both now disguised as Syrian doctors, made their way to the center. Along the route they rested at Riyadh, the capital of the Nejd. Then they traveled to Hofuf, a town near the Persian Gulf. From there they proceeded to Al Qatīf on the coast. On reaching Al Qatīf, Palgrave became the first European explorer to cross the Arabian Peninsula from west to east. It had taken eight months from Gaza, on the Mediterranean coast, to Al Qatīf, on the Persian Gulf.

Charles Montagu Doughty was among the next to venture into the Nejd. He too was an Englishman and had already traveled widely in Europe and the Middle East. In 1876, he set out from Damascus. For the first stage of the journey to the Nejd, Doughty traveled with a pilgrim caravan. But at Medā'in Sālih he left the caravan, and after four months there set out eastward into the heart of Arabia. Doughty was alone, except when he joined groups of Bedouin. He traveled slowly from place to place, spending in all two years in

Below: the An Nafūd, the vast red sand desert of Arabia, an enormous expanse of desolation lying to the north of the Nejd. It was in the An Nafūd that Palgrave encountered the burning desert wind, the *simoom*.

Right: Charles Montagu Doughty (1843–1926) as an old man. In the late 1870's he spent two years traveling in Arabia, crossing the Nejd accompanied only by his Bedouin guides.

Arabia. He visited Taymā', Hā'il, Buraydah, and 'Unayzah. Finally he turned southwest and, skirting the holy city of Mecca, reached the Red Sea port of Juddah.

Doughty was anxious to live the life of the Arabs. He traveled as a Christian, sharing as far as he could the life of the tribesmen, experiencing the heat, hunger, and thirst, joining in the quarrels of the nomads' life. After returning exhausted to England in 1878, he worked for nearly 10 years turning his notes into *Travels in Arabia Deserta,* an important book about Arabia and the Arabs.

In 1878, just a few months after Doughty had completed his wanderings, an English couple set out on an expedition into the Nejd. Wilfrid Scawen Blunt was then 38 years of age. As a British diplomat, he had served in Athens, Madrid, Paris, and Lisbon. With his wife, Lady Ann Blunt, and a party of Bedouins, he set out from Damascus to reach the Nejd. Also in the party was a young sheik who was returning to his tribe to find himself a wife. His presence was a protection for the Blunts, who never pretended to be Moslems. The fact that they were traveling with the sheik probably also enabled them to carry instruments such as a compass and a

395

Above: Wilfrid Scawen Blunt, shown mounted on his Arabian horse, Pharaoh. Right: although the Blunts' journey was generally peaceful, there was one frightening incident, when they were attacked by mounted horsemen in the desert. They were saved only by the intervention of a young sheik traveling with them. This water color by Lady Anne shows the moment before the sheik rode up to rescue them.

barometer, and to take notes openly without provoking the Arabs.

The Blunts, like Doughty, visited the city of Hā'il in the northern Nejd. There they were received by the ruler of the region, Mohammed ibn Rashid. He seemed to respect their lack of disguise, but some of the Wahhabis in Hā'il were hostile toward the party, especially to Blunt's wife.

One of the Blunts' reasons for going to the Nejd was to buy Arab horses to take back to England for breeding. They were delighted, therefore, when Ibn Rashid showed them his stable, which was one of the most famous in Arabia. As it was winter, the horses were ungroomed, and the Blunts' first impression was very disappointing. "We made the mistake, too common, of judging horses by condition, for, mounted and in motion, these at once became transfigured," wrote Lady Anne.

The Blunts' travels through the Nejd were on the whole peaceful, perhaps because they were accompanied by the sheik. They were, however, attacked by tribesmen in Wadi Sirhan. The rest of the party had gone on ahead. The Blunts dismounted and sat on the ground to rest. Suddenly they heard the thunder of hooves and looked up to see a group of horsemen charging down on them with lances. Lady Anne had sprained her knee and could not mount her

horse fast enough to escape. The horsemen rode up to Blunt, grabbed his gun, and began to hit him over the head with it. Lady Anne pleaded that she and her husband meant no harm and would surrender. Fortunately the young sheik who was accompanying the Blunts soon arrived on the scene. The attackers recognized that he was from a friendly tribe. The danger was over and peace was restored.

On their journey through the An Nafūd to the Persian Gulf coast, the Blunts were able, as they had hoped, to buy a number of magnificent horses from the Arab tribesmen. The stud that Blunt established with these horses at his home in England is still one of the most famous in the world.

More than 30 years passed between the Blunts' journey and the next visit of a woman explorer to Hā'il. Between 1899 and 1913, Gertrude Bell had made many journeys in the Middle East, but her ambition was to travel in Arabia itself. In 1913, she achieved this aim when she became the second woman to visit Hā'il. Miss Bell wrote many books about her travels, but none of them give a full account of this Arabian journey. During her journeys, however, she gained enough knowledge of Arabia and the Middle East to be appointed to the Arab intelligence bureau during World War I.

Above: a phtograph of Lady Anne Blunt in Arab dress. Lady Anne took a vigorous part in the expedition, and kept a careful record of the sights they saw. Her exquisite water color paintings capture the barren beauty of the heart of Arabia – the Nejd.

The Empty Quarter

The last great area of Arabia to defy the explorer was the 250,000 square miles of the Rub' al Khali, the Empty Quarter. This waterless region of sandy desert fills much of the southern half of the Arabian Peninsula. Besides the formidable physical hazards of the land, the Bedouin tribes here, as elsewhere in Arabia, often resented the intrusion of the Europeans.

In the early 1930's, the crossing of the Empty Quarter became a race between two Englishmen—Bertram Thomas and St. John Philby. Both men had started their careers as British officials in the Middle East—Thomas in Iraq and Transjordan and Philby in Iraq. Both had later transferred to the service of Arab rulers in lands bordering on the Empty Quarter. Thomas became adviser to the Sultan of Muscat and Oman. Philby converted to Islam and became an adviser to King Abdul Aziz ibn Saud of Saudi Arabia.

By chance, both Thomas and Philby planned to cross the Empty Quarter in the winter of 1930–1931. Thomas was the first to set out. The lands of the sultan for whom he worked bordered the southeast corner of the Empty Quarter. Thomas decided to start from Dhofar, the fertile region in the west of Muscat and Oman, and cross the

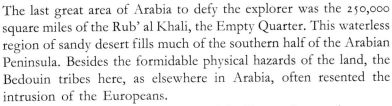

Left: wind-blown sand dunes in the vast Empty Quarter of Arabia, the Rub' al Khali. Survival in the Arabian desert, even for the most experienced Bedouin, remains a test of endurance, a battle with hunger and thirst, the bitter cold at night and burning heat by day.

Right: Bertram Thomas in 1926, four years before he became the first European to cross the Rub' al Khali.

Above: a group of desert travelers prepare for the onslaught of a sandstorm. When the first explorers ventured into the Rub' al Khali, the desert tribesmen were still hostile to Europeans and attack was always possible. Even today, desert travelers still carry arms.

Empty Quarter from south to north with a Bedouin escort. Early in December, 1930, 40 Bedouin Rashidis arrived in Dhofar, led by Sheik Salih bin Yakut. Thomas proceeded to argue and bargain with the sheik about the terms under which the Bedouins would agree to accompany him. In due course agreement was reached, and on December 10 the expedition set out.

Thomas' route was to be first north across the mountains behind Dhofar, then westward for some distance over the firm, steppe country—a large, empty, and cool area—along the edge of the sands. He then intended to head north again, directly across the sands toward the Qatar Peninsula on the Persian Gulf, a total distance of 700 miles. As they traveled along the edge of the sands the Bedouins pointed out tracks though the dunes. These, they said, led in two days to the site of a city called Ubar, which had been swallowed up by the sand. There is no doubt, says Thomas, that the sand had encroached southward, and might have engulfed a town in such a place. He wondered if there could have been some old trade route in those parts when physical conditions were less severe. He also wondered whether "Ubar" could be the Arabs' name for Ophir,

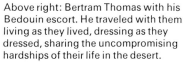

Above right: Bertram Thomas with his Bedouin escort. He traveled with them living as they lived, dressing as they dressed, sharing the uncompromising hardships of their life in the desert.

Below: St. John Philby with his camel in Riyadh, shortly before he made his crossing of the Rub' al Khali.

according to the Bible the source of much of King Solomon's treasure of gold and jewels.

By early January Thomas' party had left the firm steppe for the exhausting, shifting sand. At the water hole of Shanna, they were inside the Empty Quarter. The Rashidi escort was on the alert for Seiar raiders from the country north of the Hadhramaut, who were reported to be in the neighbourhood. Although there were false alarms, no fighting took place. Thomas had decided on Shanna as the starting point for the most difficult part of the trip, the final 400 miles. The party for this last stretch consisted of 13 men and their camels, and 5 pack animals carrying rations for 25 days.

On January 10, 1931, Thomas and the Rashidi set out from Shanna. Two weeks later there was a severe sandstorm. Another day or two brought them to the well of Banaiyan, on the northern fringe of the Empty Quarter and little more than 80 miles from the Persian Gulf. They had covered the 270 miles from Shanna in 18 days, an average of 15 miles a day. The job was virtually done.

On February 5, they saw the towers of Doha silhouetted against the waters of the Persian Gulf. "Half an hour later," records

Above: a photograph by Philby showing his car in Wadi Luja, to the east of At Tā'if. The photographs Philby gave to the Royal Geographical Society in London were the first glimpses the outside world had of many of the remote areas of Arabia.

Right: part of Thesiger's party in the Rub' al Khali. Thesiger entered whole-heartedly into the life of his Bedouin companions, even going barefoot as they did. He was the last of the old-fashioned explorers of the deserts of Arabia.

Above: an Arabian coffeepot. Even in the desert, the serving and drinking of coffee remain a ritual for the Arabs.

Below: Philby's desert coffee mill and roaster. The coffee was roasted in the ladle over the open campfire.

Thomas, "we entered the walls of the fort. The Rub' al Khali had been crossed." It was a remarkable achievement. Only two years earlier a man who knew the Arabian deserts well—the Englishman T. E. Lawrence, "Lawrence of Arabia"—had written of the Empty Quarter that "only an airship could cross it."

Only chance prevented St. John Philby from attacking the Empty Quarter from the northern side during that same winter of 1930–1931. To his disappointment, the Saudi Arabian government refused him vacation to make the crossing. Instead, he heard of Thomas' success when he was on the point of starting nearly a year later. But although Philby could not now be the first, his achievement is in many ways as great as that of Thomas. Thomas was first, and made the journey at his own cost. He traveled as a Christian and his journey was well planned. Philby, on the other hand, did not do enough planning. He had the advantage of being a Moslem, and of having the backing of the powerful Saudi king. But he also spent longer in the Empty Quarter and made a more sensational crossing.

Philby's party set out from Hofuf on January 7, 1931. They traveled southeast toward the Qatar Peninsula and then southwest across the Al Jāfūrah desert to the Jabrin Oasis. From there, they followed a zigzag course that brought them onto Thomas' route at roughly the halfway point through the sands. Philby then went southward to the Shanna water hole from which Thomas' party had started out. Then, having almost completed the crossing from north to south, Philby decided to go westward from Shanna through the Empty Quarter. His target was As Sulayyil, nearly 400 miles away, at the southernmost point of the great Tuwayq mountain range.

This first attempt on "the veritable desert," as Philby calls it, nearly ended in disaster. The party made the mistake of taking heavily laden pack animals with them. When they were just over 100 miles from Shanna, and the same distance away from any other water, even the hardy camels began to suffer from heat and exhaustion. The expedition had to turn back, making for Naifa, north of Shanna and almost on Thomas' route. This first thrust westward

40°

50°

60°

40°

MEDITERRANEAN
SEA

Euphrates

2a

2a

2a

2a

2a

2a

2a

4c

Baghdad

3

3

1a

3

1a

Damascus

2b

3

1a

2b

Tigris

2b

1b

1a

1a

1b

1a

4c

2b

4c

Euphrates

4b

1a

Petra

4c

2b

2b

4b

30°

1a

3

An Nafud

4b

1b

2b

PERSIAN

2b

1a,b

3

PERSIAN GULF

3

1b

4b

GULF OF OMA

Taymā

1b

1b

Hā'il

4b

Ash Shāriqah

6d

1b

Medā in Sālih

1b

Qatar

6d

GULF OF OMA

1b

1b

Buraydah

4b

Pena.

6d

1b

Unayzah

4b

4a

Hofuf

4a

Doha

5a

TROPIC OF CANCER

1b

4b

Riyadh

4d

Al Jafūrah

5c

Abū Zaby

6e

TROPIC OF CA

1b

4a

4b

4d

6d

6e

6c

6e

1b

4a

Jabrin

Banaiyan

6c

Liwa

6e

6c

Juddah

4a

4b

6d

Oasis

6e

E6c

1b Mecca

4e

1b

4b

6d

4b

5c

6c

As Sulayyil

6d

Naifa

Rub' a Khali

6c

4d

4d

Mughshin

5b

6c

4e

6d

5c

5b

Dhofar

4e

Shanna

4d

5c

5b

6c

4e

6d

6b

6b

5b

Manwakh

6b

6d

5b

4e

4e

6b

4e

H a d h r a m a u t

6d

4e

4d e h

6d

4e

4e

Al Mukallā

6d

GULF OF ADEN

INDIAN

6a

OCEAN

6a

6a

© Geographical Projects

40°

50°

0   100   200   300   400

Below: a swarm of locusts filling the sky. These voracious insects descend in their millions, completely destroying crops. Thesiger first became interested in the Rub' al Khali when he visited Arabia to investigate locust breeding grounds. Below right: a single locust. Locusts eat green leaves and stalks and, because they travel in such huge numbers, a swarm can destroy the vegetation over a large area.

and the subsequent retreat made two long sides of a triangle with Philby's route to Shanna as the base. From Naifa, in the first days of March, Philby led a smaller, more mobile party to make a second strike westward. The party reached As Sulayyil on March 15. It was a desperate effort—"375 miles or more between water and water," says Philby—and it tested men and animals to the utmost. Over 6 successive days, 3 of them very hot, they had kept up an average of 40 miles a day. One march lasted 21 hours, including rest periods totaling 3 hours, and covered 70 miles. Small wonder that Philby later remarked that crossing the Empty Quarter was "an adventure not to be lightly undertaken by the uninitiated."

Like Thomas, with his interest in the buried city of Ubar, Philby became fascinated by tales of a legendary city called Wabar that was reported to be hidden somewhere in the Empty Quarter. Many years before, Bedouin tribesmen had told him about a city which had been destroyed by fire because its wicked ruler would not heed the warnings of the prophet Hud. The story stuck in Philby's mind. When he and his party eventually reached the supposed site, however, they found no ruined city. All that Philby could find were two huge craters caused by meteorites.

Thomas and Philby both crossed the Empty Quarter in the early 1930's. By that time, many people thought that the day of the old-fashioned Arabian explorer, depending for his mobility on his animals and his own feet, had gone. But one more of the same type did appear in Arabia—a man of the highest ability by any standards. This was Wilfred Thesiger, an Englishman whose crossings of the Empty Quarter are only a small part of his great achievements as explorer and traveler.

Thesiger was born in 1910 in Addis Ababa, capital of Ethiopia, where his father was the British minister. The event took place, he says, in "one of the mud huts which in those days housed the Legation." Thesiger continued all his life to prefer mud huts to the conventional dwellings of European civilization. By serving as a government official in the Sudan in the 1930's and a soldier in the Middle East during World War II, he became thoroughly familiar with the desert and its people. After the war he volunteered for further service in Arabia, this time joining a group whose aim was to control the spread of locusts in the desert. Experts believed that

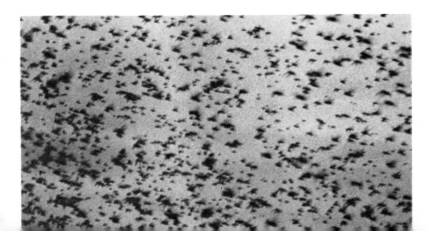

these grasshopper-like insects that descend in swarms upon vegetation, devouring every scrap, bred in areas north of Dhofar. It was while investigating these breeding grounds that Thesiger, like Thomas and Philby before him, became fascinated by the challenge of the Empty Quarter.

Thesiger crossed the Empty Quarter twice. The first time he took with him an escort of four Rashidi, members of the same tribe Thomas had found so cooperative. The small party crossed from Mughshin, north of Dhofar, to the Liwa Oasis, not far from Abū Zaby on the Persian Gulf. This route lay well to the east of that taken by Thomas more than 10 years before. On the return journey, Thesiger skirted the sands by traveling in a semicircle through the gravel desert of Oman.

In 1947, Thesiger decided to complete the exploration of the Empty Quarter by investigating the western sands. He set out across the desert from the well of Manwakh in the far north of the Hadhramaut country, aiming for the town of As Sulayyil nearly 400 miles north. It took Thesiger 16 days to make the journey across a completely waterless stretch of desert. There was constant fear of attack from tribesmen who were still, even in the 1940's, hostile to travelers from outside. When at last Thesiger and his companions reached As Sulayyil, they were arrested by the Saudi authorities. The precise reason for their arrest was never made clear to them. Only after Philby, at that time still an official of the Saudi Arabian government, had used his influence with the king were they finally released. From As Sulayyil, Thesiger traveled east, through Jabrin to the Trucial States.

While Thesiger was traveling in the Empty Quarter, a new kind of explorer was moving into Arabia. In 1942, in the middle of World War II, the United States government, in cooperation with the King of Saudi Arabia, sent an expedition to the Hejaz, the Nejd, and Yemen. Its aim was to investigate the natural resources of the desert. When World War II ended in 1945, foreign technicians, agricultural experts, and geologists flooded into Arabia. The most fateful discovery had, however, been made some years before.

In 1932, oil was first discovered in Bahrain. Shortly afterward, the Arabian American Oil Company was formed to survey vast areas in the eastern coastal region along the Persian Gulf. They, too, were soon successful, and the oil they found brought unexpected wealth to this otherwise poor region. Further important finds were made under the waters of the Persian Gulf in 1951, 1958, and 1960. By 1970, the Arabian American Oil Company alone was paying Saudi Arabia $500 million a year for its oil.

The discovery and exploitation of the oil and the subsequent introduction of modern technology soon changed the life of the Bedouins. Thesiger stayed in Arabia for a few more years, but life became increasingly difficult for the old-fashioned explorer investigating the desert for its own sake. The Saudis, traditionally suspicious, denounced him as a spy in radio broadcasts. "Few people,"

Thesiger wrote, "accepted the fact that I traveled there for my own pleasure, certainly not the American oil companies or the Saudi government." He saw too that the Bedouin way of life was changing The nomadic Bedouins were signing on as unskilled laborers in the oil fields. When Thesiger said good-by to the two Bedouins who had been his companions since he first came to Arabia, they rode away, not on camels, but perched on gasoline drums on the back of a truck. Thesiger himself was driven to the airfield at Ash Shāriqah on the Persian Gulf, and flew out. The year was 1950. The last great phase of Arabian exploration was over.

Left: a truck drives across the desert. Today, mechanized transportation is replacing the camel and is irrevocably altering the life of the Bedouin.

Below: a desert oil rig. The discovery of oil has brought wealth to Arabia.

The Vast Sahara
7

Like the Arabian Peninsula, the arid wastes of the Sahara desert long fascinated the peoples of Europe. Explorers were attracted by the challenge of the hostile climate and the difficult terrain. Merchants wanted to share in the trade on caravan routes over the Sahara. Historians and scholars were interested in the relics of the past. But there was another pressing reason for the Europeans' interest in the Sahara. It lay between Europe and the great river that Europeans called the Niger—the *black river*. Although in the 1700's Europeans knew of the existence of the river, no one had yet charted its course. Many of the adventurers who set out to explore the Niger

believed the best way to reach the river was to travel south over the vast, burning expanse of the Sahara.

Most people think of the Sahara as an unending sea of sand. In the west, this is true enough. The dune areas—called *ergs,* from an Arabic word—are vast. In Algeria, the Grand Erg Occidental and the Grand Erg Oriental each covers 20,000 square miles. But these sandy regions make up only one third of the whole Sahara area. Elsewhere are gravelly wastes, huge plains of stones and boulders, and high mountain ranges such as the Ahaggar, the Tassili-n-Ajjer, the Aïr, and the Tibesti. Scattered across this barren land are the

Above: part of the almost endless expanse of sandy waste that forms much of the Sahara – this area is near the oasis of Siwah, on the old route of the Cairo-Marzūq caravan.

409

Above: a Tuareg, one of the veiled men of the desert. The Tuareg people — proud and often hostile to outsiders — are nomadic tribesmen who used to control the routes across the Sahara.

Right: the Souf oasis in the Algerian Sahara. Oases are places in the desert where there is water. The water usually comes from springs, which are fed from water underground. Today, wells have been dug at many oases, and the surrounding land irrigated so that crops can be grown.

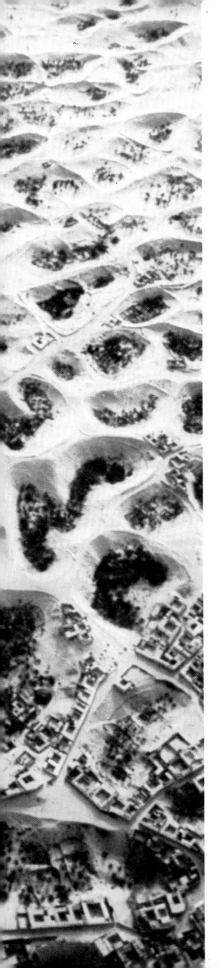

Right: the Sahara was probably not always as arid as it is today. There is evidence that plants and animals that could no longer survive in the barren land flourished there comparatively recently. This desert rock painting of about 3500 B.C. shows men hunting giraffes and an ostrich.

life-supporting oases. These isolated green patches cover only some 780 square miles—that is, less than 3 per cent of the entire area of the Sahara.

South of the Aïr and Tibesti mountains lies the great geographical region known as the Sudan. This, too, is usually considered as part of the Sahara. Stretching right across Africa, the Sudan forms a broad transitional belt between the dry desert to the north and the rain forests of equatorial Africa to the south. It is an area of savanna grasslands, with vegetation ranging from scrub and small desert plants in the north to tall grass interspersed with trees farther south. And through the west of the Sudan flows the Niger River. To get there, however, the explorers first had to conquer the hostile Sahara and its still more hostile tribesmen.

The total population of the Sahara evens out at less than one person for every square mile. Much of the desert is, however, completely uninhabited, save for the wandering tribesmen, while in the oases overpopulation is common. Only some two-thirds of the people of the oasis townships live there all the time. The rest of the population is constantly changing, as the nomadic groups wander from place to place. The peoples of the northern desert are Arabs and Berbers, while in the extreme south live Negro tribesmen, and in the southeast the Tibbu people, Negroes of mixed ancestry. The desert nomads are mainly Berbers, and in the Ahaggar and Tassili-n-Ajjer mountain regions they are called *Tuareg*. It is the Tuareg who for centuries have controlled the oasis settlements and the caravan routes between them. It was the Tuareg who frequently determined the success or failure of European expeditions.

The vegetation of the Sahara, however varied it may appear, has two common characteristics. First, it can withstand long dry periods. Second, it is able to race through life processes when water is available. This is particularly necessary in the Sahara, where rain falls only infrequently. In a year, an average of four inches of rain falls

Above: Algerian street sellers squat on the ground, surrounded by their heaped piles of dates. The best dates reportedly come from Jarbah, a small island off Tunisia.

on the Sahara. The rainfall is not, however, spread evenly over the year, but occurs in occasional torrential downpours. When rain falls, it quickly seeps through the parched surface to the subterranean deposits of water from which many of the oases in the sahara draw their reserves.

Although the Sahara is often thought of simply as a hot region, temperatures there do in fact vary widely. On a winter night the temperature may drop to freezing point, while in the heat of a summer day it can reach 130°F. In 24 hours the temperature can change by as much as 60° or 70°. To withstand the brutal changes of weather, man must be hardy and properly clothed. A nomad's robes of thick cloth are ideal, because they insulate him from extremes of both heat and cold.

More frequent than rain in the Sahara are sandstorms, which often have disastrous effects on vegetation, animals, and people. Sandstorms occur when the hot air above the sand rises and is replaced by colder air. A fierce wind results, which can be either constant or intermittent and turbulent. The wind picks up the sand and carries it like a large trembling net over the ground. The sun is hidden, and a wall of sand blots out the horizon. At this point it becomes impossible to see and difficult to stand upright. A sandstorm usually dies down at sunset, but it may start again the following morning, and repeat this cycle over several days.

The Sahara as a whole produces a rich variety of cultivated fruits and vegetables, but these are unevenly distributed because of variations in climate and soil. Tropical fruits and even grain are grown where irrigation has been carried out near oases, but neither ever becomes a regular cash crop. The only really valuable fruit grown in the desert is the date. Except at altitudes of over 4,500 feet, in the southern half of the desert, and along the Atlantic coast, the date palm tree supplies the basic food of the desert people. It also provides valuable exports.

Above: traces of the Roman past exist in many parts of North Africa. The Romans settled mainly in the more inviting coastal areas, but a number of military expeditions did venture into parts of the Sahara itself.

Left: the inscription of King Djer, who ruled Egypt about 3000 B.C. The inscription tells of an expedition into the Sahara, which conquered a local ruler. It is the earliest known reference to the Sahara.

In the southern part of the Sahara, the date becomes a luxury. Salt-mining is the livelihood of the people there, and salt is the chief export. Today the principal salt deposits are at Tisempt, Djado, and Taoudenni. During the Middle Ages, salt mined from these deposits was traded to merchants for gold. Today, it is still one of the desert's most important resources.

As in Arabia, life in the Sahara is largely dependent upon the camel. Even 50 years ago, the camel was still the only safe means of crossing the desert, and it has naturally played an important part in the story of exploration. Along some stretches of the Sahara caravan routes there are no wells for more than 300 miles. Only the camel enabled explorers to cross these waterless wastes.

Also like Arabia, the Sahara has never been completely unknown, or culturally stagnant. Seven thousand years ago it was probably

Left: two travelers before a village, from an Arabic manuscript of 1237. The villagers in the background are busy with the sort of tasks that Ibn-Batuta would have seen carried out.

not a desert at all. The people of the area knew the arts of farming and of domesticating animals. In about 2000 B.C. the climate became drier, and the farmers were forced to move south. Even at that time, however, the desert was crossed by commercial caravans.

Since the time of the Roman Empire the people of the western Sahara have been in almost constant touch commercially with southern Europe and the Middle East. With the coming of the traders, the influence of European ideas and culture began to penetrate the Sahara. The Roman settlement at Ghirza (175 miles southeast of Tripoli) consisted of large fortified farms, which must have employed local Saharans as laborers and so passed on some elements of Roman life. But although a few Roman military expeditions did venture into the interior of the Sahara, the Romans seem to have been principally concerned with the Mediterranean coastal areas of Africa.

Far more widespread than the influence of Rome was the influence of the Islamic religion. In A.D. 642, the Arabs invaded northern Africa. The northern African coastlands became part of the Moslem Empire, and Islam the predominant religion of their people. As time passed, Arab Moslem traders traveled ever more frequently over the Sahara caravan routes. They spread Islam throughout western Africa, and Arabic became the common language of the area.

By the Middle Ages merchants went regularly back and forth across the Sahara to trade. Ibn-Batuta provides evidence of this. He set out in 1349 from Tangier, and crossed the western Sahara to Silla. On his return journey he traveled with a commercial caravan. In Ibn-Batuta's time, the caravan trade across the Sahara was a rich one. Sugar, brassware, books, and horses were transported south

Below: Ptolemy's map of North Africa. Ptolemy lived in the A.D. 100's, in Alexandria in Egypt. His map is most accurate in depicting the coastal areas well known to the classical world. Farther south and inland the map is either speculative or blank.

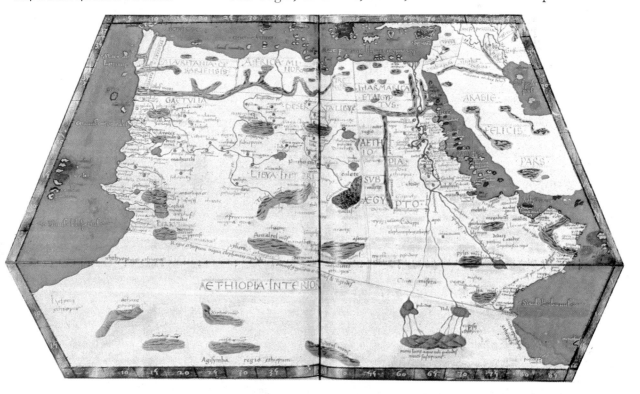

Above: el-Qara oasis, a small cluster of mud houses in the desert. It was originally founded by runaway slaves who escaped from one of the Cairo-Marzūq caravans. Slaves were one of the greatest riches of the African continent, and the slave trade there had a brutal history.

across the desert to the cities of Timbuktu and Goa. Export goods such as dates, gold, ivory, and ostrich feathers were sent north to be shipped to the kings and princes of Europe.

In the 1400's a new treasure made its first appearance in the northbound camel caravans—slaves. Portuguese sea traders first brought slaves to sell in Europe in the mid-1400's, and slave caravans were soon making regular journeys north from Timbuktu to Fez, Tunis, and Cairo. After the discovery of the Americas, the slave trade began to take on a much greater importance. The Negroes were accustomed to tropical climate and disease, and could therefore live and work in the Caribbean area. Instead of traveling north, many slave caravans now worked their way westward to the coast, and the ports of embarkation for the Americas.

The new market for African slaves in the Americas meant a new pattern of trade in the Sahara. Shortly afterward, the Moroccans

captured the salt trade of the southwestern desert and the commercial centers along the Niger, and European interest began to shift away from the southern Sahara. But stories which had reached Europe in the 1500's of the vast wealth of Timbuktu and the other Niger cities still persisted. They were to prove an added incentive for travelers to visit these cities when Europeans began to take an interest in African exploration in the late 1700's.

The eastern Sahara, however, presents quite a different picture. Following the collapse of Roman power in Africa, the area became almost completely isolated from outside influence and trade. It was not until the 1700's that trade once again became important there, and even then it grew up only slowly.

By the 1800's, trade in the area was well under way. Caravans traveling southward through Fezzan, Cyrenaica (today part of Libya), and Egypt carried such items as cloth, rugs, sheet tin, iron and steel tools, needles, firearms, and gunpowder. Luxury goods, too, were transported across the desert to the sultans of the Sudan kingdoms. These included silks, silver and gold thread, embroidered cloth, gold and silver jewelry, mirrors, sugar, and perfumes. In the eastern Sahara, as in the west, slaves were the most important and valuable of the goods carried north across the desert. Others included ivory, gold, cotton cloth, leather goods, pepper, honey, and even live parrots.

Right: a slave caravan, drawn by George Lyon. In 1818 and 1819, Lyon traveled south from Tripoli with an expedition to find out more about the course of the Niger River. He saw several slave caravans, one consisting of 1,400 slaves of all ages.

Above: Tuareg tribesmen gathered around the light of their campfire. With the arrival of the Europeans in the Sahara, the tribesmen's hold on the caravan routes was broken. But Tuareg raiding parties still roam over the vast Sahara.
Below: Tuareg bodyguard of the Sheik of Bornu, drawn by Denham in 1826.

For centuries the success of Saharan trade was at the mercy of the warlike nomadic tribesmen who controlled the territories through which the caravans passed. Of the many Saharan peoples, the Tuareg are the most important. They have adopted the Moslem religion but preserved their own language. The Tuareg are the legendary veiled men, some of whom consider themselves to be the aristocrats of the desert.

When the European explorers first looked toward the Sahara in the late 1700's, the eastern caravan route from Ghāt northward through Fezzan was controlled by the Ajjer Tuareg confederation. The central Saharan route from In Salah southward was in the hands of the Ahaggar tribesmen. The western caravan route seems to have been periodically under Tuareg control, although at various times it was ruled by other tribes and by the Moors (the Moslem Arabic-speaking peoples of northwestern Africa). The country around Timbuktu and the Niger bend was almost constantly dominated by the Tuareg of the southwest.

The Tuareg based their method of controlling commercial caravans and exploring parties on a system of furnishing armed escorts to the groups which had to pass through areas under Tuareg domination. For these services, they charged a fee calculated either on the estimated value of the cargo or the reputed wealth of the travelers who needed to be protected and directed along the route. When caravans refused to pay the money demanded, or brought their own guides and armed guards, the Tuareg would harass the caravans by raiding or by killing the travelers.

During the European exploration of the Sahara, the Tuareg felt increasingly threatened by the prospect of outside control. They saw the possibility of European domination as threatening their very existence, and they became increasingly hostile to explorers. The Tuareg tribal concept of an "eye for an eye" in settling disputes extended to their dealings with Europeans. And they used the Moslem religion as a convenient excuse for resisting and often murdering Christian travelers.

The conquest of the African continent held the same fascination for the Europeans of the 1800's as the exploration of space did for Americans and Russians in the 1960's. And despite the rigors of the desert climate and the ferocious Tuareg tribesmen, the exploration of the Sahara became a passion for many adventurers. Scientists, geographers, politicians, soldiers, and merchants from Europe—and in particular from Britain and France—were eager to learn about the Niger region. They believed that this mysterious area would lead them on to an even more fabulous land in the African interior. Above all, they still believed the stories which had been handed down about the huge wealth of Timbuktu and the other Niger cities. To reach this legendary treasure house they had to cross the Sahara or sail up the Niger River. But at the dawn of the 1800's no one yet knew where the mouth of the Niger lay.

Below: caravan routes in the Sahara and the Sudan. As in Arabia, caravans in the Sahara followed routes across the desert which had been used from time immemorial. The routes led across the burning sands from one oasis or water hole to the next. The distance between water and water could be several hundred miles, and the terrible journeys between taxed men and animals to the utmost.

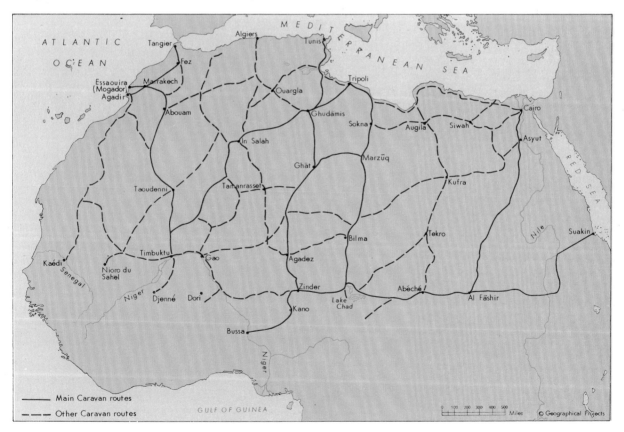

Main Caravan routes
Other Caravan routes

© Geographical Projects

The African Association

8

Left: Sir Joseph Banks (1743–1820). At the time Banks founded the African Association, he was Britain's most eminent scientist, with personal experience of organized exploration with Captain Cook in the Pacific. The association first met as the Saturday Club at Banks's own house in London.

The systematic exploration of the Sahara and the area around the Niger River began in 1788 with the formation in London of the Association for Promoting the Discovery of the Interior Parts of Africa. Sir Joseph Banks, who had explored the Pacific with Captain Cook and was the most famous British scientist of that period, founded the association. It first directed its attention to the scientific exploration of the mysterious Niger River.

At that time, little was known about the interior of Africa. No one knew for certain where the Niger River rose, in which direction it flowed, and in particular where it emptied into the sea. No one in Europe connected this river with the great delta in the Gulf of Guinea which had been known to Europeans for more than 300 years. Some people even believed that the Niger—which does in fact flow eastward in its upper reaches—flowed right across Africa to join the Nile. Others thought it might empty itself into a vast inland lake.

Banks and his colleagues quickly recruited explorers. In the same year that the association was founded, the members agreed to back an American, John Ledyard, in a journey to Timbuktu. Ledyard was an adventurer who had sailed with Captain Cook on his final

Below: Soho Square in London about 1800. Banks lived in Soho Square at the time he was organizing the Association for Promoting the Discovery of the Interior Parts of Africa (the African Association).

Above: a miniature portrait of Mungo Park (1771–1806). He was the third man the African Association recruited to explore Africa. His assignment was to find the source of the Niger, and to discover the river's mouth.

voyage in the Pacific. He responded enthusiastically to the association's challenging assignment to cross the Sahara from Egypt to Timbuktu. He set out almost immediately for Cairo to find a caravan that would take him across the desert. But in Cairo Ledyard fell ill with dysentery and died.

In spite of this initial failure, the African Association determined to continue their program of exploration. During this period there was much speculation about the great wealth of the trading cities in the Niger region and in particular of Timbuktu. Two Moslems who claimed that they had visited Timbuktu described its fantastic wealth and flourishing trade to the African Association. Their story confirmed the British in their belief that both the Niger and Timbuktu should be explored.

Daniel Houghton was the next man commissioned to find Timbuktu. He was an impoverished officer in the British Army who in 1790 answered the African Association's advertisement for someone to journey to "the Cities of Houssa and Tombouctoo." Houghton landed at the entrance to the Gambia River and set out east, thinking that he would be able to get safely to Timbuktu in about a month. He sent one letter home to his wife in England from the Gambia River, and a short note to the African Association in

Left: a West African village, shown in an engraving taken from a sketch by Mungo Park. The village is the typical cluster of round huts which Park must have seen many times as he traveled deep into the interior. The figure with the little goatee beard was added by the engraver, probably to represent Mungo Park himself.

Above: a pocket sextant of about 1800, probably similar to the one Park took along to determine his position in the unmapped interior.

London. But that was the last news ever heard of him.

In London, the association was eager to find a successor to Houghton. Finally, in 1794, a suitable candidate offered his services. He was Mungo Park, a 23-year-old Scottish surgeon, who had a passion for natural history. After qualifying as a doctor at Edinburgh University, Park had taken a job as a surgeon on an East India Company ship. This enabled him to pursue his hobby in the tropical waters of the Indian and Pacific oceans. In the waters around Sumatra, Park discovered and studied a new species of fish, and when he returned to London he published his description of the fish in a scientific journal. The article brought Park to the attention of Sir Joseph Banks and the African Association.

The association proposed that Park should explore the Niger River to find out where it rose and whether it flowed into the sea or some large lake. He accepted the offer at once and sailed from Portsmouth, England, in May, 1795, arriving at Pisania on the Gambia River in July. Pisania was a small village established by the British as a trading post. It was inhabited solely by British merchants and their Negro slaves. There, Park settled down to learn the Mandingo language and to collect as much information as possible about the regions he was to visit.

423

Right: three men silhouetted against the Bornu horizon, recalling the little group of Park, his servant Johnson, and the slave boy riding off into completely unknown territory.

Below: the bridge over the Bafing River, taken from a sketch by Park. Park began his journey in Gambia, and traveled east, crossing the Bafing River. He finally reached the Niger at Ségou, after spending three months in prison at Benown.

Toward the end of July, Park came down with fever and delirium which confined him to his home during most of August. Subsequent bouts of the fever continued to beset him. But early in December, 1795, he set out for the interior of Africa. With him went a Negro servant named Johnson, who acted as interpreter, and a slave boy who was Park's personal servant. For the first few days of the journey the three travelers were accompanied by some slave merchants, a Negro returning to his home inland, and several other domestic slaves. Then they left the company of the merchants and slaves and set off on their own. Park rode a horse, while Johnson and the slave boy rode donkeys. They carried food for two days, beads and tobacco for bartering, a compass and pocket sextant, a thermometer, some firearms, and an umbrella. Their route was to be northeastward from the Gambia River across the Senegal River, then eastward toward Timbuktu.

After three days, Park met a local king who told him that he

should go no farther. Tribesmen of the interior had never seen a white man before and would certainly kill him. But Park paid no attention to the warnings and continued eastward, traveling at night for safety. Despite all his precautions, however, he was robbed of many of his possessions during this period. When he reached Mali, which was Moslem country, the slave boy refused to go any farther. Park and Johnson started alone into the unknown and hostile interior. It was at this point that Park passed through the village of Simbing where, according to a story told by Johnson, a party of Moors—in his journal Park used the term *Moors* to describe all non-Negro Moslems—had robbed Daniel Houghton of all his possessions and perhaps killed him. Park was shown the place in the bush where Houghton's body had been thrown and left to rot.

It was not long before Park himself encountered the Moors. After some days, he was captured by a party of horsemen and taken to their headquarters at Benown, on the edge of the desert. For three months he was detained by them in very unpleasant conditions. "Never did any period of my life pass away so heavily; from sunrise to sunset I was obliged to suffer, with an unruffled countenance, the insults of the rudest savages on earth!"

Throughout this ordeal, however, Park maintained his determination to find the Niger River. He resolved to escape from the Moors, but to his disappointment Johnson was not prepared to go with him. The Negro wanted to return to his wife and family. Park recorded his feelings at the time: "Having no hopes therefore of persuading him to accompany me, I resolved to proceed by myself.

Below: the Niger River, from which the modern state of Nigeria takes its name. In the early 1800's, expedition after expedition set off into the African interior to try to solve the problem of the source and mouth of the River Niger.

About midnight I got my clothes in readiness, which consisted of two shirts, two pair of trousers, two pocket handkerchiefs, an upper and under waistcoat, a hat, and a pair of half boots: these, with a cloak, constituted my whole wardrobe. And I had not one single bead, nor any other article of value in my possession, to purchase victuals for myself, or corn for my horse." That same night, Park managed to slip away from the hut where he had been imprisoned.

When Park had got safely away from the Moors, he journeyed into the forest to avoid being noticed. But his progress was slow because his horse, which had also been badly treated by the Moors, was in very poor condition.

Starvation and death from thirst became real possibilities, but as Park resigned himself to his end, there was a sudden thunderstorm. It continued long enough for him to spread out his clean clothes to catch the rain water and then quench his thirst by wringing and

Above: the early explorers of Africa found the strangeness of everything they saw one of the most disconcerting aspects of their travels. Here, Mungo Park is startled by the sight of a lion lurking in the undergrowth.

Right: on his return journey from Silla on the banks of the Niger, Park was set upon by thieves who robbed him of all his possessions except the clothes he was wearing and his hat, in which, fortunately, he was carrying his irreplaceable notes.

sucking them. A few hours later he managed to beg a bowl of *kouskous* (a dish made from flour) from a woman who lived in one of a group of huts in the forest.

About three weeks after his escape from the Moors, Park joined a party of refugees. They assured him that he was getting near the Niger River and the great market town of Ségou. On July 20, 1796, nearly eight months after leaving the Gambia, Park had his first glimpse of the Niger at Ségou. He wrote: "I saw with infinite pleasure the great object of my mission—the long sought for majestic Niger, glittering in the morning sun, as broad as the Thames at Westminster, and flowing slowly *to the eastward*. I hastened to the brink and, having drunk of the water, lifted up my fervent thanks in prayer to the Great Ruler of all things for having thus far crowned my endeavours with success."

The fact that the Niger flowed eastward confirmed the reports Park had gathered along the way. He had made frequent inquiries about the river's direction from Negroes he had met, and they had all assured him that it flowed toward the rising sun.

Park waited for several days at Ségou in the hope of being able to visit the ruler of the area, King Mansong of Bambara. King Mansong was unwilling to receive the explorer, but eventually he sent Park a gift of money to enable him to buy provisions in the course of his journey. It seems as if this gift was meant primarily to speed the Scotsman on his way out of the kingdom.

Leaving Ségou, Park rode along the banks of the Niger for six days until he reached the town of Silla. There he realized that he could travel no farther down the river. The money which Mansong had given him was beginning to run out, but, more serious still, Park was too worn out and sick to go farther. Also, after his experience at Benown, Park was afraid of the Moors.

At the end of July, 1796, he began his return journey. After almost a month of uneventful travel, he was attacked by some robbers who took all his possessions except his trousers, his shirt, and his hat, in the crown of which he had hidden his notes. Then, in September, Park fell seriously ill with malaria at Kamalia. He was treated with kindness by a Negro slave dealer, and remained there for seven months before he set off with a slave caravan for Pisania. The caravan reached the trading post on June 10, 1797, almost 11 months after Park had first seen the Niger River.

Below: a view from the north edge of Qattara Depression, looking to the southwest. Caravans traveling from Cairo across the desert used to cross the depression and Frederick Hornemann would have followed this route to Siwah.

Above: the western end of Siwah Oasis. In ancient times, Siwah was the seat of the oracle of Zeus-Ammon. Alexander the Great visited the oracle when he was in Egypt, to consult it about his plans to conquer the Persian Empire.

Just before Christmas, 1797, Park arrived back in England. The publication of his account of his journeys two years later made him a famous man. Soon after, he returned to Scotland, where he married and set up in practice as a doctor.

In June, 1796, when Park had been a prisoner of the Moors and had not yet seen the Niger, another explorer had presented his proposed itinerary to the African Association for their approval. This man was a theological student from the University of Göttingen named Frederick Hornemann. Hornemann's plan was to join a caravan in Cairo for the Marzūq Oasis and then travel south to Katsina, a commercial and caravan center similar to Timbuktu. In order to prepare himself for the journey he spent a year learning Arabic. Then, on his way to Egypt, he passed through Paris where he received letters of introduction to Moslem merchants in Cairo, whose caravans made the desert crossing. In the autumn of 1797, Hornemann sailed from Marseille to Egypt.

In Cairo, Hornemann received a letter from Sir Joseph Banks reporting Park's safe return to the Gambia River after his journey to the Niger. Banks explained that Park had "penetrated till within

14 days of Tombouctoo, and might have enter'd that Town could he
have pass'd for a Mahometan; but he desisted from the attempt on
being told by all the persons he met that the Mahometans, who have
the Rule of the Town, would certainly put him to death as a Christian, if he entered it. . . ." Banks's letter doubtless confirmed Hornemann's decision to travel as a Moslem. In Cairo he had met a
German convert to Islam named Frendenburgh, who agreed to be
his servant on the journey to Katsina. Frederick Hornemann was
the first of the modern Sahara travelers to pose as a Moslem. Just as
Di Varthema centuries earlier had joined a Mameluke regiment in

Above: remains of the stonework of the Temple of Zeus-Ammon at Siwah Oasis. It was Hornemann's interest in this temple which aroused the suspicion of his traveling companions that he was not, as he claimed, a Mameluke.

order to make the journey to Mecca, Hornemann claimed to be a member of a Mameluke family to help explain his fair complexion and imperfect Arabic.

Hornemann left Cairo with the caravan of 1798. It included merchants, and pilgrims who were returning from the hajj. The first important stopping place was the oasis of Siwah, where Hornemann was the second European visitor after Alexander the Great. (The first had been an Englishman, William Browne, who had visited Siwah in 1792 while exploring the western Egyptian desert.) At Siwah, Hornemann showed too obvious an interest in the remains of the Temple of Zeus-Ammon, and was accused of being non-Moslem. Some days later a party of Moslems from Siwah followed the caravan in order to challenge Hornemann's belief in Islam. They questioned him again, but the German gave a convincing enough display of his sincerity to be allowed to continue with the caravan. The route took them through the Fezzan oases at Temissa, and they reached Marzūq on November 17, 1798, about $2\frac{1}{2}$ months after leaving Cairo. The distance, in a direct line, is around 1,100 miles. At Marzūq, the Sultan of Fezzan formally received the merchants and pilgrims.

Hornemann spent seven months in and around Marzūq, traveling to Tripoli to send off his reports, meeting people from many of the Saharan tribes and doubtless accumulating much information about life and travel in the desert. But journeys in the desert in the late 1700's inevitably meant disease, and in Marzūq Frendenburgh died of fever and Hornemann himself became very ill. He probably had malaria, although at that time the explorers did not always know from what form of "fever" they suffered.

By early 1800, Hornemann must have been well enough to continue his travels, and on April 6 he wrote his last letter to the African Association saying that he was about to join the Bornu caravan. At Bornu he intended to join the regular caravan to Katsina, and from there he would somehow travel southward to the coast of the Gulf of Guinea. But the association never heard from him again.

When later explorers followed Hornemann's projected route they established that he had indeed crossed the Sahara to Bornu, then traveled westward to Katsina, and south again toward the Niger. Sometime early in 1801 this courageous German had died a lonely death in an obscure village called Bokani, only a day's journey short of the Niger River. His achievement is in no way diminished by the fact that no record of his journey remains. Hornemann was the first European to cross the desert since the Romans.

Below: the castle of Marzūq, drawn by George Lyon in 1821, 23 years after Hornemann was there. Hornemann spent seven months in the area of Marzūq, but while he was there both he and Frendenburgh, his traveling companion, became sick. Frendenburgh died, but Hornemann managed to push on as far as the village of Bokani, near the Niger. There, in 1801, he too died.

Sansanding 1 Novr 1805

(Dear Megaw   63

Thunder, Death & Lightning :— the Devil
to pay: lost by disease Mr Scott, two Sailors, four Carpenters
& thirty one of the Royal African Corps, which reduces our
numbers to seven, out of which Doctor Anderson & two of
the Soldiers are quite useless, the former from one disease
or other has been for four months disabled; — we every
day suppose he'll kick it —— Capt Park has not been
unwell since we left Goree: I was one of the first taken sick
of the fever & ague, had a hard pull for a few days, but
my constitution soon got the better — had not an hours
illness since — I send you for the information of the
inquisitive, the names of the four men with me, viz
Abraham Bolton, John Connor, Thos Higgins & Joseph
Mills (the two last sick but recovering fast — Higgins
from a Fever & Mills from an old wound in the ancle)
— Capt Park has made every enquiry concerning the
River Niger, & from what he can learn there remains
no doubt but it is the Congo — we hope to get there in
about three Months or less — We had no fun on the road;
— met no opposition the whole way — We were well
received by Mansong, King of Sego; to whom Capt Park
made very handsome presents, & at our arrival at the
River, he sent Canoes upwards of 200 Miles to carry
us & baggage, & also made us a present of one which
we are now fitting out, as we intend going down the
river in it — Capt P. is this day fixing the Masts &c
— Schooner rigged — 40 feet long — 6 feet wide, &
5 feet high on the side all in the clear. —— Excellent
...... (since we came here Aug. 22) the Beef & Mutton

The Mystery of the Niger

9

Left: a letter from Lieutenant Martyn to a girl back home, describing the march under Mungo Park. At the time of this letter, the expedition had been underway almost six months and had reached Sansanding, where Park's brother-in-law, Anderson, had died. Below: a British soldier in the kind of uniform Park's men wore. It was totally unsuited to the climate and conditions which they encountered.

When Frederick Hornemann disappeared in 1800, the states of Europe were largely absorbed with the Napoleonic Wars. And until the Battle of Waterloo brought peace to Europe in 1815, there were no important developments in the exploration of the Niger. The one expedition that the British government did finance during those years resulted from a scare that Napoleon was about to expand his empire in Africa. In 1805, Mungo Park was invited to lead an expedition to sail along the Niger and somehow find the mouth of the river. In this way, the British government hoped to gain an important foothold in western Africa.

Park's second expedition was on a much grander scale than his first. On January 30, 1805, he and his brother-in-law Alexander Anderson sailed from Portsmouth well supplied with equipment and money. At Gorée, north of the Gambia River, they picked up a Lieutenant Martyn, 30 volunteer soldiers, 4 carpenters, and 2 sailors. Park himself had been given the rank and pay of a captain in the army, and Anderson, who was second-in-command, was made a lieutenant. The expedition also included a surgeon and a draughtsman.

With this large party, Park set out from the Gambia River in May, 1805. The soldiers, clad in the red coats then worn by the British Army on active duty, added a touch of color to the group. But unfortunately the rainy season was just beginning. Before very long the men began to suffer from the inevitable diseases—dysentery and malaria. But Park was ruthless, and determined to go on. Those of the party too ill to keep up with the rest were left behind to die. Only 10 men survived the dreadful journey to the Niger which they reached at Bamako in August, 1805.

Extracts from Park's diary convey something of the atmosphere of the trip. He seemed to have an indestructible will to carry on. "August 10, William Ashton declared that he was unable to travel. At half past four I arrived . . . at a stream flowing to the westwards. Here I found many of the soldiers sitting, and Mr. Anderson lying under a bush, apparently dying. Took him on my back, and carried him across the stream, which came up to my middle. Carried over the load of the ass which I drove, got over the ass, Mr. Anderson's horse, etc. Found myself much fatigued, having crossed the stream sixteen times. Left here four soldiers with their asses, being unable to carry over their loads . . . August 11th . . . This morning

433

Left: an Ibo canoe. It was from two such local craft that Mungo Park made his H.M.S. *Joliba.* In the *Joliba,* he and his party sailed down the Niger to the falls of Bussa. There they were ambushed, and all but one died.

Right: one of Mungo Park's last letters, written from Sansanding to Sir Joseph Banks. In this letter he explains the plan for the expedition's next stage: "It is my intention to keep [to] the middle of the River and make the best use I can of Winds and Currents till I reach the termination of this mysterious Stream."

Below: the early explorers found that the peoples of Africa had developed many highly skilled crafts. The sophisticated techniques of their metalworkers can be seen in these weapons made around Timbuktu.

hired Isaaco's people to go back and bring up the loads of soldiers who had halted by the side of the stream. In the course of the day all the loads arrived; but was sorry to find out that in the course of the last two marches we lost four men ... Cox, Cahill, Bird, and Ashton. Mr. Anderson still in a very dangerous way. . . ."

Accompanied by his 10 survivors, Park got permission to pass through the Bambara territory. At Sansanding, they managed to build a large boat by breaking up two big local canoes. The H.M.S. *Joliba* (the local name for the Niger) was 40 feet long and 6 feet wide. Park filled it with all the provisions he could, so as to be able to sail down the river without having to stop for food. The party for the journey to the unknown mouth of the Niger consisted of Lieutenant Martyn, three soldiers, three slaves to paddle the boat, and a well-qualified, newly engaged guide and interpreter named Amadi Fatouma. Lieutenant Anderson had died during the two-month stay at Sansanding and Park's last letter to his wife, dated November 19, 1805, conveys the news of her brother's death.

On the day Park wrote to his wife he left Sansanding. For more than five years nothing more was heard about him. In 1810, the guide Isaaco, who had returned to Gambia with Park's letter to

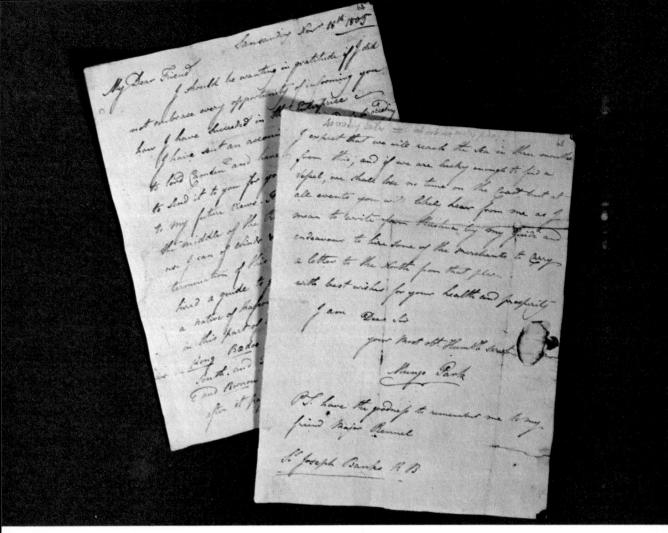

his wife, was sent out to discover what had happened to the missing *Joliba* and its party. He found Amadi Fatouma. On the journey down the Niger Fatouma had been captured by one of the kings through whose territory the *Joliba* had passed. He told Isaaco that not one of the Europeans had survived Park's expedition. He said that they had passed Kabara, the port of Timbuktu, and had managed to reach the falls of Bussa. The rapids were impassable because it was the season of low water before the monsoon (March or April, 1806), and the boat jammed in the rocks. The party was then attacked by Africans. Although they had until then been able to defend themselves with their muskets, this time the odds were too great. Park and Martyn tried to make a dash for it and jumped overboard into the rocks and shallow water, each carrying or helping one of the soldiers. They were, however, drowned during their desperate effort to escape. One of their slaves was taken prisoner, and it was he who told the story to Fatouma.

Mungo Park had shown, as well as exceptional physical strength and endurance, an outstanding courage and determination. With a little more luck the *Joliba* might have sailed on to the sea and found the mouth of the Niger River. But throughout the expedition

Above: the falls of Bussa, the place where a fierce army of Africans swept down on the *Joliba* which had become jammed in the rocky shallows. The entire expedition, except for one slave, was killed in the attack.

Park made a number of serious mistakes. He should not have started the march from Gambia to Bamako in the rainy season. Later, when the *Joliba* was afloat, he should have taken a less hostile attitude toward the local tribesmen. Instead he did all he could to avoid them. When approached by African boats he fired at the crews and killed many men.

Mungo Park's imprisonment by the Moors at Benown during his first African expedition had made him very much aware of the kind of reception he was likely to meet on the journey down the Niger. He might have managed to get to the sea if he had been willing to be delayed and indulge in the customs of parleying and present-giving at the boundary of each small kingdom. (Ironically, before he got to the area of the falls at Bussa, Park had apparently presented a gift to a chieftain. But that chieftain had not passed on the present to the ruler of Bussa, who ordered the attack on Park's party.) As Park progressed down the Niger, he left destruction and bitterness. The hostility of the local tribesmen, who were not fanatically religious but were strongly opposed to the intrusion of Europeans was to remain a problem for succeeding explorers.

Because of the dangerous condition of the west coast approach to the Niger, the British government decided that future explorers should use the route from the north across the Sahara. In 1818, another Scottish doctor, Joseph Ritchie, was chosen to lead an expedition which included a naval captain, George Lyon, and a shipwright named Belford. They planned to travel through Tripoli to Fezzan so that they could estimate the prospects of travel farther south. They also intended to find out more about the course of the Niger River.

Almost immediately after they entered the desert, the three men caught malaria. At Marzūq, Ritchie died and Belford became dangerously ill. Although he recovered sufficiently to continue his journey with Lyon, the two men eventually decided that it was

Above: George Lyon in African dress. When he returned from Africa, Lyon stated firmly that for any serious attempt at exploration there an explorer would have to be able to travel disguised as a Moslem.

Below: a sand wind of the desert, drawn by George Lyon. Lyon accompanied Ritchie and Belford in an unsuccessful attempt to reach the Niger from Tripoli in 1818. Lyon did manage to travel more than 500 miles, but then ran out of money. He had to return across the desert with a slave caravan, and wrote an account of the appalling march.

hopeless to proceed. They joined a slave caravan to take them to the north again. On the way back, Lyon was appalled by what he saw of the transsaharan slave trade and its brutalities. He found that many of the slaves believed they were being taken as cattle, to be slaughtered as meat for cannibals across the sea. Mungo Park had reported that slaves on the west coast destined for the West Indies and America had the same ghastly fear.

To his questions about the Niger, Lyon received confusing answers. He came to the conclusion that the river must enter Lake Chad and then flow on to join the Nile. He reported this mistaken theory to the British government—it was to influence the route of the next expedition. This time the plan was to go to Bornu, the kingdom around Lake Chad, by the caravan route that Hornemann had taken. This was the least difficult and dangerous of the ways across the Sahara because political links existed between Fezzan and Bornu. The Sultan of Bornu was at war with several neighboring states and managed to buy the support of the Sultan of Fezzan by allowing Fezzanese slave raids against his enemies.

A three-man team for the expedition to Bornu and Lake Chad was selected in London. The explorers were an Edinburgh doctor and

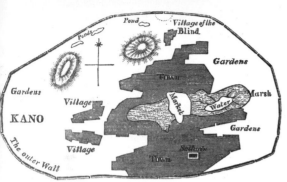

Left: Denham's map of Kano. He described it as "an eye sketch of the plan of the town," which he had drawn from the top of the eastern hill lying within the town wall.

botanist, Walter Oudney; a naval lieutenant, also from Edinburgh, Hugh Clapperton; and an army officer, Dixon Denham. They left Tripoli early in 1822, and began their journey across the desert with a caravan of camels and equipment. But before they left Marzūq they too caught malaria. Although they were really too ill to cross the desert, Oudney, Clapperton, and Denham struggled on until they reached Lake Chad. The journey from Tripoli took them 11 months, but the result made it worthwhile. They were the first Europeans to see the lake.

At Kukawa, the capital of the Kingdom of Bornu, the party camped. They then explored the lake and concluded that it was not the key to the mystery of the Niger. None of the rivers flowing into the lake from the west was big enough to be the Niger, and no great river flowed out of it to the east.

Having found and explored Lake Chad, the party split up. Denham set off to the southeast to follow the Chari River. Clapperton and Oudney decided to make for the Niger by going west through the Hausa states. They joined a caravan traveling westward to Kano under the direction of a merchant named Fezzan. Clapperton and Oudney were still following in the footsteps of Hornemann, though his objective had been Katsina, not Kano. Oudney, however, died before they reached their destination. Clapperton pressed on to Kano, the capital of the Hausa kingdom and a trading center with a reputation as legendary as that of Timbuktu. During the journey Clapperton must have learned much about Kano from the merchants in the caravan and particularly from its leader. At first, Clapperton was disappointed with the city. But he soon became interested in the life around him. And he recorded numerous details about the life and customs of Kano.

On leaving Kano, Clapperton went on to Sokoto, the Fulani capital. Sokoto was a more powerful city than the older and more famous Kano. The ruler of the Fulani, Mohammed Bello, was the most powerful man in the whole of the western Sudan, and knew something of the outside world. He received Clapperton kindly, but refused to let him pursue his journey to the Niger, which was less than 150 miles away. When Clapperton asked about the course of the river, Mohammed Bello sketched in the sand a diagram showing the river entering the sea. But a map later shown to Clapperton, apparently drawn according to Bello's instructions, and perhaps

Above: Dixon Denham, an army major who had fought in the Battle of Waterloo. He took great pride in the fact that the expedition traveled "in our real character as Britons and Christians and [in] our English dress."

designed to confuse him, showed that the Niger flowed northeast to reach Egypt. Clapperton thought that this second map was a deliberate fake prepared to put him off going south to the river.

Mohammed Bello and his advisers put heavy pressure on Clapperton to dissuade him from pressing on to the Niger. It was perfectly true that the country was disturbed and that there would have been danger. However, all the evidence suggests that Mohammed Bello decided to discourage inquisitive strangers. But he was anxious to establish good relations with Britain, especially if they would enable him to improve trade, purchase muskets, and obtain a British physician for his court. Eventually, having convinced Clapperton of the futility of heading in any other direction, Mohammed Bello provided him with an escort and set him on the eastward road. He sent a letter to the British king with Clapperton, expressing his willingness to cooperate in ending the slave trade and a wish to establish trade with Britain.

On his return journey Clapperton met Denham at Kukawa. Denham had been searching for him. The trek from Lake Chad back to Tripoli through Marzūq took them from mid-September, 1824, to the end of January, 1825. Unluckily, in spite of all they had been through together, they disliked each other intensely. But there they were, alone together in the middle of the Sahara, forced to spend day after day in each other's company. It was a difficult situation for both men, and to make matters worse Clapperton was going back

Above: Bornu horsemen, riding across the desert today much as they would have done when Clapperton was at Mohammed Bello's court. The war Mohammed Bello was then waging with Bornu prevented Clapperton from continuing to the Niger.

Above: the reception of the mission by the Sultan of Bornu, as drawn by Dixon Denham. He reported that the sultan sat "in a sort of cage of cane or wood, near the door of his garden." Below: Hugh Clapperton, a naval lieutenant from Edinburgh, was the most important explorer in the party. His endurance must have been remarkable—he set out again for Africa after only two months in England.

to Tripoli without having reached the city of Timbuktu or even having gazed upon the Niger. Denham, too, became depressed by the intense hardships of the return journey. He wrote: "the fatigue and difficulty of a journey to Bornu are not to be compared with a return to Fezzan: the nine days from Izhya to Teghery, without either forage or wood, is distressing beyond description, to both camels and men, at the end of a journey such as this. . . ." At long last the two dejected explorers reached Tripoli.

In Tripoli, Clapperton learned from the British consul, Hanmer Warrington, that Alexander Laing had received official backing in London for a journey to the Niger. The government wanted Laing to travel across the Sahara. After reaching the great city, he was to go on and explore the Niger to its mouth. Clapperton was absolutely sure he had learned the secret of the Niger from the map which Mohammed Bello had originally drawn in the sand. He felt convinced that if only he could get to the Niger, he could sail to the sea. It would be a bitter disappointment to be forestalled by Laing.

Back in London, Clapperton's success in reaching Kano made him famous. The letter he carried from the sultan also impressed the government officials. Two months after his arrival in England from Tripoli, Hugh Clapperton sailed for Africa in H.M.S. *Brazen* with a party consisting of two doctors, two black servants, a Captain Pearce, and Richard Lander, who was Clapperton's manservant. By November, 1825, they had reached the Bight of Benin and had landed at Badagri on the coast of what is now Nigeria. By the time Clapperton had journeyed 200 miles inland, three of his English companions, including Pearce, had died of malaria, and he was alone with Lander.

By coincidence, Clapperton's route northward to Sokoto took him past the falls of Bussa where Mungo Park had died. There he first saw the Niger. He crossed the river and struggled on northeastward to Kano. From Kano, he traveled on to Sokoto, where Mohammed Bello was involved in a new war against Bornu, but was no longer interested in entering diplomatic relations with England. Bello was still against Clapperton's continuing to the Bornu country. And he was also opposed to Clapperton's having anything to do with the enemies of the Fulani. It eventually transpired that Bello was really upset about the letters of introduction and presents for the Sultan of Bornu which Clapperton and Lander had in their baggage. At an audience with the Sultan in February, 1827, the Sultan agrees to send Clapperton to the sea by way of the Niger. Success was in sight. But soon afterward, Clapperton became very ill with malaria and dysentery. In March, he was completely incapacitated by dysentery and had to be looked after constantly by Lander. In spite of Lander's care he died on April 13, 1827.

The death of Clapperton left Lander in a very difficult situation. He was now completely without anyone he could trust. He was also deep in country where the local tribesmen were hostile to European travelers. His duty to Clapperton was to return to England with his

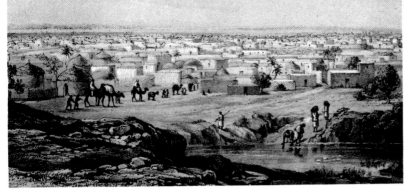

Left: the town of Kano, drawn by Heinrich Barth, the German explorer who was in the town 25 years after Clapperton's second visit there. From Kano, Clapperton went on to Mohammed Bello's court. He found Bello once again at war with Bornu.

Above: a member of the Dawada tribe, which Clapperton visited. They lived then as now around salt lakes, fishing for what they describe as worms—in fact a kind of shrimp. They live on these shrimps and dates.

papers. Lander did not trust the Arabs with whom he would have to travel if he went north across the desert. He badly wanted to try to find the Niger and trace its course, but it was now May and the rainy season. He did set out toward the upper Niger, but gave up any idea of exploring the river and returned to Kano. From Kano, accompanied by only one slave and a servant boy, he made his way back to Badagri. There, he boarded a ship for home. Lander was back in England at the end of April, 1828, a year after Clapperton's death. He delivered his master's papers to the officials in London and then began to write an account of their adventures.

Lander was a determined young man and was greatly fired with the idea of African exploration. He managed to convince the government of his sincerity and ability to trace the course of the Niger from Bussa to the sea. He received official backing for such an expedition, and at the end of January, 1830, he left England again, this time with his brother John. They had arrived at Bussa by the end of May, but did not begin their journey by canoe down river until the end of September. By mid-November the Landers had reached the coast at a small settlement called Brass Town.

The task which Mungo Park had set out to accomplish in 1805

Above: Richard Lander. He was from Cornwall, and went to Africa as Clapperton's manservant. After Clapperton's death, he managed to get himself out of the interior and reached England again in April, 1828. Below: John Lander. He joined his brother on the expedition which was finally successful in tracing the course of the Niger River from Bussa, where Park had died, to the sea.

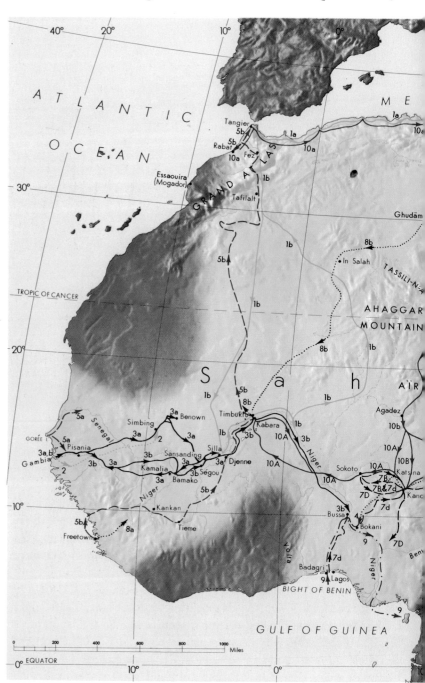

was now complete. The mouth of the Niger had been discovered, and the river's course was known from Bamako to the coast. Though the British no longer needed to forestall Napoleon's plans, they had all the same gained a foothold in western Africa which they had sought so long ago. Now they could expand their trade in the area, and could at last attempt to end the brutal traffic in slaves. More than 50 years were to pass before the true start of the colonial era. When that age dawned the long-standing British presence on the Niger helped to bring the entire area under European rule.

Below: northern Africa, showing the routes of explorers in the Sahara and the Niger region. Toward the end of the 1700's, European adventurers became interested in exploring the Niger region, and in tracing the river's course. Some chose to reach the Niger from the west coast of Africa. Others crossed the Sahara to the river. In so doing they carried out the first exploration of the vast desert.

Ibn-Batuta (part of journey)	1a	1325-32
Ibn-Batuta	1b	1349-53
Houghton	2	1790-1
Park	3a	1795-7
	3b	1805-6
Hornemann	4	1798-1801
Caillie	5a	1818-1824
	5b	1827-8
Ritchie & Lyon	6	1819
Clapperton (with Oudney & Denham)	7A	1822
Clapperton (with Oudney)	7B	1822
Clapperton (after death of Oudney)	7B	1823
Denham	7C	1823-4
Clapperton (with R. Lander)	7d	1825-7
Lander R. (after death of Clapperton)	7D	1827-
Laing	8a	1822
	8b	1825-6
Lander, R. (with J. Lander)	9	1830-2
Barth	10a	1845-7
Barth	10b	1850-5
Barth (with Richardson & Overweg)	10A	
Overweg (after explorers	10B	
Richardson separated	10C	

TROPIC OF CANCER

443

Timbuktu, the Lure of Legend

10

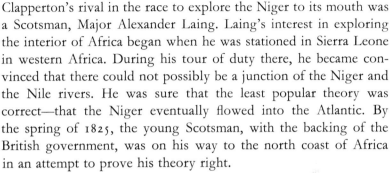

Left: Alexander Laing on patrol in Sierra Leone. He was born and educated in Scotland. He first planned to become a schoolteacher, but his love of adventure led him to join the army. While serving in West Africa, Laing became interested in exploring the Niger, and discovering its true mouth.

Clapperton's rival in the race to explore the Niger to its mouth was a Scotsman, Major Alexander Laing. Laing's interest in exploring the interior of Africa began when he was stationed in Sierra Leone in western Africa. During his tour of duty there, he became convinced that there could not possibly be a junction of the Niger and the Nile rivers. He was sure that the least popular theory was correct—that the Niger eventually flowed into the Atlantic. By the spring of 1825, the young Scotsman, with the backing of the British government, was on his way to the north coast of Africa in an attempt to prove his theory right.

In Tripoli, Laing was delayed by sickness. He was anxious to move on, but the British consul, Hanmer Warrington—the man who had informed Clapperton about Laing's projected journey—urged Laing to rest and get well before going on to Timbuktu.

During this period of enforced rest, Laing spent much of his time with Warrington's daughter Emma and eventually fell in love with her. Warrington considered that "a more wild, enthusiastic and romantic attachment never before existed," but he did not succeed in discouraging his daughter from marrying Laing. After their marriage, Laing started his risky journey.

Laing set off on July 18, 1825. His journey became a race with Clapperton to reach Timbuktu—he was fully aware of Clapperton's plans, and the rivalry was mutual. He left Tripoli accompanied by a small caravan, his servant Jack Le Bore, two West Indian boat-builders, and an interpreter. He was well provided with funds, and carried with him an impressive letter of introduction to the Sultan of Timbuktu.

Two months after leaving Tripoli, the caravan reached the oasis of Ghudāmis. It was less than 300 miles from Tripoli, but Laing had had to make a detour of 600 miles to avoid a local war. He was continually plagued by inquisitive and greedy tribesmen who forced him to pay bribes. The Turkish clothes which he had brought with him and eventually began wearing did little to make the journey easier. In spite of his treatment, Laing liked Ghudāmis very much. But as each day passed he became more depressed by a sense of loneliness and isolation. He worried about his guides and money and felt generally bitter about the lack of concern with which he seemed to be regarded by officials in London. There was also his intense longing for his wife, Emma.

Above: the typical clothing of women in Tripoli at the time that Laing was in the city preparing for his expedition across the desert. It was during his stay that he fell in love with the British consul's daughter.

Above: Alexander Laing. Laing was not a strong man, and throughout his life was plagued by ill health. His expedition to Timbuktu proved that he had the will to endure crushing hardship. Nevertheless the great loneliness of desert travel preyed on his mind and, he was constantly worried about the hostility of the nomad tribes.

The journey from Ghudāmis to the next oasis, In Salah, took Laing and his party a month and led them into the very heart of the Sahara. The caravan was outside any protection the Pasha of Tripoli could give, and was completely dependent on the nomad Tuareg tribes who controlled the desert routes. Laing wrote: "Whatever they demand, must be given them; a refusal would be a signal for plunder and murder; but if once satisfied they will . . . be your guides and protectors through their desert, dreary country. . . ." At In Salah, Laing was received with amazement by the natives, who had never set eyes on a European before. At one point he was requested to appear on the roof of his house so that he could be

seen by as many as possible of the fascinated townspeople.

A rumor began to spread through the town that Laing was in fact Mungo Park. A Moslem who had been wounded in one of the clashes with the *Joliba* was prepared to swear that Laing was the man who had been in command. The rumor naturally made Laing realize how unwise Park had been to leave such a trail of hostility behind him in his journey down the Niger. He was afraid that the Africans would become more hostile as he drew nearer the river, and that his journey would be even more dangerous than he had feared.

Nearly everything that is known of Laing's trek comes from the

Above: the typical Sahara terrain which Laing described in one letter as "provokingly monotonous." The distinctive desert plants, which look like dead brown sticks when dry, turn green when even a little rain falls. They provided almost the only source of food for the camels then used by all the travelers in the desert.

letters he sent back to Tripoli by courier. He was obviously worried about his safety even at In Salah. There, the Tuareg were irritated by the presence of a Christian who could speak only a few words of Arabic. Though his letters reveal little of the hardships of day-to-day life, we do know from them that his departure from In Salah was delayed because of rumors of the capture of another caravan to Timbuktu.

At last, in early January, 1826, a large caravan, including Laing's party, left In Salah. The route through the desert had no sizable oases or resting places. In his enthusiasm Laing had no idea of Timbuktu's exact position or that it was still nearly 900 miles farther on across the desert.

After two or three weeks of difficult travel, Laing's section of the caravan was attacked by a band of Tuareg tribesmen. Laing was severely wounded and only three members of his party survived. The caravan would not wait to accompany the wounded men to Timbuktu, but nevertheless they managed to travel some 400 miles across the desert to the lands of a friendly Arab chieftain called Sidi Mohammed Muktar. Sidi Mohammed treated Laing with great generosity and kindness, and the wounded man spent four months with him. While he was there, however, a plague he described as similar to yellow fever struck the town, killing all three remaining

Below: desert Arabs exercising, drawn by George Lyon some time before Laing's expedition. Laing soon encountered the aggressiveness and then warlike spirit of the Tuareg nomads.

members of the party, and the Arab chieftain Sidi Mohammed. Laing, too, nearly died of the disease. When he had recovered, he arranged for a guide to take him on to Timbuktu.

Early in August, 1826, Alexander Laing arrived at the far side of the desert, and on August 13 he entered Timbuktu. He had traveled 2,650 miles since leaving Tripoli and had endured countless difficulties and hardships.

There is one letter from Timbuktu in existence, written to "Consul Warrington and My dear Emma." It contains news of Laing's arrival in Timbuktu and his plans for leaving. He wrote:

Above: a Timbuktu water hole. Laing expected Timbuktu to be a great metropolis, but all he found was a small slave market in an undistinguished town. He had great difficulty in leaving Timbuktu as hostile Arabs surrounded the town.

449

Above: a caravan moves across the desert at night. It was with such a caravan that Laing left Timbuktu. On the third night, the sheik under whose protection Laing was traveling killed him and his servant as they slept. The bodies were left under a tree, and the caravan moved on.

". . . my situation in Timbuktu [has been] rendered exceedingly unsafe by the unfriendly disposition of the Foolahs of Massine, who have this year upset the dominion of the Tuaric & made themselves patrons of Timbuctu & as a party of Foolahs are hourly expected, Al Kaidi Boubokar, who is an excellent good man, & who trembles for my safety, has strongly urged my immediate departure, and I am sorry to say that the notice has been so short, and I have so much to do previous to going away, that this is the only communication I shall for the present be able to make. My destination is Sego [Ségou], whither I hope to arrive in fifteen days, but I regret to say that the road is a vile one and my perils are not yet at an end, but my trust is in God Who has hitherto bore me up amidst the severest trials & protected me amid the numerous dangers to which I have been exposed. . . ."

Despite Al Kaidi's warning, and his own plans for a speedy

departure, Laing stayed five weeks in Timbuktu. He had freedom to go about as he wished, making notes for his journal. But there was always the problem of how to get out of the city safely. It was almost completely surrounded by unfriendly tribesmen. He was urged by leaders in the city to return to Tripoli by the way he had come. Laing, however, persisted in his wish to go out by a south-west route which would take him through hostile country.

Late in September, 1826, Laing joined a small caravan going toward Arouan. According to tribesmen in that area, the third night out from Timbuktu he and his Arab servant boy were killed by the fanatical sheik who had charge of the caravan in which they were traveling. The bodies were left beneath a tree and all of Laing's baggage was burned.

In March, 1827, six months after Alexander Laing's murder and just a few weeks before Clapperton's death at Sokoto, a Frenchman named René Caillié set out from Sierra Leone for Timbuktu. He was hoping to be the first Frenchman to reach the famous city and so receive a prize of 10,000 francs which was being offered by the French Geographical Society.

Born the son of a poor baker, Caillié had been fascinated by stories of travel almost as soon as he had learned to read. As he grew up he began to study geography books and maps. It was the map of Africa which particularly excited him. On it he saw nothing

Below: the French official enquiry of 1910 digging for Laing's remains. After the murders, a passing Arab had buried the bodies. The nephew of the sheik who had killed Laing was still alive, but by then 82 years old. He still possessed the golden brooch which the sheik had taken from the explorer's body—it had been a parting gift from Laing's wife, Emma.

Above: René Caillié. The son of a baker who had died in prison, Caillié had a passion for travel from the time he was small. He had no particular scientific interest in exploration, but he was determined to be the first Frenchman to reach Timbuktu.

but desert or areas marked "unknown". Very soon his interest in reading about Africa developed into a passion to explore it.

At the age of 16, Caillié got a job as a servant on a French ship which was going to Senegal. From Senegal, he eventually managed to join an expedition which had been organized to go inland to search for any sign of Mungo Park's second expedition on the Niger. During this time, Caillié had also got hold of a copy of Park's account of his first journey. This strengthened his desire to explore the interior of Africa himself, and he began working to save money for the journey. He went to live for nine months in a primitive Moorish village called Brakna, where he learned to speak Arabic and studied the Koran. The stories he had heard and read about the hostility of Moslems toward European travelers had made him realize that he would have to travel as a Moslem. When he left Brakna, Caillié could pass as an Arab.

After he had saved some money, Caillié was able to buy the supplies he would need for the journey to Timbuktu. In March, 1827, he embarked at Freetown in Sierra Leone. His destination was the Rio Nunez estuary between Sierra Leone and Senegal. From there he would proceed inland. He traveled as an Arab and explained to his guides and companions that he had been born in Egypt, where he had been captured and deported by the French. Now he was on his way to make the pilgrimage to Mecca and search for his family.

Caillié arrived at the Rio Nunez nine days after leaving Freetown. After a few miles he managed to join a caravan which was going to Timbuktu. Early in June the caravan reached the Niger at Kouroussa. There Caillié and his three servants joined another caravan which would take them to Kankan and Djenné. Fever had already begun to attack him, but he managed to keep up with the caravan which was very much delayed by continual crossings of the tributaries of the Niger. In his journal Caillié seldom mentions his difficulties during this period, but concentrates instead on noting the names of places.

In August, Caillié walked wearily into the town of Tieme which—unknown to him—was less than a quarter of the way to Timbuktu. There he developed scurvy and was unfortunate enough to catch malaria as well. To add to his troubles, his foot was very painful and he was unable to walk. He was taken into a primitive grass

Right: a drawing of the Niger River taken from René Caillié's own book. This was probably Caillié's very first sight of the Niger River on his journey across Africa on the way to Timbuktu. Caillié started his journey from the west coast of Africa.

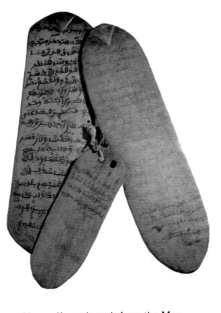

Above: Koran boards from the Mandingo area, near Timbuktu. Caillié spent nine months in a Moorish village, preparing for his journey by studying the Koran and learning Arab and African customs. When he left there, he could pass as an Arab.
Below: Caillié in Arab dress. Not everyone he met believed that he was really an Arab, but all the same he was generally received kindly.

hut at Tieme and cared for by an old Negro woman, who kept him alive for five months.

"I soon experienced all the horrors of that dreadful disease [scurvy]. The roof of my mouth became quite bare, a part of the bones exfoliated [peeled off] and fell away, and my teeth seemed ready to drop out of their sockets. I feared that my brain would be affected by the agonizing pains I felt in my head, and I was more than a fortnight without sleep. To crown my misery, the sore in my foot broke out afresh and all hope of my departure vanished. . . . Alone, in the interior of a wild country, stretched on the damp ground, with no pillow but the leather bag which contained my luggage, with no medicine. . . . This good creature [the old Negro woman] brought me twice a day a little rice water, which she forced me to drink, for I could eat nothing. I soon reduced to a skeleton. . . . Suffering had deprived me of all energy. One thought alone absorbed my mind—that of Death. I wished for it, and prayed for it to God."

Despite Caillié's prayers, the old Negro's care eventually had its effect. In January, 1828, with a new guide, he was fit enough to continue his journey. In early March he arrived at Djenné. He was just a little more than 200 miles from Timbuktu. Caillié had walked nearly all the way—1,000 miles. During his journey he had received kind treatment from Moslem and non-Moslem alike.

At Djenné, which is situated on a tributary of the Niger, Caillié boarded a boat for Timbuktu. This proved to be the worst experience of his journey. He was very sick much of the time. He was also ranked with slaves and forced to lie in the most cramped quarters below deck. When they entered the country where the Tuareg roamed the banks of the river, Caillié had to remain out of

sight below deck during the day. After a month of dreadful heat and fear of being discovered by the Tuareg, he caught sight of Kabara, the port of Timbuktu. His first glimpse of the city of Timbuktu a few hours later proved to be an unexpected anticlimax.

"I looked around and found that the sight before me did not answer my expectations. I had formed a totally different idea of the grandeur and wealth of Timbuktu . . . the city presented, at first view, nothing but a mass of ill-looking houses, built of earth. Nothing was to be seen in all directions but immense plains of quicksand of a yellowish-white color. The sky was a pale red as far as the horizon; all nature wore a dreary aspect, and the most profound silence prevailed; not even the warbling of a bird was to be heard."

Caillié strolled round the city the next day. Timbuktu was a

Above: a drawing of Timbuktu from the book by René Caillié. Like Laing, he found that the famous city was a typical desert town, not particularly wealthy, and less impressive than other towns he had traveled through. He complained that "Timbuktu and its environs present the most monotonous and barren scene I ever beheld."

454

Left: a brickmaker in modern Timbuktu. As when Laing and Caillié saw the city, many of the houses in the center of Timbuktu are still made of mud bricks.

dying place. Little business was being done, and unlike Djenné, the streets were empty of foreign travelers. "I was surprised," says Caillié, "at the inactivity, I might even say, indolence, displayed in the city." He saw three shops, which were really small rooms, with good stocks of European cloth, and also a warehouse with European merchandise, including muskets. But there was no local agriculture whatsoever, and the city's only substantial source of income was as a distributing center for the salt brought in from the mines in the far north.

Caillié's lodgings were opposite the house where Laing had stayed, and he made such discreet enquiries about Laing's death as he could without arousing too much suspicion. He spent much time studying and sketching architectural details of the three principal mosques in the city.

Caillié's visit lasted for two weeks. He left on May 4 for Morocco with a caravan of 1,200 camels, numerous slaves, and other merchandise. Four days out from Timbuktu the scene of Laing's murder was pointed out to him by members of the party.

During his arduous journey across the Sahara, Caillié encountered all the horrors of desert travel. He experienced such thirst that he thought of nothing but water, and would go about begging for an extra mouthful to add to the tiny ration issued in the evening to each member of the caravan. Besides, his disguise was now becoming less convincing, probably because of the stress of the intolerable conditions. His guide was a malicious and mischievous individual who teased Caillié and gave him ridiculous nicknames. The guide and his companions further terrified the Frenchman by saying that he looked like a Christian. This taunting naturally made him think of Laing's death. Finally they reached the oasis of Tafilalt on the south side of the Grand Atlas on July 23, 1828. Caillié was another six weeks getting across the Atlas through Fez and Rabat to reach Tangier, where he could ask the help of the French consul.

It was not easy, however, to prove to the French authorities that he really had gone to Timbuktu. They eventually acknowledged his claim, but only after a special committee had been formed to investigate it. Back in France, Caillié received the award of 10,000 francs from the Geographical Society. He was the first Frenchman to have reached the city of legendary wealth and the first man to have survived to tell of his experiences there.

Above: the house in which René Caillié lived in Timbuktu—it is opposite the house where Laing stayed. Above the door a plaque has been placed commemorating the fact that Caillié lived there. The French held the city for many years, and placed several such plaques in memory of early explorers.

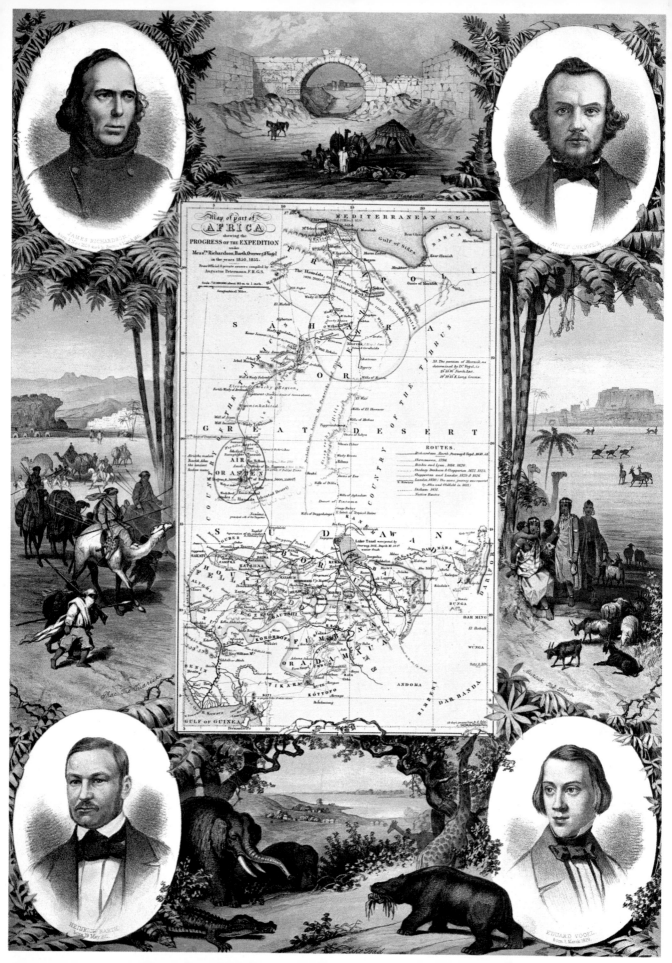

Conquering the Sahara

11

Left: an 1854 map of Africa, showing the portraits and routes of Richardson (top left); Barth (bottom left); Overweg (top right); and Vogel (bottom right). The other pictures show scenes reported by the four explorers.

Above: James Richardson, wearing the costume of the people of Ghudāmis. He did not attempt to disguise himself for his journey, but traveled openly as a European as far as Ghāt, about 600 miles from Tripoli.

During the 50 years that followed René Caillié's return from Timbuktu, a succession of travelers tried to cross the Sahara to Timbuktu and the other cities along the Niger. Many of those who attempted this journey never came back. Of about 200 who set out, 165 died from disease or were killed by the Tuareg. But those who did survive the terrible hardships of the desert brought back reports and information which would eventually help to open up barren wastes of the Sahara.

Many of the unsuccessful Saharan travelers in the 1800's were wealthy young men who engaged in semiscientific exploration in many parts of the world. Typical of these explorers was a British doctor, John Davidson. He had already traveled widely in eastern Europe and North and Central America before he turned his attention to the Sahara. His plan was to cross the desert by the caravan route through the wasteland of Mauritania. Davidson was warned that he had chosen a very dangerous route, and that, at that time, the hazards were made worse by tribal fighting. But he would not be put off. In 1836 he set out from Mogador (now Essaouira), on the coast of Morocco, and had traveled barely six weeks with a caravan when he was killed.

It seems probable that Davidson's murderers were paid by powerful Arab merchants, worried that their monopoly of that caravan route would be broken if Europeans were allowed to interfere. The Arab merchants had good reason for their fears. During the 1800's, merchants in Europe—and particularly in Britain—became increasingly interested in the caravan routes across the Sahara, and in the possibilities for trade in that part of Africa. But the next European to venture across the burning sands was employed, not by merchants, but by a British Bible society whose chief aim was to find out more about the slave trade across the Sahara. That man was James Richardson. He set out from Tripoli in August, 1845, traveling openly as a European and a Christian, and first headed southwest to the oasis of Ghudāmis. From there, he struck due south, nearly 400 miles to the city of Ghāt. There he was warmly welcomed by the sultan, who gave him presents to take back to Queen Victoria. After observing and recording details of the slave trade, Richardson set out on the return trek to the Mediterranean coast, where he took a ship to London. Although his journey had been a limited one—he had penetrated only about 700 miles into the

Below: the antislavery convention of 1840. Notice that there is a Negro in the audience. The horrors of the slave trade in Africa struck each of the explorers with enormous force. Their reports gave a new impulse to demands for the abolition of slavery, but even after slavery was officially abolished, slaving continued in Africa. Below right: a gang of Negro slaves with their Arab captors. This Victorian engraving shows a mother and child dying on the ground, while the vultures wheel overhead.

Sahara—Richardson's account of his travels aroused great interest in London. In particular, his reports of the cruelties of the slave trade stirred up strong feelings in Britain.

The British government now became interested in the idea of investigating the great caravan routes between the oases of the Sahara and the cities on the southern fringe of the desert. A few years after Richardson's return, they authorized an official expedition to explore these routes and to gain more information about the slave trade. They appointed Richardson to lead the expedition. Richardson wanted to make his team as international as possible. He also wanted to recruit men with a more scientific approach to African exploration than the romantic adventurers of the past.

The Prussian ambassador in London suggested to Richardson the name of a young German, Heinrich Barth, who already had experience of exploration in the Middle East and in northern Africa. Barth had studied archaeology, history, geography, and law at the University of Berlin. He had also spent some time in London learning Arabic. He seemed an ideal candidate, and Richardson quickly asked him to join the expedition. Barth eagerly agreed, and at once began

459

Left: a drawing of Ghāt by Heinrich Barth. He spent five years in all traveling around the southern fringe of the Sahara between Lake Chad and Timbuktu. Barth was a methodical, humorless, and unemotional man who was well prepared, physically and practically, for his African adventure. He allowed nothing to deter him.

Below: the *monster of Sefar*, one of the notable Neolithic rock paintings found in the Tassili-n-Ajjer.

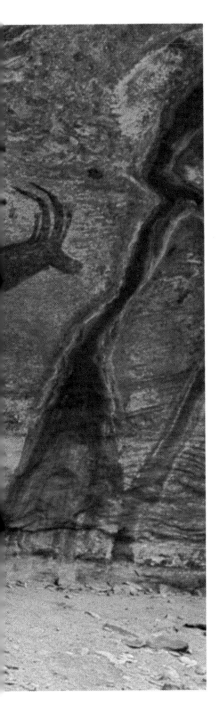

a strenuous course of physical training to get himself in good shape for the rigorous months ahead. The third member of Richardson's party was a young German geologist named Adolf Overweg.

The expedition which left Tripoli in 1850 appears to have been the best organized and equipped ever to have ventured across the Sahara. The three Europeans were accompanied by the usual retinue of guides and servants. They had with them great quantities of stores and equipment, including a large wooden boat in which they planned to explore Lake Chad. The boat was in two sections to make it easier to carry.

The explorers themselves were particularly well suited to the job in hand. Barth especially was very well trained, and Richardson, the leader, was familiar with the desert and its dangers. Unfortunately, soon after they set out these two men seem to have developed a strong personal dislike for each other. From the beginning the party was split into distinct national groups. During the heat of the day the two Germans rode ahead, followed at a considerable distance by Richardson and a British sailor who had been sent along to manage the boat. Even in the cool of the evening the two groups and their servants settled down to eat and sleep in separate camps.

In this unfriendly atmosphere the party arrived in Marzuq in May, 1850. From there they went on to Ghāt. A few days out from Ghāt, Barth decided to climb the mysterious Mount Idinen, which according to the Tuareg was inhabited by evil spirits. He reached the summit of the mountain but was so exhausted and thirsty that, by the time he made his descent, he had drunk all of the water he had with him. He then lost his way and eventually fell to the ground in a state of semiconsciousness. On regaining his senses, he managed to prevent himself from panicking, and cut open one of his veins to quench his thirst by drinking his own blood. A Tuareg found him and helped him to get back to Overweg and the expedition. His companions bound up his wound and Barth quickly recovered.

From Ghāt the party traveled through the Tassili-n-Ajjer where, nearly a century later, thousands of Neolithic rock paintings were to be discovered. Barth himself saw some rock carvings there. The party had a rough passage through the mountains. They were frequently attacked by marauders, forced to pay ransom money, and even so had to defend themselves by firing on their attackers. As they made their way through the Aïr Mountains they were threatened

Left: men on the shore of Lake Chad building a reed boat following traditional construction methods. Richardson died before reaching Kukawa, but Barth and Overweg went on to explore the lake and its shores.

by the hostile Tuareg tribesmen, who demanded that they renounce their Christian religion or die by sundown. Luckily the Tuareg were willing to strike a bargain, and their religious fervor evaporated when they were offered one-third of the belongings of the British expedition.

From the Aïr Mountains Barth traveled south to Agadez, once one of the great centers of commerce in the Sahara. By the mid-1800's, however, Agadez' prosperity had declined and Barth describes it as an abandoned city whose population had dwindled from 50,000 to 7,000. Everywhere he saw traces of vanished splendor.

It was soon after this that the three men decided to separate. Richardson headed directly for Lake Chad, and the two Germans set off to find a more westerly route to the lake. Shortly afterward, Barth parted from Overweg, and made an expedition on his own to Katsina and Kano. The three men had arranged to meet at Kukawa in April, 1851. But Richardson never kept the rendezvous. Three weeks before Barth arrived at Kukawa to meet his companions, Richardson died of fever.

Overweg was the last of the party to reach Lake Chad. When he finally arrived there in May he was exhausted and suffering from fever. Nevertheless, while Barth explored the territory to the south and east of Lake Chad, Overweg recovered sufficiently to explore the lake itself in the boat they had brought with them across the Sahara. The two men stayed for about 15 months in the Lake Chad region. When the British government heard that Richardson had died, they appointed Barth the new leader of the expedition. They also sent sufficient funds for the two men to continue to their next objective—Timbuktu. But before they started on this stretch of their journey, Overweg died of malaria. He was only 29 years old.

Barth, too, had suffered numerous attacks of dysentery and fever. But, despite his own illnesses and the deaths of Richardson and Overweg, he was determined to go on. At the end of November, 1852, he left the capital of Bornu. He had now been 32 months on the journey out from Tripoli. He knew the next stretch to Timbuktu might take him another two years. Barth was confident, however, that he would reach his destination. He was certainly fortunate in his dealings with local tribesmen, and he attributes his luck to a single incident. One day when he was surrounded by a hostile group of fierce-looking townspeople, Barth fired off six rounds from his

Above: Barth's drawing of the interior of a Mugsu dwelling. Barth initially specified that he would undertake only scientific work on the expedition. However, after Richardson's death, he was appointed leader, and, although a German, he became Britain's representative. The expedition was to investigate routes across the Sahara, and to learn more about the slave trade.

revolver into the air. In his journal he says that this show of force had great influence over his future safety. The Africans were afraid, believing he had guns hidden in all his pockets and could fire them as and when he wished.

When Barth finally reached Timbuktu in September, 1853, he found the city slightly more prosperous than Caillié had done 25 years earlier. But it had never regained the position as a trading center for the Sahara that it had held in the 1500's and before.

Early in 1854 Barth left Timbuktu and began working his way eastward to Lake Chad. On the way he learned that a party of Europeans had been sent out by the British government to look for him and had already arrived at the lake. This party was led by another German, Edward Vogel, who when he met Barth explained that people in London had given him up for dead. After a brief discussion, it was decided that Barth should go on to Kukawa. Vogel, meanwhile, would make for Zinder, a town almost 300 miles west of Lake Chad. He was to rejoin Barth before starting the journey north across the desert.

Barth, however, eventually made the desert crossing without Vogel — the latter decided to stay in Africa and explore the Lower Niger. Barth left for the desert in May, 1855, and, despite the fact that it was the hottest time of the year, he managed to get back to

Tripoli and on to London by early September. He had been away over five years. Vogel was murdered in 1856 on his way to the Nile.

The success of the British expedition of 1850–1855 was due almost entirely to Barth's single-mindedness. Despite innumerable difficulties and the very real threat of death from the fanatically religious tribesmen, he fulfilled his mission, and brought back a vast amount of information about northern Africa. It was Barth's scientific thoroughness which made him unique—no other explorer of the same area managed to accomplish as much as he had. He was the first man to make reliable maps of huge areas of Africa, and the first man to study the customs of the Negro tribes he encountered.

Barth was to have great influence on all future explorers of the Sahara. And he was most generous in giving them the benefit of his advice and encouragement. Three Germans—Gerhard Rohlfs, Gustav Nachtigal, and Oscar Lenz—and a Frenchman—Henri Duveyrier—are probably the most important of his successors.

Gerhard Rohlfs was a German soldier who, in order to prepare himself for travel in the desert, joined the Foreign Legion in Algiers. In 1862, he disguised himself as a religious official and set out for the interior of Morocco. On this first journey Rohlfs traveled to the oasis of Tafilalt—he was the first European since René Caillié to report on this area. Rohlf's second journey was far more ambitious. From Tafilalt he pushed southeastward to In Salah, in the very heart of the desert. Rohlf's dream was to visit Timbuktu, but at In Salah he ran short of money and was forced to abandon his plan. Instead he traveled north through Ghudāmis to Tripoli.

Below: a drawing based on the reports of Edward Vogel, a young German who was sent by the British government to look for Heinrich Barth. His descriptions of the vegetation of the Chad area were highly imaginative.

The second German expedition to the Sahara resulted from King Wilhelm of Prussia's desire to join the European race for trade and influence in Africa. He commissioned Gustav Nachtigal to cross the Sahara with numerous elaborate presents for the Sultan of Bornu—Nachtigal needed eight camels simply to carry the gifts. However, he made the journey across the Sahara safely, and reported that the Sultan was delighted with the presents. Nachtigal was an explorer as well as an envoy. He traveled widely in the Tibesti Massif, and also managed to visit Darfur and Kordofan (in the west

Above: Gustav Nachtigal, who traveled across the Sahara carrying with him the most remarkable collection of presents from the King of Prussia to the Sultan of Bornu. Nachtigal was fortunate to arrive unmolested.

of what is now Sudan), and explore the valley of the Nile.

Oscar Lenz's achievement was to cross the Sahara from Morocco to the mouth of the Senegal River—in effect, this was very like Caillié's route, but in reverse. With only a small party, Lenz made good time, and only 40 days or so after leaving the slopes of the Grand Atlas he arrived at Timbuktu. To his great astonishment he was well received there, and the 18 days he spent in the city were, he says, among the best in his life. From his account, it is clear that Timbuktu was still in decline, although the political situation was less tense. Lenz left Timbuktu in mid-July, 1880, and by November he had reached a French outpost on the Senegal River.

Perhaps the most famous of all Barth's successors was Henri Duveyrier. Duveyrier first visited North Africa in 1857 when he was 17 years old. He was fascinated by what he saw, and returned to France determined to prepare himself properly for a more am-

466

bitious expedition. He traveled first to London, to get Barth's advice, and to continue his studies of geology, natural sciences, and languages.

In 1859, when he was still only 19 years old, Duveyrier set out from the French colony of Algeria for the oasis of El Goléa, which was a stronghold of Moslem tribesmen. When he finally reached there, the Moslems drove him away from the oasis and threatened to kill him if he came back. But in spite of this treatment, Duveyrier refused to show any sign of fear in his dealings with the tribesmen.

His courage even succeeded in the end in winning their respect.

Duveyrier next went south from Tripoli to the Tassili-n-Ajjer, where he made friends with two powerful Ajjer chiefs. He lived a year among the Ajjer Tuareg, sharing their hard way of life, and learning their language and writing. During this time he remained fascinated by the people—he took copious notes and asked questions on every subject relating to their way of life.

When Duveyrier eventually returned to Tripoli, he had in mind another expedition to the Tuareg of the Ahaggar Mountains. But before he carried out his plan, he returned to Paris. There he edited his notes and fitted himself out with new equipment. He had hardly finished writing up his notes when he became ill with a recurrence of typhoid fever, which he had first contracted while living with the Tuareg. He temporarily lost his memory and from that time onward was unable to continue any serious explorations. Neverthe-

Above: a water hole, drawn by Barth. The lives of explorers in the desert depended on oases and water holes, and if, as often happened, a water hole went dry, the party faced almost certain death from thirst.

Left: Henri Duveyrier (1840–1892) went to Africa and lived among the Tuareg, sharing their difficult life. He refused to be afraid of them, and succeeded in gaining their respect.

Above: two Tuareg tribesmen of Ghāt, drawn in 1821 by George Lyon. These fierce warriors used to roam across the Sahara. The possibility of attack by Tuareg nomads was one of the greatest hazards facing travelers crossing the desert to Timbuktu.

less, his book *The Tuareg of the North* remains a standard work.

Early in 1869, 10 years after Duveyrier had set out to study the Tuareg, a young Dutchwoman called Alexandrine Tinné reached Marzūq with a large caravan, and a bodyguard of two Dutch sailors. Miss Tinné was a wealthy heiress, who had already spent some years in Africa, exploring in the Bahr el Ghazal region, in Algeria, and in Tunisia. Now she planned to cross the Sahara.

Soon after leaving Marzūq, Miss Tinné fell in with an Ahaggar

PORTRET van ALEXANDRINE TINNE
1835   1869
C? ... MONTPEZAT 1849

Tuareg chieftain, who persuaded her to let him escort her to the Oasis of Ghāt. After a few days, she was attacked by the chieftain and his Tuareg. Her hand was slashed off, probably to prevent her from drawing a revolver, and she was left lying in the hot sun to bleed slowly to death. Knowing the hazards of desert travel, Miss Tinné had taken two water tanks with her. It seems probable that her escort believed they were full of gold, and murdered her to steal them. The Sahara had claimed another victim.

Above: Alexandrine Tinné, the rich young Dutchwoman who used her fortune to finance her expeditions. She traveled lavishly, carrying curtains, cushion covers, and a small library as part of her equipment. On her last expedition, she was killed by the Tuareg.

The Desert Tamed
12

On April 4, 1881, a handful of survivors from a French expedition to the Sahara crawled into the oasis of El Meseggem. They were half-dead from thirst, hunger, and exposure. Some were badly wounded. When they had recovered, they gave a horrifying account of their journey. They had set out from Ouargla in December, 1880, the strongest military expedition that France had ever sent deep into the desert—10 officers, 46 soldiers, and 36 tribesmen. Their aim was to explore and survey the desert northeast of the Ahaggar Mountains. But this was the land of the hostile Ahaggar Tuareg who particularly disliked the French.

Scarcity of water was a great problem because of the large number of men and camels. It was this need for water that provided the Tuareg with the perfect trap. A band of tribesmen who were shadowing the expedition approached the French commander, Colonel Paul-Xavier Flatters. They told him that they would take him to a well where the camels could be watered and from which he could take a supply back to the main camp. Flatters, with a small party and most of the camels, went with them. He left a Lieutenant Dianous behind in charge of the main party.

At the well, a band of Tuareg swooped down on Flatters and his men. They shot and killed everyone except for a few Arab camel men who fled back to the camp. When Dianous heard what had

Left: one of the French Saharan regiments. The officer on horseback is the colonel of the regiment. It was this rank that Flatters held on the catastrophic mission to explore and survey the desert northeast of the Ahaggar Mountains.

Right: Paul-Xavier Flatters (1832–1881). Flatters made the fatal mistake of allowing his party to be split, and the Tuareg killed them almost to a man

Above: an early photograph of the Foureau-Lamy mission. Their exped-ition across the desert proved that it was possible for a well-armed force to challenge the fierce Tuareg tribesmen in their own territory.

happened, he was faced with the terrifying task of returning to Ouargla with the survivors. They would have to walk because the Tuareg had driven away the few remaining camels.

All the way back across the desert the wretched, exhausted Frenchmen were hounded by the Tuareg. Dianous was killed, and most of the men died on the way of wounds, thirst, or starvation. When food and water had run out, the demented survivors resorted to eating the bodies of their dead companions.

The story of the disastrous Flatters expedition had an overwhelming effect on French morale. The French government had planned to build a railroad across the Sahara. Now they gave up the idea and concentrated instead upon establishing control over the areas around the desert. Tunisia became a French protectorate in 1881. In 1895, the area around Timbuktu, including much of what is now Mali, became the French colony of Sudan.

But during this period one man still dreamed of establishing a definite link across the Sahara. His name was Fernand Foureau. Between 1868 and 1898, Foureau made numerous journeys into the Sahara on his own. Altogether he covered more than 12,000 miles over the desert in preparation for the day when the French government would once again sponsor an official expedition.

Foureau's chance came in 1898. In that year the French Geographical Society, which had heard of his achievements, offered him financial backing if he would lead an expedition to explore the Sahara between Algeria and the Sudan. Foureau jumped at the opportunity. A military escort was provided under the command of a Major Lamy. Soon the expedition grew until it was more like a small army. The soldiers were armed with rifles, machine guns, and light cannon. The French government was determined that this time the Tuareg would attack at their own peril.

At last the expedition set out. The long column made its way slowly southward to the central plateau and the fearsome Ahaggar Mountains. The Tuareg, armed with swords and spears and occasionally rifles, never attacked the French. They used a more subtle way of terrorizing them. They refused to supply food or water for the camels. As the Frenchmen pushed on through the territory between the Tassili-n-Ajjer and Ahaggar Mountains, they were losing over 100 camels a week.

By the time the French had got halfway across the Aïr Mountains, all the camels were dead. Most of the luggage had to be burned, and the bulk of the ammunition buried. The men continued their march, many of them by now in rags and almost starving. At last they struggled into Zinder. The march between Algeria and the Sudan was accomplished, but their trials were not yet over. The expedition moved eastward to Lake Chad where they were attacked by an army from the kingdom of Bornu. The French managed to win the battle at Kousseri, which was renamed Fort-Lamy in memory of Major Lamy who was killed in the battle.

The Foureau-Lamy mission showed that a well-armed force of men could cross the desert. But it had not managed to overcome the Tuareg. By the end of the 1800's, the French still had no real control over their Saharan possessions or the desert tribes. They persisted in their belief that an army could subdue the tribesmen. In 1901, however, a French officer was put in charge of the Sahara who knew how to pacify the angry Tuareg and achieve the linking up of Algeria with the French Sudan.

Above: disk-lipped women of Kyabe, Chad. A traditional method of the people living near Fort-Lamy for enhancing the beauty of their women, the practice has now been forbidden. Only a handful of these women can still be found in the area.

Below: the Foureau-Lamy mission, crossing the Sahara in 1899.

Right: between 1859 and 1900, a
number of Europeans set out into the
Sahara, either to explore the desert,
or to study the Tuareg tribesmen who
lived there. This map shows the
routes followed during this time by
some of those who, by their journeys, helped to open up the desert.

Below: a Tuareg caravan. It was by
enlisting rival desert tribesmen that
the French finally succeeded in cur-
bing the power of the Tuareg nomads.

....	Duveyrier	1	1859-61
————	Rohlfs	2a	1862
		2b	1863
		2c	1865
		2d	1867-8
		2e	1869
		2f	1874
		2g	1878
		2h	1880-1
— — — —	Nachtigal	3	1869-74
....	Lenz	4a	1879-80
		4b	1885-7
————	Flatters	5a	1880
	Flatters (with Dianous)	5b	1880-1
————	Foureau	6a	1895-6
	Foureau (part with Lamy)	6b	1898-1900

© Geographical Projects

This man was Marie Joseph François Henri Laperrine. When he
was sent out to be commander in chief of the Saharan Oases, his
job was merely to patrol the Saharan bases. But he had the ingenious
idea of recruiting a force of desert tribesmen who were traditional
enemies of the Tuareg. He formed them into three large camel
companies. These were to be well trained and supplied with arms and
food. After a number of successful brushes with the Tuareg, the
camel corps began crossing the desert without fear of attack.

In May, 1902, a battle took place which finally broke the strength
of the Ahaggar Tuareg. Early that year, a heavily armed French
expedition had opened fire on some tribesmen who were determined
to prevent them from approaching In Salah, the traditional meeting
place of their chiefs. The Tuareg responded by their very effective
practice of attacking French caravans traveling in their territory.
The French, and their corps of desert tribesmen, took up arms
against the Ahaggar Tuareg. At the Battle of Tit, in the Ahaggar
Mountains, the Tuareg were heavily defeated.

Laperrine's camel corps, each usually made up of about 20 riders,
continued their journeys across the Sahara. Within a few years,
they hardly ever had to fire a shot. Their regular crossings of
the desert paved the way for better communications. By 1910 a

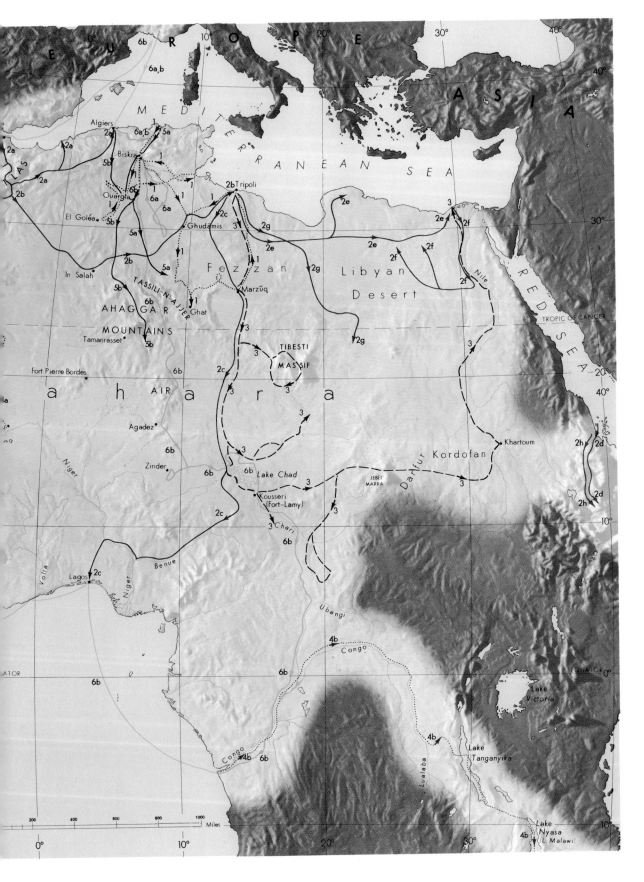

E U R O P E

ASIA

M E D I T E R R A N E A N   S E A

6b

6a,b

Algiers
6a,b 5a
2a
Biskra 1
5b
6b 1
Ouargla 6a
1 6a
El Goléa 5b
In Salah

2a
2a
2a
2b

2b Tripoli
Ghudamis 3
2c
2e
2g
2e

2e
2f
2f

3
2e 2f

Nile

R E D   S E A

TROPIC OF CANCER

5b
5a
2b
5a
Ghat
5a
Marzūq
1
1
1

F e z z a n

L i b y a n

D e s e r t

2g
2g

2g

TASSILI-N-AJJER
AHAGGAR
MOUNTAINS
Tamanrasset
5b
6b

1

3

3
TIBESTI
MASSIF
3
3

Fort Pierre Bordes
6b
2c
3
3

3

3

S a h a r a

A I R

Agadez
6b
Zinder
6b
6b
Lake Chad
Kousseri
(Fort-Lamy)
2c
3 Chari
6b

Khartoum

Darfur Kordofan
3

JEBET
MARRA

3
3
2h 2d

2h 2d

N i g e r

6b
Benue
Niger
Lagos 2c
2c
Volta

Congo

Ubangi

4b
Congo

EQUATOR 0°

Lake
Victoria

ATOR
6b

6b
Congo 4b 6b

Lualaba

4b
Lake
Tanganyika

200 400 600 800 1000 Miles

0°
10°
20°
30°

Lake
Nyasa
(L. Malawi)
4b

475

regular postal service operated across the Sahara from Timbuktu via the Ahaggar Mountains, In Salah, and El Goléa to Algiers.

Laperrine had adopted the desert way of life and had built on desert customs and rivalries in order to achieve his success. He transformed the French officers of the camel corps into a band of desert nomads. They had no headquarters, but lived with their camels wherever there was pastureland. By 1905, one of Laperrine's small groups had crossed the desert four times in the hottest season of the year without losing a single man or camel—a truly remarkable feat considering how many had died in attempting one crossing.

Ironically, Laperrine, who did so much to bring the Sahara under control, died there. In 1920, he was a passenger in one of two airplanes on an official mission to establish an air route across the Sahara from Algiers to Dakar. Somewhere near Fort Pierre Bordes, the plane Laperrine was traveling in ran out of fuel, and was forced to crash-land in the desert. The plane turned over as it struck the ground, and the general's shoulder was badly injured. The temperature in the desert was over 100°F and they had only a small supply of water. The three survivors managed to keep alive for several weeks, hoping that someone would find them. Eventually, Laperrine crawled away from the wreckage of the plane and died in the sand. Ten days later, a party of the camel corps found the general's body and the two half-dead survivors.

Unlike other parts of Africa, the work of missionaries played only a small part in the opening up of the Sahara. One reason was that the Moslem religion was well established there, and the Moslem tribesmen did not take kindly to Christian intruders. Cardinal Lavigerie, a Roman Catholic prelate, aimed to create a network of mission stations in the desert oases through the missionary White Fathers. But one group of three was murdered in 1876, and 6 years later 3 more missionaries met their deaths. Both groups had felt that they were in no danger, and it is difficult to know whether they were killed as infidel, or for the money they were carrying.

One priest who did manage to live peaceably among the Tuareg was Father Charles de Foucauld, once a classmate of Laperrine's at military school in France. Instead of going into the Saharan army De Foucauld decided to explore Morocco. There he became increasingly interested in the life of the nomadic tribesmen. Finally he decided to live the life of a monk in the Sahara. He built himself a hermitage at Tamanrasset in the heart of the Ahaggar Tuareg country, and settled down to a life devoted to prayer and the study of the desert tribesmen. He learned their language, translated their poetry, and compiled a dictionary of Tuareg words. His only difficulty in dealing with the Tuareg was that he was also a friend of the French soldiers in the Sahara, who were committed to the idea of controlling the Tuareg through French military might.

During World War I, the Turks encouraged Tuareg tribesmen to join in a "holy war" against the French posts in the desert. Although De Foucauld's hermitage at Tamanrasset seemed impregnable, it

Above: Marie Joseph Francois Henri Laperrine, who trained and armed the desert tribesmen. The camel corps he formed put an end to the absolute control the Tuareg had maintained over their desert territory.
Below: Father Charles de Foucauld, who chose to live an austere life in the desert, among the Tuareg tribesmen.

476

was attacked one evening and De Foucauld was shot by a band of angry nomads. In Europe he was mourned as a Christian martyr.

The murder of Charles de Foucauld marks the end of an era in Saharan exploration. World War I brought the automobile and the airplane to the Sahara—machines which were to further the conquest of the desert and foreshadow the disappearance of the camel caravan. The 1920 flight in which General Laperrine had taken part had included two primitive planes, the second one piloted by a Major Vuillemin, who did manage to complete the trip. Although Vuillemin's achievement was overshadowed by the death of the general in the desert, his crossing represented the first triumph of the machine age in northern Africa.

The first crossing of the Sahara in an automobile took place some two years later. A group of French Citroën tracked vehicles left the Mediterranean coast in December, 1922, and arrived in Timbuktu one month later. It had taken Alexander Laing 11 months to do the same crossing, and even a fast camel caravan could not manage it in less than six months. The success of the Citroën mission convinced the French that they had really conquered the desert.

By this time, the exploration of the Sahara was no longer simply a question of overcoming the difficulties of climate and terrain. The desert's fascinating history was to occupy the next generation of adventurers. In 1933, a French officer, Lieutenant Brenans, discovered carvings of human figures and animals on the walls of

Above: Cardinal Lavigerie (1825–1892). He founded the White Fathers, a Roman Catholic order of priests who went to the Sahara to seek converts. His portrait now hangs in Versailles. Below: a White Father talking to a group of local children. Behind them is a typical example of the buildings of the area, constructed of dried mud.

Above: a plaque commemorating the Citroën expedition over the Sahara, which consisted of five caterpillar-wheeled Citroën cars. They arrived at Timbuktu on January 7, 1923, having taken only a month on their journey.

a rocky gorge in the Tassili-n-Ajjer. In the caverns beneath the walls of the gorge he found rock paintings. These amazing works of art were subsequently examined by scholars and established as part of the Sahara's prehistoric culture. The rock paintings showed the different races of men which had once lived in the Sahara, and the different kinds of animals which had roamed there. Most important were the clues the paintings gave about the desert's climate. There were pictures of elephants, some blowing water out of their trunks, rhinoceroses, hippopotamuses—all animals which live in tropical regions rather than in deserts. Archaeologists, speculating on the age of the Sahara, used the evidence of the cave paintings to support their theory that about 40,000 years ago the Sahara was a tropical region with rivers, lakes, and swamps.

Alongside the investigation of the history and art of the Sahara, other vitally important exploration was being carried out in the desert. In the 1930's, scientists were already predicting that large deposits of oil, gas, and minerals existed under the desert. It was

Right: the customs of centuries and the present-day world rub shoulders in North Africa today. Here a woman dressed as her great-grandmother would have dressed takes her child in a modern pushchair past a modern truck.

Below: the countries of northern Africa and the Arabian Peninsula in 1970. As the European explorers spread into Africa, they took with them the influence of European culture and civilization. Gradually almost the entire continent was brought under European rule. After World War II, however, a move toward self-government began in Africa, and by 1970 almost all the African countries had gained independence.

not until after World War II, however, that oil companies from the United States, France, and Britain began to drill for oil. Within about a year (1955–1956), enough oil fields were found to establish the Sahara as one of the major oil-producing areas of the world.

The period after World War II was also a time of political change. From 1922, the Sahara had remained largely under French control. But by the 1950's Africa was changing from a continent of European-ruled colonies to one of self-governing countries. Morocco and Tunisia became independent countries in 1956, while Algeria gained her independence in 1962 after a long and bitter war.

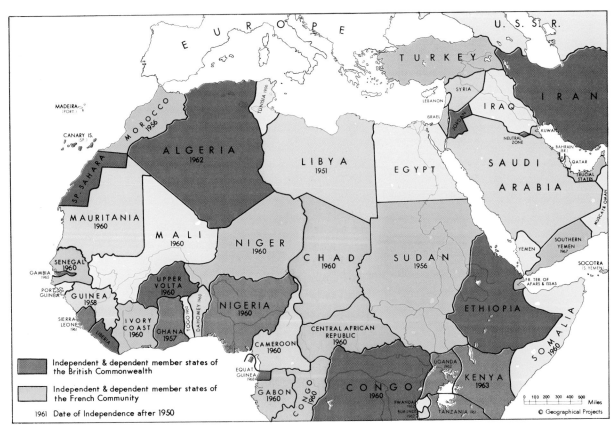

Above: the empty wastes of the Sahara, for so long thought to be valueless, are at last revealing their hidden wealth. Under the sand lie vast deposits of minerals and oil, and it is on these that the future of the desert rests. Here, an oil jet flames against the desert sky, symbolizing the challenge modern technology presents to the people of the area.

The courage and determination of the early explorers in the face of overwhelming odds helped to conquer the great "seas of sand." But what started as an exploration of unknown and mysterious regions will continue in other ways. The Sahara, with its vast hidden resources, and its great development potential, is now on the threshold of an exciting future. Further exploration in the desert will involve businessmen, politicians, scientists, technicians, and engineers. Together, they will devise new schemes for developing this rich area. Their achievements will yield further secrets to a scientific and technological age. The story has not yet ended.

Acknowledgments

Aldus Archives 353(T)(B), 354, 355, 357(L)(R), 361(T), 363, 365(B), 372(B), 376, 378(T)(B), 383(T), 422(R), 424(B), 440(T), 453(BL), 456; Photo Bibliothèque Nationale, Paris 338, 339, 341, 414; Reproduced by permission of the Trustees of the British Museum 346, 393(T), 432, 435(T), 451; British Museum/Photo A. C. Cooper © Aldus Books 347, 349, 350(B); British Museum/Photo Michael Holford © Aldus Books 375, 381(B), 435(B), 453(TL); Chateau de Versailles/Photo Giraudon © S.P.A.D.E.M., Paris 477(T); Photo Ray L. Cleveland of the American Foundation for the Study of Man 343(L)(R); Photo Barbara Cooper 356; Photo Wilfred Thesiger from his book, *Arabian Sands,* courtesy Curtis Brown Ltd. 403; *Daily Telegraph* Colour Library 418(T); Edinburgh University Library 351; Mary Evans Picture Library 421, 444, 459; Photo Graham Finlayson 424(T), 439, 450, 462; Photo Tony Walker © Aldus Books courtesy Foreign and Commonwealth Office, London 377; © Geographical 424(T), 439, 450, 462; Photo Tony Walker © Aldus Books courtesy Foreign and Commonwealth Office, London 377; © Geographical Projects Limited, London 335, 337, 385, 404, 419, 443, 475, 479(B); Dipl. Inc. Richard Gerlach, Berlin 369, 370–71, 374, 379; R. J. Griffith, New Zealand 408–09, 416, 428, 429, 430; Collection Haags Gemeentemuseum, The Hague 469; Sonia Halliday 336; Historisches Museum, Basel 358(L); Photo Hopker, München 407(B), 413, 480; India Office Library and Records 348; Courtesy Mrs. D. Ingrams 387, 390, 391; Photo Peter Keen 331, 340, 352, 398, 400, 405(T)(B), 410(L), 447; Document Henri Lhote's Expedition 411(R); Photo Henri Lhote 455(R); Photo Mike Busselle © Aldus Books courtesy London Borough of Richmond upon Thames 360(T)(BR); Photo Mike Busselle © Aldus Books, by permission of Lady Anne Lytton 326, 394, 396(L), 396–97, 397(R); Georg Gerster/Magnum Photos 410–11, 412(B), 479(T); Mansell Collection 358(R), 362, 368(L), 434, 442(T)(B); George Metcalfe 426, 427; Middle East Archive 350(T), 359, 402(T), 406–07; Musée de l'Armée, Paris/Photo Denise Bourbonnais © Aldus Books 330, 470; National Maritime Museum, Greenwich/Photo Michael Holford © Aldus Books 380–81(T); National Maritime Museum, Greenwich/Michael Holford Library 361(B); National Portrait Gallery, London 360, 420, 422(L), 436–37, 438(B), 458; Nationalmuseum, Copenhagen (Ethnographical Department) 368(R); Nationalmuseum, Stockholm 372(T); Manuscript Division, The New York Public Library, Astor, Leonox and Tilden Foundations 328, 415; Loaned by the Parker Gallery, London 433; Picturepoint, London 345, 412(T), 425, 449, 455(L), 473(T); Radio Times Hulton Picture Library 393(B); Reproduced by permission of the Royal Geographical Society 395, 401(R), 446; Photo Mike Busselle © Aldus Books reproduced by permission of the Royal Geographical Society 402(B); Photo Tony Walker © Aldus Books reproduced by permission of the Royal Geographical Society 364–65(T), 364(B), 401(L); Photo John Webb © Aldus Books reproduced by permission of the Royal Geographical Society 399, 402–03, 436(L), 440(B), 457; The Royal Library, Copenhagen 370(L); By courtesy of Sammlung für Völkerkunde der Universität, Zürich 333; British Crown Copyright, Science Musuem, London 423; By courtesy of Archives de la Société de Géographie, Paris 452; Photo Denise Bourbonnais © Aldus Books courtesy Archives de la Société de Géographie, Paris 468(T); Photo Sonia Halliday courtesy Topkapi Saray Museum, Instanbul 342, 356; Ullstein Bilderdienst, Berlin 465, 466(L); Photo D. Van Der Meulen 332, 372–73, 382–83(B), 388, 389(T)(B); Roger Viollet, Paris 453(TR), 471, 472, 473(B), 476(T), 478; Photo John Webb © Aldus Books 417, 418(B), 431, 437(B), 438(T), 441(T), 445, 448, 454, 460(L), 464, 466–67, 468(B); © James Wellard 441(B), 460(R), 474; Courtesy The White Fathers 476(B), 477(B).

Index

484

Quelimane, 229, 231
quinine, 296, 297

Rainmaker, 291
Rashidi Bedouins, 400, 401, 406
Razin, Frolka, 45
Razin, Stenka, 41–5
Rebmann, Johann, 243–45, 246, 247
Red Sea, Greek mariners' guide to, 181
Regensburg, Russian embassy at, 37
reincarnation, 80, 111
rhinoceros, 221; trade in horns of, 171
Rhodesia, 316
Ricci, Fr. Matteo, 92, 93, 97
Richardson, James, in Sahara, 456–59
Riebeeck, Jan van, 202
rinderpest, 303
Ripon Falls, Lake Victoria, 256, 288, 306
Ritchie Dr. J., in Sahara, 436
rock paintings, 411, 460–61, 478
Rohlfs, Gerhard, in Sahara, 465
Romans, in N. Africa, 413
Roth, Fr. Henri, 84
Royal Geographical Society, 231, 232, 235, 236, 238, 253, 256, 258, 259, 280, 300, 358
Rub'al Khali desert, Arabia, 330, 378, 381, 386, 391; exploration of, 399–407
Rudolf Lake, 313
Russel, Dr. Patrick, 191
Russia, 8–29, 41–9; and Britain, 120–39, 140–52; Siberia added to 30–41, 50–3
Ruvuma River, 236, 271
Ruwanika, Karagwe king, 254
Runwenzori Mts., 311–12
Ruzizi river, 251, 277, 288

Sabaeans, in Arabia, 367, 375, 383
Sahara, 330; travelers in, 408–80
Said ibn Sultan, Sayyid, 188
St. Petersburg, 48, 49
Salih bin Yakut, Sheik of Rashidis, 400
salt mines, in Sahara, 413, 417
Samarkand, taken by Russia, 135
Samoyed tribes, Siberia, 31, 35, 36–7
San'a, 344, 352, 367; capital of Yemen, 374, 375, 376, 378–79
sand dunes, 398, 409

sandstorm, 153–54, 400, 401, 412
Sang Farsh road, North Persia, 63
Santos, J. dos, describes Bantu kingdoms 187-88
Saudi Arabia, oil revenues of, 406
Saudi family, 354
saydis, 384
Say 'un, Hadhramaut, 386, 388
Schweinfurth, G. A., 296–99
Sebituane, Makololo chief, 224, 227
Seetzen, U. J., travels to Mecca, 353, 354
Ségou, on Niger, 424, 427, 450
Seiar Bedouins, 391, 401
Sekeletu, Makololo chief, 229, 235
Selim Bimbashi, 242, 243
Selous, F. C., big game hunter, 313
Semliki River, 308, 311
Senegal R., 424, 466
Sennar, Bruce at, 196, 197–99
serai, 101–02
serfdom, in Russia, 16, 41, 45
Shamakha, Persia, 57
shamans, 39
Shandi, market at, 197, 239, 241
Shanna, water hole in Rub'al Khali, 401, 402
shawls, made in Kashmir, 84
Sheba, Queen of, 169, 186, 332–33, 336–37
sheiks, 400
Sherley, Sir Anthony and Sir Robert 60, 62–3
Shibam, Hadhramaut, 384, 386
Shiel, Lady, in Persia, 126, 127, 128
Shigatse, Tibet, 77, 108, 155
Shihr, on Arabian coast, 386–390
Shire Highlands, 232, 236, 237
Shire River, 232, 270; *Ma-Robert steamboat on,* 232, 234
Shirwa, Lake, 232
Shupanga, Mary Livingstone's grave at, 237
Siberia, 28. 30–41, 50–3
Sibir, Mongol capital 35, 36
Sidi Bombay, 248, 258, 280, 283
Sidi Mohammed Muktar, befriends Laing, 448–49
Sierra Leone, 451, 452
silk, in Persia, 55, 56, 69
Silk Road, 157
Silla, on Niger, 415, 427
Silveira, G. da, missionary, 187
Silver, 187
simoom, 199, 393, 394
Singh, Kishen, pundit, 116, 118
Singh, Nain, pundit, 116, 118
Siwah oasis, Shara, 409; temple of

Zeus Ammon at, 430
slave chains, 272
slave trade, 171; to Angola 230, 282–83; in Congo, 309; in E. Africa, 188, 197; at Khartoum, 296, Livingstone and, 230, 234–35, 236–37, 272; at Shandi, 241; in S. Africa, 227; suppression of, 315; in W. Africa, 188, across Sahara, 416–17, 437, 439, 443, 455, 457, 458–59
sledges, 13, 20
smallpox, 192, 250, 262
social security, tribal system of, 178
Socotra, Portuguese take, 354
Sofala E. Africa. 182, 183, 185
Sokoto, Fulani capital, 438–440
Soltykoff, Prince, in Persia, 132–33
Somalis, 248, 313
Souf oasis, Algerian Sahara, 410, 411
South Africa, 320; Dutch in, 169, ' 174, 177, 202–04, 315
Spanish Sahara, 315
Sparrman, Anders, in S. Africa, 205–06
Speke, J. H., 178, 248–49, 262
spice trade, 9
Srinagar, Kashmir, 74
Stanley, Lady Dorothy, 311, 313
Stanley, H. M., 276–77, 283, 284–86, 288–93, 309, 312–13
Stanley Falls, Congo, 309
Stein, Sir Aurel, 153, 157–59
Stel, Simon van der, 203
Steller, G. W., naturalist, 51
Stephanie Lake 313
steppes, 31, 32
stool, ceremonial, 264
Strahlenburg, explorer for Peter the Great, 50
Strogonov, Maxim, 31, 32
Strutt, W. T., 214
Struys, Jan, Dutch traveler, 44
Sudan, 174, 175, 176, 260, 411, 417
sudd, in Nile, 242, 258, 260, 262, 295
Suk people, 303
as Sulayyil, Arabia, 402, 405, 406
Susi, with Livingstone, 273, 274, 276, 279
Sykes, Sir Percy, 77, 134, 136
Syr-Darya R., 135

Table Mountain, 202, 206–07
Tafilalt oasis, Sahara, 455, 465
Tahmasp, Shah of Persia, 59
Ta'izz, Arabia, 353, 374
takhtrawan (grandee's litter), 362–63
Takla Haymanot, King of Ethiopia, 193

WATERFORD CITY AND COUNTY

WITHDRAWN

LIBRARIES